French Free-Thought
from Gassendi to Voltaire

French Free-Thought
from Gassendi to Voltaire

by

J. S. SPINK

GREENWOOD PRESS, PUBLISHERS
NEW YORK

Foreword

FRENCH free-thought was remarkably consistent and substantial during the century which preceded the main manifestations of the Enlightenment. It evolved, but it evolved according to its own inner nature. It was never dependent upon foreign inspiration. Even the ideas received from sixteenth-century Italy were rigorously trimmed according to a peculiarly French model, whilst Spinoza can hardly be said to have been acclimatized at all and in Locke the French 'libertins' found only what they already knew. That is not to say that French free-thought was inflexible or impervious to new matter. It assimilated the information produced in the laboratories and studies of Europe, keeping well abreast at a time when the total sum of sound knowledge was rapidly increasing from decade to decade. It never petrified into a creed. The original scepticism gave ground at first to Epicurean empiricism and Cartesian rationalism, but by the end of the century these three elements had amalgamated to form the rational scepticism of Bayle and Fontenelle. Free-thought was neither aggressive nor dogmatic, though constantly faced with aggressive and violent enemies who had the civil power at their disposal. The main effect it had on the intellects which surrendered to it was to keep them open, flexible and mobile. It was this very mobility, this readiness to question accepted beliefs time and time again and constantly reassess them, which enabled the French 'philosophes' to become Europe's purveyors of general ideas. England provided more sound knowledge than did the French, both in the sciences and in scholarship, but the French were none the less destined to hold the intellectual hegemony of Europe. Their books, clearly written, with a minimum of jargon and specialized vocabulary, handled general ideas courageously and radically, with the lucidity of mind and expression which the 'libertins' had created. French free-thought was essentially *social* at all times. This does not mean that it was the attribute of a particular class, at least not in the seventeenth and early eighteenth centuries—later in the eighteenth century it was adopted by the financial, commercial and industrial 'bourgeoisie'; nor does it mean that free-thought was a by-product of a

drawing-room culture: it was the creation of men of science and
men of learning and of an intelligentsia which kept closely in touch
with men of science and men of learning, but it readily found expression in the assemblies, academies, salons, taverns and coffee-
houses, where ideas were an eagerly accepted currency. In spite of
a repressive censorship, it produced an intellectual environment in
which men of genius could flourish.

In this book I have attempted to follow the course of French free-
thought from the time when Gassendi began to write to the time
when Voltaire reached maturity. There are no real beginnings and
endings in the constantly-moving panorama of intellectual life, and
the dates I have chosen are no more than convenient dates for the
making of a book. Before the time of Gassendi the Renaissance mentality is still so involved that a special guide is needed in order to
tread its maze;[1] after Voltaire's *Lettres philosophiques* comes the main
highway of the Encyclopaedist movement. Between the two lies the
open but varied countryside through which French rationalism and
naturalism are two roughly parallel, but sometimes divergent, sometimes convergent, sometimes intersecting paths, and these I have
attempted to follow.

1959   J. S. S.

[1] The best we have so far are J.-R. Charbonnel's *La Pensée italienne au seizième
siècle et le courant libertin* (Paris, 1917) and H. Busson's *Les Sources et le développement
du rationalisme dans la littérature française* (Paris, 1922).

Contents

Part One: *Gassendi and the 'Libertins'*

Part Two: *Descartes and the Rationalists*

Part One

Gassendi and the 'Libertins'

I

The Crisis of 1619–25: The Erudite Sceptics

BOTH the English word 'libertine' and the French word 'libertin', from which it is derived, were already reserved for the sexually vicious at the time when Richardson created his Lovelace and Laclos his Valmont; the term referred to a man's bad morals and not his mental outlook, although the belief that chastity is a 'prejudice' might conceivably be looked upon as a philosophical tenet.[1] Voltaire referred to Helen of Troy as 'une vieille femme fort libertine'; Rousseau described himself as 'polisson mais non libertin' in his adolescent years. The word 'libertin' had been used to describe loose morals as early as the end of the sixteenth century and the first French–English dictionary, that of Cotgrave, published in 1611, translated 'libertinage' as 'libertinage, Epicurism, sensualitie, licentiousnesse, dissolutenesse', but 'libertinage' was not used only, or even primarily, to speak of depravity at that time, as it was when Malthus wrote, in 1798, of women whose 'libertinage must render them . . . unfit for bearing children'. The dictionaries, both the *Oxford English Dictionary* and the *Littré*, enable us to follow the semantic development of the words we have mentioned. In the middle of the sixteenth century, the name 'libertins' was given to a Protestant sect, in the Low Countries and northern France, whose characteristic tenet was a belief, based on such texts as Acts xvii. 28 ('. . . in him we live, move and have our being'), that a divine spirit permeates all things and is the cause of all things, so that all that is is good.[2] This theme, reminiscent of ancient Stoicism, reappears

---

[1] Cf. Duclos: 'Cette vertu, si précieuse à vos yeux, n'est qu'un préjugé chimérique, que les hommes, par un autre préjugé, exigent dans leurs femmes ou dans leurs maîtresses, et dont ils font peu de cas dans les autres.' (*Histoire de madame de Luz*, *Œuvres*, 1820–1, ii, p. 234) and the marquis de Sade: 'Cette vertu dont vous faites un si grand étalage ne sert à rien dans le monde . . . La chose qui flatte le moins les hommes, celle dont ils font le moins de cas, celle qu'ils méprisent le plus souverainement, c'est la sagesse de votre sexe.' (*Justine*, Paris, 1950, i, p. 22.)

[2] The sect was strongly condemned by Calvin in his *Contre la secte fantastique et furieuse des libertins qui se nomment spirituels*, n.p., 1547 (*Opera*, Amsterdam, 1657, viii, pp. 374–408: *Instructio adversus fanaticam et furiosam sectam libertinorum, qui se spirituales vocant*).

constantly in the history of libertine thought and, in the Netherlands particularly, it was still looked upon, in the second half of the seventeenth century, as the distinguishing feature of the 'libertins',[1] but it is not possible to establish a link between this early use of the term and its more general use in the seventeenth century. From before 1600 until the second half of the seventeenth century, it meant first and foremost a man who refused to accept current beliefs and desired to free himself especially from the bonds of Christian doctrine.[2] From the first, however, the adversaries of the free-thinkers assumed that from free-thinking followed inevitably free living, and in spite of efforts made (by Pierre Bayle in particular) to show that this was a *non-sequitur*, dissolute morals and free-thinking became so firmly associated in the public mind that the term 'libertin' had lost its philosophical sense by the beginning of the eighteenth century and was replaced by the equivalent of the English expression 'free-thinker', namely 'libre penseur', or, quite simply, by the word 'philosophe'. Bayle himself used the term 'libertin d'esprit' to mark the difference, but this expression did not become common and the word 'libertin' came to mean only a debauchee and a profligate. In the early nineteenth century Victor Cousin hinted that even the austere Gassendi was morally suspect. As for Vanini, Cousin believed, on the evidence of a document fabricated by a clever forger, that he was a wanton sodomite, a slur which still clings to Vanini's name, in spite of the fact that such an accusation was not mentioned by Vanini's seventeenth- and eighteenth-century biographers.[3] The morals of the seventeenth century were not, it is true, of the kind that a moralist of Cousin's day was likely to approve of, and one look at the licentious verses composed by such a staid poet as Malherbe is apt to make a modern reader's hair stand on end, if he is not inured to seventeenth-century coarseness and obscenity, but to maintain that speculative beliefs are the cause of good or bad moral conduct would amount merely to re-opening the old question to which Pierre Bayle gave such a telling negative reply in his *Pensées sur la comète de 1680*.[4] Only the negative permits of tolerance: to affirm that a

---

[1] Stouppe, *La Religion des Hollandais*, Paris, 1672, p. 88.
[2] H. Busson notes examples earlier than those quoted by Littré. Viret used the word 'libertin' in the sense of 'free-thinker' in 1585. (*La Pensée religieuse française de Charron à Pascal*, Paris, 1933, pp. 5–6 and 'Les noms des incrédules au XVIe siècle', in *Bibliothèque d'humanisme et renaissance*, xvi (1954), p. 281.)   [3] See below, p. 29.
[4] This was a century in which the following stories were in circulation; true or false they were told with no obvious anti-clerical intention: 'L'Angeli étant entré un matin

man must necessarily be a villain because he is a Protestant, a Catholic, a Jew or a free-thinker is to open the way to strife and oppression; Nero was devout to the point of superstition; Vanini on the other hand lived the life of an honest man. A survey of contemporary manners would have borne out Bayle's assertion. France was overwhelmingly Catholic in the seventeenth century, but morals were coarse and dissolute. The 'underside' of the age of Louis XIV, as Félix Gaiffe called it,[1] was so dark that it could hardly have been darker, though what is referred to as the 'crisis' of 'libertinage' was then long past and piety was fashionable. The history of the 'libertins' is not the history of vice;[2] the student of dissolute manners is referred to Gaiffe's book or to the Memoirs of the duchess of Orleans, sister-in-law of Louis XIV.

There was indeed a 'crisis' in French intellectual life at the beginning of the seventeenth century. It has been located between the years 1619 and 1625 because these were the years when Vanini was burnt at the stake and the poet Théophile narrowly escaped a like fate. In 1619 Vanini was condemned to death by the Parlement of Toulouse.[3] In 1622 a certain Fontanier, a wanderer who had been as far as Constantinople, was burnt at the stake in Paris for having given lessons in some occult or mystic doctrine which it is difficult to identify. In 1624 the Parlement of Paris forbade the teaching of new doctrines, on the occasion of an attempt by two chemists or alchemists to sustain anti-Aristotelian theses in the town. In 1623 Théophile de Viau was accused of atheism and in 1625 condemned to banishment. Works of Catholic apologetics were not noticeably more numerous in these years than at other times; such works came out in their usual regular stream at the rate of about two a year. But three particularly aggressive attacks on free-thought were published

chez monseigneur l'archevêque de Harlay, on lui dit à l'antichambre que monseigneur était malade. Il attendit et vit sortir de la chambre une jeune fille habillée de vert. Enfin il entra, et monseigneur lui dit qu'il avait eu trois ou quatre évanouissements la nuit. "C'est donc cela, dit-il, que j'en ai vu passer un habillé de vert?"'; 'Maldachin étant amant et favori de donna Olympia et partageant ses plus douces faveurs avec le pape, elle lui dit un jour dans ses transports les plus violents: "Coraggio, mi' Maldachin, ti farò cardinale", mais il lui répondit: "Quando sarebbe per esser papa non posso più."' (Published in Monmerqué's edition of Tallemant des Réaux's Historiettes, second edition, Paris, 1840, ix, p. 41 and pp. 44–5.)

[1] L'Envers du grand siècle, Paris, 1924.

[2] The weakness of the book by F.-T. Perrens, Les Libertins en France au dix-septième siècle, Paris, 1899, is that it makes of the subject a collection of anecdotes and gossip drawn from contemporary correspondence and memoirs.

[3] See below, pp. 28 sqq.

between 1623 and 1625, two of them mean and violent, by the Jesuit writer Garasse, and one more dignified and moderate in tone, by the Minim Friar Mersenne.[1] Garasse's efforts were the expression of a co-ordinated Jesuit move which met with a good deal of resistance in the Parlement of Paris, luckily for Théophile.[2]

The 'crisis' of 1619–25 was, in effect, a repressive reaction on the part of the authorities, namely the Parlements, and was a symptom of a much more general crisis through which intellectual life was passing. It is the transformation that marks the beginnings of modern times. The collapse of mediaeval teaching was becoming unmistakable; it was to hold sway in the colleges for the next hundred years, but outside the classrooms it was already discredited. To fill the gap there was as yet only the revised version of Aristotle professed in the University of Padua by Pomponazzi and Cremonini and certain themes of hylozoic or panpsychistic naturalism, also of Italian origin and propagated in the works of Cardano and Bruno. Even these were under fire before their position was established; Renaissance science, the science of the astrologers and alchemists was following Scholasticism in collapse, while the new science, the science of modern times, was only just at its beginnings. The traditional picture of the world, which placed the earth in the centre and arranged the skies in concentric spheres around it, still held good in the minds of most men; it was to disappear only in the middle years of the century, and was shared alike by the Schoolmen and the astrologers. Only a handful of specialists in mechanics and astronomy were acquainted with the new physics of Copernicus, Tycho-Brahe, Kepler and Galileo, and they refrained discreetly from public expression of their views. In one case at least, that of Marin Mersenne, opposition to 'libertinage' was the equivalent of support for the mechanistic physics of Galileo against other manifestations of Italian influence. Moderately progressive and liberal-minded men had difficulty in maintaining their position in face of a determined effort by the Jesuits to establish themselves in the University of Paris; the Jesuits did not hesitate to accuse their adversaries of encouraging depravity and lawless living. The situation was confused and intricate; it is difficult to determine the real direction in which blows carried.

[1] F. Garasse, *Les Recherches des recherches et autres œuvres de M. Etienne Pasquier* . . ., Paris, 1622; *La Doctrine curieuse des beaux esprits de ce temps ou prétendus tels* . . . *combattue et renversée*, Paris, 1623; M. Mersenne, *L'Impiété des déistes, athées et libertins de ce temps*, Paris, 1624 (chiefly against the 'Quatrains du déiste' and against Bruno).
[2] cf. below, pp. 42–5.

To add to the disarray had come the sceptical criticism of which Montaigne had made himself the mouthpiece. Preceded by Cornelius Agrippa's *De vanitate scientiarum* and Etienne's Latin edition of Sextus Empiricus, and seconded by Charron's *Sagesse*, Montaigne's *Essays* had pushed home the assault on each and every claim to certain knowledge that the Italian philosophers, equally with the schoolmen, had advanced. The bewildering variety of human opinions, the deceptive nature of the senses whereby our knowledge of the outside world comes to us, the vacillations of our reason, made nonsense of the vaunting pretensions of the learned. Only in the domain of morals had Montaigne sought to reconstruct, and then only a modest doctrine to be arrived at by experience, an art of living or a moral hygiene rather than a doctrine, a purely practical means by which the limited resources of our nature may be exploited. His conception of experience was confined to the moral sphere; he had not applied it, as Bacon did in England, to the restoration of natural philosophy.

The main positive contribution of Italian naturalism was the belief that the operations of nature are regular and unvarying, a conception which vied with that of divine providence and contradicted belief in miracles. It was to be the central theme also of the new mechanistic science of the seventeenth century, but the new science stripped it of its metaphysical associations and replaced them by a simple and straightforward deism which separated God radically from his creation. For the Italians God was implicated in every part of nature.

The belief that an Intelligence is suffused throughout the universe and that the laws of nature are modes of that Intelligence is probably the most attractive of all beliefs for the human mind; it enables the mind to rediscover itself in the outside world. It was handed on by the sixteenth century to the seventeenth and persisted all the way through the seventeenth century, although it was greatly weakened by the impact of the mechanical sciences and by the trenchant argument by which the Cartesians distinguished between minds, the divine and the human, on the one hand, and the extended material world on the other. It attached itself to the old cosmology with the Italians Vanini and Campanella, both of whom brought Italian naturalism with them to France. It attached itself to the new cosmology with Cyrano de Bergerac and, to some extent, in the works of Gassendi. It reappeared in the later years of the century with the accounts of Indian and Chinese beliefs given by travellers and missionaries. It associated itself with extreme sensationalism and materialism in the fantasies of Cyrano and with extreme intellectualism in the purely rational system of Spinoza. It influenced Christian thought, from which it had never been entirely alien. It christianized Cartesianism in the mind of Malebranche and with Leibniz served to re-introduce into the universe the psychical activity which Descartes had expelled therefrom. It crept into the dictionaries amongst the definitions of the word 'nature'.[1] In England it took one form with the Cambridge Platonists and another with John Toland, who invented the term 'pantheist'. In the eighteenth century it was known as 'neo-Spinozism'. Throughout both centuries it was always present in the minds of the astrologers, occultists, cabalists and alchemists.

Various intellectual themes current in the seventeenth century were modes of this central theme: the belief that the motions of the planets determine all the motions which take place on earth and that the planets symbolize the general truths which are the primary expression of divine thought; the belief that all true ideas are modes of the divine mind, the belief in a world soul of which all souls are parts; the belief that all nature is sensitive, the belief that plants possess by intuition a knowledge of the general scheme of things, the belief that the sun is the source of all animation and feeling in the world, belief in telepathy and divination. Many of these beliefs are mutually exclusive and they cover the whole range of thought from intellectualism to sensationalism, but all are directly connected with the ancient and fundamental belief that an Intelligence permeates the whole world. Even Lucretius was interpreted in this sense in a conversation recorded by Boulainviller (c. 1700), when it was argued that the chance collisions of an infinite number of particles over an infinite length of time, are the equivalent of an Intelligence in the universe.[2]

French scepticism applied itself to the Italian philosophers as well as to the scholastic tradition, and particularly to the claims of astrology and occultism. As for magic, the sceptics looked upon it as being beyond the pale of critical controversy and the accusation of

[1] Academy dictionary of 1694: 'Il se prend aussi pour cet esprit universel qui est répandu dans chaque chose créée et par lequel toutes choses ont leur commencement et leur fin.'
[2] Boulainviller's reading notes at the Bibliothèque nationale (MSS 11071–6 of the Nouv. acq. fr.), ii, pp. 1–6: 'Origine des êtres et espèces, fruit d'une conversation retenue imparfaitement.'

having practised it as a charge against which the Italian philosophers had to be defended. But a certain number of essential ideas distillé and elaborated by the Italians were adopted by the French sceptics. It was from the Italians that they learned to distinguish between the virtue which the philosopher pursues for its own sake and the pragmatic rules which the mass of the people must be induced to observe if public order is to be preserved. They learned to look upon themselves as initiates (*déniaisés*), to distinguish between the *élite* and the vulgar herd, between rational knowledge and implicit faith, between philosophy and religion. The sceptics who are known to us were for the most part prudent and conservative scholars, safely ensconced in comfortable niches in the intellectual world. They showed no inclination to proselytize or parade their views before the public. They were academic in outlook and as exclusive as were the polite and literary salons surrounding the court. Their assumption of superiority led to the term 'esprit fort' being used as a term of abuse, to imply a presumptuous disdain for popular beliefs, but they were not dogmatizers and their motto was that of Cremonini: *intus ut libet, foris ut moris est.*[1]

The Jesuit writer Garasse would have preferred the free-thinkers to come out into the open so that they could the more easily be dealt with. For Garasse the suppression of free thought was simply a matter for the police, there being no Inquisition in Paris. His first book, published in 1622, was devoted to an attack on the memory of Etienne Pasquier, the famous lawyer-historian, who had defended the rights of the University of Paris against the Jesuits. The second was a more general onslaught. Both were uniformly violent and often merely grotesque, and they probably did more harm than good to the Jesuit cause in the University and Parlement of Paris, but Garasse was not without a certain understanding of the mental make-up of his adversaries. He gives a recognizable sketch of libertine thought as it must have appeared to an unsympathetic observer; it is out of focus but the main features are represented. The libertine (says Garasse) practises secrecy and dissimulation; he professes to believe in God, but really worships nature only and submits to the immutable laws of destiny; he rejects popular superstitions, but is

---

[1] *Naudaeana et Patiniana*, Paris, 1701, p. 16: cf. Gui Patin, *Lettres*, ed. Reveillé-Parise, Paris, 1864, ii, p. 277: 'M. Naudé ... disait qu'il fallait faire comme les Italiens, bonne mine sans bruit, et prendre dans ce cas-là pour devise: *Intus ut libet, foris ut moris est.*'

careful not to give offence to simple folk who hold them; he claims
that the Bible contains both good and bad precepts; he believes in
neither angels nor devils, is sceptical of the immortality of the soul
and believes that in some ways the brutes are superior to men.[1] In
his book against Pasquier he defines the term *libertin*: 'By the word
libertine I mean neither a Huguenot, nor an atheist, nor a Catholic,
nor a heretic, nor a *politique*, but a certain combination of all these
qualities.' The word *politique* may sound strange here, but it must
be remembered that it was used to describe the moderate Catholic
politicians who had put a stop to the wars of religion and were prepared to subordinate religious interests to the preservation of public
order. Garasse then continues:

After protesting that he is a Catholic so as to insert his venom the more
effectively, he will say that he does not however believe all the petty nonsense they instil into the minds of simple folk; as for ceremonies and
ecclesiastical traditions, visions, apparitions and such like, he will call
them in mockery the offal of religion; should he hear told some difficult
story, hard to believe and of doubtful authenticity, he will call it Saint
Bridget's revelation; if some ancient or modern marvel performed by a
saint comes to his ears, he will ask whether he will be damned if he does
not believe it; to give a ridiculous turn to an idea he will invent a saying
full of scorn and profanation of sacred things, as for example to describe
somebody's zig-zag gait he will say that he walks like a dog just come from
vespers; to say that a poem is ridiculously rhymed, a libertine will say that
it rhymes like *Beatiquorum*;[2] to say that a person is stout, he will say that
he is as fat as a monk; to mark the light-headedness of a poor fool, he
will say that he is as light-headed as the first stroke of the matin-bell; to
describe the slothful humour of a man who is careless in what he performs,
he will say that he passes his duties and affairs through a *Fidelium*; to
mock a man without judgment, he will say that he is a poor priest, a man or
a horse covered with mud, that he is befouled like an archdeacon; if it is a
question of praying to God or reciting the breviary, he will say it is time
to do the *Briborium* [*Breviarium*[3]] and similar expressions which can only
have seen the light of day in a tavern. If it is a matter of expressing his
opinion on a religious topic, he will straightway step in and go right into
the thick of it, like a fly into glue. So you will hear him say, 'For my part
I am for the marriage of priests and against celibacy; Gregory of Nazian-
zus was wrong in attacking the reputation of the Emperor Julian;[4] Con-

[1] *La Doctrine curieuse*, pp. [v–vi].
[2] "Que cela ryme comme *Beatiquorum*.' The reference is doubtless to the Beatitudes.
[3] The word *brimborion* (bauble) in modern French is derived from *Breviarium*.
[4] Garasse accused his former pupil Guez de Balzac of holding this opinion: 'Celui
que vous appeliez autrefois le petit Grégoire de Nazianze reconnut aux lettres de Julien

stantine was a canting humbug; Saint Louis nearly ruined France with his bigotry; the popes have gradually obtained possession of the temporal power, etc.' At the end of every sentence he will pronounce with emphasis the words 'Gallican Liberties'; he will maintain that Clovis was never a Catholic and died an Arian, that de Bèze was an intelligent man, that Calvin was an important figure, that Marot was the ornament of his age, that heretics should be treated with leniency, that it is barbarous to persecute the Huguenots, that the Inquisition is a barbarously cruel thing. As for the ruinous state of the country, he will blame the Catholics for it and absolve the heretics from blame; there are doubtless erroneous beliefs held in France, but what is their source if not the wicked life led by the priests and ecclesiastics? The Huguenots broke the images and the crosses and demolished churches, it is true, but think of the abuses that had crept in! How much idolatry and superstitions of the common people! Were not the monasteries and cloisters all places of ill fame? And then, so as not to be suspected of heresy, he will add with an assured gesture and tone of voice, 'I say all this, not because I am favourably inclined towards the Huguenots; I am more Catholic than the Pope, but I am a good Frenchman.

> As far as I am concerned, the Huguenots could work miracles,
> Raise the dead, pronounce true oracles,
> Without my being able to believe them to be true;
> On all matters of opinion I dislike novelty,
> So we ought rather to imitate our forbears
> Than to chase after the new chimeras of the new generation.[1]

But I remember (he will say) that when I was young our forebears were better than we are to-day; there was more true piety, more frankness, more Gallic sincerity, and there were not so many Capuchins, monks and Jesuits about as there are now.' There you have the ordinary talk of the libertine, and, actions and conduct following the same bent as speech, a libertine will mock at acts of piety, blame frequent confession and communion, asceticism, monasticism, and will only fast when the mood takes him. In sickness and at the approach of death, to console himself in Jesus Christ, he will have Plato's *Phaedo* read to him, concerning the immortality

l'Apostat (que vous nommiez le grand empereur) les fougues enragées de son esprit furieux, et permettez-moi de vous dire que j'ai découvert à la lecture des vôtres la trempe très aigre de votre âme un peu farouche.' (*Réponse du sieur Hydaspe au sieur de Balzac*, 1624, p. 1.)

[1] Pour moi les Huguenots pourraient faire miracles,
Ressusciter les morts, rendre de vrais oracles,
Que je ne pourrais pas croire à leur vérité;
En toute opinion je fuis la nouveauté;
Aussi doit-on plutôt imiter nos vieux pères
Que suivre des nouveaux les nouvelles chimères.

of the soul, as did Pasquier. As for confession, the pardon of wrongs, an
the reparation of honour, when exhorted to see to these things at his la:
hour, he will reply, as Pasquier did, that they are mere weakness of min
and will talk only of Seneca, Plato, his own works, a flea that bites hin
or his hand, or his amorous exploits, and with such spiritual discourse w
surrender his soul to his maker.[1]

Garasse, who was out to throw mud at as many adversaries of th
Jesuits as possible, makes no distinction between the libertines whos
attitude was essentially sceptical and those who adopted pantheist
naturalism or 'atheism', as it was called, as a positive creed, o
rather who could be looked upon as tending in this direction, seein
that it is difficult to distinguish between pantheistic naturalism an
orthodox scholastic theology: God and *Natura naturans* could b
taken as identical in a perfectly orthodox manner and laymen wer
often inclined to see simpler distinctions between ideas than wer
seen by theologians. Garasse himself used the term 'atheist' as
general term of abuse; he called Luther a 'perfect atheist'.[2] We sha
need to make a distinction between two types of libertinage, i
attempting to answer the question, who were the *libertins*? We sha
need to distinguish between pure scepticism on the one hand and th
naturalistic tendencies we have just mentioned on the other. Ther
is another distinction one can make and it follows the same lines a
the first. On the one hand we find the professional erudites, librarian
in the houses of the great, tutors to the sons of the great, professo
at the Royal College, holding stable positions in society. On th
other we find the wanderers, the irregulars, the independents, resent
ful of authority, unsubmissive in spirit. It was the members of thi
latter group who ran a real risk of the galleys and the stake.

Scepticism itself was not sufficient to make an erudite libertine
Philosophical scepticism, coupled with theological orthodoxy, wa
openly professed by some ecclesiastics. Huet, for instance, bisho
of Avranches, adopted a sceptical position and defended it agains
Cartesianism over a long period of years. Simon Foucher defende
the ancient Academy and refuted Malebranche's rationalism. Ma
gnan, as a student, showed himself to be sceptical in philosophy bu
submissive in theology. Scepticism also nourished Christian though
in the writings of Pascal, who drew heavily on Montaigne in hi
effort to humble the human reason. What made the academic liber
tine was the fact that he was a scholar, an erudite, with a full shar

[1] *Les Recherches des recherches*, pp. 681 sqq.   [2] *La Doctrine curieuse*, p. 42.

of *libido sciendi*. He coupled a pronounced interest in what was strange and unaccepted in the intellectual world, with a noticeable inaptitude for belief, religious or other.

It was the presence of men of unbounded intellectual curiosity in the learned assemblies, in private libraries and studies (*cabinets*), their correspondence with each other, their travels to Italy, their contacts with scholars in England and the Low Countries which gave to intellectual life in Paris, in the early seventeenth century, the thrill of inquiry and speculation, an excitement which was shared by even that pronounced enemy of 'deism' and 'atheism' Marin Mersenne. Marin Mersenne's free-thinking went no further than the acceptance of the physics of Galileo, but he took pleasure in open-minded research.[1] In the closed academic circles a liberal atmosphere was maintained; Protestants like Elie Diodati were on good terms with Catholics like Gassendi; a noted free-thinker such as Théophile and a bishop such as Coëffeteau could meet at the abbé de Marolles's house and take part in the same conversations.[2] In De Thou's library, administered by Jacques and Pierre Du Puy, where philologists and bibliophiles foregathered, at Mersenne's, where the mathematicians congregated, at Marolles's house, where conversations were literary as well as philosophical, at Bassompierre's house, where an 'honest liberty' prevailed in the discussions,[3] ideas were exchanged with greater freedom than would have been possible in public places. Personal contacts between scholars, maintained by a very active correspondence, constituted a network of exchanges in which certain nodal points or a rudimentary organization can be discerned. Certain men, who were not necessarily in the forefront of learned inquiry, served as collectors and retailers of news, activators and patrons. Fabri de Peiresc was one such person. He was in contact with Galileo, Campanella, Holstenius (the librarian of the Vatican), Gassendi, Naudé, Mersenne, Camden, Barclay, Cotton.[4] His house at Aix-en-Provence was a place of learned pilgrimage; his study was used for anatomical dissections and his roof for astronomical observations. For mathematicians and physicists Mersenne served as a sort of postmaster: he was in touch with Galileo, Descartes,

---

[1] R. Lenoble, *Mersenne ou la naissance du mécanisme*, Paris, 1943.

[2] R. Pintard, *Le Libertinage érudit dans la première moitié du dix-septième siècle*, Paris, 1943, p. 90.

[3] The term 'une honnête liberté' is used by Arnauld d'Andilly, with approbation, 'bien qu'un Vanini en ait été bénéficiaire' (ibid.).

[4] *Correspondance*, ed. Tamizey de Larroque, Paris, 1889-97, 7 vols.

Constantine and Christian Huyghens, Gassendi, Beeckmann, Fermat and Hobbes.[1]

The mere fact of taking part in these intellectual exchanges implies independence of thought in the wide sense, but when we come to narrow down our definition of free-thinking to such historical, moral and philosophical speculation as carried its authors into opposition to Christian beliefs, we find (and this doubtless is to be expected at a time when the right to free discussion did not exist) that the number of persons to whom we can attach the name 'erudite libertine' is a small one. Mersenne affirmed in 1623 that there were fifty thousand atheists in Paris, but he withdrew the statement later, so its value is open to question.[2] There were doubtless far more freethinkers than we can name, seeing that the open profession of free-thinking was fraught with perils, but the fact remains that we cannot quote more than a few names and even these must be pronounced with as much caution as the erudite libertines themselves displayed.

The first names to catch our eye are those of three friends, Pierre Gassend, François de la Mothe le Vayer and Gabriel Naudé. To these we can add a fourth well-known name, that of Gui Patin, and those of a few less well-known scholars, Claude Belurgey, François Guyet, Gui de la Brosse, René de Chantecler and the scholar-gentleman Philippe Fortin de la Hoguette.

Pierre Gassend, or Gassendi, as he has always been called, was the oldest of the group.[3] He was born in 1592, at Champtercier, near Digne, and spent most of his life in the south. The fact that he was a southerner probably explains the form Gassendi, which is more likely to have been a Provençal form of Gassend than a mistaken use of the genitive of the Latin form of the name, Gassendus. Gassendi was elected to a chair of philosophy and theology at Aix in 1616, entered holy orders in 1617, became provost of the cathedral of Digne in 1623 and professor of mathematics (astronomy) at the Royal College in Paris in 1645. He died in 1655.

Gassendi was an erudite in all his works; even in his most scientific writings he was essentially a commentator, and the great respect he showed for experience, as against pure ratiocination, did not lead

---

[1] *Correspondance*, ed. de Waard, Paris, 1933.

[2] *Quaestiones celeberrimae in Genesim*, Paris, 1623, col. 671. In most copies the passage is suppressed, but it is in the Bibliothèque nationale copy: A 952 (1).

[3] For an account of Gassendi's doctrine, as contained in the *Syntagma philosophicum*, see Chapter VI below.

him to take more than a minor part in the work of the experimental scientists. His place is therefore certainly amongst the erudites, but to what extent was he an erudite libertine? The answer lies in the profound independence of mind with which he criticized current doctrines in the first part of his career and championed the philosophy of Epicurus in the second part. Gassendi was a free-thinker in the simplest and noblest sense of the term. His attitude at the outset of his career was that of the sceptics as defined by Sextus Empiricus; he was a searcher: he did not think that the truth had been attained, nor did he think that it was unattainable.[1] His first publications were attacks on the three main philosophical positions held in seventeenth-century France, the scholastic, the occultist and the Cartesian. He began with a series of essays entitled *Exercitationum paradoxicarum adversus Aristoteleos libri septem* in 1624.[2] He followed these with an *Exercitatio* against the English occultist Robert Fludd in 1629 and when Descartes published his *Meditations*, in 1641, it was Gassendi who contributed the 'Fifth Objections' followed by a *Disquisitio metaphysica, seu Dubitationes et Instantiae adversus Renati Cartesii metaphysicam* in 1644.

Meanwhile, alongside this purely negative criticism, he had undertaken a study of Epicurus and gradually the whole of the time which

[1] For a fuller treatment see B. Rochot, *Les Travaux de Gassendi sur Epicure et sur l'atomisme*, Paris, 1944, ch. I 'Contre Aristote'. Sextus Empiricus's description of the three possible philosophical attitudes runs as follows, 'The natural result of any investigation is that the investigators either discover the object of search, or deny that it is discoverable and confess it to be inapprehensible, or persist in their search. So too with the objects investigated by philosophy; this is probably why some have claimed to have discovered the truth, others have asserted that it cannot be apprehended, while others again go on inquiring. Those who believe they have discovered it are the dogmatists. . . . Aristotle for example and Epicurus and the Stoics and certain others; . . . [the] Academics treat it as inapprehensible; the Sceptics keep on searching. Hence it seems reasonable to hold that the main types of philosophy are three—the Dogmatic, the Academic and the Sceptic.' (Trans. R. G. Bury, Loeb Classics, London & Cambridge, Mass., 1933, ch. i.)

[2] He explained his method of teaching in his preface: 'and thus it came about that when the charge of professing philosophy and indeed the philosophy of Aristotle was laid upon me for a period of six years in the Academy at Aix, I always saw to it carefully that my pupils were in a position to defend Aristotle fittingly, but I proposed to them nevertheless by way of appendices the opinions by which Aristotle's dogmatic teaching is weakened. Truth to tell, it was, so to speak, necessary to teach the former, because of the nature of the place and the persons present and the time, but fairness of mind required me not to omit the latter, so that the real reason for suspending the judgment might appear. By this means my pupils were warned not to decide too hastily, seeing that they would never meet with an opinion or proposition so admitted and so plausible that its opposite could not be shown to be equally probable, if not more probable still.' (Trans. from *Opera*, 1658, iii, p. 100.)

his ecclesiastical duties left at his disposal became absorbed in an effort to present the natural and moral philosophy of Epicurus in a form acceptable to the reason and conscience of his contemporaries, an ambition which he realized in the *De vita et moribus Epicuri libri octo* (1647), the *Animadversiones in decimum librum Diogenis Laertii* together with the *Philosophiae Epicuri Syntagma* (1649) and the *Syntagma philosophicum* published posthumously in 1658.

Gassendi's attacks on the three main philosophical positions held by his contemporaries provoked reactions from three different quarters. The astrologer J.-B. Morin, a professor at the Royal College, declared that he ought to be burnt alive, but Morin was not a man whose opinions were taken very seriously and his judgment was repeated only by the practical joker Dassoucy.[1] The Jesuit professors Rapin and Daniel declared him to be a sceptic, but did so in the most moderate of terms.[2] The Cartesians, on the other hand, looked upon him as dangerous. Descartes himself made no such suggestion; the controversy between Mr Mens and Mr Caro (as they called each other) was polite and considerate and neither of the two men endeavoured to embroil the other with the theologians of the Sorbonne. The serious campaign began in the Port-Royal grammar of 1662 with the contention that Gassendi's theory of the origin of ideas was absurd and contrary both to religion and true philosophy.[3] It was carried on by another member of the Port-Royal group, the pugnacious theologian Antoine Arnauld, who deplored Gassendi's teaching as a danger for the young and presented the coming of Descartes as an act of Providence exercised in defence of Christian doctrine.[4] This was the time (at the end of the century) when the Cartesians were making their successful bid for recognition as defenders of the faith and Gassendi provided Arnauld with a useful flogging boy. The hint of immorality in Arnauld's accusations was, however, a very veiled one and he did not suggest that Gassendi had himself taken part in any debauchery. In fact, the only place where the word 'debauch' was used in connection with Gassendi was in a collection of remarks and anecdotes published at Amsterdam in 1710 under the title *L'Esprit de Gui Patin*, and even

[1] '[Chapelle] avait sucé le lait auprès d'un grand philosophe, athée parfait et accompli. (*Les Pensées de Dassoucy*, 1672; *Aventures burlesques* (with text of *Pensées*), ed. Colombey Paris, 1858, p. 359).

[2] F. Bouillier, *Histoire de la philosophie cartésienne*, Paris, 1854, i, pp. 558-9.

[3] Part I, ch. i.

[4] *Difficultés proposées à M. Steyaert* (1692), *Œuvres*, 1776, ix, pp. 305-6.

ere the word was used in such a way that no one could mistake its meaning: it referred to uninhibited private discussion amongst intimate friends and had nothing whatsoever to do with wine-bibbing r delicate supper parties.[1] Two serious studies of Gassendi published in 1737 discountenanced any suggestion that Gassendi had een other than a man of the purest morals.[2] But the story had taken oot. Grimarest, in his life of Molière (1705), had given the puritanically minded a pretext for thinking that if all was not well from heir point of view in the famous comedian's plays, the reason was hat he had taken private lessons from Gassendi, along with Chapelle,)ehénault, Cyrano de Bergerac and Bernier. Diderot, in the article n Epicureanism in the *Encyclopédie*, went further and presented Jassendi as the founder of that delicate and voluptuous way of living which graced aristocratic life at the end of the seventeenth century and during the greater part of his own. In doing so he was far rom any desire to harm Gassendi's reputation and far from disapproving of the activities he described, but when the story reappears under the pens of the nineteenth-century devotees of Descartes, and particularly of Descartes the spiritualist metaphysician, how different s their attitude! Gassendi has become 'suspect'; the disapproving ones of Arnauld reappear with Cousin and Bouillier and the picture f Gassendi as a debauchee in clerical garb wandering from drawing-oom to drawing-room preaching the pleasures of the flesh becomes n accepted feature of literary history. So Gassendi's reputation as a ibertine has not been founded on his original sceptical approach to hilosophical inquiry so much as on tendentious interpretations of he Epicureanism by which he sought to overcome his original excess f intellectual caution.

François de la Mothe le Vayer (1588–1672) presents a far simpler problem. Throughout his long career La Mothe maintained an

---

[1] The passage in question was from a letter of Patin addressed to Falconet in 1648 27 August). It runs as follows: 'Monsieur Naudé, bibliothécaire de Monsieur le Cartinal Mazarin, intime ami de Monsieur Gassendi, comme il est le mien, nous a engagés our dimanche prochain, à aller souper et coucher en sa maison de Gentilly, à la harge que nous y ferons la débauche! Monsieur Naudé n'a jamais bu que de l'eau; 4. Gassendi est si délicat qu'il n'oserait boire du vin; il s'imagine que son corps rûlerait s'il en avait bu; c'est pourquoi je puis appliquer à l'un et à l'autre ce vers 'Ovide: Vina fugit, gaudetque meris abstemius undis. Pour moi, je ne puis que jeter e la poudre sur l'écriture de ces deux grands hommes; je bois fort peu: ce sera pourtant ne débauche; nous l'avons ainsi résolu, mais une débauche philosophique, et peut-être uelque chose davantage.' (cf. *Lettres*, ed. Reveillé-Parise, ii, p. 508.)

[2] Bougerel, *Vie de Gassendi*, Paris, 1737; La Varde (abbé de), *Lettre critique et his-rique à l'auteur de la vie de Gassendi*, Paris, 1737.

attitude of pure Pyrrhonic doubt which was reflected in his enigmatic smile[1] and his detached, absentminded manner. He lived
quietly, affected a rude simplicity of dress and avoided any show of
dogmatism or any attempt to attract public attention to himself. He
followed the law for a time; but gave it up to devote himself entirely
to learning and the range of his erudition became tremendous. He
was eventually appointed tutor to the duke of Orleans in 1649 and
to the young king in 1651. Political pamphlets in favour of Richelieu's policy, pedagogical treatises and moral essays make up his
literary production. We are concerned only with the moral essays.
The *Dialogues d'Orasius Tubero* were first published in 1630, in a
limited edition for the author's friends, though they were more
widely diffused in further editions later in the century. They begin
with *De la Philosophie sceptique*, followed by *Le Banquet sceptique* or
De l'Ignorance louable. The fifth dialogue is entitled *De la Diversité
des religions*.[2] *De la Vertu des païens*, published in 1642, defends
Socrates, Aristotle, Diogenes, Zeno the Stoic (though with no great
warmth), Pyrrho, Epicurus and Confucius. Socrates and Confucius
are placed in the first rank and the author suggests that, pagans
though they were, these two men were worthy of salvation, but of
them all it is Pyrrho who is placed nearest to Christianity. The
Pyrrhonic theme is stated again in the titles of the later works, the
*Deux Discours, le premier du peu de certitude qu'il y a dans l'histoire,
le second de la connaissance de soi-même* of 1668 and the *Soliloques
sceptiques* of 1670. La Mothe's gaze ranges over the world from China
to Peru and through the centuries from ancient Egypt to modern
Italy: what is right? what is wrong? what is true? what is false? No
one knows and no one will ever know. There is no rational ethics, no
rational metaphysics, no rational theology; there is only a mass of
conflicting opinions to which the vagaries of the human mind have
given birth. The search for truth is vain and the wise man severely
limits his pursuit of it. True wisdom lies not in a persistent search
for the truth, but in the quiet of a mind freed from idle curiosity, in
the suspension of the judgment and in conduct guided always by
prudent moderation. Judging by La Mothe's preaching rather than
by his practice, one could say that, while being obviously indepen-

---

[1] See his portrait at the head of his collected works, Paris, 1662.
[2] For a fuller treatment see H. Busson, *La Pensée religieuse française de Charron à
Pascal*, 1933; F. Wickelgren, *La Mothe le Vayer*, 1934; A. Boase, *The Fortunes of
Montaigne*, London, 1935; R. Pintard, *Le Libertinage érudit*, 1943.

dent of Christian thought, he was not actually opposed to it and that the point he stopped at could provide the starting point for the sort of religious belief which follows the abdication of the human reason and exults in its own blindness.[1] La Mothe did not actually take this step, which, once taken, should silence the believer for ever: his acceptance of orthodox belief had the coldness which, in this particular predicament, makes of it a mere conservatism. His attitude was however one of acquiescent neutrality and, if one took account of his conclusions only, one might even say that he was less of a disturbing element in the intellectual life of his time than a man like Mersenne, who priest as he was and enemy of free-thought, was none the less a mathematician and therefore a searcher for the sort of truth that is always consistent with itself. But La Mothe's conclusions are one thing and the insatiable curiosity which amassed the erudition on which they are founded is another. Such knowledge as La Mothe accumulated does not necessarily lead to the humiliation of the human reason. A century later Montesquieu was to use the same knowledge of the diversity of human beliefs and customs in order to constitute a science of human legislations. Montesquieu based his comparative method on precisely those variations and contradictions which for La Mothe's generation were proof of the weakness of the human reason. But for La Mothe there was no real science. It was not until the rationalism of the new philosophy had imposed its methods in every field of inquiry that the work of Montesquieu was to become possible; it could not grow out of mere erudite curiosity. La Mothe's curiosity led nowhere; it resolved itself in immobility and acquiescence. Small wonder is it therefore that he was not singled out for attack by the enemies of free-thought.

The attitude of Gabriel Naudé (1600–53), doctor to Louis XIII, then Mazarin's librarian, was very similar to that of La Mothe except that a certain common-sense rationalism was united to his critical

---

[1] La Mothe says so explicitly: 'elle [la philosophie sceptique] est possible l'une des moins contraires au christianisme et celle qui peut recevoir le plus docilement les mystères de notre religion . . . Notre religion est fondée sur l'humilité, ou sur cette respectueuse abjection d'esprit que Dieu récompense de ses grâces extraordinaires. Et l'on peut assurer que la pauvreté d'esprit bien expliquée est une richesse chrétienne, puisque le Royaume des Cieux est si expressément promis aux pauvres d'entendement. Ce n'est donc pas sans sujet que nous croyons le système sceptique, fondé sur une naïve reconnaissance de l'ignorance humaine, le moins contraire de tous à notre créance et le plus approprié à recevoir les lumières surnaturelles de la foi. Nous ne disons en cela que ce qui est conforme à la meilleure théologie.' (*De la Vertu des païens, Œuvres*, 1662, i, p. 665.)

historical method. He studied medicine in Paris and spent one year at Padua attending the lectures of Cremonini. One of his first publications was a satirical attack on the Rosicrucians who were very much in evidence about 1620 in spite of their being a secret society of the learned, and with his attack on the Rosicrucians he coupled scorn for all occult 'science', astrology, alchemy, magic and cabalistic lore.[1] He followed this in 1625 with a book intended to prove that a number of famous men who had been looked upon as magicians were nothing of the kind.[2] Plato was not amongst them; he looked upon the Platonic tradition as the cause of all occultist and cabalistic aberrations and reserved his respect for Aristotle, interpreted by Cremonini, as the founder of natural science. His interest did not however lead him towards the natural sciences, though he was sufficiently abreast of current speculation to be able to decide for Copernicus against the old cosmology.[3] He devoted his life to erudition and published some fifty historical studies and editions of learned works. He was a destroyer of myths and legends,[4] a forerunner of the brilliant generation of erudites and chronologists who worked in Paris, the Low Countries, England and Germany later in the century and at the beginning of the next, Isaac Vossius, Bayle, Mabillon, Simon, Baillet, Morhof, Moréri, Basnage de Beauval, Leclerc, Lacroze, La Monnoie, Fontenelle, Fréret, Desmaizeaux, Dumarsais, Mirabaud, Marchand, Bernard and many more beside, who completely changed the aspect of historical studies and made possible such a work as Voltaire's *Essai sur les mœurs et l'esprit des nations*.

However, Naudé was not the founder of the critical rationalism of the next generation, which was to come from a fusion of the Cartesian spirit with its very opposite, the original scepticism of the disciples of Montaigne. He was a forerunner of it, but not its founder. He realized that a revolution was taking place in the intellectual world and he did not hesitate to praise the instigators of it, but he did not share with the men of the new science the hope of indefinite progress

---

[1] *Instruction à la France sur la vérité de l'histoire des frères de la Rose-Croix*, Paris, 1623.
[2] *Apologie pour tous les grands personnages qui ont été faussement soupçonnés de magie*, Paris, 1625.
[3] And to add that most 'great men' do so also (*Naudaeana*, Paris, 1701, p. 17).
[4] Concerning Naudé's attitude as an historian, Patin wrote, 'Je suis fort de l'avis de M. Naudé qui disait qu'il y avait quatre choses dont il fallait se garder afin de n'être pas trompé, savoir: de prophéties, de miracles, de révélations et d'apparitions.' (*Lettres*, ed. Reveillé-Parise, ii, p. 490.)

towards the truth and would not have been surprised to see a further revolution bring back the old philosophy to replace the new. Naudé was one of the last humanists rather than one of the first 'philosophers'. His very scepticism led him to prefer the old to the new in religious matters; all dogmatizers and provokers of disputes, Huguenots, Jansenists and promoters of new fashions of piety or belief were anathema to him, *tantum relligio potuit suadere malorum*. He knew his Machiavelli as well as his Lucretius and accepted the skilful maintenance in the popular conscience of notions conducive to the public order as a necessary part of the art of government. He was an absolutist through fear of popular passions. The pursuit of virtue for its own sake was the prerogative of princes and learned inquiry was the privilege of an intellectual *élite*. He addressed himself to the learned and for the most part wrote in Latin.

As for Gui Patin (1600–72), who was dean of the faculty of medicine of the University of Paris from 1652 and professor at the Royal College from 1654, his reputation as a free-thinker depends on a few stories and was hardly merited in a philosophical sense, though he was certainly of a cautious turn of mind, difficult to convince and possessed of a dry and critical wit. He did not believe in the dire effects of comets; he thought that the prophesies of Nostradamus were nonsense; he did not believe there were any real sorcerers or magicians; he thought the Golden Legend was full of superstitious stories and, after relating the story of a belief held in Java that the soul suffers as long as there is flesh left on the bones, remarked that a big book could be written on the ridiculous beliefs of men; he disliked the Jesuits; he was capable of joking about going to a sermon and of saying that it did not happen to him often; he could also joke about belief in immortality, relating how he asked a patient who was dying to return and report on the after-life and how the patient did indeed return but refused to speak, so that he (Patin) had to remain in his former ignorance; he was even capable of saying that doctors profit by their patients' credulity and that the authority of Hippocrates and Galen is not everything in medicine, but he was in no wise a forward-looking thinker. In his own profession he was one of the most conservative persons of his generation; he lived through a revolutionary period in the history of medicine without participating in any of the new developments. He resisted the use of quinquina as a febrifuge, was a great believer in bleeding and did not even declare his acceptance of the circulation of the blood. His physiology remained that of the middle ages even when he expressed scepticism about it: he was content to believe, he said, that the heart is the seat of natural heat, that the lungs produce respiration, that the bile is the excrement of the liver, that the spleen draws the melancholy humours to itself, without attributing any other powers to these organs, such as giving rise to various passions. This can be understood as a sort of positivism,[1] but it is also a refusal to have anything to do with unusual opinions. He was also very attached to established forms; on one occasion, as a young *docteur-régent*, he held up a religious procession in order to argue about his right of precedence. He delighted in Latin literature and was very scornful of any attempt to translate it for the benefit of non-latinists. His scorn for surgeons and apothecaries was unbounded. He had a lively interest in the free-thinking of others, but he was in no sense an originator of ideas.[2]

We are, unfortunately, obliged to resort to contemporary gossip in attempting to describe the minor figures of the group of sceptical erudites. The most one can claim for such evidence is that it gives a general impression of the intellectual atmosphere, whether the stories told are true or not; the mere fact that they were told is sufficient for that. But it would be hazardous to use them to attempt to probe into individual consciences. Of Claude Belurgey (b. 1568), a regent at the Collège de Navarre in the University of Paris, of whom Naudé was a pupil, Patin writes as follows:

I have met people who used to know this teacher of rhetoric and told me that he cared nothing for any religion, set great store on the figures of antiquity, Homer and Aristotle, mocked at the Scriptures and especially Moses and all the prophets, hated Jews and monks, believed in neither miracles nor prophecies, visions or revelations, laughed at the idea of purgatory, which he called a *chimera buzzing in the void and consuming second intentions* [a scholastic term]. He used to say that the two silliest books in the world were Genesis and the Golden Legend, that the Empyrean was a mere fiction, *heaven and hell were a fable*. He set great store on a passage

---

[1] Patin said that in theology he was prepared to take much on trust, but in medicine only believed what he saw with his own eyes. *Esprit de Gui Patin*, Amsterdam, 1710, p. 118. The *Esprit de Gui Patin*, like the *Patiniana* of 1701, is a collection of extracts from Patin's correspondence and private papers.)

[2] *Esprit de Gui Patin*, pp. 90 (comets), 23 (Nostradamus), 65 (sorcerers), 57 (Golden Legend), 185 (Java), 41 (sermons), 77 (Hippocrates), 1–2 (physiology), 45 (credulity), 43 (procession), 59 (surgeons); *Lettres*, ed. Reveillé-Parise, iii, p. 758 (Jesuits); Tallemand des Réaux, *Historiettes*, ed. Monmerqué (1840), ii, p. 193 (immortality); *Patiniana*, Paris, 1701, p. 9 (magicians).

from Seneca: *What makes hell terrible to us is a fable; the poets counter-feited it to affright us with vain terrors etc.* One day, on account of some remark he had made, he was asked what was his religion and replied that it was the religion of the greatest men of antiquity, Homer, Aristotle, Cicero, Pliny, Seneca, whom he rated highly by reason of a chorus in the *Troades* which begins with these words: *Is it true, or does a fable deceive the timid that the shades live on when the bodies are buried?*[1]

Of François Guyet (1575–1655), a grammarian of the Collège de Bourgogne in the University of Paris, and an intimate of the Du Puy brothers, Guez de Balzac wrote that he proclaimed his atheism on the public squares whereas La Mothe le Vayer was content to whisper in his disciples' ears, but Balzac was not preparing to denounce Guyet; on the contrary he claimed at the same time to have made Guyet's peace with the Cardinal de la Vallette, the grammarian's pupil.[2]

A further story, which we owe to Gui Patin, concerns Gui de la Brosse, the naturalist and director of the Jardin du Roi. When he died in 1641, Patin, who hated him, called him an atheist and a hypocrite and told the following story. When La Brosse was showing some ladies round his house in the Jardin du Roi, he said, on coming to the chapel, 'this is the salting-house where they will put the hog

---

[1] Patin to Spon((1662) in *Lettres de Gui Patin*, ed. Reveillé-Parise, ii, pp. 478–9: 'J'ai vu des gens qui ont autrefois connu ce maître de rhétorique, lesquels m'ont dit qu'il ne se souciait d'aucune religion, faisait un état extraordinaire de deux hommes de l'antiquité, qui ont été Homère et Aristote, se moquait de la Sainte Ecriture, surtout de Moïse et de tous les prophètes, haïssait les Juifs et les moines, n'admettait aucun miracle, prophétie, vision ni révélation, se moquait du purgatoire qu'il appelait *chimera bombinans in vacuo et comedens secundas intentiones*. Il disait que les deux plus sots livres du monde étaient la Genèse et la Vie des Saints, que le ciel empirée était une pure fiction, *illi fabula erant caelum et inferi*. Il faisait grand état d'un passage de Sénèque: *Quae nobis inferos faciunt terribiles, fabula est; luserunt ista poetae ut vanis nos agitarent terroribus* etc. On lui demanda un jour, sur quelque mot qu'il avait lâché, de quelle religion il était; il répondit qu'il était de la religion des plus grands hommes de l'antiquité, Homère, Aristote, Cicéron, Pline, Sénèque, duquel il faisait grand cas pour un *chorus* qui est *in Troadibus* qui commence par ces mots: *Verum est an timidos fabula decepit umbras corporibus vivere conditis?* etc.

[2] 'Celui-ci [La Mothe] n'est pas meilleur ami de Jésus-Christ que celui-là que nous voulons châtier [Guyet]. A la vérité son athéisme a un peu plus de discrétion et il se contente de siffler à l'oreille de ses disciples ce que l'autre voudrait faire savoir à son de trompe dans les places et sur les théâtres. L'un et l'autre méritent l'indignation des fidèles. Mais le Campané Grammairien doit être publiquement foudroyé. Il faut de nécessité en faire un exemple:

> Ne se jus commune hominum, ne quicquid ubique
> Augusti sanctique colunt, laetetur ineptus
> Grammaticus violasse, et spreto insultet Olympo.'

(*Lettres de J.-L. Guez de Balzac*, publ. by Ph. Tamizey de Larroque, in *Mélanges historiques*, i, Imprimerie nationale, 1873, pp. 802, 808.)

when it dies', applying Horace's famous expression 'Epicuri de grege porcum' to himself by implication. How much worthier a man was Epicurus than La Brosse, goes on Patin; Epicurus did not follow Christ because he had no knowledge of him, La Brosse did not follow him though he had that knowledge.[1] Whether La Brosse was an atheist or not it is difficult to ascertain independently of Patin's statement, which it would be hazardous to accept at its face value. From his published work *De la Nature des plantes* (1628) one can only conclude that he applied uncompromisingly the method of pure observation, refusing to proceed from the observed facts in the direction of any systematic philosophy. Though impressed by the obvious dependence of plant life on the action of the sun, he was not prepared to make of the sun's heat the soul of the plant or admit of any knowledge whatsoever concerning such a soul. However, on the title-page of his book he had printed the words 'la vérité non l'autorité' and a flaming sun which does not look like a mere printer's trademark; one finds it also on Campanella's title-pages. Furthermore, he had a precise conception of what was meant by living according to nature. At the dawn of history, nature and virtue were closely related, virtue merely holding nature with a gentle rein, but since that happy time law and particularly religion have drawn the rein tighter and now pull in the opposite direction.[2] Neither La Brosse's scientific empiricism nor his ethical naturalism had any

[1] After saying that La Brosse refused to be bled and called the doctors sanguinary pedants, Patin goes on: 'Le diable le saignera en l'autre monde, comme mérite un fourbe, un athée, un imposteur, un homicide et bourreau public tel qu'il était, qui même en mourant n'a eu non plus le sentiment de Dieu qu'un pourceau, duquel il imitait la vie, et s'en donnait le nom. Comme un jour il montrait sa maison à des dames, quand il vint à la chapelle du logis, il leur dit: "Voilà le saloir où l'on mettra le pourceau quand il sera mort", en se montrant, et se nommait assez souvent "pourceau d'Epicure", combien qu'Epicure valût bien mieux que lui quem scribunt Galenus et Seneca fuisse vitae sanctissimae et continentissimae: Epicurus non coluit Christum quia non novit, Brossaeus non coluit quem noverat.' (*Lettres*, ed. Reveillé-Parise, i, pp. 81–2, to Belin, 4 Sept. 1641.)

[2] 'La nature et la vertu ne naquirent pas ensemble. Il y avait déjà longtemps que la première gouvernait le monde par la simplicité de ses lois quand la vertu parut; quelques prud'hommes du vieux siècle lui donnèrent premièrement l'être au plus près des intentions et des désirs de la nature: lors il y avait peu de vicieux; mais depuis, la vertu ayant été jointe à la loi, la religion l'a faite son esclave et l'a mise à l'étroit: elle lui a rendu la nature suspecte, de sorte que d'amis qu'elles étaient, elles ne font plus que se picoter; elle était grandement libre et fort universelle: prise pour action, c'était un usage modéré des appétits de l'homme selon la simple et parfaite nature; et ores ce n'est qu'une habitude qui dresse les facultés intellectuelles, les sens internes et les appétits sensuels au bien. (*Traité contre la médisance*, 1624, pp. 183–4; cf. Pintard, *Le Libertinage érudit*, p. 198.)

great need of the religious beliefs of the times. Of that one can be certain without the help of Patin's gossip.

Patin is again the source of a story concerning a lawyer friend of La Mothe named René de Chantecler, president since 1633 of the Parlement of Metz. Chantecler, wrote Patin, died a bachelor in August 1641. He was very learned and widely read, but had a particular hatred for monks. Having made his confession, he said these words, 'A man should die κατὰ πατρίους νόμους, that is to say accepting the laws and religion of his own country.' Charron, adds Patin, said that it is normal to belong to the same religion as the king, or one's family or the country, Malherbe that he understood not at all the religion he was taught, but did like other people, provisionally, and often said one should worship the deity worshipped by the state.[1]

Patin also tells us that Naudé held the same views about remaining in the religion in which one was born and considered that changes of religion were a sign of wrong-headedness and that it was not worth while to change anyway. He attributed this attitude to the fact that Naudé had spent several years in Italy, where the only good Christians are Jesuits and monks (he adds with heavy sarcasm),[2] but it is readily understandable that sceptical men of a generation born soon after the end of the wars of religion should have been disinclined

---

[1] 'M. de Chantecler, Président au Parlement de Metz, fils d'un maître des Requêtes et frère de feue madame des Portes Bevilliers, est mort vieux garçon, sans avoir jamais été marié, l'an 1641, au mois d'août. Comme il avait été fantasque toute sa vie, aussi a-t-il laissé un testament fort bizarre par lequel il a laissé entre autres à M. de la Mothe le Vayer son ami 8.000 livres. Il était fort savant et homme de grande lecture, mais qui haïssait extrêmement les moines. Ayant été confessé et communié, il dit ces mots: "Il faut qu'un honnête homme meure κατὰ πατρίους νόμους, c'est-à-dire dans la loi et la religion de son pays." Charron, en sa *Sagesse*, liv. Ier, chap. 5, a dit qu'ordinairement on est de la religion de son prince, de ses parents ou de son pays. Malherbe disait qu'il n'entendait rien à la religion qu'on nous prêchait, mais que par provision il fallait faire comme les autres, et avait ordinairement à la bouche ce mot qu'il tenait pour fort bon: *cole daemonium quod colit civitas* qu'on dit être d'un ancien empereur romain nommé Galienus. Mais cette maxime est très dangereuse.' (Pintard, *Le Libertinage érudit*, p. 180.)

[2] 'M. Naudé disait qu'il fallait demeurer comme l'on était, et que c'était la marque d'un esprit mal tourné de changer souvent de religion, que le tout n'en valait pas la peine: *nota* qu'il avait demeuré treize ans en Italie auprès du cardinal Bagni et qu'il avait été l'intime ami de Cremonini, qui n'était point meilleur chrétien que Pomponace, que Machiavel, que Cardan et telles autres âmes moutonnières dont le pays abonde, j'entends l'Italie, où il y a bien plus de rusés et fins politiques que de bons chrétiens, excepté les jésuites et les moines, gens d'honneur et de probité, grands serviteurs de Dieu, gens de charité et de conscience, qui aiment et servent Dieu et ne veulent que *votre bien*.' (*Lettres*, ed. Reveillé-Parise, iii, p. 758; August 1670.) Naudé had spent twelve years, not thirteen, in Italy.

to leave the Catholic religion in order to embrace the Protestant; in that respect one may well say that the Catholic church derived benefit from the sceptical traditionalism of the *libertins*.

Concerning Philippe Fortin de la Hoguette (1585–*c*.1670), tutor to the duc de Longueville's sons, we have the direct evidence of his *Testament ou conseils fidèles d'un bon père à ses enfants*, a little treatise published at Leyden in 1655 on natural religion and the wisdom of following the religion of one's own country; there has been a long uninterrupted series of Catholic kings, writes La Hoguette, and the peace of the country depends on the continuance of Catholicism as the religion of the country. Natural religion shows us the existence of a God who is the originator of all nature, but a God whose nature is unknown to us; he may be imagined by analogy with the sun, which (according to the 'moderns') is the centre of our world. The *libertins*, he adds, distinguishing himself pointedly from them and calling down the law upon them, see the ordered actions of nature, but cannot rise above this conception to the universal harmony and its sovereign principle. To this sketch of his deism and traditionalist Catholicism, he adds a little treatise of morals for the gentleman: moderate one's appetites, know oneself and a little of nature, but leave the study of astronomy to the specialists, study history, read novels with circumspection, follow the career of arms, study society and the court, be flexible, study social organization based on the family as the social unit. All this is very circumspect and conservative, but there is a clear realization implied in it that only by circumspection can questions be avoided which might upset a gentleman's peace of mind.

This brings us to the end of the short list of scholarly sceptics of the first half of the seventeenth century who are known to us; there were doubtless many more sceptically minded scholars whose trace has been entirely lost and a host of men of inquiring mind whose individual existence the public was not aware of,[1] but in this study we can devote our attention only to the men who for good or ill left behind them a name to which an idea may be attached.

[1] Such a person was J.-J. Bouchard whose strange physiognomy has been resurrected by Professor Pintard. He was a friend of Gassendi, Naudé, Luillier, the Du Puy brothers and looked upon as being highly intelligent, but his ideas seem never to have had any sort of consistency.

II

The Crisis of 1619–1625: The Radical Naturalists

THE sceptics were prudent men of settled and stable character. When we turn to those who continued the naturalistic tradition, we find ourselves in the company of men of a different stamp, restless, proud and unsubmissive in spirit. Two such men of the early years of the century were Giulio Cesare Vanini and Théophile de Viau. Vanini was executed in 1619; Théophile narrowly escaped a like fate in 1625. In the intervening years an unknown author wrote the proud catechism of libertine ethics known as the *Quatrains du déiste*. The line of these radical thinkers continues intermittently throughout the century. The authors of utopias and imaginary travel stories, Cyrano de Bergerac, Foigny, Vairasse, maintained the tradition cloaked in fictional guise. The author of the enigmatic *Theophrastus redivivus* in the middle years and Jean Meslier in the closing years of the century or the first years of the next, systematized the tenets of philosophical and political radicalism in the most downright and uncompromising manner. It is with such an attitude of protest, and not with the acquiescent open-mindedness of a La Mothe or a Naudé, that can be associated also the negations of a number of noblemen who had a reputation for unbelief without making any positive contribution to the intellectual life of their times, Roquelaure Romainville, Haudessens, Cramail, Savary (marquis of Brèves).[1] Guez de Balzac and Tallemant des Réaux also tell the story of a foreign nobleman, reputed to be Maurice of Nassau (d. 1625), who died saying that he believed that two and two make four and that the only certain truth is the truth of mathematics.[2] It is to this com-

[1] Most of our information concerning them comes from Tallemant des Réaux, *Historiettes*. Cf. H. Busson, *La Pensée religieuse française de Charron à Pascal*, Paris, 1933, p. 452.

[2] 'Une heure avant que ce prince rendît l'esprit, le théologien protestant qui prêchait d'ordinaire devant lui l'était venu visiter accompagné de deux ou trois autres de la même communion. S'approchant de son lit avec une profonde révérence, il le conjura au nom de toute leur église de vouloir rendre quelque témoignage de la religion qu'il professait et de faire une espèce de confession de foi qui pût être recueillie de la compagnie, afin, disait-il, que les dernières paroles d'un si grand personnage se conservassent dans la mémoire des hommes, et donnassent de l'autorité à l'opinion qu'il avait suivie. A cette

pany that Molière's Don Juan belongs rather than to the company of the sceptics or the Epicureans, who in their various ways took life very much as they found it. An impulse towards self-assertion and a craving after the absolute, be it merely the absolute of complete negation, is common to both the plebeian and the aristocratic radicals.

The reputation of Giulio Cesare Vanini[1] (1585-1619) has suffered many vicissitudes since he was brutally done to death by order of the Parlement of Toulouse. A strange figure, tall and pale, with a large nose and bald head, this Carmelite monk frightened the youthful Gui Patin when he met him in Paris in the years before 1612.[2] He lived the life of a wanderer. After studying medicine and theology in Naples, Rome and Padua, he travelled through Europe, visiting Geneva, Germany, the Low Countries, England, France, incapable of keeping the favour of wealthy patrons like Bassompierre, in whose household he served for a time as almoner, never enjoying the safety afforded by the colleges and the libraries of the great to unorthodox scholars. He was restless; he was poor; he tried to live by currying favour, by displaying talent and charm. He was involved in at least one serious fight and there is reason for thinking that he killed his assailant, a certain Henry Silvius.[3] He lived in Paris for some years

demande le prince se mit un peu à sourire et lui répondit incontinent après: "Monsieur mon ami, j'ai bien du déplaisir de ne vous pouvoir donner le contentement que vous désirez de moi. Mais vous voyez que je ne suis pas en état de faire de longs discours ni de vous rendre compte de ma créance par le menu. Je vous dirai seulement en peu de mots que je crois que deux et deux font quatre et quatre et quatre font huit. Monsieur Tel (montrant du doigt un mathématicien qui était là présent) vous pourra éclaircir des autres points de notre créance." ' (Balzac, *Socrate chrétien*, 1652, p. 181, *Œuvres*, ed. Moreau, Paris, 1854, pp. 95-6); 'Etant à l'extrémité, il fit venir un ministre et un prêtre et les fit disputer de la religion et après les avoir ouïs assez longtemps: "Je vois bien, dit-il, qu'il n'y a rien de certain que les mathématiques." ' In a note at the foot of the page: 'On conte d'un prince d'Allemagne fort adonné aux mathématiques qu'interrogé à l'article de la mort par un confesseur s'il ne croyait pas etc.: "Nous autres mathématiciens, lui dit-il, croyons que deux et deux font quatre et quatre et quatre font huit." ' (Tallemant des Réaux, *Historiettes*, ed. Monmerqué, 2nd edn., Paris, 1840, ii, pp. 131 and 493 n.)

[1] This, and not Lucilio, was his real name; for a discussion on this point, see A. Baudouin, *Histoire critique de Jules-César Vanini* (*Revue des Pyrénées*, xv, 1902, p. 111).

[2] Patin, *Correspondance*, 26 Dec. 1653. Cf. 'Cet homme grand de taille, un peu maigre, au poil châtain, au nez long et recourbé, aux yeux brillants et aucunement hagards.' (*Annales manuscrites de l'hôtel de ville de Toulouse*, vi, f. 13, quoted by V. Cousin in *Revue des Deux Mondes*, 1843, pp. 719-20.)

[3] Baudouin, op. cit., p. 286. Baudouin's biographical sketch is the best available, but it is marred by a tendency to embroider on the few known facts of Vanini's career. F. Strowski embroiders far more on the few facts supplied by Baudouin, and with obvious ill-will as far as Vanini is concerned. (*Pascal et son temps*, Paris, 1907, i, p. 145.)

before 1612; then he came to England, possibly after the Silvius affair, and abjured the Catholic faith, only to flee the country when ecclesiastical favour cooled towards him. He travelled in the south of France under the assumed name of Pompeio Usiglio, in secular dress and earning his living by giving private lessons in philosophy and medicine. He was foolhardy enough to choose, of all places in which to seek pupils, Toulouse, a town famous for its zeal in the suppression of heresy, and, being without protection from a man of rank, fell an easy prey to his persecutors. He was arrested, kept in prison for six months and finally condemned on the evidence of one of his pupils, a member of the local gentry, who came forward at the last moment to bear witness against him. His judges were, presumably, convinced that they were putting an end to a public scandal, but the 'corruption of youth' of which he was accused was not claimed to be of a sexual nature. The accusation of homosexual practices was not made at the time, nor in any seventeenth- or eighteenth-century account of Vanini's life; it appeared first in an article by Victor Cousin in the *Revue des Deux Mondes* in 1843 and was based on a document which has since been shown to be a forgery perpetrated by Cousin's 'informant'.[1] Vanini was condemned for 'atheism', as both the text of the sentence, discovered by Cousin, and the account of an eye-witness, B. de Grammont, make quite clear. Grammont's account of the proceedings runs as follows.

He professed to teach medicine, but in reality poisoned the minds of imprudent youths; he mocked at sacred things, vilified the Incarnation, knew no God, attributed all things to fate, adored Nature as the bounteous mother and source of all being. Such was the origin of all his errors and he dogmatized persistently on the subject in the devout city of Toulouse. The unfailing attraction of novelty for the young brought him many disciples, especially from amongst the young men fresh from school. Of Italian origin, he had studied first in Rome and had applied himself with success to philosophy and theology, but had fallen into impiety and sacrilege and disgraced his priest's habit by the publication of an infamous book entitled the *Secrets of Nature*, in which he shamelessly proclaimed nature as the goddess of the universe. Accused of crime in Italy, he came to Toulouse. There is no town in France where the law is stricter with regard to heretics, and, although the Edict of Nantes accords protection to the Calvinists, and they have the right to trade and participate in public administration, they have never trusted themselves to Toulouse, so that Toulouse, of all the towns in France, is free of heresy and has never admitted to its

[1] See Baudouin, op. cit., p. 517 n.

freedom any person suspect by the Holy See. Vanini kept quiet for some time, but vanity led him to cast doubts upon the mysteries of the Catholic faith and then to vilify them, applauded by your young men, who like nothing better than novel opinions, especially such as are held by a small minority only. They admired all he said and they imitated and followed him. He was accused of corrupting young men by his new doctrines. He pretended at first to be an orthodox Catholic, in order to gain time; he was even about to be set at liberty, when a gentleman of the name of Francon, a man of great integrity, as can be seen from the mere fact that he took this action, bore witness that Vanini had often denied the existence of God and had mocked the mysteries of the Christian religion. The accused was confronted with the witness. Francon maintained his assertions. Vanini was brought before the court and in the box, when asked what he held concerning God, replied that he worshipped one God in three persons as did the Church and that Nature herself proved clearly the existence of God. As he said this, his eye fell on a piece of straw lying on the floor, and picking it up and showing it to the judges, he said, 'this piece of straw commands me to believe there is a God'. Then, passing to the question of divine providence, he added, 'the seed cast into the ground seems at first to languish and die, to whiten by decay, but then it turns green, is reborn, increases imperceptibly, feeds on the morning dew, draws strength from the rain, puts out its barbed ears to drive away the birds, swells and rises tubelike, shoots out leaves, ripens to yellow, bends its head and dies. Thrashed, and the grain separated from the chaff, it serves as food for man and the beasts intended for man's use.' From all this he concluded that God was the author of nature, replying to the objection that nature could be the cause of all by passing from the seed itself to the cause which produced the seed, in this manner, 'if nature produces this particular seed, who produced the seed from which it sprang? And if this is the product of nature, what of its predecessor, etc., until he reached the first seed, which must have been produced by creation, there being no anterior principle from which to derive it. And thus he concluded that God is the creator of all things. Lucilio spoke thus to show his learning, or else by fear, rather than by conviction, but the evidence against him was overwhelming and he was duly condemned to death, after an enquiry lasting six months. I saw him in the cart which bore him to the stake, mocking at the Franciscan monk who sought to soften his obdurate soul. He refused the consolation offered by the monk, pushed aside the proffered crucifix and insulted Christ in these words, 'He sweated with fear at his last hour, while I die unafraid.' He spoke false; I saw him give the lie to the philosophy he professed to teach. At the last moment, his face was wild and horrible, his soul tormented, his speech confused, and though he frequently proclaimed that he would die like a philosopher, he died like a beast. Before the fire was lit, being ordered to submit his sacrilegious tongue to the knife, he refused, and pincers had to be used to drag it out; having seized it, the executioner sliced it off. Never was more horrible cry; one would have said the bellow of a stricken ox. The fire consumed the remains; the ashes were scattered to the winds. Such was Lucilio Vanini's end. How much constancy was his is shown by the bestial clamour he made at his death. I saw him in prison; I saw him at the stake; I had seen him before he was arrested. While he was at liberty he lived loosely and was an ardent pleasure-seeker. In prison he was a Catholic, but at the last moment, abandoned by his philosophy, he died raving. During his life he sought the secrets of nature and made a profession of medicine rather than theology, although he liked to pass for a theologian. When his goods were seized at his arrest, an enormous toad was found in a glass bowl full of water. Accused of sorcery on this account, he replied that a toad, burnt alive, provided a cure for a disease which would otherwise be fatal. In prison he took the sacrament regularly, hiding his real opinions, but when he saw that all was lost, he dropped his mask and died as he had lived.[1]

The *Mercure françois* of 1619 (v, p. 63) gave other details, but without stating the source of its information. According to the *Mercure*, Vanini taught, in his private lessons, that men were without souls and died like brute beasts, and that the Virgin had carnal relations like other women. It added that when Vanini was brought out of prison, to be taken to the Place du Salin for execution, he cried out in Italian, 'Let us die cheerfully as a philosopher!' and that on the way to the stake he replied, on being ordered to ask mercy of God, that there was neither God nor Devil, for had there been a God, he would have begged him to strike with his lightning the unjust and iniquitous Parlement of Toulouse, and he would have begged the Devil, had there been one, to engulf it in the underworld, but as there was neither, he would pray to neither.

Garasse descended like a vulture on his reputation as a man and made no effort to understand him as a thinker, being content to accuse him of hypocrisy. In his books and in private, says Garasse, Vanini professed a hatred of atheism and his conduct was devout, but all that was mere dissimulation. His one great fear was to be taken for a libertine, but that was mere cowardice. He did not believe in possession by devils, because, when one of the speakers in the *Dialogues on Nature* (*De admirandis naturae . . . arcanis*) explained such conditions by the effects of a melancholy humour, the other was content to submit to the decisions of the Church. Garasse himself

[1] *Historiarum Galliae ab excessu Henrici IV libri XVIII*, Toulouse, 1643, iii, pp. 208-10.

did not need to make any such sacrifice of his reason; he was firmly convinced, for instance, that Luther was possessed of a devil and was scratched about the face by him; so, for Garasse, submission on such a point was obvious humbug. It is true that Garasse himself calls Vanini a 'hypochondriac' and at the same time accuses him of being possessed of a devil, but for the Jesuit both the medical and the theological explanations were rational. As for Vanini's suggestion that the calming effect of holy water on one possessed might well come from the cooling effect of water on an overheated brain, Garasse professed to be mightily shocked by it.[1]

There is no evidence of any attempt having been made to call in question the judgment of the Parlement of Toulouse before Pierre Bayle did so in 1682. Descartes came nearest to it by suggesting that the verdict was motivated only by the evidence given before the court, there being no justification for it in Vanini's writings; he did not, however, actually express doubt about the judgment.[2] All the others who mentioned the case added their word of condemnation. Mersenne's favourite epithet for Vanini was 'stultissimus'.[3] Dabillon[4] and Grenaille[5] were content with vituperation. Guez de Balzac varied this with astonishment at the constancy shown by Vanini in his last hours, but called it 'obstinacy' and 'obduracy'; there was no trace of pity in his remarks.[6] Patin threw his stone like the rest, with the possible, but not probable, intention that it should ricochet (the dean of the faculty of Medicine did not like 'cads' and 'gutter-snipes'); he declared that Vanini's book, the De admirandis naturae . . . arcanis, was nothing more than a compilation drawn from the works of Scaliger, Cardano, Frascator and Pomponazzi.[7] For

---

[1] La Doctrine curieuse des beaux esprits de ce temps, 1623, pp. 350, 853, 858, 972–3.

[2] Letter to Voet (1642) (Œuvres, ed. Cousin, xi, p. 185; ed. Adam and Tannery, viii (2), p. 182).

[3] Quaestiones in Genesim, 1623, passim; or 'brutal' (Impiété des déistes, i, 237 e.g.).

[4] 'Cet avorton d'Italie que la piété de nos cours souveraines condamna justement au feu pour l'impiété de ses dogmes et pour ses impuretés diaboliques.' (La Divinité défendue contre les athées, 1641, quoted by H. Busson in La Pensée religieuse française de Charron à Pascal, p. 39.)

[5] 'Sa langue allait causer un grand incendie si le Parlement de Toulouse en le laissant brûler tout vif n'eût éteint un feu par l'autre. Il faut que des âmes si damnées que celle-là sentent leur enfer dès cette vie.' (La Mode ou Caractère de la religion . . . Paris, 1642, quoted by H. Busson, op. cit., p. 39.)

[6] Socrate chrétien (1652), p. 179; Œuvres, ed. Moreau, 1854, p. 95 (ed. Souriau, p. 260).

[7] Naudaeana et Patiniana (1701), p. 31. 'Ce misérable était las de vivre et enragé à mourir, parce qu'il était gueux ou du moins parce qu'il n'avait pas autant d'argent qu'il voulait.'

Rosset[1] and for Spitzel,[2] as for Grammont, he had attributed to nature what ought to be attributed to God. The name Vanini became a synonym for 'atheist'. Gisbert Voet, a professor at Utrecht, used it thus when he accused Descartes of atheism, but, as Descartes pointed out, Voet constantly spelled Vanini's name wrongly, calling him Vaninius, instead of Vaninus,[3] so Descartes was probably justified in claiming that Voet was ill-acquainted with the subject. Knowledge of Vanini was coming to depend on hearsay. The compilers of historical dictionaries, Moréri and Jeremy Collier, merely stated that he was a blasphemer who deserved his fate. Collier repeated the story retailed by Garasse and Mersenne to the effect that Vanini set out with twelve companions from Italy on a tour of atheistic proselytizing throughout Europe. Samuel Parker, bishop of Oxford, claimed that with Vanini's death a pest had been extirpated and called Vanini's constancy in the face of death an 'indecoram et beluinam quandam fortitudinem'.[4]

Except for Descartes's reservations, the chorus of vituperation was universal until the *Pensées sur la comète de* 1680 struck a new and discordant note. After this, writings devoted to Vanini, though disagreeing with Bayle for the most part, adopted a much more moderate attitude and language. The language of hate and fear reappears, it is true, in an academic diatribe by a certain Thomas Jenkins, printed in Basel in 1709, but this is an isolated outburst.

One of Bayle's main contentions in the *Pensées sur la comète* was that speculative beliefs are quite independent of morals, and *vice versa*, so that an atheist may well be an honest man and a superstitious man a villain. Vanini was an atheist, but he was not a villain; he was charged with no crime other than atheism, so any person who had referred to him as a villain might well have found himself sued for slander.[5]

[1] 'Vanini composa un livre des causes naturelles, il donnait à la nature ce qui n'appartient proprement qu'au créateur de l'univers et de la nature même' (*Histoires tragiques*, p. 203, quoted by Deutsche, *Dissertatio prior de Vanini scriptis*, Jena, 1708). The passage is to be found in one edition only according to Baudouin, op. cit., p. 377 n.

[2] [Vaninus in Dialogis] Naturae omnia (excluso Numine) in solidum tribuere, eam Deae instar colere et venerari, ac simul regiam atheismo viam sternere non dubitavit. (*De atheismi radice epistola*, Augsburg, 1666, p. 50.)

[3] *Letter to Voet* (*Œuvres*, ed. Cousin, xi, p. 185; ed. Adam & Tannery, viii (2), p. 182).

[4] *Disputationes de Deo et providentia divina*, London, 1678, p. 86.

[5] 'Le détestable Vanini qui fut brûlé à Toulouse pour son athéisme l'an 1619 avoit toujours été assez réglé dans ses mœurs et quiconque eût entrepris de lui faire un procès criminel sur toute autre chose que sur ses dogmes auroit couru grand risque d'être convaincu de calomnie.' (*Pensées sur la comète*, ed. Prat, 1912, ii, p. 111).

Another new note was struck in 1683 by a Lutheran theologian of Wittenberg, Diecmann, who remarked on the fact that the greatest uncertainty reigned as to what Vanini had actually taught in his books. Diecmann was firmly convinced of Vanini's villainy by the account given by Grammont and repeated by Parker, but he realized, having read Vanini's works, that an explicit proclamation of 'naturalism' was not to be found in them. 'The great rarity of his books,' he declared, 'has been the cause whereby many people have judged incorrectly of his writings as though they distributed this same naturalism from a full store; having examined these famous books of Vanini with more care, we do not agree.'[1]

At the beginning of the eighteenth century several attempts were made by Protestant writers to re-examine the question of Vanini's life and teaching. Three of these were academic theses sustained by students of theology in German universities. They are straightforward accounts of Vanini's life and works and are moderate in tone.[2] One of them concludes with Descartes that there must have been secret evidence to explain the verdict.[3] Leibniz suggested that the real reason was a personal rivalry between the *procureur général* of the Parlement of Toulouse and the first president of the court: Vanini was tutor to the president's children and the *procureur* had him arrested in order to spite his colleague.[4] This is mere surmise, but it is none the less significant of a profound change of attitude. In 1712 a Protestant writer named Arpe published in Rotterdam a closely reasoned reply to Garasse's accusations of blasphemy and impiety and refused to discuss the charge of atheism on the ground that the word 'atheist' was a general term of abuse bandied about indiscriminately by the Jesuit.[5] The *Journal des savants*, at the end of a long analysis of Arpe's book, was content to point out that the Parlement of Toulouse had a great reputation for zeal in defence of

[1] *De naturalismo*, 1683, p. 22.

[2] J. W. Apel, *De vita et fatis Julii Caesaris Vanini, dissertatio prior*, Jena, 1708; J. Deutsche, *Dissertatio posterior de Vanini scriptis et opinionibus . . .*, Jena, 1708; J. M. Schramm, *De Vita et scriptis famosi athei Julii Caesaris Vanini tractatus*, Custrin, 1719.

[3] Deutsche, op. cit., p. 15.

[4] 'Quand on lui demanda s'il y avait un Dieu, il arracha l'herbe, en disant: Et levis est cespes qui probat esse Deum. Mais le procureur général du Parlement de Toulouse, voulant chagriner le premier président (à ce qu'on dit), chez qui Vanini avait beaucoup d'accès, et enseignait la philosophie aux enfants de ce magistrat, s'il n'était pas tout à fait son domestique, l'inquisition fut poussée avec rigueur.' (*Remarques sur le livre de l'origine du mal* [de W. King], in *Œuvres*, ed. P. Janet, ii, pp. 410–11.)

[5] *Apologia pro Jul. Caesare Vanino, Neapolitano*, 'Cosmopoli', 1711.

the faith![1] Such discretion could have only one significance, namely that the reviewer was impressed by Arpe's arguments. Arpe's apologia was nothing if not thorough-going; his aim was to show that not only had Vanini's character been slandered, but that he was not even an unorthodox thinker. He tried to prove too much for Voltaire's liking, as we shall see. The fact of the matter is that the greatest uncertainty reigned as to what Vanini's teaching had actually been and the result was at times paradoxical; Vanini was accused of atheism on the basis of statements to which a doctor of the Sorbonne would not have refused assent. An interesting example is provided by David Durand, a Calvinist minister from Rotterdam, living in London, who wrote in reply to Bayle an attack on Vanini entitled *La Vie et les sentiments de Lucilio Vanini*.[2] Durand admitted ingenuously that he did not understand Vanini's metaphysics, and some of his remarks do indeed betray a complete ignorance of the traditional teaching of the schools. He quotes, for instance, a sentence in which God is described as a Being in whom all is actual and nothing is merely potential ('en qui rien n'est en puissance et tout est en acte') and adds the remark that this is a falsehood which would deprive God of his sovereign liberty and introduce complete naturalism (p. 87). The only proof of the existence of God which Durand was prepared to accept was that drawn from the necessity of supposing a prime-mover in the universe and this was precisely the argument which Vanini rejected with scorn as limiting the being of God and situating him in time and space. Vanini preferred to argue that the existence of contingent beings presupposes the existence of a necessary Being, and for Durand this implies 'naturalism' or 'spinozism' as it was called at the time. Another Protestant minister, Jacques Saurin of The Hague, seized upon the same passage, in which Vanini attempts to express the idea of Absolute Being, and held it up as a proof of Vanini's hypocrisy. Saurin was so self-conscious about such statements as that God exists outside time and yet through countless ages and others equally self-contradictory (for Vanini the idea of Absolute Being resolves all contradictions), that he concluded that Vanini had intended by their

[1] *Journal des savants*, 6 February 1713.
[2] Rotterdam, 1719 (written in 1714—Preface); an English translation was published in London in 1730 under the title *The Life of Lucilio (alias Julius Caesar) Vanini, burnt for atheism at Toulouse with an abstract of his writings being the sum of the atheistical doctrine taken from Plato, Aristotle, Averroes, Cardano and Pomponazzius's philosophy with a confutation of the same; and Mr. Bayle's arguments in behalf of Vanini completely answered.*

mere exposition to prove their absurdity: but, adds Saurin, we are proud to believe such things.[1]

On one issue, however, even Durand represents a change of front as compared with seventeenth-century opinion. He condemned the action of the Parlement of Toulouse: 'The Parliament of Toulouse drove things a little too far. It is, I confess, the interest of princes and republics to suppress impiety when it dogmatizes because of the fatal consequences it may have among a society of Christians, but I cannot tell whether that should not be moderated by prudence.'[2] This is a half-hearted condemnation, but a condemnation none the less. The Protestant erudite La Croze, who taught philosophy at the French College at Berlin, was more decided; he affirmed that a recantation should have been judged sufficient.[3] Leibniz, as we have seen, condemned the conduct of the court by implication. Chauffepié, in a note added to an otherwise hostile article on Vanini in his translation of an augmented English version of Bayle's dictionary (1756), said explicitly that the procedure followed by the Parlement of Toulouse and its harshness towards a wretched man were inexcusable 'whatever Vanini was'.

So far the discussion had gone on, albeit in French for the most part, in the Protestant world beyond the French frontiers. In France itself silence was maintained except for a statement in one of the clandestine tracts which circulated in manuscript to the effect that Vanini had always lived honourably.[4] It remained for the common sense of Voltaire to point out that the story handed down from writer to writer since the time of Mersenne and Garasse and according to which Vanini set off from Italy with a band of twelve

---

[1] 'Un homme infâme, qui vivait au commencement du siècle passé, un homme qui avait formé le plus abominable dessein qui fût jamais, qui avait levé avec onze personnes de sa trempe un collège d'incrédulité, d'où il devait répandre ses émissaires dans tout l'univers, pour déraciner de tous les cœurs le dogme de l'existence de Dieu, cet homme, dis-je, se prit d'une façon bien singulière à prouver qu'il n'y a point de Dieu, ce fut d'en donner l'idée. Il crut que le définir c'était le réfuter, et que le meilleur moyen de faire voir qu'il n'y a point de Dieu c'était de dire ce que Dieu est.' (*Sermons sur divers textes de l'écriture sainte*, Geneva, 1745, i, p. 200.) Saurin died in 1730.

[2] English version, p. 100.

[3] 'Au reste je n'ai pu traduire le Président Gramont sans être plus d'une fois frappé d'horreur, et même, si j'ose le dire, de compassion pour Vanini. Il est certain qu'on le traita avec trop de cruauté. L'Inquisition même, toute formidable qu'elle est, ne lui aurait point ôté la vie: une sincère rétractation des ses erreurs l'aurait délivré du supplice.' (Veyssières de la Croze, *Entretiens sur divers sujets*, Cologne, 1733, pp. 374–5.)

[4] Arsenal Library MS no. 2239 (*Traité de la religion*, by 'Philotheos philolotheos', composed *c.* 1720).

disciples on a tour of atheistic proselytizing in Europe was hardly likely to be true: how did a penniless monk come to have twelve men in his service? Voltaire was not particularly attracted by Vanini and spoke of him without sympathy, the reason being that he saw in Vanini, not a free-thinker of his own turn of mind, but a scholastic pedant, 'a quibbling disputant on quiddities and universals'. 'His notion of God,' he adds, 'is in keeping with the most approved theology.' Here Voltaire quotes the passage which had been so strongly disapproved of by Durand (in whose book Voltaire had doubtless made its acquaintance) adding, 'This is not very philosophical, but it is in keeping with the most approved theology.' For Voltaire, the burning of Vanini was merely one of the ordinary judicial crimes in which history abounds.[1] Vanini's judges were on trial before him and the case was decided against them with the laconic remarks, 'he was unfortunate enough to make enemies . . . he was too frank in debate'. The wheel had gone full circle.

Voltaire was right in refusing to call Vanini an atheist, if by the term 'atheist' one means, not merely a person who does not distinguish sharply between the ideas of God and Nature, but a person whose mind rejects as absurd, unworthy and unacceptable all possible interpretations of the word 'God'. Not only did Vanini's understanding accept the idea of God as the idea of an Absolute Being, that is to say of a Being limited in no way whatsoever, not even by the idea of non-being, but also his understanding placed the idea of such an Absolute Being above the idea 'Nature' in the order of perfection. For Vanini, the idea 'Nature', even when expanded as far as the imagination and the understanding can take it, remained a limited idea. Nature was the manifestation of God, but the two ideas 'Nature' and 'God' were not identical. Nature manifested God through the various motions, beginning with the regular motions of the stars in their courses, which were transmitted downwards through the scale of being and governed the destinies of men and of all creatures on the earth. This view of the world was, reduced to its simplest expression, the world-view elaborated by the Italian philosophers of the previous century. It may be called a 'pantheistic naturalism', because the distinction between God and Nature can only be made on the highest level of abstract thought. Below that level, and therefore throughout the whole field of inquiry referred to as 'physics', that is to say the whole field which we now include in

[1] *Dictionnaire philosophique, Athée.*

the natural and human sciences, no distinction is necessary between the two ideas of God and Nature; the will of God and the operations of Nature are one and the same thing.

Such is the view of the world which underlies Vanini's first published book entitled *Amphitheatrum aeternae providentiae divinomagicum, christiano-physicum, nec non astrologo-catholicum, adversus veteres philosophos, atheos, Epicurios, Peripateticos et Stoicos, auctore Julio Caesare Vanino, philosopho, theologo, ac juris utriusque doctore*, published at Lyons in 1615, with an authorization and a privilege. This work introduces at the outset the notion of the Absolute Being or the One, and rejects at the same time the Aristotelian proof of the existence of God drawn from the necessity of supposing a primemover in the universe. But the notion of an Absolute Being is associated immediately afterwards with the traditional Scale of Being, by means of an ingenious analogy between the nine numerals and the ascending order of perfection in which everything is arranged in this world, and also between the unit which must be added to nine to complete the decade and the One who is both the efficient and the final cause of all things. Nine is the highest and most perfect of the numbers, but it is made up of units and it needs an unit in order to form the last number; so unity is the principle and the end, the efficient and the final cause of all numbers, including the most perfect. One is to nine as God is to Nature.

Numerical analogies of this kind had been worked out at great length by all those who were interested in cabalistic lore. Vanini here borrows from Scaliger. He goes fully into the mysteries of the numbers 3, 9 and 27, and is obviously impressed by the symmetries which it is possible to establish by various arithmetical operations. Such preoccupations in no way distinguished him from his contemporaries; he shared them with his enemy Mersenne; but at the opening of Vanini's *Amphitheatrum* they give a clear indication of a mind craving for unity, simplicity and logical consistency, and such a craving is the mark of the radical thinker.

The work is concerned particularly with the idea of divine providence and, more generally, with that of an intelligent ordering of the universe. Vanini had, very evidently, no sympathy whatsoever with Epicurean modes of thought; he brushes them aside with an allusion to the obvious ordering of the heavens. He was prepared to give a meaning not only to the term 'Providence', but also to the terms 'Creation' and 'Miracle'. 'Providence' he defines as the eternal power of God preceding each and every event, unchanging in itself, but producing changes in all things. 'Creation' is the operation of the intelligent cause of the world; its operations consist in producing forms identical with, or analogous with those which are already existent, or 'actual', in God, the source of all forms, in whom nothing is merely potential and all is actual. Creation does not consist in the production of 'existences' corresponding to 'essences' in the divine mind; if this platonic notion was valid there would be two substantial worlds instead of the one there really is; there would be a world of 'essences' and a world of 'existences'. Vanini rejects such a dualism; for him only 'existences' are real: the world is neither an emanation from God, nor a reflection of the divine mind; it is simply what it is.

As for miracles, they are the effects of the motion of the stars, this motion being itself the effect of the divine arrangement of the world:

Pietro Pomponazzi, in a work printed in Basel . . . gives as the cause [of miracles] either the stars or our imagination: that is true of the stars, for they act upon the order and arrangement of the world; even religious institutions, the universal source of order. As the people would not give credence to a new legislator not sanctioned by miracles, the stars unite together all the virtues which they impart separately to animals, herbs and stones, and attribute them to the new law-giver who, equipped and blessed with all these celestial gifts, is enabled to accomplish a host of miracles.[1]

God is the source of good, but is not the source of evil. Evil is not a reality; it is an absence, a privation. God is the source of being, not of privation; all being is good and comes from God, the source of all being. Evil is always the effect of man's will. This cosmic optimism, this insistence on the intelligent order and organization of the world, is the keynote of the book. Such pessimism as appears in it applies to human conduct only: the world is a harmonious ensemble in which man alone strikes a discordant note. Even 'monsters' are 'perfect in their genus' (Ex. XLI); they manifest the variety and diversity which make the beauty of the universe.

Vanini's second work was entitled *Julii Caesaris Vanini neapolitani, theologi, philosophi et juris utriusque doctoris de admirandis naturae reginaeque, deaeque mortalium arcanis libri quatuor* (Paris, 1616). It was published by two doctors of the Sorbonne. It is written in a much more familiar manner than the *Amphitheatrum* and consists of a series of discussions, jocular in tone, between the author and his

1 *Exercitatio* viii. But see below, p. 40 n.

pupil on various questions of physics and natural theology (the sky, its motions, the phenomena of nature, plants, animals, reproduction, the affects, ethnical religion, God, oracles, sybils, auguries). The discussions are conducted with a certain wanton freedom of expression which smacks of the tutor's study. The various topics succeed each other apparently at random and the tone and style are those of a familiar and personal conversation. One gathers as one reads that Vanini was interested in the theories, put forward by Diodorus of Sicily, that men sprang from the mud of the earth, that animals can be generated by heat from rotting matter and that man descended from the apes. One gathers also that he rejected the belief that man's part on earth is to be lord of the brutes and that the story of Adam's fall did not seem to him to be an adequate explanation of the human predicament. One gathers that he looked upon Christ as a skilful teacher whose aim was to establish the rule of virtue and goodness, that he did not believe in the reality of devils, apparitions, oracles and miracles,[1] that he considered certain moral laws to be universal truths, but that the majority of such laws are the inventions of men for the purpose of governing ignorant populaces, that he believed man's fate to be governed by the stars, that he looked upon the stars as the channel by which both motion and intelligence come into the world from the eternal and infinite Being and as the intermediary between the primum mobile and the earth and believed that they are the primary manifestations of absolute reason, that they are the general ideas under which are subsumed the particular ideas which we refer to as human minds. In Vanini's scale of being the superior is in a causal relationship with the inferior; God is the cause of the Intelligences (the stars); the Intelligences are the causes of human minds or rational souls; the rational soul is the cause of the sensitive soul and the vegetative soul; the lower is in each case subsumed by the higher, contained within it as a sub-section is contained in a clause, a subordinate clause in a sentence. Below the vegetative soul in the scale of being come the 'principles' (rest, motion, harmony, accident, privation, the final cause, the efficient cause, the form and, at the bottom of the scale of real things, primary matter). Primary matter, or mere potentiality is at the bottom; at the top is the Absolute Being, whom we cannot conceive in a positive way, because our minds are contained in the divine mind and the content cannot

---

[1] He goes back, in the *De admirandis*, on what he had affirmed in the *Amphitheatrum* concerning miracles; in the *Amphitheatrum* he was prepared to give a meaning to the word miracle, but admitted in the *De admirandis* that he had done so without conviction.

conceive of the container; but we can understand the being of God negatively as not being limited in any way whatsoever.

It is difficult to understand nowadays why so many writers from Garasse to Victor Cousin looked upon this work as being (to use Cousin's terms) 'guilty before God and before morality', unless it be on account of a certain pedantic jocularity with which Vanini treats some of the (purely scholastic) topics he deals with. He made short work of oracles, it is true:

Alexander: What do you hold concerning oracles?
J.C.: That they were priestly impostures.
Alexander: But how was the fraud not discovered?
J.C.: Because the fear of authority prevented the philosophers from pro-
testing.

He was flippant on the subject of martyrdom:

Alexander: When I argued with the atheist from Amsterdam that Christians are not feeble-minded, as many glorious martyrdoms attest, this
blasphemer attributed such martyrdoms to an exalted imagination, or
the thirst for glory, or even a hypochondriacal humour. He added that
all religions, even the most absurd, had their martyrs, that the Turks,
the Indians and, in our own day, the heretics had produced believers
whom no torture could daunt. How many English Protestants during
the reign of Mary had suffered death for their beliefs? In my zeal for
the faith I began to revile him, calling him the Antichrist.
J.C.: And what did he reply?
Alexander: He burst out laughing.

Such passages are the expression of a mind working freely and without restraint to the point of imprudence, but Vanini was not prepared to treat the stories of sybils in the same way; he thought it was not impossible that an Intelligence should make use of a human mind in order to prophesy. Vanini's mind was far from being an un-believing one and the main structures of scholastic thought still held firm in it. His imprudence consisted especially in following the arguments of medicine or physics to the point where only a declara-tion of submission could extricate him from an anti-religious posi-tion, and being at bottom a theologian, and not a man of science, he was foolhardy to expect his submission to be accepted. His acute mind was probably too mobile to admit of real conviction, but his habits of thought led him along the well-worn paths of sixteenth-century speculation and did not open up the new vistas of seventeenth-century scientific inquiry. He knew nothing of the new physics of Galileo and his learning was that of the generation of Cardano and Scaliger. He fell a victim to the zealots of Toulouse who were very easy to convince that they had a blasphemer in their grasp. Voltaire's estimate was the correct one; the death of Vanini was due to a sordid display of intolerant zeal.

In Paris the *procureur général* picked on Théophile de Viau, one of the best lyric and dramatic poets of his generation and denounced him to the Parlement in July 1623. During the long inquiry which lasted until 1625, the main burden of the charges preferred against the poet was that he was a worshipper of nature and taught men to live like the brutes. His interrogation was preceded by a campaign against him by the Jesuits Garasse and Voisin and violent sermons were preached against him by a Minim friar named Guérin.[1] Garasse's main contribution to the affair was the publication of his *Doctrine curieuse des beaux esprits de ce temps* in August 1623; Voisin was the real instigator of the proceedings, which have been looked upon by the scholar who has given most attention to the subject, M. F. Lachèvre, as a move in the Jesuits' campaign to fasten their hold on the University and the Parlement.[2] According to M. Lachèvre, the Jesuits took the initiative in denouncing the *libertins* and forced the Parlement to follow them. Since 1618, when the Jesuit Collège de Clermont had been re-opened and had been given the right to prepare candidates for the Paris degrees, in spite of the opposition of the University, the Jesuits had been making headway. They had their supporters in the Parlement but they also had their opponents, and the two parties were divided over the case of Théophile; in the end the opponents of the Jesuits were strong enough to prevent a burning at the stake.

Théophile was a poet who preferred to haunt taverns such as the Pomme de Pin, near the Pont Notre-Dame, rather than drawing-rooms and to sing the charms of a vulgar Venus rather than those of Madame de Rambouillet's daughter Julie, as did the gallant rhymsters who courted the reigning hostess. He was not alone. Desbarreaux, Des Yveteaux, Tristan l'Hermite, Maynard, Boisrobert, Berthelot, Colletet, Motin, Frenicle, Saint-Amant, de la Porte, and Bergeron all belonged to this cloven-footed herd, and Malherbe was not unknown amongst them. They were poets, not philosophers or

[1] F. Lachèvre, *Le Procès du poète Théophile de Viau*, Paris, 1909, 2 vols., i, p. 206.
[2] ibid., pp. xxxvii–xlvi.

moralists, but their imperious need for independence led them to adopt attitudes which have a moral significance. They affirmed the existence of a Virtue not founded on law or creed and in the face of the social domination of the noble, and the intellectual domination of the cleric, their attitude was not one of prudent acquiescence but of scorn and exasperated blasphemy. With ferocious cynicism they vied with each other in the production of licentious verse and enterprising printers frequently published, without their consent, collections of their poems, love poems for the most part, varying from the merely sensual to the most grossly obscene, with no scruple as far as the attribution of the various works was concerned. Of the many collections of this kind, one in particular, the *Parnasse des poètes satiriques*, published in 1623 (dated 1622) provoked a violent reaction on the part of the authorities, without being in any way different from its numerous predecessors. Théophile, Frenicle, Colletet and Berthelot were held responsible for it and, as they could not be apprehended, they were tried *in absentia*, and condemned, Théophile to be burnt, Berthelot to be hanged, Colletet to be banished; more information was requested concerning Frenicle. Further proceedings were taken against Théophile only. Only one of the poems, a sonnet, was actually attributed to him in the *Parnasse satirique* and at most twenty-four poems out of a total of 385 can be ascribed to him: the other names mentioned were those of Bergeron, Berthelot, Colletet, Frenicle, Maynard, Motin, Rapin, Regnier, Ronsard (eight poems), Sigognes. One can only conclude that the *procureur général*, prompted by Voisin, intended to strike at the man he looked upon as the ringleader. Théophile protested against the action of the printer in publishing the *Parnasse*, but thought doubtless that he would be safer out of the clutches of the Parlement and fled from Paris; he was however arrested at Saint-Quentin and brought back to Paris in September 1623. His patron Montmorency strove to protect him; his fellow poets published poems bewailing his plight; François Ogier, a priest who was also a literary critic, published a scathing attack on Garasse's *Doctrine curieuse*, but Théophile's position was serious when the interrogation was opened in March 1624.

Like Vanini, Théophile was an unsettled man, without fixed roots; he lived by his talent as a poet and a wit. He was without fortune and had to seek a living as the paid poet of a troupe of actors and as a major domo in the house of a wealthy patron (the comte de Candale from 1613, the duc de Montmorency from 1619). Born of a Protestant family, at Clairac near Agen, in 1590, he studied in three Protestant academies, those of Nérac, Montauban and Saumur, before going to Leyden. His studies at Saumur seem to have ended with the rhetoric class. Whether he followed a philosophy course elsewhere is not known and he probably studied no theology. He claimed a knowledge of Latin, Greek, English, Spanish and Italian,[1] but on several occasions during his interrogation he denied all knowledge of theology. He published no doctrinal works and such knowledge of his beliefs as we can acquire must be inferred from the themes and imagery of his verse and from the fact that he made a translation of Plato's *Phaedo*. There is no trace in his works of Lucretian materialism; his naturalism is pantheistic and mystical, not mechanistic and scientific. Nature for Théophile was a mysterious energy unfolding and manifesting itself in the manifold forms of the world of sense. He desired to live in accordance with nature's laws, but rebutted the charge that he desired men to live like the brutes.[2] He claimed to desire neither wealth nor place, but only independence. He admitted no distinctions of birth and mocked the pride of honour and military glory. But, like the Stoics, he affirmed that virtue and courage raise a man to the level of the gods, and, as the divine spark of ethereal flame which makes man's soul is dulled by servile imitation in society, it is only by following nature that man achieves his true stature. Such is the radicalism expressed by Théophile or which is implicit in the themes and imagery of his poetry, while no characteristically Christian themes are present.[3] But to attempt to co-ordinate his ideas into a coherent whole as a matter of academic interest is one thing, to indulge in such an

---

[1] *Fragments d'une histoire comique, Œuvres, Seconde partie*, 1623, ch. iii; Lachèvre, *Le Procès du poète Théophile de Viau*, i, p. 50.

[2] In the first interrogation. '*Demande*: Lui avons remontré qu'il résulte de la plupart de ses poésies qu'il veut faire croire qu'il ne faut reconnaître autre Dieu que la nature à laquelle il se faut abandonner entièrement et, oubliant le christianisme, la suivre en tout comme une bête, même par l'ode qui commence:

> Heureux tandis qu'il est vivant
> Qui va toujours suivant
> Le grand maître de la nature.

Réponse: A dit qu'il n'a jamais parlé qu'il fallût s'abandonner à la nature ni oublier le christianisme et vivre comme les bêtes et a toujours fait profession de chrétien.' (Lachèvre, op. cit., i, p. 375.)

[3] For a fuller treatment see A. Adam, *Théophile de Viau et la libre pensée française en 1620*, Paris, 1935.

exercise with the object of leading a man to the stake is another. Yet this is precisely what was done during the long interrogations to which Théophile was subjected in order to build up the charge that he attributed everything to nature and nothing to God in his poetry. Théophile replied that he knew nothing of theology and believed what the Church told him to believe. He was no more veracious than his accusers were fair, but during a gruelling ordeal, which lasted until September 1625, he made no damning admissions, and, all attempts to produce serious witnesses against him having failed, he was condemned to perpetual banishment and not to the scaffold. He was allowed to remain in the country, but his health had been undermined[1] and he died the following year.

In one of the long didactic poems which were popular in the early seventeenth century and seem to have formed a link between the erudite world and a larger educated public, the attitude to life which is implicit in Théophile's poetry is expressed with the greatest directness and consistency. The *Anti-Bigot ou le faux dévotieux* (also referred to as 'les Quatrains du déiste') was composed before 1623 by a 'philosophy master', doubtless a regent in one of the Paris colleges.[2] The deist rejects impatiently all anthropomorphic conceptions of God and will have no truck with belief in heaven, hell, rewards and punishments after death. His mind craves for logical consistency and refuses to accept contradictions or obscurity; he insists that if statements are made concerning the nature of God and God's relationship to man, such statements must be consistent with each other. If God is defined as 'pure act' or 'pure essence', eternal, anterior to all contingent things, in whom to know and to will are one and the same thing, for whom past, present and future are all equally present, one cannot also represent him as changing his will, or as angry or in any way affected by the actions of men: one must admit that all that happens happens by God's will and that all that

---

[1] By his imprisonment, according to the *Mercure* (1626) which quotes a *Discours remarquable de la vie et mort de Théophile*, published in 1626.

[2] The date 1623 is fixed by a reference to the Quatrains in Mersenne's *Quaestiones celeberrimae in Genesim* which was published in that year. Mersenne says in his preface that the poem was composed by a philosophy master. In the following year Mersenne devoted 1,340 pages to a refutation of the Quatrains in his *L'Impiété des déistes*. They had doubtless been in circulation for some time, but were evidently still a matter of topical interest, so it is reasonable to suppose that they were composed in the five or so years before 1624. The complete text of the poem is to be found in F. Lachèvre's *Le Procès de Théophile*, ii, pp. 105-26. I do not understand why M. Lachèvre refers to the aim of the deist as the satisfaction of the appetites (p. 100); the poem is austere and intellectual.

is is good and forms part of the general order of things. True virtue consists in conformity with that order; it has no need of legal sanction and is not prompted by any mercenary motive; virtue is its own reward. The deist is a perfectionist and indeed such moral perfectionism is characteristic of the form of libertine thought which can be called radical or anarchistic. It is the counterpart of the blasphemy and obscenity with which it was wilfully sullied. There is a note of despair and rage in much of the obscene poetry of this young generation and an absence of full-blooded lust. The grounds for it are a matter for conjecture. It may have been in individual cases a revolt against a severe upbringing and a repressive parental control. More generally it could be seen as a protest against the ever-increasing importance given to birth, rank and position in a society which was becoming more stratified and rigid. But it has some similarity also with the current vogue of the Stoic philosophy. Epictetus's manual had a great vogue at the beginning of the century. The readers of Du Vair's *Philosophie morale des Stoïques* could find therein a christianized Stoicism. The works of Seneca were in great demand, particularly his Letters to Lucilius. Gomberville made and published a magnificent picture-book of Stoic morals for the young king Louis XIV in 1646 under the title *La Philosophie des mœurs*; the vogue continued until about 1660 and then waned sharply. P. A. Mascaron's discourse *La Mort et les dernières paroles de Sénèque* in 1637, Tristan's tragedy *La Mort de Sénèque* in 1645, Desmaret's *Morales d'Epictète, de Socrate, de Plutarque et de Sénèque* in 1653, Gilbert's tragedy *Arie et Petus ou la mort de Néron* in 1660, Le Grand's defence of Stoicism against Jansenist accusations of vaingloriousness (1662),[1] d'Aubignac's didactic novel *Macarise* (1663) all made of Stoicism primarily an affirmation of man's capacity for virtue. Pascal, in his famous conversation with Sacy, the learned disciple of St Augustine, at Port-Royal, in 1655 or thereabouts, still manifested great admiration for Stoic virtue, although he detected in it an overweening pride. Corneille's heroes and the magnanimous man according to Descartes share a Stoic confidence in the human mind and the human will. A more headstrong generation than that of Richelieu and his enemies, male and female, could hardly be imagined. For both sexes the highest moral value was represented by the word 'gloire', which meant the radiation of one's personality; duty was duty to one's own glory first and foremost; aristocratic

[1] *Les Caractères de l'homme sans passions.*

morality was an idealized egotism. Vanini, Théophile and the Deist were part and parcel of their generation; they lived with it and died with it. They did not dominate it intellectually, nor did they shape the free-thinking of the future.

III

The Ideas of Cyrano de Bergerac

SAVINIEN DE CYRANO, known as Cyrano de Bergerac, was one of the most daring speculative thinkers of his generation. It used to be thought that he was born at Bergerac in the South of France, but he was born in Paris in 1619, Bergerac being, in this case, not the town in the South of France, but a small family property near Paris. He was educated in Paris, possibly at the Collège de Beauvais. If so, he is not likely to have come in contact with many new ideas there, seeing that Grangier (a doughty champion of the University's rights but notorious as a narrow pedant) was at the head of it. The ferocity with which Cyrano berated him in his satirical comedy *Le Pedant joué* (1645) excludes any possibility of influence from that direction. Gassendi was teaching astronomy at the Royal College from 1645 to 1655 and it is possible, to say the least of it, that Cyrano was introduced to Gassendi by his friend and Gassendi's pupil Chapelle, although, as in the case of Molière and Dehénault, there is nothing to support the story that he joined Chapelle at private lessons.[1] In his imaginary travel story, the *Empires de la lune*, one of the philosophers whom his traveller in inter-stellar space meets on the moon says that he used to associate with La Mothe le Vayer and Gassendi. Cyrano also knew and admired Marolles, the translator of Lucretius, and Rohault, a Cartesian physicist, but reading was his chief source of information. His friend and first editor Lebret says he knew all the systems of the ancient philosophers and he was certainly acquainted with the new cosmology. He was also thoroughly acquainted with the Italians Cardano and Campanella. Italian naturalism was but dimly reflected in the poems of Théophile, and Vanini's two badly printed books had no more than one edition and cannot have reached a wide public. The *Anti-bigot* was not published and can only have been known to a wide public thanks to Mersenne's refutation, but the original works of the Italian philosophers were still available. Cardano was not forgotten in seventeenth-century France and his reputation was still high. As late as 1663 a complete edition

---

[1] This story was told by Molière's first biographer, Grimarest, in 1705. It was severely shaken by G. Michaut in *La Jeunesse de Molière* (1923); but cf. below, p. 146.

of his works was published in French, with a life of Cardano by Naudé by way of introduction. Naudé, who had already devoted a study to Cardano in his *Apologie des grands personn'ages*, looked upon the Italian philosopher as a man of genius, albeit somewhat mad, and explained away his wilder fantasies as the temporary aberrations of an over-active brain. He took Cardano's part against J.-C. Scaliger, who had called him a 'jingling fortune-teller'. So did Bayle, and Vossius (whom Bayle quotes in this context), though Bayle agreed with Naudé that Cardano was unbalanced; according to Bayle, Cardano's fault was not incredulity but an excess of superstitious belief in astrology, magic, necromancy and all the pseudo-sciences of the Renaissance. But readers of Cardano's works could find therein a coherent picture of the world. The world for Cardano was an immense animate being, whose soul, the *Anima mundi*, was the seat of intelligence and motion, while space was a mode of its existence. It is possible to make an abstract distinction between the extended universe and its soul, just as one can make an abstract distinction between the matter of a particular object, which is part of universal matter, and the form of a particular object, which is part of the universal soul, but it should not be thought that there are two substances, the world and its soul; there is only one world and the distinctions we make do not affect reality. We can distinguish between the universal intelligence and the universal soul, provided that we remember that such a distinction is an abstract one. In so far as an individual soul participates in the universal intelligence it is immortal; man's soul does so participate in so far as it comprehends the truth. But the doctrine of immortality is not necessary as a sanction for morality; the notion of justice is sufficient by itself; virtue is not dependent on the supposed rewards and punishments meted out in a future life. As far as the material world is concerned, Cardano continued to see it as it had been seen in the middle ages; he knew nothing of the new cosmology; for him the sky moved by itself and determined the motions of terrestrial things; the stars guided the course of history. The sun was the source of light and life and by its action produced living things from the earth in rich and varied profusion. Nature was wonderful, beneficent and worthy of man's adoration.

The Calabrian monk Tommaso Campanella forms a solid link between Cyrano and Italian naturalism. When Cyrano's traveller explores the surface of the sun, the philosopher who undertakes to explain the nature of this abode of light and life is none other than Campanella. Campanella was a focus for ideas coming from many different points of the intellectual horizon, and his books were widely disseminated: they were in all the bookshops in London in the middle of the century according to the translator of one of his political tracts.[1] He learnt much from Telesio, one of the greatest thinkers of the Italian renaissance, but he added to Telesio's sensationalism and materialism, the Stoic doctrine of the soul of the world, occultism and suggestions of oriental philosophy and finally Copernican cosmology. The placing of the sun in the centre of the world gave it an added importance for a philosopher who was used to considering the sky and the stars as the source of light, life, feeling, motion and all those superior influences which act upon the heavy, damp, dark principles whose seat is the earth. The sun became the great source of animation in a nature every part of which had soul, every part of which was sensitive. It is little wonder therefore that this man, who combined with philosophical speculations which brought him near to the stake in 1595[2] an active political idealism which landed him in the prisons of Naples for twenty-five years from 1599 to 1624, should have entitled a utopian treatise written in a Neapolitan prison in 1602 *Civitas solis*. This book envisages a state organized in a strictly hierarchical fashion in concentric circles round a temple dedicated to the sun, but the sun is not actually worshipped for itself; it is worshipped as the 'image, the face, the living statue' of God.[3] The Solarians are therefore Deists, rather than sunworshippers or even pantheists, but they are said to originate from India and to have drawn their religious ideas from the Brahmans, doubtless because Campanella was acquainted with the pantheism and universal animism of the Hindus and had studied some such account as that of Strabo who expressly describes them as being dedicated to the sun.

Campanella was in Paris from 1634 until his death in 1639 and it may be reasonable to believe that Cyrano, who was educated in Paris and was fifteen years old when Campanella arrived and nineteen when he joined the Guards, may have come in contact with the illustrious Italian at some time during the years 1634–8.

[1] *Advice to the Spanish monarchy*, London, 1659, p. 8.
[2] See L. Blanchet, *Campanella*, Paris, Alcan, 1920.
[3] Cf. *De Sensu rerum* (Frankfurt, 1623, p. 370): 'Mundus ergo totus est sensus, vita, anima, corpus, statua Dei altissimi ad ipsius gloriam, in potestate, sapientia et amore.' (Epilogue.)

Be that as it may, the direct reference to Campanella towards the end of the *Empires du Soleil* is an explicit acknowledgment of a debt. Cyrano was acquainted with Campanella's work, both the *Civitas solis* and the *De sensu rerum*, by the time he came to write his imaginary journeys to the moon and the sun, about 1648.

The early part of Cyrano's career was given to soldiering, not to philosophizing. At the age of nineteen he took service with the Guards, in a company composed almost entirely of Gascon gentlemen, and became renowned for duelling. The *Menagiana* of 1695 says that he killed more than ten men for making fun of his nose, which as his portrait shows was very long, but the *Menagiana* is not a very reliable witness. His friend and first editor Lebret merely says: 'les Gascons, qui composaient presque seuls cette compagnie, le considéraient comme le démon de la bravoure, et lui comptaient autant de combats que de jours qu'il y était entré'. The thirty years war was in progress and Cyrano fought and was wounded at Mouzon in Champagne in 1639 and again at Arras in 1640. He must have left the army soon afterwards seeing that we find him in Paris in 1643 in the company of the facetious poet Dassoucy and Gassendi's pupil, Chapelle. He had a room at the Collège de Lisieux, but it is not known what sort of post, if any, he held in the college. He lived simply, according to Lebret, drank little, ate soberly and was extremely chaste. Lebret tells the story of how, on one occasion, Cyrano was set upon by a band of armed men near the Porte de Nesle and how he killed two, wounded seven and put the rest to flight. But Lebret does not vouch for this story and it has left no other echo in contemporary records. Meanwhile Cyrano had become a playwright. His *Le Pédant joué*, a comedy of the schools and colleges, was played by the *Illustre théâtre* in 1645. Molière may well have prepared it for the stage; at any rate he claimed a scene from it ('Qu'allait-il donc faire dans cette galère?') as his own property, when later he made use of it in his own *Fourberies de Scapin*. Cyrano's one tragedy, *La Mort d'Agrippine*, played in 1654, gave him the reputation of being an atheist, or confirmed the reputation he already had, because of certain ideas expressed in the play. There seems to have been some hesitation on the part of the spectators as to which passages contained these ideas and on one occasion certain members of the audience, eager to be scandalized, but not knowing which were the scandalous lines, missed them in the second act,[1] but cried, 'Ah! le scélérat! Ah! l'athée!' when Séjanus, in the fourth act, pointing out Tiberius as the man to be struck down, spoke the words, 'Frappons, voilà l'hostie.'

Lebret says that Socrates and Pyrrho shared his approval with Democritus. In his satire *Contre le Pédant*, he declared that he believed in God, and in his letter *Contre le carême* he claimed to be a good Catholic, but the argument he used in *Contre le Pédant* to prove the existence of God was precisely the same as the one used by Séjanus in *La Mort d'Agrippine* to prove the non-existence of the gods. If a kind God did not exist, you would have ceased to exist long ago, says Cyrano to the pedant, and, if the gods existed they would have destroyed me long ago, says Séjanus. In his epistle *Contre un jésuite assassin et médisant*, he declared that he believed in providence and asked the question, how can chance explain the order of the universe and inert matter produce human reason? in such a way as to suggest that he disagreed with Lucretius, but he took the opposite view in the *Empires de la lune*. In spite of these vagaries, there is evidence in these shorter works, and particularly in his letters on sorcery, of an eminently sane and courageous mind. He believed in neither black magic nor in possession by devils. A witch according to him was a sufferer from sexual disorders of the mind

---

[1] The lines they missed in the second act were the following:

> Ces enfants de l'effroi,
> Ces beaux riens qu'on adore, et sans savoir pourquoi,
> Ces altérés du sang de bêtes qu'on assomme,
> Ces dieux que l'homme a faits, et qui n'ont point fait l'homme,
> Des plus fermes états ce fantastique soutien,
> Va, va, Térentius, qui les craint ne craint rien.

Cf. V, vi:

> J'ai beau plonger mon âme et mes regards funèbres
> Dans ce vaste néant et ces longues ténèbres,
> J'y recontre partout un état sans douleur,
> Qui n'élève à mon front ni trouble ni terreur;
> Car, puisque l'on ne reste, après ce grand passage,
> Que le songe léger d'une légère image,
> Et que le coup fatal ne fait ni mal ni bien;
> Vivant, parce qu'on est, mort, parce qu'on n'est rien,
> Pourquoi perdre à regret la lumière reçue,
> Qu'on ne peut regretter, après qu'elle est perdue?
> Pensez-vous m'étonner par ce faible moyen,
> Par l'horreur du tableau d'un être qui n'est rien?

These lines are spoken by Séjanus and cannot of course be looked upon as a direct expression of Cyrano's opinions, although the author of the *Theophrastus redivivus*, writing in 1659, assumed that they could be so interpreted.

who might be given a beating but not burnt alive. As for the cross used for exorcising demons, his opinion was merely that a cross is length considered in relation to breadth'. His thinking was plain, straightforward, radical, modern: in none of his writings did he adopt an historical approach to the problem in hand or show any respect for tradition, established belief, accepted values. He was the first French writer to adopt the device of the 'philosophical novel' which permits of a total disregard for current standards of judgment and a fresh and ingenuous, or supposedly ingenuous attitude towards contemporary manners, customs, institutions and controversies. It also enables the author to pass off serious thinking as harmless fantasy. As an adept of the technique of the philosophical novel Cyrano is a forerunner of Montesquieu, Swift and Voltaire.

The *Etats et Empires de la lune* was written by 1649, in which year it was commented upon in a poem by Royer de Prades to whom Cyrano had communicated it in manuscript form. It was not published however until 1657, two years after Cyrano's death, when it was published by Cyrano's friend Lebret. Lebret chose as a title *Histoire comique ou Etats et Empires de la lune*, but Prades refers to it as *L'Autre monde* so it is possible that such was its original title. The idea of a journey to the moon may have been suggested by an English work entitled *The Man in the Moon, or a discourse of a voyage thither by D. Gonsales*, by Francis Godwin, bishop of Llandaff and Hereford. This English work was translated into French in 1648 and Cyrano must have been acquainted with it because his traveller to the moon finds a Spaniard there and this Spaniard has, like Godwin's D. Gonsales, used birds to make the trip. Cyrano seems also to have used a manuscript copy of Pierre Borel's *Discours nouveau prouvant la pluralité des mondes* before it was published at Geneva in 1657. Borel claimed in his preface that a copy of his book, which was completed by 1648, had been stolen and that his ideas had been used by another author. There is a copy of Borel's book at the Arsenal library in Paris which bears on the title page the words 'Fait à Castres en haut Languedoc en 1647.'[1] This is, on the face of it, evidence to show that the work existed early enough for Cyrano to have made use of it. Borel, who was a physician to the king, set out to prove in his discourse, by means of a heterogeneous collection of arguments, including the existence of birds of paradise and many quotations from Copernicus, Cardano, Tycho-Brahe, Galileo, and Kepler, that

[1] Arsenal 2858, ff. 316–35.

the earth is an animate being, possessed of reason and a soul,[1] and that it is not in the centre of the world but in the third heaven. He believed the stars to be inhabited. He argued that the moon must be inhabited seeing that, like the earth, it has mountains and rivers. Pythagoras called the earth a moon . . .' some Stoics believed that there were people not only on the moon but also in the body of the sun, and Campanella says that these bright and shining mansions may have their inhabitants who are possibly more learned than we and better informed of the things we cannot comprehend'.[2] At the end of his book Borel maintains that it would be possible to invent a machine to fly to the moon and promises an *ars volandi* in a proposed book of natural magic which, however, he does not seem to have written.

Cyrano relates, at the beginning of the *Etats et Empires de la lune*, how, during a conversation with some friends one moonlight night he maintained, in spite of their incredulous jests, that the moon was an inhabited world like our own. Perhaps even now, he cried, they are laughing in the moon at someone who thinks our own globe to be a world. But in vain did he quote Pythagoras, Democritus, Epicurus, Copernicus and Kepler, his friends only laughed the louder. On returning home, he found a volume of Cardano mysteriously open at the page where the author describes his meeting with two men from the moon. Forthwith he began to plan a voyage of discovery thither.

His first attempt, made with the aid of bottles of dew strapped around his body, ended in Canada, where he discussed his plans with the governor. 'The sun', said Cyrano, 'is in the centre of the world, like the pips in the centre of an apple. In the pips is concentrated the life and heat of the fruit, and similarly the sun gives life, light, heat and energy to the world.' 'I agree with Copernicus,' replies the governor, 'that the sun is in the centre of the world and I agree that the earth turns; one of my priests explains this motion by saying it is due to the efforts of the damned down in hell; they try to climb up the inside to get away from the fire and make the earth go round like a tread-mill. But if, as you suggest, the stars are

[1] This is not for lack of knowledge of Descartes; in 1656 he published a life of Descartes (*Vitae Renati Cartesii, summi philosophi, compendium*, Paris).

[2] Text from the English translation entitled *A New Treatise proving a multiplicity of worlds. That the Planets are Regions Inhabited, and the Earth a Star, and that it is out of the Centre of the World in the third Heaven, and turns round before the Sun which is fixed . . .* London, 1658.

inhabited, then the world must be infinite, because the inhabitants of each star will see other stars beyond their own and so on indefinitely.' 'Why should not the world be infinite?' replied Cyrano. 'For one thing complete nothingness is unthinkable; for another, if the world is finite, God is finite, because where nothing existed God would not exist.'

This last remark can only have one meaning, namely that God is to the World what the intelligence is to the body; space and intelligence are two aspects of the same infinite Being. Cyrano does not, however, develop his argument in this sense and henceforward keeps within the realm of physics, and does not venture into metaphysics.

At the second attempt, propelled by rockets firing in succession, Cyrano's traveller reaches the moon and there falls into the Garden of Eden, but is not killed by his fall because he falls on the tree of life and one of its fruits is forced down his throat. The inhabitants of the moon are four-footed creatures and they refuse to admit that he has a soul because he is a biped. Luckily he is discovered by Socrates's daemon who converses with him in Greek. Socrates's daemon has had many adventures since the death of his original charge. He has appeared to Cardano, Cornelius Agrippa, John Tritheme, Faustus, Nostradamus, the knights of the Rosy Cross, La Mothe le Vayer, La Brosse, Tristan l'Hermite and Gassendi, as well as to Campanella, whose *De sensu rerum* he has inspired. He taught Campanella, at that time a prisoner of the Inquisition, how to guess his enemies' secret thoughts by imitating their physical attitudes and gestures: seeing that the thoughts in our minds correspond to the physical states of our bodies it is possible to reproduce the ones by adopting the others. Socrates's daemon, who is really an inhabitant of the sun, sent to the moon as one might be sent to a colony, is very wise because he possesses many sense organs a Tellurian, or even a Selenian, is not possessed of. Because he has many more sense organs he has many more impressions and more knowledge than others not so gifted; he knows for instance by purely sensitive intuition the nature of the magnet's attractive power. The Selenians also differ from earth-bound man. They use an intoned speech, like music, feed only on the odours of viands and (a fantastic detail but doubtless near to Cyrano's heart) a lunar poet is allowed to pay his bills in sonnets and quatrains.

At the lunar court Cyrano's traveller is put in the same cage as a Spaniard who has been carried to the moon by a flight of birds. This

Spaniard complains that the doctors of the University of Paris think that no one besides themselves knows anything at all; he propounds a theory whereby the four elements can be reduced to one and the differences between things explained by the varying amounts of matter and void in them. There is the same matter in everything, though we should doubtless need another Prometheus to be able to separate matter from the things it composes. There is the same matter in a tree as in a man; everything is in everything; nature is one.

Our traveller soon learns to speak the lunar language and would have been taken for a man, albeit a deformed one, if the doctors of the country had not scorned the idea that God should give a two-footed beast the privilege of manhood and an immortal soul. He is at last freed from his cage on condition that he recants after the manner of Galileo, and admits that the earth is the moon and the moon the earth.

On the moon the old respect the young and a son has no filial duties towards his father. Some of the philosophers of the moon eat only vegetables and the flesh of animals which have died a natural death, because in all things there is life and feeling and they would think it a crime to wound even a cabbage. Why should Nature prefer bloodthirsty creatures to this inoffensive plant? There is no right of birth in nature; all God's children are equal; therefore, if man has an immortal soul to his share, surely vegetative life must also have its bounty, and why should that bounty not be an intuitive knowledge of all nature, a share in the universal consciousness? Is not the possession of sense organs a limiting factor in the exercise of sensation? Does not the absence of such organs imply an immediate union with all nature?

The universe is an immense animate being (says a lunar philosopher) and we ourselves are universes for the minute animals that live in us, and these in their turn are universes for animals more minute. We are entirely composed of living beings; we are societies of microbes.

The conversation is interrupted because the whole town is being moved on wheels in order to obtain a change of air. When it is resumed, the subject is the eternity of the world and there is no doubt that Cyrano rejects the doctrine of creation in favour of Epicurus's eternal atoms. The roundest and most mobile of the atoms are those of fire, the formative or constructive principle in the universe. Fire forms and organizes the things we see around us, but fire is not a sort of providence. Cyrano takes up a resolutely anti-teleological position. The existence of any particular object is not to be marvelled at. Given a certain arrangement of the atoms, some object or other had to be formed and there is no need to marvel that it should be this rather than that, an oak-tree rather than an ash-tree. A different arrangement and different motion would have produced a sensitive plant, an oyster, a worm, a fly, a frog, a sparrow, a monkey, a man. It is no miracle that a pair of deuces comes up in dicing; so why should it be a miracle that a certain species, such as man, appears in nature? There is no problem to be solved, when one considers an infinite number of atoms in eternal motion.

All the senses, touch, sight, hearing, taste and smell are produced by emanation of particles from bodies. The lunar philosopher knows his Lucretius, but quietly neglects (as did all the physicists of the seventeenth century) the 'idols' or material images which, according to Lucretius, detach themselves from objects like a fine skin and come floating through the air to our organs of sense. On the other hand he applies his theory of the radiation of particles to astrology, and explains by this means the influence of the stars, whereas Lucretius had refused to admit any influence of these tranquil, imperturbable gods upon the affairs of men. But Lucretius's world is a world mechanically ordered, whereas Cyrano, like Campanella, and the Italian philosophers generally, pictured the world as suffused throughout with sensation and every object as sensitive to the radiations vibrating through it. Light and heat are radiations of smooth round particles like a fine dust. On the sun the dust *is* light and heat, and can be gathered up into flasks; indeed Socrates's daemon has brought several such flasks to the moon and produces them in order to replace the usual source of artificial light on the moon, namely glow-worms in glass bowls.

Only criminals are buried when they die. Other Selenians are cremated so that their souls, composed of fire, may be given added strength in the burning and thus enabled to rise to some planet nearer the sun, the divine centre of light and life. Sometimes how-ever, when a Selenian takes leave of life, his friends drink his blood and eat his flesh, after which they pass the night with a girl of sixteen or seventeen years of age in the hope that the spirit of their friend will live again in the offspring they engender. Even Cyrano's long nose plays its part in the strange lunar customs. On the moon a

long nose is a sign of intelligence and all those whose noses are not
of the requisite length are castrated so that they cannot reproduce
their unworthy kind. Chastity is a grave offence and a phallic symbol
worn at the waist is a mark of nobility, to be preferred to the sword,
because it is nobler to create life than it is to destroy it. No one
believes in miracles on the moon; no one believes in doctors. The
imagination is, by nature, capable of healing the body and doctors
destroy this natural property by means of their drugs. When our
traveller hears of this he attempts to see in it a proof of the soul's
rationality and immortality, but the lunar philosopher will have none
of such arguments. The soul without the body would be without
sense and therefore without understanding; if it were not so, the soul
of a blind man would not need eyes in order to see. But the traveller
will hear no more of this impious talk and, being homesick for the
earth, he asks for and is given a passport by the lunar authorities and
is transported back to earth by Socrates's daemon. At least that is
how the story ends in Lebret's edition. But the manuscript gives
another version according to which the lunar philosopher gets as far
as denying God before a black and hairy devil snatches up both
philosopher and traveller and away up the chimney with them and
towards hell. Fortunately our traveller just has time to say Jesu
Maria and so finds himself lying in the heather near Mount
Vesuvius.[1]

In the *Etats et Empires de la lune* are already several hints to the
effect that there is a still more interesting place to be visited, so we
are not surprised to find Cyrano pen in hand again by 1650 com-
posing the *Etats et Empires du Soleil*,[2] which takes up the story
precisely where the early work leaves off. Having reached France,
the author relates how, while staying with a friend near Toulouse,
he is taken for a sorcerer by some peasants, incited against him by
their parish priest. When they find him riding along one day with
a copy of Descartes's *Principia* among his baggage, they take this
book for a book of magic because of all the circles and other diagrams it contains; they think Cyrano has come to bewitch the crops.
He is imprisoned in a high tower and there makes a machine with
a huge crystal bowl on the top of it. The action of the sun, creating

[1] F. Lachèvre, *Œuvres libertines de Cyrano de Bergerac*, Paris, 1921, i, p. 98 and 98 n.
[2] Published in 1662. Cyrano himself (or Lebret his editor) refers to it as *l'Histoire de la
république du soleil* at the end of the edition of the *Etats et Empires de la lune* published
by Lebret in 1657.

a continual vacuum in this bowl, causes the air to rush in and fill up the void and push the machine upward. So off goes the traveller towards the sun. He does not experience hunger during his journey and this fact intrigues him. He knows perfectly well that the sun's heat is sufficient to nourish the soul within him provided it has some 'radical moisture' to attach itself to, as the flame of a lamp adheres to oil. But where is the *humide radical* coming from? Then he remembers that both heat and the *humide radical* are the same thing in substance, both being composed of mobile atoms. Furthermore, when one nears the sun there is sufficient heat for one to be able to dispense with the *humide radical*, whose function on earth is to hold the heat and prevent it from being rapidly dissipated. And so he journeys on for four months without food, past the moon and Venus and Mercury. As he journeys, he imagines that when matter was created, all the particles sorted themselves out by a sort of sympathy, like tending to like, and then all the planets so formed went spinning round the sun, pushed along by the sun's heat. Perhaps the sun spots will one day break away from the sun and form new planets. Perhaps the earth was once a sun; at all events it still retains enough heat to cause the moon to turn around it.

At last the traveller alights on a little planet near the sun, 'one of those which the mathematicians call maculae', and there he meets a man whose language he understands at once, because every word in it corresponds exactly to the essence of the thing it refers to. This man is a scientist; he prefers an inductive to a deductive method of reasoning, proceeding always from effects to causes and never from causes to effects. His natural history is better informed than that of Lucretius, but is conceived in exactly the same spirit. The planet he lives on was cast off by the sun and thereafter so sweated out vapours that rain fell for forty days and formed the seas. The ground was covered with a thick coat of fertile mud, in which, by the action of the sun, a series of coctions took place. It needed three coctions to produce a man, one for the liver, one for the heart and one for the brain. Two coctions were sufficient to produce a beast and one to produce a plant. At this point in his explanation, he points to a protuberance which is forming in the palpitating mud in front of him: the ground is about to bring forth a man[1] and he goes forward to act as midwife, while our traveller regains his flying machine. Up he goes towards the bright orb of the sun, his body now drawn to it

[1] Cf. Lucretius, *De rerum natura*, v, 806–15.

by a natural attraction and impelled onwards by a natural desire. His body becomes transparent, except for the red of the life-blood within him, and his machine likewise. At length, nature, speaking within him by the voice of instinct, and without any recourse to reason, tells him to leap from his machine. He does so, breaking the crystal bowl as he goes, and the machine falls away behind him, becoming opaque again as it falls. He now feels perfectly happy, because joy is a flame within him and burns the more brightly as it approaches the luminous source from whence it flows. He falls at length on the surface of the sun.

Now the author's imagination is put to a hard test in which it weakens sadly. The novel begins to read at this point like a mediaeval allegory. We see the traveller awakening under a golden tree of which the fruits are diamonds, rubies and other precious stones and discover that the tree is a whole colony of minute beings who have taken on the form of a tree in order to cool the ardour of a nightingale who now sings disconsolately on the topmost branch: the unfortunate bird had fallen in love with the king of the colony at a time when he had assumed the form of a nightingale. As the traveller watches, the tree again changes its shape; after disintegrating into a myriad tiny creatures who perform a dance like that of motes in the sunbeams, it reassembles as a man!

These metamorphoses have a philosophical significance. They are Cyrano's strained effort to express in narrative form the very abstract conception of 'pure act'. The traveller is now at the centre of the universe and at the beginning of things. He cannot go beyond in search of causes and principles without supposing the existence of a world beyond. Whilst on earth he had two opposing principles to work with, gross and sluggish matter (a principle of inertia) and rapidly moving fire (a principle of activity), and could combine them more or less in the same way as the schoolmen combined matter and form, in order to explain the nature of things, but the earthly principle of inertia has now been left behind. The beings he meets with on the surface of the sun are all activity; they are what men call 'spirits', although they refuse to call themselves by this name. They are, like everything else in the universe, composed of atoms, each one of which is spontaneously active; that is why the tree disintegrates before assuming a different form; it is a colony of minute autonomous beings. But though the tree is made of minute creatures, it is not moulded into shape or constructed by any outside agent; it is self-constructing. Its metamorphoses are pure acts. Cyrano is not content with a purely abstract notion of 'pure act', nor is he content with a mechanistic materialism. He applies his corpuscular principle to all the dualisms current in his time ('form' and 'matter' in the schools, 'mind' and 'matter' in Descartes's *Meditations*, 'heat' and 'cold', 'contraction' and 'expansion', the notions used by the 'chemists' and the Italian philosophers) and aims at a thorough-going monism. The forms which the solar beings take on must not be separate from their matter, otherwise Cyrano is as far as ever from realizing the perfect unity of nature. Their form must be an arrangement of atoms and at the same time a spontaneous act, not imposed from without; its psychical and physical aspects must be identical; mobility and consciousness must be one and the same function; panpsychism must be reduced to dynamic atomism, other-wise the arrangement of the atoms will be the effect of an outside cause and the old dualism of intelligence and matter will reappear in all its obstinacy.

The passage makes strange reading, but it is not the fanciful product of an overheated imagination (a term which had a perfectly literal meaning for Cyrano); it is the sustained effort of a systematic thinker to clothe his most abstract conceptions in concrete language. A failure, certainly, as literature, but a *tour de force* of expression none the less.

The next episode repeats some of the effects of the *Etats et Empires de la lune*. The traveller is tried by a sort of 'parliament of fowls' and would certainly have been pecked to death as a represen-tative of man's tyrannical breed, had he not been saved by the soul of his parrot, who frequently heard him declare on earth that the brutes have souls. He is escorted out of the land of birds into that of trees, which sense his presence amongst them and speak to each other in their murmurous language as he approaches. Trees have sense, just as beasts and men have sense. Sense exists at all stages in the scale of being, as the following episode is doubtless intended to illustrate. It is a struggle between the two opposing elements, heat and cold, the one represented by the salamander the other by the lemur. Heat being the active principle of Cyrano's universe in its simplest form, we have now reached the point at which Campanella can appear to add an explanatory comment. Campanella has retained his identity on the surface of the sun, whereas most human souls are merely united to the sun's heat and lose all individual personality.

Campanella has been saved from such extinction by the fact that he had knowledge of the truth; the human soul is immortal in so far as it contains within itself true ideas, but other souls disintegrate into their component atoms and sooner or later these atoms radiate out once more from the sun and go to exercise in animate bodies on various planets the functions of sense and memory. Descartes's name is now mentioned and Campanella expresses great admiration for his rival's mental powers, but Cyrano adds a remark which is sufficient to show that he prefers Lucretius's atoms to Descartes's 'extended substance'. Unfortunately the text left by Cyrano stops abruptly at the point when Descartes arrives. According to the last sentences of the *Etats et Empires de la lune* in Lebret's edition of 1657, the manuscript of the *Etats et Empires du soleil* and of a third part entitled *Histoire de l'Etincelle* (the soul) was stolen; it is therefore likely that the final section of it, including the whole of the *Histoire de l'Etincelle*, was lost or suppressed before the publication of the manuscript in 1662.

In 1662, in a volume entitled *Nouvelles œuvres de Cyrano de Bergerac*, appeared a fragment entitled *Physique ou science des choses naturelles* which at first sight gives the impression that Cyrano held at some time very different beliefs from those explicitly or implicitly contained in the *Autre Monde*. This fragment, which contains a detailed table of contents of a treatise of physics, together with a draft of the first chapters, follows Descartes, with the exception that Descartes's metaphysical introduction to physics is replaced by a sketch of an empiricist psychology, and might lead one to believe that Cyrano had come under the strong influence of Descartes. But the fragment bears such a close resemblance to Rohault's *Traité de physique*, published in 1671, that one is obliged to conclude that one or other of the writers of these two works merely followed the thought of the other and as Rohault's treatise consists of the lectures which he had been giving for some years, it is reasonable to assume that the real author of the system is Rohault. There is a resemblance between the ideas expressed in the opening sections and those expressed by Cyrano elsewhere, but not in the later sections. The opening sections are empiricist; they state the necessity of proceeding from effects to causes; they propose the use of an experimental method; the rest is purely Cartesian: matter is reduced to extension, the possibility of vacuum is denied, figure and motion are the only two properties of matter used in the explanation of natural phenomena. These theories are far from being in accord with Cyrano's thinking as expressed elsewhere, while the combination of an experimental method with Cartesian theories of matter and motion characterizes Rohault as a scientist. Cyrano may have come under the influence of Rohault at some time; Lebret says that the two men were friends. Cyrano's notes may be the outcome of their relationship. It is very unlikely that they are the fruit of independent inquiry or speculation on Cyrano's part and they did not have any marked effect on the rest of his work.

Apart from these notes there is no trace of Cartesianism in Cyrano's writings. That he knew the *Principia* is not in doubt: was it not this work of Descartes which led to his hero's being accused of sorcery? But such ideas expressed by Cyrano (elsewhere than in the *Physique ou science des choses naturelles*) which do not conflict with Cartesianism were commonplaces for the physicists of the time.

Cyrano is much nearer to Gassendi and he may well have discussed his ideas with Gassendi seeing that he was a friend of Gassendi's pupil Chapelle. He may also have followed Gassendi's lectures on astronomy at the Royal College. It is from such personal contact that the influence of Gassendi must have come seeing that Gassendi's *Animadversiones in decimum librum Diogenis Laertii* were not published until 1649 and the *Syntagma philosophicum* until 1658. A general encouragement to pursue his speculations in the direction of dynamic atomism was probably the form Gassendi's influence took, rather than the precise teaching of particular theories. Cyrano brings modifications to the doctrine of Lucretius, it is true, which are made also by Gassendi in the *Animadversiones*, particularly as regards the theory of vision, but they were so expected at the time that even Marolles, who was no physicist, makes them in the notes to his translation of the *De rerum natura* published in 1650. It would have been strange indeed had Cyrano taken over from Lucretius the material images or 'idols' which come through the air from the things of the outside world to the organs of sense. He could have found these 'intentional species' rejected by others than by Gassendi. He was a voracious reader and one of his complaints according to Lebret was that book after book repeated the same ideas. Conversation with Gassendi, whose erudition embraced all that Cyrano took from Lucretius and the Italians (and how much else besides!), may well have orientated his speculations. The bold integration of panpsychism with atomism which Cyrano carries through with such vigour, had been cautiously explored by the master, beside whose work that of Cyrano is a mere rapid sketch. But, whereas the Provost of Digne never forgot that he was a cleric and was constantly pre-occupied with the claims of Christian doctrine, Cyrano followed the lead of the Italians and Lucretius in so totally a non-Christian spirit that his independence of Gassendi is also evident.

Cyrano was as non-pagan as he was non-Christian. There is no trace of religious feeling in his work at all. He does not replace Christianity by the religion of nature. As far as he is concerned therefore, a little satirical essay published by Zacharie de Lisieux, in *Gyges Gallus* (1658), misses its mark. Zacharie de Lisieux imagined an assembly of men engaged in the worship of a statue all covered with breasts like the Roman goddess of fertility, or, more exactly, the suckling of young, Ruminia. The argument implied by this allegory is that the putting of intelligence into nature (as against making it transcendent) comes to the same thing as the worshipping of nature. But Cyrano shows no inclination to worship nature or any other being, real or imaginary. His physics are strictly atomistic, and his psychology strictly sensationalist. The one substance in Cyrano's cosmos is the atoms and, however fine and 'subtle' they may be on the sun and in the rays of light and heat, they have one fundamental property which may be called either motion or sensation. Intelligence is sensation and all nature participates in it; the less it is limited by particular sense organs or stereotyped by reason and the ordinary forms of language, the more nearly does it correspond to the nature of things: sensitive intuition, far from being the lowest form of understanding is the purest and the most authentic. Although Cyrano does not say so explicitly, one can infer from what he does say that pure intelligence and the simple motion of the atoms are one and the same thing. The total motion and the total intelligence of the universe are one and the same thing. There is no falsehood in his world, no evil. He is no more a dualist in morals than he is in physics or psychology. There is no negation in his world. Everything can be conceived and can exist; nothing is impossible.[1] If the word

---

[1] In the *Grand Œuvre des Philosophes*, which Socrates's daemon leaves behind, the author 'proves that all things are true, and explains the means of uniting physically the truths of each contradiction, as, for instance, that white is black and that black is white, that one can be and not be at the same time, that there can be a mountain without a valley, that non-being is being, that all things which are are not. But notice that he proves all these strange paradoxes without any fanciful or sophistic reasons.' (*Œuvres libertines*, ed. Lachèvre, Paris, 1921, i, p. 83.)

miracle is not used in the 'other world', it is not because some things are impossible, but because, all things being possible, nothing is miraculous. The danger of such an attitude would have been a belief in magic such as Cardano had entertained, but Cyrano's thinking was too close to that of Lucretius for the danger to be grave. That he considered black magic to be an illusion of a disordered mind is shown by his letters on witchcraft. If he believed in magic, it was natural magic, the magic of science. He speculates, it is true, on the power of divination and attributes such a gift to Campanella, but his speculations are scientific in spirit. He begins from observation. He has observed that twins not only have the same physical characteristics but also the same mental characteristics and think and act in harmony even when they are at a distance from each other. Applying to these observed facts, or what he took for observed facts, his speculative principle which identifies the physical with the psychical, he argues that in two persons who are physically identical the same mental states must occur. If therefore by imitation one can bring one's physical state into harmony with that of another person, one may well be able to reproduce in one's own mind the thoughts and feelings of that person. By imitating their attitudes and gestures Campanella discovered the most secret thoughts of the inquisitors. When Cyrano goes further, on the very last page of the *Etats et Empires du Soleil*, and attributes to Campanella a real second sight, the modern reader is justified in raising his eyebrows. Campanella knows immediately when Descartes arrives on the sun (Descartes died in 1650), although he is three leagues or more away. He knows by intuition; he sees Descartes arrive in a 'dream'. On this issue scientific rationalism was to take a very different attitude from that of Cyrano, but even here there is no suggestion of a conquest of nature by the easy way which was the magicians' aim; there is no mention of magic formulae, incantations or rites. Campanella's insight can be rationally explained by Cyrano's physical principles: his imagination is so receptive that it registers purely physical impulses received from three leagues away. Doubtless a severe lesson in geometry from the newly arrived Descartes would have helped to bridle such speculation, just as a stern lesson in mechanics would have convinced Cyrano at the outset that his machine could never have reached the moon, but prophetic dreams were not unheard of occurrences in Cyrano's time and did not Pierre Borel promise an *ars volandi* which would make a flight to the moon feasible? It would be idle to suggest that Cyrano submits his thinking to rigorous scientific discipline; on the contrary he allows speculation unfettered play, but his speculation is far from aimless; it is coherent and purposeful.

Cyrano's mentality was sane and vigorous; it had a vulgar strength and pugnacity. He openly derided the professors of the University of Paris, a corporation to be feared in the intellectual world. He could imagine the putting of a town on wheels so as to obtain a change of air. He could imagine the settlement of international disputes by arbitration. He was sometimes coarse but never obscene. Confident in himself, he was capable of good-natured satire which could strike deeper than earnest indignation. Confident with the self-confidence of an amateur and a cavalier, but also of natural genius, he could drive straight to the heart of the matter, albeit rough-shod over the susceptibilities of the learned.

He died at the early age of thirty-five. Was he in danger from the ecclesiastical authorities? Did the Jesuits steal the manuscript of the *Histoire de l'Etincelle*? The bibliophile Lacroix suggested as much in his edition of 1858, but there is no documentary evidence to support the suggestion, so it would be idle to discuss it. Cyrano may well have been considered too eccentric to be dangerous. All the same Lebret thought it prudent to omit a number of long paragraphs from his edition of the *Etats et Empires de la lune*. Cyrano was not quickly forgotten, though his name aroused little controversy. His book was parodied by the Italian players in 1684, in an *Arlequin, Empereur de la lune*. It was frequently reprinted until the middle of the eighteenth century. In 1748 Benoît de Maillet dedicated his *Telliamed*, a book of geological essays, to Cyrano, and this was a fitting honour to pay to the author of so lively an imaginative theory of the moon.

IV

Atheism and Political Radicalism

THE *Theophrastus redivivus* (1659)[1] is far from having the smiling appearance of Cyrano's romances. It is a vast and immensely erudite compendium in Latin, of the type which does not seem to expect a reader and is content with its own existence. A professor or regent in one of the colleges may have written it, a true radical in the intellectual world. There is nothing lighthearted or satirical about it; it is the work of a forceful and systematic thinker of great intellectual ruthlessness; from that point of view there was no intellect in seventeenth-century France to compete with him; only the Englishman Thomas Hobbes of Malmesbury was his equal. It would be difficult to imagine him in the polite circle of the scholarly Du Puy brothers, or at the other private academies such as those of Montmor or Bourdelot; his erudition lacks the necessary polish and worldly grace for such company. That he worked in Paris seems fairly probable seeing that the only contemporary references he makes are French. Amongst a welter of quotations from Plato, Aristotle, Lucretius,[2] Plutarch, Macrobius, Diodorus and a host of other ancient philosophers and historians, and from Pico della Mirandola, Machiavelli, Pomponazzi, Cardano, Henri Etienne, Bodin amongst the Renaissance writers, his only seventeenth-century references are to Vanini, Campanella, Saumaise, Fabrot and Cyrano de Bergerac. His quotation from Cyrano is the only close link which connects him with contemporary affairs; in many ways he is a man of the sixteenth century rather than of the seventeenth. Cyrano's tragedy, *La Mort d'Agrippine* was played in 1654 and the lines which caused a scandal and which I have quoted above[3] are the lines which the author of the *Theophrastus* quotes. All the thinkers of Antiquity and the Renaissance who were or could be considered as atheists, who denied the immortality of the soul, the existence of hell, demons, spirits and apparitions figure in this compilation, but it is not merely a compilation; its two thousand folio pages of historical references

[1] The date is clearly indicated on p. 351 of the MS in the Bibliothèque nationale (fonds latin 9324). Cf. my article in the *Revue d'Histoire littéraire de la France*, 1937.
[2] The quotations from the *De rerum natura* are particularly numerous.
[3] Ces beaux riens . . . ne craint rien, see above, p. 52.

are all made to bear uncompromisingly on the following implacably developed argument. There is no God, unless the sun be referred to by that name. The sun gives life and, with the other heavenly bodies, directs the destinies of living things. *O sol omnipotens, mundi anima, mundi vis, mundi lux!* This invocation runs like a refrain through the first part of the work (*De Diis*) and is frequently written very large so as to stand out on the page. The author is an astrologer (he draws the horoscope of Christ) and in this respect, as in every other respect, continues the traditions of the sixteenth century. He will have no God, if it be not the sun. The popular idea of God is a mere expression of human fear; the God of the theologians is a mere 'thing of reason', a pure abstraction; he will not admit its existence. Nor will he admit the possibility of a creation. The second part (*de Mundo*) is devoted to proving the eternity of the world, and again we are on ground familiar to the sixteenth century, as we are also in the third *Tractatus* (*de religione*) of which the object is to prove that all religions, with all their miracles, oracles, prophesies and revelations, are a colossal deception practised by expert rulers on their superstitious peoples for purely political ends, that is to say in order to maintain order and govern. The Christian religion is no exception, and the author here refers to the old tradition of the Three Impostors and attributes to Frederick II of the Empire the proposition that Moses, Christ and Mahomet were three remarkable impostors who seduced the human race.[1] The author does not mean to imply that all religions are bad, but merely that all religions are false, and the sixth chapter of the same *Tractatus* is summarized as follows in the table of contents: Each and every religion is shown to be good, none indeed but has a political origin, instituted by men and not by God as the peoples are led to believe.[2] The fourth *Tractatus* (*de anima et inferis*) finds a mere jumble of incomprehensible affirmations in all that has been said about the nature of the soul and is completely and uncompromisingly negative as far as the existence of ghosts, apparitions, the resurrection of the dead and a future life are concerned. The fifth (*de contemnenda morte*) draws the correct conclusion that death is not to be feared and the last (*de vita secundum naturam*) develops a naturalistic philosophy of life on the following lines. Everybody wishes to be happy, but few know how to accomp-

[1] p. 613.
[2] Omnis religio bona esse ostenditur, enim nulla est quae a politica ortus non habeat tabe hominibus instituta sit, non vero a Deo data, ut vulgo persuasum est.' (p. 613.)

lish such an ambition. Some seek happiness in pleasure (*voluptas*) or the absence of pain (*indolentia*), others in riches and purely external things, others in virtue and the avoidance of all agitation,[1] but the true way to live happily is to live according to nature and to follow nature's law as it is revealed to us by experience.[2] Nature's first law is that every animal seeks its own preservation and well-being. The first law of society is not to do to others what you would not they should do unto you, and this is not man's law or the gods' law, but nature's, for evil naturally begets evil in the form of revenge.[3] One's character, as Aristotle says, is formed by one's temperament, and nothing is by nature good or evil but thinking makes it so, as the variety of existing laws and customs amply shows.[4] A people adopts the customs to which nature inclines it and in relation to those customs actions become good or bad which are not so in nature. Man is an animal amongst other animals and is not by nature a superior being; he differs from others only as one species differs from another; each species excels by some particular faculty and in the case of man this faculty is the use of speech and of that internal form of speech named reason.[5] But the other animals are not without the use of speech entirely and as for reason, which is not to be separated radically from sensation, and is a form of discourse whereby we distinguish between what is true and what is false, what is good for us and what is bad for us, the other animals, being also capable of distinguishing between what is good for them and what is bad for them, are not totally deprived of it. So the commonly accepted opinion which places man on a superior plane is an erroneous opinion and not borne out by nature.

The English reader may well ask whether the author of the *Theophrastus redivivus* was acquainted with Hobbes, the contemporary philosopher with whom he had most in common. Hobbes was known in France, where he lived in exile from 1640 to 1653 and had taken part in the controversy over Descartes's *Meditations*; he was well known in Gassendi's circle, and Mersenne's, and Sorbière had

---

[1] p. 913.   [2] p. 915.   [3] p. 917.   [4] pp. 927–8.
[5] 'Praeterea nihil est propter quod hominis intellectus et alii sensus interiores perfectiores caeterorum animalium sensibus dici possint, nisi quod sermone intrinseco et enunciativo, id est ratione, et extrinseco, id est loquela utitur . . . nam ratio nihil aliud est quam discursus quo verum a falso et bonum a malo discernimus . . .' (pp. 945–6); 'Igitur intelligere, ratiocinari et sentire unum idemque sunt, nec ullum ab altero ullomodo separari potest; qui intelligere et ratiocinari dicit, sentire dicit; intellectus enim nullus est absque sensibus; similiter, qui sentire dicit is etiam et intelligere dicit, cum absque intellectu sensus nihil prorsus sit.' (p. 947.)

published two editions and a translation of *De cive* and a translation of *Human nature*. But the fact that no mention of Hobbes is made in the *Theophrastus redivivus*, a work interlarded with quotations from innumerable authors, seems to rule out the possibility of his having learnt anything from Hobbes's publications; it remains possible, of course, that he met Hobbes in Paris between 1640 and 1653. But there is more to it. The one idea of Hobbes which had repercussions in France was a political one. Pascal knew Hobbes's political work and was not afraid of the terrible formula *homo homini lupus*, which he in effect adopted as his own. But Hobbes the metaphysician and logician was rarely referred to. Poiret refuted him with Cartesian arguments towards the end of the century.[1] Ideas similar to those of Hobbes appear in the *Lettre de Thrasibule*,[2] but without any mention of Hobbes by name. Huet refuted his biblical criticism. His name appears occasionally in the clandestine tracts of the early eighteenth century,[3] and in reviews such as the *Bibliothèque raisonnée* which were interested in English writers. Brucker's history of philosophy supplied Diderot with information for an article in the *Encyclopédie*,[4] but Voltaire knew little about Hobbes[5] and when Diderot came finally to read Hobbes for himself he had the experience of a positive revelation.[6] D'Holbach merely mentions him in passing in the *Système de la nature*.[7] Naigeon was the only conscious and enthusiastic Hobbesian and he had to discover Hobbes for himself; there was no unbroken Hobbesian tradition in France. The reason may well be that, apart from his political theory, the content of Hobbes's ideas was not sufficiently unusual to cause a stir in France in his own day, and thereafter he was overshadowed by Locke. Be it as it may, the author of the *Theophrastus redivivus* writes as though he

[1] *Cogitationes rationales*, I, cap. II. Cf. Pillon, *Bayle critique du spiritualisme* in *Année philosophique*, 1901, p. 68.

[2] Sometimes attributed to Fréret; cf. below, p. 302.

[3] One of these ms treatises, in the municipal library at Rouen (N. 74), is called *Notes de Hobbes sur le Nouveau Testament*, but it is spurious. It was written about 1735.

[4] Cf. J. E. Barker, *Diderot's Treatment of the Christian religion in the Encyclopédie*, New York, 1941, p. 22.

[5] He mentions him in the Introduction to the *Traité de métaphysique* as one of the small number of 'esprits sages'; in a letter to Formont of August 1733 he names him as having taught before Locke that God could create matter capable of thinking.

[6] 'Hobbes qui longtemps avant Locke avait déduit, dans son petit et sublime *Traité de la Nature humaine*, du principe d'Aristote (nihil est in intellectu quod prius non fuerit in sensu), toutes les conséquences qu'on en pouvait tirer.' (*Réfutation de l'ouvrage d'Helvétius intitulé L'Homme*, *Œuvres*, ed. Assézat, ii, 296.)

[7] Part II, ch. III.

were unaware of Hobbes's existence; he never refers to him any more than he refers to Gassendi or Descartes. He was a man of an earlier generation in outlook; he seems to have been affected little by his contemporaries and it is likewise true that his powerful synthesis of naturalism had no influence that one can detect on even a narrow circle. When his work was mentioned again, or rather for the first time outside his own manuscript, by one or two scholarly free-thinkers of the early eighteenth century, he had become an object of erudite curiosity. Three of the little treatises which were handed round in secret at the beginning of the eighteenth century claim to be partial translations of the mysterious Latin manuscript, which was said to have been bought by Prince Eugene and hidden in the most secret part of his library. One copy, bound in two volumes with gilt and marbled edges was in actual fact in the library of Baron Hohendorf, commander of Eugene's guards, in 1722, while the one which remains to us was doubtless already standing on the shelves of the royal library, as it stands now in the Bibliothèque nationale, somewhat remote and solitary amongst the leather-bound and parch-ment-bound volumes.

Similarities between Hobbes and the Jansenists have been noted more than once,[1] and such similarities are to be expected seeing that the Jansenists denied that all men receive grace in the fallen state. Before the fall Adam was in a state of grace, but this grace having been lost on account of the original sin, and its loss having been per-petuated by all men's participation in the concupiscence which con-stituted that sin, no man has any right to grace and those men who do in fact receive it do not receive it as a reward for any merit on their part. The others have no principle of charity in them and are therefore only motivated by the self-regarding passions. This being the state of affairs which Hobbes referred to as the 'state of nature', it is not surprising to find that the state which Hobbes describes as being anterior to the social state is that which men without grace are actually now in according to the Jansenists. All men hate each other naturally, wrote Pascal. Self-love has been made to serve the common weal, but it is but a feint, a false image of charity and at the bottom is but hatred.[2] Law and government are founded on force:

[1] Condorcet in his edition of the *Pensées*, Sainte-Beuve in *Port Royal* and particularly G. Chinard in *En lisant Pascal*, Geneva, 1948.

[2] 'Tous les hommes se haïssent naturellement l'un l'autre. On s'est servi comme on a pu de la concupiscence pour la faire servir au bien public; mais ce n'est que feindre, et une fausse image de la charité; car au fond ce n'est que haine.' *Pensées* (Brunschvicg), 451.

all rule is usurpation.[1] One might read into such statements a spirit of revolt, but Pascal had no desire to inspire revolt: on the contrary he saw no remedy for the state of affairs he describes and was only interested in it as a proof of man's wretchedness. He was satisfied to think that the existence of rule is its own justification and thought it dangerous to inquire into the origin of law, to talk of fundamental laws and so forth, for to inquire into the origin of laws is merely to show that they are not founded in justice; laws are to be obeyed, not because they are just but because they are laws.[2] The saying is borrowed from Montaigne, but there is more than the scepticism of a Montaigne or a Charron here, resigned spectators of the vagaries of human conduct; there is a bitter and positive denial of the existence of any justice among men based on reason or experience. True, Pascal sets against this a possible state in which all the members of the community would merge their individual selves in a general self and find in the common good the good of each;[3] true, he also affirms that in the Church the state of charity does indeed exist, but in the civil society he had before his eyes he found no germ of rational justice and was content that force should rule and tame the self-seeking impulses of the men subjected to it, lest anarchy destroy all. The state of nature as Hobbes understood it was still in being as far as Pascal was concerned, whereas Hobbes, by means of his social compact establishes laws and a government which men can accept not only as existent but as right. Pascal admits that self-interest has been used to establish efficient social administration but claims that the rules thus established merely hide the evil essence of human nature without changing the herd or pack into a society.[4] There is good reason for thinking that Pascal borrowed many of his remarks

---

[1] '*Mien, tien.* Ce chien est à moi, disaient ces pauvres enfants; c'est là ma place au soleil. Voilà le commencement et l'image de l'usurpation de toute la terre.' ibid., 295.

[2] 'Il est dangereux de dire au peuple que les lois ne sont pas justes, car il n'y obéit qu'à cause qu'il les croit justes. C'est pourquoi il lui faut dire en même temps qu'il y faut obéir parce qu'elles sont lois, comme il faut obéir aux supérieurs, non parce qu'ils sont justes, mais parce qu'ils sont supérieurs. Par là, voilà toute sédition prévenue si on peut faire entendre cela et ce que c'est proprement que la définition de la justice.' (ibid., 326.) Cf. Montaigne: 'Or les lois se maintiennent en crédit, non parce qu'elles sont justes, mais parce qu'elles sont lois: c'est le fondement mystique de leur autorité.' (*Essais,* III. xiii.)

[3] In several fragments he uses the traditional metaphor of the body and the members, *Pensées* (Brunschvicg), 474–83.

[4] 'On a fondé et tiré de la concupiscence des règles admirables de police, de morale et de justice; mais dans le fond, ce vilain fond de l'homme, ce *figmentum malum*, n'est que couvert: il n'est pas ôté.' (ibid., 453.)

from Hobbes,[1] but he neglected completely the main framework of Hobbes's political philosophy and chose only those points which were useful for his own bitter arraignment of human nature. Hobbes postulated a state of nature in which certain rational rules of conduct guide the self-love of each individual; these purely rational principles he considered to be natural laws. Self-love having impelled men to unite together into a society, they make a compact with a man (or council of men) and sacrifice to him (or them) their right to decide what is good or bad, what aims shall be pursued by the whole community. By this process they set up standards of right; the government of the whole community is established on right, not on force. Self-love has not been transformed into charity, but a rational basis for society has nevertheless been laid down; the state of war of all against all has been done away with. For Pascal nothing of the kind has happened and man in society is natural man, prevented by force or ruse or skilful play upon his imagination from pursuing his own ends in the most brutal manner. Only in a purely hypothetical state of grace would the self-love of all men be transformed into charity and a true civil society be established. In the present state, however perfect the social organization built up upon the principle of self-interest, it is merely a pretence overlaying the essential corruption of man's nature.

Jansen himself was not so pessimistic and, indeed, there was something artificial in Pascal's argument because he was pleading a case in a book of Christian apologetics, painting the picture of man's miserable state as black as he could paint it and drawing on the sceptic Montaigne on the one hand and the rationalistic Hobbes on the other and making of them an unnatural mixture. Jansen allowed man in the fallen state the form of intellectual enlightenment which St Paul referred to as the 'old law', which does not replace self-love by charity but may yet provide a rational guide to conduct.[2] The Jansenist jurist Domat was prepared to admit certain basic principles of equity as being accessible to the natural reason and permitting of the establishment of just societies without religion. To render unto each his due, to keep one's word, and to avoid wronging one's fellows would be examples of such purely rational principles. Men, even in the corrupt state, are capable of a love of humanity which

[1] See particularly G. Chinard's *En lisant Pascal*, Geneva, 1948.
[2] *Augustinus*, vol. iii, bk. 1; N. Abercrombie, *The Origins of Jansenism*, Oxford, 1936, p. 144.

binds them together; it is an extension of self-love, a tendency to love in others the resemblance of one's own nature. The universal society which Christianity can in theory establish is paralleled by a universal society founded on the principle of humanity. Thus does Domat, in the preface to his *Traité de droit public* (1689), build a bridge between his religious speculation as a Jansenist and the speculations he shares with contemporary philosophers of law, and, far from agreeing with Hobbes as did Pascal, he agreed rather with Grotius and Pufendorf. Arnauld, a Jansenist, but also a Cartesian, suppressed Pascal's remarks concerning Justice from the Port Royal edition of the *Pensées* (1670), declaring simply that it was false and dangerous to declare that there was nothing essentially just amongst men.[1] Nicole, another spokesman of Port-Royal, went further than Domat in admitting that a society based on enlightened self-interest would to all intents and purposes function like a society based on charity. The Jansenists had indeed speculated so earnestly on the moral basis of the state and had so assimilated naturalistic speculation to their own ways of thinking that it is understandable that they did not feel the necessity of refuting Hobbes.[2]

---

[1] 'Il est faux et très dangereux de dire qu'il n'y ait rien parmi les hommes d'essentiellement juste; et ce qu'en dit M. Pascal peut être venu d'une impression qui lui est restée d'une maxime de Montaigne, que les lois ne sont pas justes en elles-mêmes, mais seulement parce qu'elles sont lois.' (Letter to Pascal's brother-in-law, Périer. *Œuvres*, 1775–83, i, 644; cf. Sainte-Beuve, *Port-Royal*, Paris, 1848, iii, 302.)

[2] 'On peut conclure de tout ce que l'on a dit que pour réformer entièrement le monde, c'est-à-dire pour en bannir tous les vices et tous les désordres grossiers, et pour rendre les hommes heureux dès cette vie même, il ne faudrait, au défaut de la charité, que leur donner à tous un amour-propre éclairé, qui sût discerner ses vrais intérêts, et y tendre par les voies que la droite raison lui découvrirait. Quelque corrompue que cette société fût au-dedans et aux yeux de Dieu, il n'y aurait rien au-dehors de mieux réglé, de plus civil, de plus juste, de plus pacifique, de plus honnête, de plus généreux; et ce qui serait de plus admirable, c'est que n'étant animée et remuée que par l'amour-propre, l'amour-propre n'y paraîtrait point, et qu'étant entièrement vide de charité, on ne verrait partout que la forme et les caractères de la charité.' ((*De la Charité et de l'amour-propre*, cf. Chinard, op. cit., p. 115.)

V

Between Aristotle and Epicurus:
Emmanuel Maignan

THE rehabilitation of Epicurus's natural philosophy to replace discredited scholastic teaching presented obvious difficulties in the seventeenth century. Did Epicurus not refuse to see any pre-ordained design in the universe? Did he not explain the present appearance of things by the fortuitous encounter of invisible, but solid germs or principles imagined by analogy 'with specks of dust in the sunlight, minute particles falling eternally through space and continually colliding and coming together to form all the things we see around us, or separating to encompass their death and destruction? Did he not bluntly deny the immortality of the soul? All these difficulties were critical under their religious aspect and had to be overcome somehow or other if Epicurus was to be made respectable.

Yet strangely enough the task was far easier at the beginning of the century than it would have been at the end of it, and, more unexpectedly still, the task was rendered possible in the first half of the century by the continued currency of two essentially scholastic notions. Gassendi considered himself an opponent of Aristotle and took up the philosophy of Epicurus as a counterblast to the teaching of the schools. But the central feature of Aristotle's conception of the world, namely the unity of all nature including man, remained with him as a tacit assumption. Cartesian dualism severed the human mind from nature. For a Cartesian, to attempt to trace back consciousness to unconscious principles was merely nonsensical. The ideas of matter and thought were for him mutually exclusive; the expression 'thinking matter' had no more sense for him than 'a conscious square'. But for the professors of the old school there was nothing absurd about a purely corporeal thing being able to think in a certain limited fashion. Were not the purely corporeal beasts capable of a high degree of intelligence? Were there not classical examples, handed down from Pliny, to prove the wisdom of birds, dogs and foxes? For the old school, conscious nature melted imperceptibly into unconscious nature. The unity of all creation was assumed by two conceptions which blended the psychical and the corporeal together. The first of these was the Universal Scale (or Chain) of Being; the second was the oft-quoted principle: *nihil est in intellectu quod prius non fuerit in sensu.*

These two notions ceased to be part of current speculation wherever Descartes's influence was felt. The second returned, it is true, and with added strength, after Locke's *Essay on Human Understanding*, but only as a 'dangerous doctrine', the very mention of which (in the unfortunate abbé de Prades's thesis in 1751 for instance) was sufficient to rouse the ire of the bishops. As for the first, it was so thoroughly destroyed that the Encyclopaedists did not manage to recreate it, though they groped towards it. Leibniz was familiar with it, but his unfortunate comparison between the mind and body on the one hand and two perfectly regulated clocks on the other ruined his reputation with the *philosophes*; they laughed at his 'pre-established harmony'. For want of the Scale of Being, or something to replace it, the *philosophes* were without a means of adequately restoring to nature a unity which their naturalistic conception of man and his place in society and the world called for. They could prove well enough that Descartes's dualism was absurd but they failed to advance beyond this purely negative position: they were anti-Cartesians first and foremost. As a way of envisaging nature, the Universal Scale of Being implied briefly this: the whole of creation is imagined as strung out vertically, with the creatures having the fewest 'perfections' (or powers, or properties, or qualities) at the bottom and those having the most 'perfections' at the top. Purely featureless matter is at the bottom, then come the stones and minerals, 'active' minerals and 'precious' stones and notably the magnet. Then plant life, then sensitive life, with man at the top of the sensitive scale and participating in the 'perfections' of the rank immediately above him, which is that of the 'intellectual beings' or angels. God is a being of all perfection and the source and headspring of all the 'perfections' in the created world, which is separated from him by being finite and imperfect. Every possible rung or degree in the scale is filled, because the expression of God's creativeness or 'goodness' would be incomplete if a gap were left unfilled. There is no gap between one degree and the next and the highest creatures of one degree share the perfections of the lowest creatures of the rank above, a principle which was expressed thus: *supremum infimi attingit infimum supremi.*

Such a view of the nature of things has very pronounced hierarchical implications such as no doubt suited the social philosophy of the middle ages, but could scarcely appeal to the social reformers of the eighteenth century: at any rate they did not revive it. Exceptionally, with Toland, Maupertuis, Buffon, Bonnet, Diderot, Robinet, Cabanis, Lacépède, and Lamarck a new conception appears, later to be called 'transformism' or 'theory of evolution' which resembled in some ways the Scale of Being, though in a new, a dynamic, not a static guise. André Chénier attempted to paint the new picture in his *Hermès*, but in the eighteenth century it remained as confused and fragmentary as the *Hermès* itself. It was still overshadowed by a simple, clear design of a vast machine or clockwork drafted by Descartes and the astronomers of the seventeenth century.

Gassendi's picture of nature was far removed from any analogy with a clock as we shall attempt to show, but, before dealing with Gassendi, who is a controversial figure, we propose first to study a contemporary of his whose Catholic orthodoxy has never been called in question, with a view to ascertaining just what *could* be said with the approval of the ecclesiastical authorities.

Emmanuel Maignan has been sadly overlooked by the historians of philosophy and is nowadays entirely forgotten, but Pierre Bayle thought him to be one of the greatest philosophers of the century and Bayle was no complaisant critic.[1] Maignan was born in 1601 and joined the order of Minim friars at the age of eighteen. Though very submissive in theology, he showed a critical mind in philosophy and soon manifested his dissatisfaction with the teaching of the schools. He taught at Rome from 1636 to 1650, when he became provincial of the Minim order at Toulouse. He lived there quietly and when the king and Mazarin visited his physical laboratory and showed themselves greatly interested in his machines, he declined the king's invitation to come to Paris, and lived on quietly in Toulouse until his death in 1676. He did however, according to Saguens, visit Paris on one occasion, in 1657, and was received with great respect by the philosophical academy which met at the house of Habert de Montmor.

---

[1] Saguens his disciple published a short biography in 1697: *De vita, moribus et scriptis R. patris Maignani Tolosatis*, Toulouse, but Brucker condemned him out of hand for having sought to reconcile scholasticism with atomism and Diderot had nothing to say about him in the *Encyclopédie*.

The part of Maignan's treatise[1] which interests us particularly is the *altera pars physicae, de corpore animato, sive de anima*, which deals with the 'vegetative' soul, the 'sensitive soul' the 'external and internal senses' (or sense organs) and the 'rational' soul. Before the second part of the Physics, Maignan has already expounded his logic and his general theory of being, and then, in the first part of the Physics, has dealt with causes, bodies (the rare, the dense, the mobile), the four elements of Empedocles (fire, air, water and earth), motion, and 'mixed bodies'. He now proceeds to deal with animate bodies.

So as not to misrepresent our author's meaning, we shall use in our summary the terms *cognition, cogitation, reflection, ratiocination* and *intellection*, rather than 'consciousness' or 'thought', because the terms *cognition . . . intellection* are used by Maignan in an ascending order of 'perfection', so that cognition may be attributed to a being which can lay no claim to *reflection* and so on. In this respect the importance of the underlying notion of the Scale of Being is apparent, as it is already in the sequence 'vegetative' soul, 'sensitive' soul and 'rational soul'. We have to consider its application to the phenomena which we call vital, sensitive and intellectual; in other words we have to consider that part of the Scale which starts with the plants (with perhaps some intrusion of the stones and metals from below) and mount steadily, genus by genus, to the point where plants intrude upon the stage above, which is that of the animals and climbing still further we reach the point where man distinguishes himself from the other animals and attains perfections characteristic of the purely intellectual beings.

Maignan takes over this traditional scheme of things from the schools and preserves it as a scale of values, but at every stage replaces the abstract terms of the schoolmen by a concrete interpretation. The schoolmen understood such terms as 'vegetative soul' in what we should call an abstract sense, more or less as we should use such terms as 'vital principle'. They started from the rudimentary analysis of experience provided by the ordinary language and proceeded by means of purely linguistic analysis, attributing however real significance (independent of the word used) to the various purely linguistic elements thus distinguished. Maignan, on the contrary attempts to analyse outside nature by a bold application of physical

---

[1] *Cursus philosophicus* . . ., Toulouse, 1653; *Philosophia Maignani scholastica* . . (ed. Saguens), Toulouse, 1703.

principles. His starting point is the same as that of the schoolmen, but while they tended towards greater and greater abstractness, he strives towards greater and greater concreteness.

He begins, as they did, with a distinction between the 'nature' of a thing and the 'soul' of a thing. The 'nature' of a thing is the principle of motion and rest in that thing. The 'soul' is also the principle of motion and rest in a thing, but in a 'higher' sense, a 'vital' sense, some actions being merely 'transitive' (transmitted from outside) and others being 'immanent' (having their cause inside). So every 'soul' is a 'nature', but every 'nature' is not a 'soul'. We are on Aristotelian ground, at the foot of the ladder. Every animated body is a natural body but every natural body is not an animated body.

Now the 'nature' of a thing is nothing more than the special composition, or special arrangements of its component parts whereby it is fitted for the exercise of certain *natural* actions, and similarly the 'soul' of a purely corporeal thing is the special composition, or special arrangement of its component parts, whereby it is fitted for the exercise of certain *vital* actions. In more concrete terms such a 'soul' is a union of 'select' particles, and is co-extended with the body, for the whole of the body is animated not just part of it. And here Maignan is careful to point out that all the philosophers before Aristotle held this view, and notably Democritus, Leucippus, Anaxagoras and Empedocles. There is no such thing as a 'form' which enters into 'matter'. The word 'form' and similarly the word 'act' may be used, provided that these abstract terms are not taken for real things. Thus the Vegetative Soul can be defined, in the abstract, as the 'primary act' of organic bodies having, potentially, vegetative life. An organic body having, potentially, vegetative life is one in which a special composition, or a special arrangement of its component parts fits it for the operations of vegetative life. It is, in short, that by which a 'vegetable' lives, feeds, grows and reproduces itself. And in concrete terms it is a union of 'select elementary particles' and particularly those which 'actuate' the organic disposition of the seed from which the vegetable grows in the first place. There are two kinds of elementary particles in the seed, those which constitute its organic disposition and are the reason for its 'matter', and those which actuate this organic disposition and are the reason for its 'form'. Some people argue that the seed is not alive, but they fail to make the distinction between actual life and potential life. The definition of the vegetative soul includes only *potential* life, the *power* to exercise the functions of life, not *actual* life, the actual exercise of those functions. Some people also argue that everything does not come from a seed or semen, and instance animals which come from decaying matter, but one must conclude that an equivalent of semen is in the decaying matter, or that the particles which constitute and vivify the semen are scattered in the air or the earth, or that semina of various kinds, uniting together, form a further kind. In any case the semen must be there either 'formally' or 'equivalently'.

There are many kinds of stones and metals in which there is vegetative soul. Some stones, such as shells and fossils, grow according to a certain shape; the rock in which fossils form is a sort of matrix and the fossils grow like subterranean plants; some stones have cavities, called veins, through which humours are distributed and which may be called organs. It is not necessary for these organs to be as perfect as in plants and animals; on the contrary the organs of an animated thing must be suited to the degree of vegetative life which it enjoys. Some people argue that stones either do, or do not reach the perfection of vegetative life, i.e. that they must all be alive or all dead, but this is not so: in any genus the highest species attains to the perfection of the lowest species in the genus immediately above, according to the principle *supremum infimi attingit infimum supremi*. So it is not surprising that some stones possess the perfections of plants, but not *all* stones, just as some plants possess the perfections of animals but not *all* plants, and some animals, namely men, attain the intellectual perfection, which is that of angels, but not *all* animals.

As for the Sensitive Soul, most people agree that the beasts have one, and that they suffer, rejoice, desire, fear and have in fact all the passions which appertain to the Sensitive Soul. Only Descartes and his followers consider the beasts to be pure automata, fitted with a marvellous mechanism for receiving impulses from without and acting upon those impulses just as though they had feeling. The Cartesians say that the beasts run without knowing that they run, feed without knowing that they feed and are awake without knowing that they are awake; they deny them, that is to say, the actions of cognition and cogitation. They agree that in the act of vision light is emitted by an object and makes an impression on the eye; that this impression is conveyed by the optic nerve to the brain and causes a motion in the brain which is in turn transmitted to the muscles of the limbs and causes the animal to pursue the object or flee from it, or, if the impulse is not strong enough to promote pursuits or flight, leaves the animal motionless. But they deny that any knowledge of the object accompanies this action, because the beasts are purely material, and the notion 'matter' implies only extension, motion and figure, and from these it is impossible to derive the notion 'sensation'. But the facts of observation are that experience refutes Descartes; the actions of the beasts resemble those of men, and some of their actions, such as building a nest, obviously require intelligence. They obviously do not enjoy 'reflective' or 'perfect' sensation, for no corporeal sense (or sense organ) reflects upon itself (the eye sees without knowing that it sees) but they have 'simple' or 'imperfect' sensation. When one considers the ordinary notion of matter, it is indeed impossible to attribute to it pleasure, or desire, or anger, but when one considers the most spirituous particles of matter, it is possible to conceive that they have these perfections, according to the principle *supremum infimi attingit infimum supremi*. And so it is that there are stones which, in a manner of speaking, grow, and plants which, in a manner of speaking, feel, and beasts which so to speak cognize, while men accede to intellection, the perfection essential to angels. If it be true, as the theologians tell us, that there are spiritual entities which move in space, which is a quality peculiar to corporeal things, why should not a certain perfection of spiritual beings be compatible with some corporeal things? And again, if it be said that God can create beast-machines, why should he not be able to create beasts capable of thought? The actions of brutes are performed, say the Cartesians, just as certain actions of man's body are performed, that is to say unconsciously, but surely this is not true of building a nest, or rearing young, actions which require industry, care, and, one might almost say, wisdom?

The Sensitive Soul is the 'primary act' of an organic body having the power of feeling. It is the principle of sensation, or that by which feeling things feel. But this abstract Aristotelian method of defining a word is insufficient; a physical significance must be given to it. The operations of the sensitive soul are corporeal and a corporeal act cannot be anything but motion. It follows then that all sensation is motion, but 'immanent' motion, not 'transitive' motion, otherwise it would not reach the level of life and no one doubts that sensitive motions are vital motions. The Sensitive Soul is compounded of elementary particles which occupy the whole body, especially the blood and have sufficient motive force within themselves to produce the sensitive motions of the body. These particles are material, but must not be understood in the Aristotelian sense of matter, which implies mere potentiality, but rather as the Aristotelians understand 'form', when they call the beasts' soul their 'substantial form'. To this 'substantial form' the Aristotelians ascribe 'sensitive cognition', and the elementary particles which compose the sensitive soul are to be considered as having this same perfection. There is no question of their having 'reflective cognition', which is beyond the sphere of corporeal activity.

It may be argued that the soul is a unity and not a collection of particles, but there is no reason for supposing that these particles cannot unite as do the elements in a 'mixed' substance. It may be argued again that animals have the same soul all their lives, but this must be understood 'equivalently' and not in a real sense, because the Sensitive Soul is co-extended with the body and must change when the body grows or shrinks or loses some of its parts.

The manner in which sensation takes place will be adequately understood when it is seen how the organs of sense transmit motion to the part of the animal where it is perceived. In the nerves there lies the power to transmit motion from the sense organs to the brain. The motion is carried by the animal spirits which flow in the nerves to that part of the brain called the *apophysis vermiformis*, and from thence to the muscles of the limbs. The motion is modified in the brain in the same way as the motion of a tennis ball is modified by the greater or less tension of the racquet from which it rebounds. Nothing but motion is transmitted in the whole operation; there is no such thing as 'intentional species', 'similitude', 'simulacrum', or any material image transmitted from the external object to the sense organ. In vision, nothing but the motion of the light is transmitted and nothing resembling the object which reflects the light.

The animal spirits flow more easily along a course which they have followed many times before, and an organ of sense becomes more easily disposed to receive and transmit motions when it has received and transmitted them many times before, just as a wheel turns more easily after several revolutions. Nothing more than this is implied by what is called a 'habit'.

It is necessary to suppose a 'common' sense which receives all the motions transmitted from the various sense organs, otherwise the animal would not be able to distinguish one sense impression from another. All the senses are kinds of touch; the sense organs are different, but the sense is the same. The Aristotelians distinguish several senses because they fail to make the necessary distinction between sense and the sense organs. Similarly *appetite* is not a different power from *sense*. The beasts have appetite for the good, and its negative form, aversion from evil, which presupposes that they *know* a thing to be good or evil in so far as it concerns them. But that does not mean that they have a separate faculty called 'appetite'. When a pleasant odour pleases an animal and impels it towards the source of the odour, that is all one and the same movement. The smell is caused by corpuscles which are carried by the air into the nostrils. It is not inherent in the object. Differences of smell are caused by differences in the object, but also by the different temperaments of different brains. A pleasant smell for one person is an unpleasant smell for another. Hearing is caused by the membrane of the ear being moved by the air, and vision by corpuscles which strike the eye. Differences of colour are to be explained by the different ways in which light is reflected from objects.

The Rational Soul is distinguished from the Sensitive Soul by having the power of reflective cognition and by its knowledge of universal ideas. The rational soul is not transmitted by the semen; it is produced by creation only and is immaterial. Man has the power of reflection; he *knows* his sensations and can modify them. But the sensitive soul of the brutes may have the *equivalent* of reflection, and some of the brutes' sensitive operations are so perfect in the material order that they accede almost to the perfection of the immaterial order, that is to say to reflective cognition. Often the brutes act in such a way that they could not act in a more suitable or opportune way if they reflected upon their actions. So, though it is not possible to attribute to them reflection in the true sense, nevertheless it would seem possible to attribute to them an accessory sort of reflection, or an equivalent of reflection, according to the axiom *supremum infimi attingit infimum supremi*. 'Mixed' substances are nearer to life than simple substances, amongst the stones is a species which can be called plants, some plants have a sort of sensation, so why should not the most perfect sensation resemble reasoning? The most perfect human reasoning approaches the intellection of the angels and the intellection of the angels approaches the Divine comprehension.

The Rational Soul is immaterial, and this is true in spite of objections such as the following. How can an immaterial soul be aware of material things? The reply is that it can do so because of its superiority, but, in any case, the power of reflection is sufficient by itself to prove the immateriality of the Rational Soul. However, in many ways, the Rational Soul is dependent upon the body. In the first place, the better the body is organized and especially the brain, the better the Rational Soul performs its functions. Secondly all rational knowledge depends upon the senses, because external objects do not affect it immediately but only through the medium of the senses. *Nihil est in intellectu quod prius non fuerit in sensu*, as can be shown from experience: who, for instance, has any notion of colour without having seen any colours? The dependence is not always direct, as we sometimes see colours in dreams, but the colours seen in dreams resemble those seen in our waking hours. Thirdly there are motions of the body over which the Rational Soul has no control and which come from the organic functioning of the body, while, on the other hand it is true that many of the actions of the body depend upon the Rational Soul, as can be seen when a man moves hither and thither at the bidding of his will.

The Rational Soul is immortal, as can be deduced from its immateriality. Material things resolve into the parts of which they are composed, but immaterial things are not composite, they are simple and therefore cannot be so resolved.

The foregoing is a summary of a text book of philosophy used in the seventeenth century, which provoked neither controversy nor even comment. The theories Maignan puts forward so unselfconsciously in it can variously be described as mechanistic, sensationalist, hylopsychistic, but the underlying concept of the Scale of Being, and the essentially Aristotelian method of proceeding from being to thinking, in contrast with the Cartesian method of proceeding from consciousness towards the outside world, place the whole doctrine outside the scope of the Cartesian distinction between spiritualism and materialism. Though for Maignan the material world merges by minute stages into the spiritual world, the existence of that spiritual world is not for a moment in doubt in his mind. He believes not only in the existence of Rational Souls, but also in the existence of Intellectual Beings and Universal Ideas. A sceptical mind might make short work of the Intellectual Beings or Angels, but there were still the Universal Ideas and the Rational Soul. In fact a whole superstructure of spiritual entities reared itself towards God above the world described by physics.

VI

Gassendi's Account of the Nature
of Things

It is difficult to determine which of several possible reasons at-tracted Gassendi to Epicurus in the first place in 1626. He had just given up, or was in process of giving up his plan for publishing a series of direct attacks on the old school in continuation of his *Exercitationes paradoxicae*. Doubtless it was prudence which caused him to do so; not that he felt menaced by the campaign of his friend Mersenne against the sceptics and deists; more probably he realized that attempts of the type of the *Exercitationes paradoxicae* were neither new nor effective. The old guard was strongly entrenched, especially in Paris and was merely irritated without being shaken by such skirmishing. Was he attracted by the idea of rehabilitating Epicurus as a means of decrying Aristotle without openly flouting the authority of his elders? Very possibly. He at any rate intended his *Epicurus* to be a sequel to his *Exercitationes paradoxicae*,[1] and such an indirect approach was entirely suited to his cautious tem-perament. He had no desire to stir up a hornets' nest, but at the same time his lively intelligence must have been tempted by the prospect of justifying, with sound evidence in hand, a man so uni-versally condemned by the unintelligent as was Epicurus: here was a 'paradox' he could victoriously force upon the adversary! Did the success of others with whom he was in contact, Galileo, Mersenne, Beeckmann, Descartes, who were achieving results by reducing the problems of physics to those of mechanics, encourage him to develop his study of a mechanistic philosophy? Was he attracted by Epi-

[1] 'Ego tanto viro paravi Apologiam, destinato ipsius doctrinae volumine integro, quod Paradoxicarum Exercitationum adversus Aristoteleos volumini, cujus ideam, primum-que librum feci jam juris publici, attexatur.' (Letter to Du Puy, *Opera*, vi, p. 11; cf. B. Rochot, *Les Travaux de Gassendi sur Epicure et sur l'atomisme*, Paris, 1944, p. 31). Gassendi's close friend Peiresc (H. Fabri de) said explicitly (according to Morhof's *Polyhistor philosophicus*, l. 1, cap. xii, § 3) that the work on Epicurus was a continuation of the campaign: 'Caeteros 5 libros, nimirum in libros Physicorum, de corpore simplici, de mixtis, in Metaphysicam et moralem Aristotelis Philosophiam, teste Honorato Fabri, ex concilio amicorum suppressit. Quam telam suam cum non posset absolvere, et vitu-perare Aristotelem amplius sine dedecore, ad alterum extremum delapsus, Epicurum laudare, ejusque Philosophiam illustrare coepit.' (Lübeck, 1708, 1714, ii, p. 68; cf. Rochot, op. cit., p. 28.)

curus's method as a means of overcoming his own natural scepticism? All these factors may have weighed with him. In 1628 he was still asserting, to both Peiresc and Mersenne, that he was of a sceptical turn of mind, but on one of these occasions he was referring to astrology and so probably meant no more than that he was intellectually cautious to a fault and found it difficult to convince himself rationally of the truth of any proposition. Such a scepticism would not be the same as Pyrrhonic doubt, content with an exact equilibrium of pro and con; it would rather be an inhibiting excess of caution, to be overcome by intellectual effort and courage. In Epicurus's 'Canons' lay a means of acquiring a reasonable degree of certainty, or at least the means of making possible an advance in philosophic inquiry beyond one's starting point. This is the attitude which Gassendi eventually reached, as is amply shown by the *Syntagma philosophicum*; it is the attitude of mind which has since become general in the scientific world, where theories which no one would claim as ultimate are nevertheless used as working hypotheses.

Gassendi's friends were from the first acquainted with his plans and Beeckmann, going straight to the heart of things, was anxious that he should tackle at once the problem of how sensitive organisms can be formed from insensitive atoms.[1] Neither of the two philosophers was worried by the religious significance of such an inquiry; at least neither mentioned it. It was indeed to Mersenne, the author of *l'Impiété des déistes*, that Beeckmann addressed his inquiry. Both he and Gassendi were prepared to take elasticity in bodies as the starting point in an attempt to proceed from the insensitive to the sensitive.

Gassendi's plan grew in scope as he worked upon it. By 1631 he intended to put into his book all that could be learned on the life and thought of Epicurus; he was planning a work of scholarship rather than of science. The first part was to be a life of the philosopher and a defence of his character. This was to be followed by the Physics of Epicurus. The Physics was to contain first an account of Epicurus's views on the nature of things in general: the atoms and their properties, motion, space, the existence of God, the existence (or rather non-existence) of demons. The second part of the Physics was to deal with the origin and structure of the world, the existence or non-existence of a Providence, the end of the world and the existence of innumerable other worlds. The third part was to deal with the

[1] Rochot, ibid., p. 38.

heavens, the stars, their motion and whether they exercise an influence on human affairs. And the last book was to deal with the Earth, with animate and inanimate beings on the Earth, the generation, nutrition and reproduction of animals, the senses; the soul or mind, its seat and functions, the appetites, animal motions, sleep, health and sickness and the immortality of the soul. A final section, on Epicurean moral philosophy, was not yet planned.

The various chapters were sent round to Gassendi's friends in manuscript form as they were written, and were read and argued about in an active philosophical correspondence. The work progressed slowly because of interruptions, occasioned by Gassendi's ecclesiastical duties and his numerous journeys. Sometimes the interruptions were of long duration, from 1637 to 1641 for example. In 1647 Gassendi allowed the first part to appear under the title *De vita et moribus Epicuri libri octo*[1] and in 1649 he edited with long philological and philosophical commentaries drawn from his voluminous notes the tenth book of Diogenes Laertius, which deals with Epicurus. His systematic treatment of the subject was as yet known only to the friends to whom he had communicated his manuscript or summaries of it.

A certain amount of opposition and doubt was expressed by his friends. In 1632 Campanella wrote to him announcing his *Atheismus triumphatus*, which sets Campanella's own picture of a world permeated with intelligence beside that described by Lucretius from which design and purpose are excluded. Gassendi replied that there were indeed aspects of Epicurus's philosophy which he would have to refute, but that he should not for that reason fail to give a complete and impartial account of it. Mersenne did not think atomism could be made acceptable to religion, nor could he accept as conceivable an atom extended in space and at the same time indivisible.[2] He had however already expressed his approval of Gassendi's *Apology*, which he had read in manuscript.[3]

Chapelain was worried both by the general idea of a defence of Epicurus[4] and by what seemed to him a contradiction affecting the whole system. If the atoms were to replace the old idea of matter, how could they at the same time be the cause of motion? 'Matter'

---

[1] Published at Lyons. Cf. below, p. 138. [2] Mersenne to Gassendi, 1 Jan. 1636.
[3] In his *Preludes*, 1634, p. 66, see R. Lenoble, *Mersenne*, Paris, 1943, pp. 419–20, and Rochot, op. cit., p. 74 n.
[4] To Gassendi, 7 Dec. 1640, Rochot, op. cit., p. 104.

was something essentially inert. Gassendi replied that the atoms are always in motion, that motion is one of their properties: his conception of the atoms was essentially 'dynamic', though he did not use the term. While making motion essential to the atoms, he was however careful to point out to Chapelain that he considered Epicurus to be in error for having assumed the existence of eternal atoms eternally in motion. God created the atoms and directed their motion according to his own design; all their movements are therefore the expression of God's providence.

Indefatigably Gassendi strove in his correspondence to show his friends how the difficulties of Epicurus's system could be removed. Epicurus assumes an infinite number of atoms in an infinite space. If that were so, God's providence would not be necessary in order to explain the present appearance of things, as an infinite number of atoms, moving eternally in an infinite space would at some time or other, in some place or other, actualize every possible combination of themselves and there would be no problem to solve in explaining why the present constitution of things as we see them has come about: it would merely be one of an endless series of possible combinations of atoms. Gassendi's reply was that God alone is absolutely infinite; Epicurus was therefore wrong in postulating an infinite number of atoms.[1]

In order to put his answer to Epicurus on a rational basis, he had to be prepared to prove at least the existence of God, and not be content with the authority of religion as sufficient grounds for affirming it, and indeed, in the years following 1631 he showed himself more and more ready to admit the importance of reasoned argument as against unquestioning faith. In 1636 he was prepared to prove the existence of God, God's providence and the immortality of the soul by reason,[2] and in 1642, in his controversy with Descartes, he had his own proofs to offer as an alternative to his adversary's.

So far, such objections as had been made against Gassendi's Epicureanism had been made by personal friends. Descartes indulged in harder hitting, but had no desire to cause his adversary any

---

[1] To the comte d'Alais, 24 Oct., 31 Oct., 7 Nov., 14 Nov. 1742; cf. Rochot, op. cit., pp. 95–6. Gassendi considered it possible to accept 'imaginary' infinite space(s), but not an infinite number of atoms: 'Si quidem et nostri [i.e. theologians] plerumque admittunt esse ultra Mundum infinita spatia quae *Imaginaria* appellant, et in quibus fatentur Deum posse condere innumeros Mundos: non perinde tamen tolerari potest infinitudo corporum.' (To the comte d'Alais, 7 Nov. 1642, *Opera*, vi, p. 158.)

[2] Cf. R. Pintard, *Le Libertinage érudit*, p. 498.

trouble with the religious authorities; the argument between him and Gassendi was purely philosophical. That was not the case with J.-B. Morin, who declared publicly that Gassendi was fit to be burnt at the stake. Morin was a teacher of the old school and an astrologer. He took up the cudgels for Aristotle against Etienne de Claves in 1624 and in 1643 published a refutation of Copernicus. A reply by Gassendi in the same year, published without the author's consent in 1649, started a violent quarrel between the two and it was in Morin's *Dissertatio de atomis et vacuo contra Gassendi philosophiam Epicuream* in 1650 that the menace of the stake occurred. Bernier continued the argument and succeeded in presenting Morin in a ridiculous light.[1] No one in authority took any notice of Morin as far as one can make out, and it was not until long after Gassendi's death in 1655 that it was again suggested that Gassendi's teaching was dangerous for the faith, by the Cartesian theologian Antoine Arnauld. By that time (1692)[2] the atmosphere had changed and Cartesian habits of thought had made possible interpretations of Gassendi's ideas which Gassendi probably never even dreamed of. Gassendi's Epicureanism was framed at a time when scholastic theology was scarcely challenged and was taken for granted in its own domain; it was Cartesianism itself, with its ruthless simplification of current ideas, which was to cut away that framework and leave the picture almost as Epicurus had originally painted it.

Apart from Lucretius himself, whose *De rerum natura* was always readily available and widely read, Gassendi seems to have had few competitors as an exponent of Epicurean atomism. Descartes was developing a corpuscular physics, but his particles of the first, second and third elements were not atoms; they were mere parts of a continuum and were divisible to infinity. It is true that at Pavia, a Frenchman by birth, Jean Chrysostome Magnen, was professing an atomic theory taken from Democritus, and that his lectures were published, but there is no evidence of his having had many readers in France.[3] One can also mention an abortive effort of two Frenchmen, Jean Bitaud and Etienne de Claves to defend in public a certain number of theses (one of them being a clear statement of atomism) in Paris in 1624. The Parlement intervened at the request of the

[1] Cf. R. Pintard, op. cit., p. 386; B. Rochot, op. cit., p. 16.   [2] Cf. above, p. 16.
[3] J. C. Magnen was born at Luxeuil and studied at Dôle. He became professor of medicine and philosophy at the university of Pavia. He published his *Democritus reviviscens sive de Atomis. Addita est vita Democriti* at Pavia in 1646 (Leyden, 1648; The Hague, 1658; London, 1688).

Sorbonne and drove the two disputants out of the confines of its jurisdiction. It was on this occasion that attacks on the 'ancient and approved authors'—meaning Aristotle—were forbidden on pain of death; the Aristotelian professors of the University of Paris had claimed and obtained the protection of the civil authorities. As for Bitaud's and Claves's claim that 'all things are composed of indivisible atoms' it was condemned by the Sorbonne as 'false, audacious and contrary to the faith'. Their statement of the principle is dogmatic enough, but they do not seem to have developed it systematically. They were interested in chemistry and not mechanics, to the point of being suspected by Peiresc of seeking in chemistry the revelation of all nature's secrets, and though they were sufficiently scientific in their attitude for us to call them 'chemists' rather than 'alchemists', they were not, of course, in a position to make a systematic application of the atomic theory to chemistry; they were still at grips with the five 'elements': water, earth, salt, sulphur and mercury, which were for them the component parts of all 'mixed' substances (theses nos. IV to X). However one looks upon it, they cannot be thought of as serious rivals of Gassendi, who, be it said by the way, seems not to have been in contact with them.

When Gassendi died on 9 November 1655 he was still engaged in putting his notes in order under the title *Syntagma philosophicum*. In 1658 the work was published by his literary executors in two volumes at the head of his complete works. Such parts as were still not written up in their final form were printed from earlier drafts dating from 1636–45. The *Syntagma* is the most complete and systematic exposition which Gassendi made of his teaching, and while it follows more or less the author's original plan (1631) for an account of Epicurus's opinions, it does not limit itself to them, but on the other hand discusses other ancient and contemporary theories relating to each question under discussion. It is indeed an account of Epicurean atomism presented in the light of seventeenth-century speculation.

The *Syntagma* begins with a discussion of philosophical method and continues through 'physics' (physics, biology and psychology) to morals. The first part, the *Institutio logica* tries to overcome the sort of scepticism which makes philosophy impossible and replace it by a 'prudent confidence' in being able to attain to truth, holding the balance evenly between reason and experience, accepting the axioms and the law of contradiction as limits beyond which the necessity of proving first principles need not be pushed and contending that to know the properties or operations of a thing is to know the thing itself. Our ideas come to us through our senses; there are no innate ideas. All the ideas we receive through our senses are singular or particular, not general; it is the mind that makes general ideas out of singular or particular ideas. But ideas can also be communicated to us by other people, so that we can say that our ideas come to us from two sources, (1) our own experience, and (2) another's teaching. A good philosophical method consists in discovering hidden relations between things, in interpreting these relations correctly and in expounding their explanation clearly.

The second part of the *Syntagma*, that is to say the *Physica*, begins with a discussion of the nature of things followed by a discussion of the causes of things. In discussing the nature of things, Gassendi deals first with the four categories of being which he calls space, time, substance and accident. Space and time are not primary substances, nor are they ideas, nor are they modes of a primary substance, nor are they mere fictions: they are categories of being. One can summarize the foregoing by saying that according to Gassendi the things which are and which we can know by experience are accidents of a primary substance existing in temporal and spatial relations with each other. Accident alone, substance alone, time alone, space alone cannot be objects of experimental knowledge; they can only be known as part of a complex of all four. The term 'substance' then disappears from Gassendi's discussions and is replaced by the term 'matter'. 'Matter' is that which is permanent under the ceaseless change and variety we see in things; it is the matrix from which all things come and to which they all return. It is not merely an indeterminate something, capable of receiving forms and qualities, as was taught in the schools. Such a being would be nothing and nothing could come from it. No purpose is served, on the other hand, by imagining four primary elements, fire, air, water and earth, because the immense variety we see in nature cannot be explained by combinations of only four elements. The most satisfactory theory is that of the atomists Democritus, Epicurus and Lucretius. The atoms can be imagined by analogy with the motes one sees in a ray of sunlight. From their innumerable combinations come all things with all their properties, which are the properties of matter. We cannot see the atoms, but we can determine their characteristics by reasoning. They must be indestructible, indivisible, solid; they must have size, however minute they be. Their essence cannot be mere extension, as Descartes says, otherwise nothing could be produced from them. They must be indivisible, because if matter was infinitely divisible there would be as many parts in a grain of sand as in a mountain. They must be very (though not infinitely) varied in shape in order to explain the great variety we see in things, and there must be a finite number of atoms and not an infinite number of each shape as Lucretius says. The atoms must have weight and they must have a tendency to movement or action by their nature. Repose is a mere illusion; everything is constantly changing, although some things change very slowly. Where the atoms are not, there is vacuum, otherwise movement would be impossible, as can be shown by reasoning and proved by experiments such as the dissolution of salt in water or the compression of air.

After discussing the *nature* of things, Gassendi deals with the *causes* of things. He distinguishes the first cause and the secondary causes. The first cause of all things is God and the existence of God must therefore be established first and foremost. For Gassendi the existence of God is proved by our having the idea of him in our minds and by the evidence of harmony and order in the universe. Of these two proofs the first is drawn from the second, so that the one great proof of the existence of God is the evidence of harmony and order in the universe. Lucretius is wrong therefore in giving fear as the source of our idea of God; we do not fear God in times of danger, we turn to him for help. The idea of God is not an innate idea, but on the other hand it does not come entirely from experience. There is in the mind a predisposition to know God, so that we readily believe what we are told about him, and form the idea of him spontaneously when we behold the harmony of nature and its laws. To say with Lucretius that the world needs no cause is unreasonable. A prosperous state presupposes a good ruler, a magnificent palace presupposes a clever architect; by analogy the world presupposes God. God must be distinct from the world and must exist *necessarily* or by himself. We cannot conceive his nature because our senses give us no help: he can be thought of as the reason for all things and as perfection, but no relative quality can be attributed to him. He must be intelligent because he is the cause of an intelligible effect; he can have nothing in common with matter because matter is limited, composite, divisible, changeable, corruptible. He is known by the intellect and not by the imagination, and as our language is never devoid of imaginative content it can never correspond with his nature. Considered in himself, or as a substance, his attributes are unity, eternity, immensity (understood as a quality and not as an extent of space). Considered as the intelligent cause of all things he is omniscient, omnipotent, good, free, wise and blessed. In the world his intelligence and activity are seen, for example, in the regularity of the crystals of which minerals are composed, in the wonders of the bodies of animals, in the return of the seasons. It is not reasonable to attribute these marvels to chance. Creation is incomprehensible, but is a fact none the less. Before the creation God was an active intelligence contemplating his own perfections; in the creation his goodness radiated outside himself for his own glory alone. Nothing thereby was added to his being because he is sufficient unto himself: creation is the expression of God's goodness. Lucretius was so preoccupied with the sight of evil, that he failed to understand that life is good (or rather a good, not an evil) and that it is better to be, than not to be, alive.

Providence in general is not inconceivable because for God to care for his creation is surely a perfection in him. Without it he would not be all perfect. Also, as action is more perfect than contemplation, he would not be all perfect if he were not active. *A posteriori* his providence can be proved by the order and harmony of the universe. Chance is no explanation of order and harmony. The idea of chance is merely an expression of our ignorance. God has a special providence for man, the most perfect of his creations. To say with Lucretius that God's felicity would be deranged thereby is sheer anthropomorphism, and to ask why there are dangerous animals in the world, and why the virtuous suffer, is to fail to see that God allows the causes he has created to act independently of himself. He allows man the liberty to do evil, but he gives him the strength to do good, and the fact that the virtuous suffer is a proof of the immortality of man's soul because the balance must be redressed in a future life.

The secondary causes of things can be reduced to one, that is to say motion. Motion according to Lucretius is the passage of a body from one place to another. The principle of motion is the atoms themselves which are naturally active and always active. When they meet an obstacle their effort is not destroyed, it continues to be exercised. Differences of movement are explainable by the different shapes of the atoms, for their motion is more or less hindered by their shape. The principle of motion is in bodies. There is no point in making a distinction between motion and what moves, as the Aristotelians do, nor is Aristotle's way of explaining motion by the desire of the world to turn towards God any more than the product of his imagination. The principle of motion is in bodies and especially in the most active of the atoms, the 'flower of matter' so to speak, the part that is usually called 'form' in the schools. Gravity is a movement of one body towards another body to be understood by analogy with the action of the magnet. One must suppose an emanation of particles (species) from one body (the earth, say) which operate on another body (a stone, say) either by squeezing from the sides, as Descartes suggests, or (and this Gassendi would prefer to believe) one can imagine a sort of feeling in the stone in response to an impression carried to it by the emanation of species from the earth, the species themselves being very fine and subtle atoms such as the sentient faculties are made of. This hylopsychistic theory Gassendi develops at length and with obvious affection. It is the first of a whole series of explanations in which he gives preference to hylopsychistic over mechanistic theories, throughout the whole of his physics and biology. The similarity with Maignan is too obvious to need to be stressed. The principle of latent sensitivity diffused throughout the whole of nature and differing only in degree from our own, is essential to the teaching of both authors, and in this respect they carry on the traditions of the philosophers of the Italian renaissance, and especially Telesio, just as Bacon had done in England. Later in this same book (book V of Section I), Gassendi compares the earth with a living creature calling back to itself the parts that become detached from it, as though by a vague sense of self-preservation, and here again his acquaintance Campanella, who had brought with him into France the ideas of sixteenth-century Italy, would certainly have approved, had he lived to read the *Syntagma*, though he was at variance with Gassendi on most other questions and particularly that of the atoms themselves. Gassendi develops the theory tentatively and as a hypothesis, but there can be no doubt that he was attracted by it, and it is indeed an attractive notion, although science has resolutely turned its back upon it ever since the seventeenth century.

Qualities can be reduced to the arrangement of the parts of a thing. 'Form' is a useless word if it does not have the same meaning. All qualitative differences are differences of quantity or arrangement.

The secondary qualities, such as heat and cold or colours, are not in things nor in us: for secondary qualities to exist, species must pass from the thing into a sense organ and be perceived.

Motive force is the resultant of all the movements of the atoms in a body. The more active atoms drag along the more sluggish and force them into positions suitable to their own rapid movement. The more sluggish atoms become fixed in such positions and thus certain movements of the body become 'habitual'.

The generation or coming into being of things is not caused, as the Aristotelians say, by a 'form' coming into 'matter', nor, on the other hand, is the problem of generation a false problem, as Epicurus says. According to Epicurus there is no idea of the whole anterior to the idea of the parts and it is obvious that the whole will act in conformity with the arrangement and movement of the atoms which compose it. Gassendi rejects the idea that the whole is merely the sum of the parts, and is not impressed by Lucretius's examples of eyes without sight, genital organs in a sterile mule, rudimentary teats in the male or by the fact that one organ can perform the functions of another organ. He has no doubts about the evidence of design or purpose in the world. He is not put off by the existence of monstrosities and thinks they are greatly exaggerated anyway and are merely relative imperfections about which our limited intelligence has no right to judge. Design is for him perfectly apparent in everything and if some organs exist before their functions, they do not exist before the *idea* of their functions in the mind of the creator. His application of the idea of design leads in the direction of hylopsychism rather than of mechanism. Everything that exists develops from a kind of semen. Gassendi not only rejects the idea of plants and animals being produced by spontaneous generation from 'dead' matter, he suggests that God arranged the atoms at the beginning in the form of 'seeds' and that metals, plants and animals grow by means of atoms collecting round the original semen under the influence of formative principles which he compares with little prudent and industrious artisans. Or God may have placed the atoms originally in such a position that the 'seeds' would be formed by the atoms' own natural motion. None of this is dogmatically stated and Gassendi frankly admits his ignorance on the subject, but his hypothesis carries him the whole way towards universal animism.

The third section of the *Physica* begins with a long historical account of the doctrine of the *Anima Mundi*, which Gassendi finally rejects, except as a way of referring figuratively to God, or of referring to the heat of the sun, or of expressing the principle of unity of the whole world, and provided that no similarity is implied between such a Soul of the World and the souls of beasts and men. The use of the term in the last of these three senses Gassendi himself finds attractive, and he is prepared to say that the world has a soul *sui generis*, as one might say that minerals have a soul *sui generis*, suited, that is to say, to their peculiar operations. Next comes a review of the opinions expressed by the ancients for and against the eternity of the world, and in this dispute Gassendi sides first with the ancient Atomists against the ancient Academicians, preferring, that is to say, the theory of a world formed from eternal matter to the theory of an eternal world, but then he sides with the Church against the ancient Atomists and decides in favour of the creation of the world from nothing. His descriptions of minerals need not detain us, nor what he has to say about rain, thunder, the rainbow and other 'meteors', but then he returns to the need for a 'formative' or 'seminal' agent in stones, especially precious stones and the magnet, and the magnet becomes the subject of a discussion concerning a sort of sensation in metals, with references taking us back to Cardano and Pliny. Cardano wrote of iron's 'appetite' for the magnet, and Pliny of the magnet's 'sense' by which it perceives the iron and the 'hands' by which it draws the iron towards itself. Of the plants Gassendi uses the word 'soul' because their *functions* allow of its use. Their roots find food, their leaves turn to the light; creepers wind round sticks, the sensitive plant reacts to touch. There is a corporeal soul in plants, like a spirit or flame, very active and industrious and spread out throughout the plant. This spirit wilts if it is deprived of food; it is exhaled if it becomes too hot; it governs the growth of the plant. But again Gassendi proceeds warily and admits that we can only stammer (*balbutiendo solum et quatenus licet*) in dealing with these matters, and Bernier adds in his analysis[1] that Gassendi is far from having given a clear idea of the soul of plants, although he has penetrated deeper into the subject than any other natural philosopher.

Gassendi's section on animals begins with a classification followed by a discussion on the nature of the soul in animals. He gives first an account of the opinions of the ancient philosophers, then examines

---

[1] *Abrégé de la philosophie de M. Gassendi*, Lyons, 1678, v, p. 395.

the solutions worthy of consideration and finally gives his own opinion. The soul of animals is known by the understanding, in an abstract manner, from its functions. It must be a real principle and not just a proportion or symmetry of the parts of the body, for in such a proportion or symmetry there would be no source of activity. It must be a contexture of very fine and mobile particles like those of heat, moving in the cavities and passages of the body. Heat is its instrument and it is inseparable from heat; it is of an igneous nature. It comes into the body in the semen.

The following sections on the formation of the foetus, nutrition and the circulation of the blood show Gassendi abreast of contemporary theory, but he was not leading the way by any means and was prepared to believe stories of men with goats' heads and the like due to cross-breeding.

In discussing sensation he begins again from the magnet and the piece of iron. Iron perceives the magnet and a stone does not; a goat perceives a branch of an ash tree and a fox does not. It can be said that iron has a 'phantasm' or 'imagination' of the magnet as something which suits it, provided that too much meaning is not read into the terms 'phantasm' and 'imagination', but only such as is fitting to the operations of iron and the magnet.

Sensation is not merely passive: it is an 'immanent' not a 'transitive' motion and consists of the self-motion of the atoms. It does not consist merely in receiving the species emanating from an object but also in apprehending them and striving towards their source. The species press upon the sense organ and their pressure is transmitted to the brain, but the sensation is in the organ as well as in the brain, an opinion Gassendi affirms while being well aware of what is said of people who lose a limb and can still imagine pain in it. The sensitive part of the soul is composed of very fine particles and is divided into parts corresponding to the various senses, the atoms of each part being variously shaped and variously mobile so that they move through different passages in the body according to their shape and mobility. Lucretius teaches that insensitive atoms combine to form sensitive things, and points to the worms which appear in dunghills and the grass which is assimilated to the substance of the cow as experimental proof, and Gassendi here seems prepared to go all the way with him and find the source of sensation in a certain ordering of the atoms. But he attempts to make sensibility fade off into insensibility by minute stages and would like to see in the way the flames devour a piece of wood a sort of rudimentary feeling of hunger. Similarly, he argues, the roots of a plant must have something like taste and the rain must give a sort of pleasure to plants. The Sensitive Plant has a sort of touch and oysters and worms slightly more. But though one can distinguish these rudimentary forms of sensation as various degrees of the same power, yet the original problem of how insensible atoms begin to feel remains and is above human understanding. For that matter, it is equally difficult to explain how atoms, which are not hot, make hot things, and how atoms, which are not white, make white things. We must conclude that a body composed of atoms has properties which the individual atoms do not have.

When he comes to discuss the Internal Sense, Gassendi is willing to start from a scholastic distinction between the Imagination, attributed to both beast and man alike, and the Understanding, reserved for man alone, but he is careful to say that, apart from what religion teaches, very little is certain concerning this distinction. He refuses to follow the schoolmen when they divide up the Internal Sense into various faculties, such as those of judging, cogitating, remembering, and is content with a *sensus communis*, in the brain, to which all the sense organs are connected by the nerves. The differences between sensation and imagination are, firstly, that the object of sensation must be present, whereas the object of imagination may be absent, and, secondly, that sensation implies no comparison between impressions, whereas imagination does. These are not however essential differences. When the impression is made by an absent object, it is made by means of a trace left previously by the spirits on the soft substance of the brain. Sometimes these traces, or 'vestiges', become confused, so that one can imagine eyes in the middle of a man's shoulders, for instance, but no new factor is involved in such fantasies. The Internal Sense can put together two images and can perceive their suitability or unsuitability to each other. In the beasts this process is implicit; in man it is explicit, because man enjoys the power of reflection and the use of language. A beast's imagination contains no universal ideas, but merely a collection of particular apprehensions. A beast has no apprehension representing *all* men, but it has a collective apprehension representing *many* men and this collective apprehension representing many men, is distinct from one representing, say, many sticks. In a dog's imagination a particular apprehension representing a particular man can appear beside the collective apprehension representing many men and suffice for a *judgment*. A dog has no abstract ideas and no use of speech, so he cannot think or say, 'This man is my master', but he can put together the concrete apprehensions *man—master* and the verb *to be* seems to be potentially present. Brutes can therefore reason in a certain manner called 'sensitive reasoning', which is used by men also in certain cases, though man is also capable of intellectual reasoning. Brutes can make inferences: a dog runs away when he sees a man pick up a stone, a fox turns back when he hears water running under the ice; a swallow wets its wings in order to mould the clay of its nest; an ass suffers blows rather than be driven over a cliff. The brute is not only able to unite and separate simple apprehensions according to their suitability or unsuitability to each other; it can also link each one with a third or separate each one from a third, and this is argumentation.

The brute's Imagination can be said to exist from the moment it receives its first sense impressions. These first sense impressions are those of pleasure and pain, from which the brute proceeds by experience to the knowledge of the useful and the noxious. The brute also learns by example and from the teaching of its parents, as when the parent birds teach their young to fear and flee from men. And knowledge is also transmitted to them by the semen, as in the case of the silkworm which knows how to spin its cocoon without instruction.

In man the Intellect (or Understanding or Rational Soul) is incorporeal and is created by God. The Intellect differs from the Imagination in that man knows things by reasoning, such as the size of the sun, which it would be impossible to know by imagination. The Intellect differs too in that it knows itself and is conscious that it knows what it knows. It differs thirdly in that it has abstract ideas as its object; the Imagination can contain a collective apprehension such as *man*, but it cannot contain an abstract and universal idea such as *humanity*. And fourthly it differs in that it comprehends not only corporeal things (which it is able to do by virtue of being a superior faculty to the Imagination and so possessed of all the powers of the Imagination 'eminently') but also incorporeal things. It knows incorporeal things *positively*, only with the aid of corporeal images, it is true, but it knows them *negatively*, by reasoning as (being *in*corporeal) and *abstractedly*. At any rate it knows them sufficiently to be sure of their existence. The imagination represents something corporeal, the intellect *understands* something incorporeal. But the intellect, when associated with the body, proceeds only by stages, from experience. Separate from the body it comprehends immediately by intuition, but when it is associated with the body it cannot function without the brain; that is why illness destroys knowledge by obliterating the traces in the brain left by previous experience. The intellect agrees with the axioms as soon as it is acquainted with them, not because of any immediate connection between the intellect and the truth, but because the axioms are in accordance with any man's previous experience. It understands general ideas by means of the particular apprehensions of the Imagination. The best method of reasoning, in the search for new truths, is the 'analytical' method, which starts from experience and proceeds from effects to causes, although it may well be true that the 'synthetic' method, typified by the syllogisms of scholastic logic, provides a useful means of demonstrating truths already attained.

The Intellect is the same in all men by nature, but differences and inequalities arise from different temperaments and especially different temperaments of the brain. The temperament of the brain which is most favourable to the Intellect is one which is neither too hot nor too cold, neither too dry nor too humid, but on the hot, dry side rather than the cold, humid side, not too rare nor too dense, but on the rare rather than the dense side.

The Will or 'Reasonable Appetite', whose seat is the same as that of the Intellect and the Imagination, differs from the 'Sensitive Appetite', or Passion, as the Intellect differs from the Imagination. The Will uses the Passions as the Intellect uses the Imagination. Passion is an agitation of the soul caused by the anticipation of something advantageous or noxious, but the Will can love and pursue the good for its own sake.

Morals is the science, or rather the art, of living according to virtue and of turning other men's will towards the virtuous. Pleasure and pain are the sources of men's actions, even though at first sight this does not seem to be so, as when men sacrifice themselves for their children or for their country. Everybody's aim is supreme happiness, and though supreme happiness cannot be attained on earth, a relative felicity can be achieved. According to some (Anaxagoras, Pythagoras, Plato) it is to be found in knowledge, which frees us from passion. According to others (Zeno and the Stoics) it is to be achieved by virtue. According to Aristippus and the Cyrenaics it is to be found in the fleeting pleasures of the body, and Epicurus is often accused of holding the same opinion, but such an accusation comes from ignorance and prejudice. Epicurus begins from the fact that every living thing seeks pleasure and flees from pain. Pleasure can be pleasure of the body or pleasure of the mind and pleasure of the mind is superior to pleasure of the body. Tranquillity of mind and health of body are the highest pleasures each of its own kind, and the Epicurean term *voluptas* means only absence of agitation in the mind and absence of pain in the body. The way to it is through virtue.

For Gassendi this means firstly meditation upon the nature of God so as to become enamoured of his perfections and to seek to please him, and meditation upon death so that death becomes, not a source of fear, but an anticipation of greater happiness. Secondly it means the making full use of the present, because constant temporizing results in making of oneself the slave of the future. Thirdly it means the schooling of oneself in wisdom, which alone can give us the true discernment of what is good for us, in fortitude, which removes the fear of death and enables us to brave misfortune, in justice, without which quiet of mind is impossible. These precepts Gassendi draws from Epicurus, making only the changes necessary to adapt them to his Christian point of view. For instance, when he speaks of the nature of God, or rather the gods, Epicurus is concerned only with getting rid of a source of fear and disquiet of mind, whereas Gassendi discourses on the positive idea of God's perfections. But Gassendi claims Aristotle also as his ally and quotes the Aristotelian definition of virtue: the elective habit of choosing the happy mean determined by reason and prudence.

Gassendi's attitude is that of a teacher whose business it is to show his disciples how to live in society, and especially the aristocratic society of his time, in a post of command. The virtues he demands are fortitude (which includes firmness of mind and constancy), temperance (which includes modesty, chastity, long-sufferance, clemency and humility), and justice. Justice is based on Right, and Right is derived from social utility. Without society there is no law and no right. Right presupposes a contract, but is 'natural' in the sense that it is natural to seek the best way of safeguarding one's interest.

Without freedom of the will there is neither virtue nor vice. But free will does not mean unmotivated choice. As long as the understanding fails to discern the truth, the will hesitates, and similarly the will suspends its action while the understanding considers first one side and then the other of a question. Freedom of the will *is* this capacity to suspend its action. Once the evidence is clear, the will acts in accordance with it. It is not possible to know the good (the advantageous) and not pursue it, but one's knowledge of the good may be destroyed by drunkenness or passion. In that case, however, one's responsibility for one's actions is not removed, as one is at liberty not to get drunk and not to give way to passion. The complete determinism of Democritus has the advantage, as against the doctrine of free will, of emphasizing the order and connectedness of all the facts of nature, but this system cannot account for man's consciousness of his own liberty. Epicurus attempts to explain why he is free to move backwards and forwards at the bidding of his will by supposing that atoms sometimes follow a curved path instead of a straight one, but such a curved path would be just as much determined by fate as a straight one. And there Gassendi leaves the matter; he is content to accept the regularity of nature's operations on the one hand and the existence of free agents on the other. He was not faced, as Leibniz was to be faced, by the knowledge that no energy is ever lost and no energy is ever gained in any operation of nature and was not therefore obliged, as was his successor, to imagine two entirely separate explanations for each event that happens in the world, the one in terms of beginnings and the other in terms of ends, the one in terms of efficient causes and the other in terms of final causes, the one entirely mechanistic, and the other entirely teleological. Gassendi's world was still *one* world and for him the world has only *one* face and that face turned towards man. For him as for Maignan the material and the psychical are mingled intimately together except at the very bottom and the very top of the scale of creation.

VII

Lucretius and the Natural Philosophers

IN the scientific world Gassendi's authority gave backing to just
those features of Lucretian mechanism which were to be of the
greatest service to the natural philosophers, namely a constant and
confident recourse to experience and a bold application of the corpuscular theory of matter. His influence did not lead to the formation of a Gassendist school, nor to the publication of numerous
works purporting to expound his doctrines. One work only could
be looked upon as an exposition of Gassendism. It was François
Bernier's *Abrégé de la philosophie de Gassendi* (1674–8). Reference to
particular writings by Gassendi, as distinct from general references
to the man and his work, are almost non-existent in the publications
of the late seventeenth century. In England, Charleton published his
Physiologia Epicuro-Gassendo-Charletoniana in 1654.[1] and Boyle had
read the *Philosophiae Epicuri Syntagma*[2] by 1658, but Gassendi's
own countrymen were content to refer to him by name and admit
his authority. His authority was exercised over a wide field by means
of his personal contacts and his teaching at the Royal College, but
the number of rival philosophers who were prepared to admit
agreement with him was small. It is moreover difficult to distinguish
between the influence of Gassendi and that of Lucretius himself,
seeing that the *De rerum natura* was as readily available as ever. On
certain specific issues such as the transmission of impressions from
outside objects to the organs of sense, Gassendi does not follow
Lucretius, but as far as the two guiding principles are concerned
(experience, atomism), he agrees with his master. The *De rerum
natura* was very popular. Apart from Latin editions (at least nine
between 1600 and 1700), three complete French translations were
published in the second half of the century, and a wicked fate deprived the public of a fourth whole or partial translation by none
other than Molière himself. There was also the abbé Cotin's

---

[1] Walter Charleton, president of the College of Physicians, *Physiologia Epicuro-
Gassendo-Charletoniana or a Fabrick of Science Natural upon the Hypothesis of Atoms,*
London, 1654. Charleton also published *Epicurus, his morals,* London, 1656. Cf. C. F.
Mayo, *Epicurus in England,* 1650-1725, The South-west Press, Dallas, 1933.

[2] Published with the *Animadversiones in decimum librum Diogenis Laertii* in 1649.

Théoclée ou la vraie philosophie des principes du monde (1646), a polite refutation interspersed with snatches of translation in verse. Cotin's main line of argument was the traditional one, namely that the world is so perfect that it cannot have been produced by the fortuitous encounters of atoms of matter, but Cotin also claimed, without apparent justification, but also without any apparent fear of official disapproval, to have carried the atomic theory further in his *Théoclée* than it had ever been carried before. The abbé Marolles's prose translation (1650) was belaboured by Chapelain as being full of mistakes,[1] but the ideas of the original find a perfectly clear expression therein and the translator's notes, intended as a refutation of such propositions as were at variance with religion, were hardly of a calibre to dull Lucretius's lustre: a seventeenth-century reader could find an adequate account of Lucretius's natural philosophy in this work and also in the verse translation, somewhat flat-footed and plodding, but perfectly clear and intelligible, which he published in 1677. Marolles accepted a good deal of what Lucretius has to say on purely physical matters, going even as far as to accept his theory of vision, whereby material images are carried by particles through the air as though they were thin skins detached from the objects of sense. He counters on metaphysical topics by argument and by recourse to faith. He refuses eternity and incorruptibility to the atoms, because God alone is eternal and incorruptible; he refuses eternal motion to the atoms, because God is the prime-mover; he claims immortality for the human soul, because the human soul can be preserved by God's grace even though it be by nature mortal; the souls of brutes are indeed mortal, composed, as they are, of smooth, round particles, but we learn from religion, rather than from philosophy, that man's rational soul is of a different nature and endures. Marolles claimed, in the preface of his second edition (1659), that Gassendi had helped him in his task as a translator, and there is no reason for disputing his claim, although his constant recourse to religious authority can hardly have had his master's approval: submissive priest as he was, and inclined to fideism, Gassendi argued as a philosopher when he was writing for the public.

Jacques Parrain, baron des Coutures (d. 1701), made even more use of religious authority in the notes to his translation of the *De rerum natura* (1685). Fideism destroys itself when it is overworked.

---

[1] *Lettres*, ed. Ph. Tamizey de Larroque, Paris, 1883, t. ii, pp. 207–8 (to Huet, 18. ii. 1662) and 225 (to Bernier, 25. iv. 1662).

It was all very well at the beginning of the century, when scepticism and theology were allied against the new philosophy, but by 1685 times had changed and rationalistic arguments were readily available for retailing to the public. Parrain's main point, in his introduction, is that ignorance alone is responsible for fear and disquiet of mind; then, after approving Lucretius's physics, he limits himself to adding that a Christian's faith is sufficient defence against belief in the eternity of the world and the mortality of the soul. In his notes (p. 420), he explains with seeming approval the argument whereby sensation cannot be explained by recourse to sensitive principles and must be derived from insensitive principles. At the end of Parrain's discussion with Lucretius, one is left (apart from religious belief) with a material world and a God who is its artisan. There is no spiritual substance, no superstructure of intellectual beings rising above the material world, no universal Ideas, only atoms moving along paths preordained by an Intelligence. Parrain's interpretation of Lucretius is eighteenth-century deism and his translation had a long run of success in the eighteenth century.

As compared with the *De rerum natura*, whose literary merit recommended it to the reader, Gassendi's works were at a disadvantage on account of the austere form in which they were published. The work on Epicurus's life and writings which he had composed[1] was presented to the public in a mutilated form in 1647 and 1649. The *Life* is straightforward enough, but the account of the works is replaced by an erudite commentary on Diogenes Laertius's summary of Epicurean doctrine and occupies 1,768 pages of dense Latin text. To this are added two appendices, the one containing articles on physiological matters and the other, entitled *Philosophiae Epicuri Syntagma*, a short account of the doctrine, without development but supplied with cross-references to various parts of the commentary on Diogenes Laertius in which such propositions as are contrary to Christian doctrine are refuted. The whole work was unattractively presented and was not likely to hold the attention of any but erudites: it resembles, from that point of view, Mersenne's *Quaestiones celeberrimae in Genesim* (hundreds of pages of commentary on the first verses of Genesis), rather than the *Discours de la méthode*. The *Syntagma philosophicum* is more systematic. It was prepared by the editors of the posthumous collected works, published in 1658,[2]

---

[1] It is still extant in its original form (Library of Tours MSS nos. 707–10).

[2] The edition was prepared under Montmor's supervision and was prefaced by a life

according to instructions left by the author and is, to a large extent, a reconstruction of the original work on Epicurus, which Gassendi had dismembered in order to form the *Animadversiones in decimum librum Diogenis Laertii*.[1] Nevertheless it still composes two stout in-folio volumes printed in two columns and was published as volumes I and II of a six-volume edition of the *Opera*.[2] The difficulty of separating what was a new contribution to physics and physiology, based on new observation, from the historical and critical appraisal of Epicureanism, is in itself a satisfactory explanation of that lack of attention accorded to the work which Sorbière was to complain of ten years later.[3] How different was the technique of a Descartes or a Robert Boyle in drawing the public's attention to their work! Descartes in France, Boyle in England both presented a limited number of ideas in varied forms to the general public; Gassendi's boundless erudition was offered in all its manifold complexity. The two short works, the *Life* and the *Philosophiae Epicuri Syntagma*, were the only exceptions and these are the two works which seem to have been noticed.

François Bernier's *Abrégé de la philosophie de Gassendi* was the most assimilable form in which Gassendi's ideas reached the general public. This work was published between 1675 and 1677 and there was a second edition in 1684. There were eight volumes of it, but they were handy duodecimo volumes and were written in an easy, flowing style intended to please Mme de la Sablière and her cultured,

of Gassendi by a doctor named Samuel Sorbière (1610–70), a restless erudite and polygraph of wide intellectual interests but few settled convictions, who liked to rub shoulders with the philosophers; he had been a practitioner in Holland and had 'interviewed' Descartes; he had translated Hobbes; he was now the head of the College of Orange and had just abjured the Reformed religion for the Roman Catholic (1653).

[1] *Petri Gassendi animadversiones in decimum librum Diogenis Laertii, qui est de vita, moribus placitisque Epicuri. Continent autem placita quas ille treis statuit philosophiae parteis: I canonicam nempe, habitam dialecticae loco. II physicam ac imprimis nobilem illius partem meteorologicam. III ethicam cujus gratia excoluit caeteras.* 3 t. in 2 vols., Lyons, 1649.

[2] *Petri Gassendi Diniensis ecclesiae praepositi et in Academia Parisiensi mathemateos regii professoris opera omnia in sex tomos divisa.* . . . 6 vols., Lyons, 1658–75.

[3] 'Je me suis souvent étonné que la manière de philosopher de M. Gassendi, admirée de tout le monde, ne fît pas plus de bruit qu'elle n'en a produit. Je pense que cela vient de sa trop grande littérature, qui a mis de plus grands intervalles qu'il ne fallait entre ses raisonnements, ce qui a dissipé la force et caché la liaison, au lieu que les autres philosophes ont toujours suivi leur pointe.' 'Je tiens pour Galilée et Gassendi et j'estime qu'à la longue ils l'emporteront par dessus Hobbes et Descartes, encore que les bricoles de ceux-ci se fassent davantage admirer sur l'adresse des autres.' 'On s'étonnera peut-être un jour que, dix ans après la publication d'un tel ouvrage (the *Syntagma*), il s'est trouvé des gens qui ont embrassé une autre philosophie.' (*Sorbieriana*, Paris, 1694, pp. 104, 102.)

but not erudite, friends. Bernier was certainly well qualified to present Gassendi's philosophy to the public. He was a doctor of medicine, well-read and well-travelled, and had served Gassendi as a private secretary. He was born at Joué in Anjou in 1620[1] and had travelled in Italy, Germany and Poland before proceeding to Montpellier to take his doctor's degree in 1652. According to Nivard's *Eloge*, read before the Academy of Angers in 1689, Bernier met Gassendi before taking his degree at Montpellier. According to Brossette, he acted as a factotum to Gassendi and looked after Chapelle. Sorbière says he was 'élevé auprès de feu Monsieur Gassendi' and Chapelain uses the terms 'votre institution sous le macarite Gassendi'. Bernier himself informs us that he met Gassendi through the good offices of Chapelle.[2] Their first meeting must have taken place by the early 'forties at least, seeing that Bernier was already twenty years of age and Chapelle fourteen in 1640. We can safely believe that Bernier was for some years Gassendi's intimate and was favourably placed for understanding the intentions of his master. Nivard says he returned to Gassendi after taking his degree in 1652 and this statement may be true in spite of the fact that by that time Gassendi had another secretary named La Poterie, seeing that the year of Gassendi's death (1655) was a year of great change for Bernier; in the December of that year he left Europe and travelled by way of Egypt to India, where he stayed until 1668 at the court of Aureng Zebe. There were some doubts in the intellectual world as to whether he was a serious student. Chapelain was worried lest his style should prove too flippant; according to Brossette, he had a good repertoire of drinking songs; but Chapelain gave him credit for having undertaken the journey to India solely with the desire to study the countries he visited and he advised him to come back equipped as a specialist on that country just as the Jesuit Martini was on China.[3] There is moreover ample evidence in his letters to his many friends that he observed his surroundings with a lively curiosity and when he returned from India he was listened to with

---

[1] According to Grimarest (*Vie de Molière*, 1705) he studied at the Collège de Clermont, but Grimarest's evidence can never be accepted unsupported.

[2] Text of Nivard's *Eloge*, MS copy at Bibliothèque publique of Angers; collection Grille S.M. 129 (1780), published with one or two omissions by L. de Lens in *Revue historique et archéologique de l'Anjou*, t. ix, 1872, pp. 168 sqq. Refs. to Sorbière and Chapelain in R. Pintard, *Libertinage érudit*, p. 625.

[3] Brossette, *Commentaire sur Boileau*, ap. Lens, *Correspondants de F. Bernier*, Angers, 1872, p. 27 n. Chapelain, Letter to Bernier, 13 Nov. 1661, ibid., pp. 24–5.

respect in the salon of Mme de la Sablière. By that time he was no longer under the exclusive influence of his late master and was soon to proclaim, first that he was a sceptic on metaphysical matters and then that he was an enthusiastic admirer of Confucius.[1] In his *Abrégé* he did not hesitate to develop at length a few suggestions concerning the soul of the world, a theme he had found very prominent in Indian religions, and to insist on the distinction between the soul and the body far more than the original warranted, because he himself had come to reject the materialist conception of the soul: he was at the same time admonishing Chapelle on the insufficiency of materialism[2] and publishing an essay in defence of the freedom of the will. Bernier's final philosophy seems to have been eclectic and his moral opinions during the latter part of his life seem to have hesitated between Epicurus and Confucius. However, in spite of infidelities and corrections,[3] and a marked lightening of the tone, Bernier's *Abrégé* followed the *Syntagma philosophicum* more or less closely and was quite capable of giving the educated public an insight into Gassendi's philosophy. For the men of science it came rather late in the day and Gassendi's own theories, as distinct from his general support of corpuscular physics, did not lead to any active discussion in the pages of the *Journal des savants*. His name was a general guarantee for the legitimacy of the Epicurean philosophy of life. As far as Epicurean physics were concerned, their central theme, that of the atoms moving in empty space, was already launched on its independent career before the *Abrégé* appeared.

One or two French physicists of the seventeenth century seem to have adopted the atomic theory without encouragement from Gassendi.[4] The two chemists Bitaud and Claves in the theses forbid-

---

[1] Cf. below, p. 246.   [2] See below, p. 161.

[3] With regard to the indifference of matter to motion and rest; cf. B. Rochot, 'Gassendi le philosophe' in *Centre international de synthèse*: Pierre Gassendi *sa vie et son œuvre*, Paris, 1956, p. 90.

[4] The first known reference to atomism in the seventeenth century is in a work published in Paris by a Londoner, Nicholas Hill, in 1601. Hill's title (*Philosophia Epicurea, Democritiana, Theophrastica proposita simpliciter, non edocta*) is misleading; his book is a disorderly collection of scholastic propositions, but various detached sentences in it state the main atomistic theses clearly, and Hill was known to his contemporaries as an atomist, as the following lines from Ben Jonson's *Epigrams* (no. 134) witness:

> . . . those Atomi ridiculous,
> Whereof old Democrite and Hill Nicholis,
> One said, the other swore, the world consists.

(Cf. *Dictionary of National Biography*.)

den by the Parlement of Paris in 1624 made use of it; J. C. Magnen, a Frenchman who taught at Pavia published a book on Democritus in 1646;[1] a Capuchin monk named Casimir, known in the Languedoc for his zeal against the Protestants, fitted atomism into a scholastic treatise for schools[2] of the type which, according to the *Journal des savants* (30 March 1676), filled the new philosophers with horror. Like Emmanuel Maignan he was caught up in an effort to reconcile the corpuscular philosophy with the teaching of the schools. So was the abbé J.-B. Du Hamel, the first secretary of the Académie des Sciences.[3] Outside France, Daniel Sennert at Wittenberg in 1618, David van Goorle of Utrecht in 1620 and a doctor named Sebastian Basso, or Basson, whose book appeared at Geneva in 1621, all published accounts of ancient atomism,[4] but none of them attempted to develop it in the direction of a universal mechanism capable of rivalling that of Descartes. In England on the other hand, Robert Boyle[5] and Isaac Newton[6] pushed forward the 'corpuscular' philosophy in precisely that direction. In his *Origin of forms and qualities according to the corpuscular philosophy* (1666), Boyle described for the English public the methods by which the new philosophy dealt with concepts previously analysed in terms of 'form' and 'matter': the idea of 'form' was reduced to that of the structure of the parts. Boyle himself did not, it is true, make systematic use of the atomic theory; having a preference for chemistry, he was content to postulate the ultimate analysis of 'chemical' elements into atoms and was, meanwhile, content to operate with the 'elements' that chemical experiments supplied him with. But Newton, having replaced Descartes's conception of a continuous matter or solid space,

---

[1] See above, p. 89.

[2] *Atomi peripateticae sive tum veterum tum recentiorum atomistarum placita ad neotericae peripateticae scholae methodum redacta*, Paris, 1674. He believed the planets to be inhabited.

[3] In his *Philosophia vetus et nova* (1678).

[4] See C. Lasswitz, *Geschichte der Atomistik vom Mittelalter bis Newton*, Hamburg, 1890, 2 vols., i, pp. 436 sqq.

[5] Already in 1661 Boyle had made a clear declaration in favour of atomism (Preface to *Some Considerations touching the style of the Holy Scriptures*) and, from the terms he uses, one gathers that he had been a convinced atomist for some time and was known as one. We know that he had studied Gassendi's *Philosophiae Epicuri syntagma* in 1658 (L. C. Moore, *Robert Boyle*, Oxford, 1944, p. 235. This author dates Boyle's first acquaintance with Gassendi's work from 1645, p. 65).

[6] We have Voltaire's evidence that Newton had said to certain Frenchmen still alive in 1738 'qu'il regardait Gassendi comme un esprit très juste et très sage, et qu'il faisait gloire d'être entièrement de son avis dans les choses dont on vient de parler' (i.e. the ideas of God, Space and Time) (*Eléments de la Philosophie de Newton*, chap. ii).

cut up into fragments by motion, by that of atoms moving in a void, was as relentless as Descartes himself in the pursuit of the laws which governed the motion of the particles. Such a policy implied the abandonment of the qualitative differences which distinguished Lucretius's atoms from each other and which could be explained by the innumerable eternal shapes with which he endowed them.[1] In a rigorously mechanical universe, capable of being described in mathematical terms, such qualitative differences could only appear as an inexplicable residue. Gassendi's physics were not those of a geometer and mathematician. He was prepared to explain the change of form by which a log of wood turns into flame by referring only to the position and motion of the atoms which composed the log of wood, but he retained Lucretius's conception of many-shaped atoms. He also endowed the atoms, and particularly the very small atoms, with spontaneous motion, upsetting thereby the picture of a completely mechanical universe. The two English philosophers knew of Gassendi's work, but they used it merely as a starting point in an inquiry which carried them far beyond in the direction taken by modern science.

When we come to consider the influence of Gassendi on the general method of inquiry adopted by the natural philosophers, we find that many French inquirers were disposed towards a cautious, tentative approach to nature, very much in keeping with Gassendi's own attitude of mind, without there being any particular reason for ascribing their leanings towards experimentalism to a direct or indirect influence of Gassendi. Pascal described an inductive method (albeit a rudimentary one, seeing that he required the observation of all possible cases) in his sketch of a treatise on vacuum (1647). The Académie des Sciences (founded in 1666) was, in a general way, animated by Cartesian faith in the application of geometry to all problems, but some of its members, such as Mariotte and Perrault, were pronounced experimentalists and the first secretary, the abbé Du Hamel, introduced a long exposé of the inductive method, taken straight from Bacon, into his *De mente humana* (1672). Amongst the Cartesians themselves, Rohault adopted an empirical approach to physics and complained in his lectures that physics were usually treated in a 'metaphysical' manner. The records of the Academy are

[1] Voltaire understood the difference between Newton's physics and those of Gassendi and supported Gassendi. (*Elements*, ch. viii: 'Des premiers principes de la matière; il n'y a point de transmutations possibles.')

records of experiments like those of the Royal Society which it sought to emulate, with a special bent towards natural history.[1] When Colbert asked Huyghens's advice as to the programme of the Academy in 1666, Huyghens replied that the best plan was to put into operation that of Bacon and to study nature by means of observation and experiment.[2] The experimental method was far from being unknown or despised in France. Torricelli's famous experiment, by which the air can be shown to have weight and vacuum can be shown to exist, had been much discussed since Pascal had had it repeated and John Locke took part in similar experiments (though of a more amateurish kind) when he visited Paris in 1678.[3] The chemist Lémery, who taught in a basement in the rue Galande brushed aside as 'too metaphysical' not only the 'spirit of nature' favoured by his fellow chemists but also the atomic theory. He was prepared to admit that his own chemical elements could be resolved into atoms, but such atoms were not the concern of chemistry; the chemist could be satisfied with water, spirit, oil, salt and earth. It is doubtless true that experimental science in France lagged behind experimental science in England,[4] and that both the old scholastic

---

[1] There were two doctors (Perrault and Cureau de la Chambre), two anatomists (Pecquet and Gayant) and two chemists (Du Clos and Bourdelin) amongst the first members.

[2] 'La principale occupation de cette assemblée et la plus utile doit être, à mon avis, de travailler à l'histoire naturelle à peu près suivant le dessein de Verulamius. Cette histoire consiste en expériences et en remarques et est l'unique moyen de parvenir à la connaissance de tout ce qu'on voit dans la nature. Comme pour savoir ce c'est que la pesanteur, le chaud, le froid, l'attraction de l'aimant, la lumière, les couleurs, de quelles parties est composé l'air, l'eau, le feu et tous les autres corps, à quoi sert la respiration des animaux, de quelle façon naissent les métaux, les pierres et les herbes, de toutes lesquelles choses on ne sait encore rien ou très peu, n'y ayant pourtant rien au monde dont la connaissance serait tant à souhaiter et plus utile . . . Outre le profit qu'on peut tirer des expériences particulières pour divers usages, l'assemblage de toutes est toujours un fondement assuré pour bâtir une philosophie naturelle, dans laquelle il faut nécessairement procéder de la connaissance des effets à celle des causes.' (*Œuvres*, La Haye, 1888–1929, t. vi, pp. 95–6, quoted by P. Mouy.)

[3] 'Water sealed up in a glass tube out of which the air is drawn, being shaked, strikes against the end of the tube and gives a knock as if it were a solid body, but if it be let stand a while, the first time you shake it, it makes no more noise than that wherein the air is included. This I tried at Mr. Hubin's in the rue St. Martin over against the rue aux Ours, in glasses about 8 or 9 or so inches long, and about an inch diameter. The cause he assigned was the parts of the liquor turned into air and upon shaking returned into liquor again. Whether this will do in all liquors and in longer tubes (they were above half full) and in all weathers alike? This was a moderate day for this time of year.' (*Locke's Travels in France* . . ., ed. J. Lough, Cambridge, 1953, pp. 187–8.)

[4] Sufficiently at any rate for England to be looked upon as the home of experimental science. La Fontaine wrote in his *Renard anglais* in 1694:

prejudice and the new Cartesian excess of conviction exercised an inhibiting effect, but the fact remains that the notions of experience and experiment were accepted as fundamental concepts. That being so, it is not possible to see the influence of Gassendi wherever one finds them.

None the less, there are some works of physics and physiology in which Gassendi's authority is openly recognized. One of these is Gilles de Launay's *Essais physiques*, published in 1677 and sold, according to one of the title pages (p. 23) by Barbin, on the steps of the Sainte Chapelle and by the author at his house near the College des Quatre Nations (nowadays the Institut). According to Pierre Bayle, De Launay gave public lectures.[1] Locke packed up De Launay's *Logique*, his *Cosmographie*, his *Introduction à la philosophie* and his *Essais physiques* in his luggage before leaving Paris in 1678 and may even have lodged at his house.[2] De Launay says quite categorically that he intends to follow the sect of Epicurus along with Gassendi.[3] He insists on the use of the experimental method,[4] claims physics to be the highest of the sciences and, although he expressly states that he is a Christian and even holds out the olive branch to the Schoolmen (provided he is only expected to submit to Aristotle when Aristotle submits to reason)[5] he often writes in the

> Les Anglais pensent profondément;
> Leur esprit en cela suit leur tempérament;
> Creusant dans les sujets et forts d'expériences,
> Ils étendent partout l'empire des sciences.

[1] Letter of 22 June 1677 in *Œuvres*, La Haye, 1737, t. i, p. 49, cf. G. Reynier, *La Femme au dix-septième siècle*, Paris, 1933, p. 162. Le Maire also mentions De Launay's lectures in his *Paris ancien et nouveau*, 1684, t. iii, p. 444. Cf. Harcourt Brown, *Scientific Organisations in seventeenth century France*, 1620–80, Baltimore, 1934, p. 72.

[2] *Locke's Travels in France*, p. 150 n.

[3] 'Comme le célèbre et savant Gassendi, l'honneur de notre France et de notre siècle, a très doctement écrit de la philosophie et très fidèlement rapporté les opinions des anciens et des modernes, je ferai gloire de le suivre et de le défendre avec lui les opinions de Démocrite et d'Epicure qu'il a accommodées au christianisme. Je me réserve pourtant la liberté philosophique d'y retrancher ce qui me paraîtra moins considérable que ce que j'y pourrai substituer et enfin d'y ajouter quelquefois de nouvelles expériences et de nouvelles observations.' (*Essais physiques*, pp. 11–12.)

[4] 'La Nature est le livre des physiciens; il n'y peut rien apprendre s'il ne la regarde que par le dehors comme les philosophes de l'école; il faut qu'il l'ouvre, qu'il la pénètre, qu'il en repasse souvent les expériences par ses mains aussi bien que par son esprit, s'il en veut découvrir les secrets.' (*Essais physiques*, p. 2.)

[5] 'Mais l'opinion péripaticienne fleurirait encore bien davantage, s'il ne s'était trouvé dans les derniers siècles et de notre temps des philosophes modernes, savants et curieux, comme ont été Bacon, Galilée, Descartes, Gassendi et les chimistes, qui ont combattu ses principes, dont on semble à présent se détromper peu à peu. Ils consentiront facile-

manner which was to be characteristic of the deists of the eighteenth century. He argued, against Lucretius, that the number of atoms is finite: were it infinite, all space would be filled by atoms and there would be no void; so there is an immense, but finite, number of atoms, enough for an infinite Intelligence to be able to build the world with them. The Soul of the World is an acceptable notion, provided that God is not identified with Nature, provided, that is to say, that God is not defined as the *informing* soul of the world. The soul of the world may be identified with the universal heat which is in everything, or with the spirit which vivifies living things and which all the chemists believe in. But God is present as a governing agent throughout infinite space; he is present throughout eternity. Eternity should not be distinguished from successive time; God always was, is now and will be for all time. There is only one world, the existing world; there is no separate 'eternal' world.

De Launay's book contains just that blend of naturalism and deism which gives the distinctive flavour to 'Gassendism' towards the end of the seventeenth century. There is the same flavour in La Fontaine's *Fables* and in Chaulieu's poems. As compared with the authentic doctrine of the *Syntagma philosophicum* it contained a somewhat increased dose of naturalism due to the increased importance given to the spirit of nature, a non-Epicurean notion.

The doctor Antoine Menjot (*c*. 1615–96), who was Mme de la Sablière's uncle, also made an explicit declaration of faith in Gassendi as against Descartes. He saw Cartesians everywhere around him and ascribed the fact that Gassendi, who, by right, ought to be looked upon as the chief of philosophers, was only known to a few, to the laziness of his contemporaries. Gassendi's books were too ample for the slothful century in which he lived. People wanted to be learned without taking the trouble to study. They could not face up to Gassendi's works and yet, if the truth were known, it would be agreed that the foundations of Cartesianism itself really came from Gassendi's teaching. Had not Gassendi taught that the explanation of all natural phenomena is to be found in the figures and motions

ment qu'il soit le prince des philosophes, mais qu'il ne règne que dans l'Université et qu'il n'entreprenne pas d'asservir les esprits qui sont libres à ses opinions et à ses seules méthodes de philosopher. Ils le feront toujours passer pour un bon prince quand ils le verront aussi pacifique que son conseil de sophistes l'a rendu chicaneur par le passé. Pour moi, je vivrai bien avec lui quand il s'accordera avec le bon sens; je le reconnaîtrai pour souverain dans l'empire des lettres quand il règnera moins par l'autorité que par la force de la raison.' (*Essais physiques*, p. 6.)

of the particles of which things are composed?[1] Menjot made an equally explicit declaration of Pyrrhonism; he looked upon Epicureanism and Pyrrhonism as naturally suited to each other. He was officially of the Protestant faith, but his keenest desire was for toleration[2] and the union of the churches. He was banished to Limoges in 1685,[3] after the revocation of the Edict of Nantes, but he considered himself too old to uproot himself and accept the chair that was offered to him in the Netherlands.[4] He eventually abjured and became a Catholic.[5] He was cautious and sceptical. He was eclectic enough in medicine to quote Hippocrates and to mistrust the application of geometrical methods to medicine. He advised modesty in attempts to penetrate Nature's secrets. Nature was for him, as for Scaliger and Vanini, the ordinary operation of the power of God and there were many secret operations of that power which man could not hope ever to decipher.[6]

A 'docteur régent' of the faculty of Medicine of the University of Paris, Guillaume Lamy (1644–82),[7] made a very outspoken and courageous defence of Lucretian anti-finalism in 1674, and can be looked upon as a thoroughgoing Lucretian, independent of Gassendi. In a course of six lectures which he was invited to give, as an introduction to a series of anatomical dissections performed in public on the body of a woman, he developed several characteristically Lucretian themes. The story went round that, according to the lecturer, God made a mistake in man's constitution and that he ought to have horns, that there was no providence, and that God took three dice when he made the world and diced to see which perfections each creature ought to have.[8] Lamy at first merely con-

---

[1] *Opuscules posthumes de M. Menjot*, Amsterdam, 1697, pp. 115–17 (letter to Puerari). In a further letter to Puerari he added: 'Je ne m'amuserai pas ici à combattre sa matière subtile, laquelle il semble n'avoir forgée que pour opposer aux petits vides d'Epicure défendus par M. Gassendi, et de devenir par là chef de parti, au lieu de se contenter d'être disciple de ce grand homme, qui est une qualité dont plusieurs savants personnages de ce siècle se sentent honorés.' (ibid., p. 119.) Elsewhere he expressed approval of Huet's attack on Descartes and of Pascal's remark to the effect that Cartesianism was 'le roman de la philosophie' (letter to Huet, ibid., 139–46).

[2] Seé, e.g., his letter to the marquise de Saint-Aignan, ibid., pp. 174–5.

[3] Archives nationales OI 29, p. 564.

[4] 'Je suis une espèce de misanthrope évangélique et mon désir ne tend qu'à déloger, étant ennuyé du genre de vie que mènent les hommes du temps présent.' (*Opuscules posthumes*, p. 103.)

[5] *Mercure galant*, Jan. 1686. Cf. Jovy, *Antoine Menjot*, Paris 1920, p. 60.

[6] *Opuscules posthumes*, p. 163 (ref. to Scaliger).

[7] H. Busson, *La Religion des classiques*, p. 147.

[8] *Discours anatomiques*, Paris, 1675, p. 6.

cluded that he had been wrong in expecting an uninitiated audience to follow him properly, but when he discovered that men whose intelligence he respected believed what rumour said, he realized that his position was serious and decided to publish the text of his lectures.[1] Meanwhile, a colleague, the professor of anatomy, Cressé, had taken up the cudgels in defence of Galen and had made an onslaught on Epicurus at the Jardin du Roi where he held his chair. The dispute became a head-on clash between finalism and anti-finalism. Lamy attended the first of his critic's lectures but could not get near enough to hear properly because of the throng of idle sightseers, but he heard enough to be convinced that Cressé was refuting a completely garbled version of what he had said. His only hope of re-establishing the position lay in the publication of a correct account, but when he came to submit his manuscript to the Faculty, whose authority to publish was required, he found that one of the senior professors, Blondel, a former dean, was determined to thwart him. This was not the first time that he had felt the effect of Blondel's displeasure. As a student, at some time before he took his doctor's degree in 1672, it had fallen to his lot to provide the objections to a fellow-student's thesis at a public examination. The candidate having mentioned the supposed motion of the skies, Lamy had taken the opportunity to expound the Copernican hypothesis in reply, only to be ruled out of order by Blondel, who was presiding as dean, on the ground that, if he wished to demonstrate the Copernican theory, he had to do it medically. There was, perhaps, something to be said for this ruling in a debate on a medical thesis, but the fact that Blondel had already tried to exclude the Copernican doctrine on the ground that it was heretical cannot be explained away so charitably. Blondel was indeed a defender of the old against the new, with a reputation for erudition rather than for science. He did not want to see Lamy's lectures in print and stooped to ruse in order to prevent their publication. The Faculty committee appointed to examine the book was not prepared to prohibit it, and (according to Lamy) it was only by persuading one of its members not to attend the meeting of the committee that Blondel managed to delay the publication indefinitely. One member in particular, Nicolas Liénard, who became dean in 1680, supported Lamy. Liénard was a Cartesian and very outspoken in his contention that only in politics and religion should authority decide matters and innovations be forbidden; for

[1] ibid., p. 8.

the philosopher the only criterion was the evidence. In the end Lamy published his book without permission, with a prefatory note, supposedly written by a Cordelier, telling an obviously invented story about the finding of the manuscript in an inn. Blondel tried to persuade the Faculty to take action against Lamy, but the Faculty refused on the ground that the book had been published without the author's permission; it even imposed a fine on one member, named Denyau, for having insulted Lamy after a warning had gone forth against such conduct. On the whole the Faculty came fairly well out of the affair, considering the political and clerical menace which always hung over the deliberations of learned bodies.

The most striking and best feature of Lamy's book is the spirit in which it is written. In the strict sense, Lamy was not a good scientist, because he allowed systematic thinking to obscure the evidence on various questions of biology which were beginning to be debated on the basis of observed fact, such as the generation of viviparous animals from eggs produced in the female ovaries,[1] and, while the anatomical descriptions given in his lectures are clear and competent, it is obvious, even to a layman, that they were unoriginal. He was content to use Sylvius, Van Helmont, Harvey, Malpighi and was not prepared to decide between these various authorities when he found them at variance with each other. Iatro-mechanists and iatro-chemists were equally acceptable to him; only Galenists and Peripateticians in general were excluded, with their 'faculties' and 'principles'. He was as wrong as was Descartes, whom he followed on this point, concerning the supposed heat of the heart; he would have been well advised to use his microscope more and his books less. Nevertheless, the attitude of mind displayed by the commentary which accompanied the descriptions was one which physiologists were to adopt more and more openly as time went by. Lamy was strictly anti-finalist, refusing to be content with facile explanations of functions in terms of purpose. His method was analytical; he believed that if the structure of the seed could be examined and understood, the structure of the grown organism would be under-

[1] He rejects Graaf's theory in the *Discours anatomiques*, p. 179, and in his *Explication mécanique et physique des fonctions de l'âme sensitive ou des sens, des passions et des mouvements volontaires*, Paris, 1678 (second dissertation entitled: 'Dissertation contre la nouvelle opinion qui prétend que tous les animaux sont engendrés d'un œuf'). In the same work (first dissertation) he refused to admit that milk comes from the blood. In a pamphlet published in 1667 he refused to admit the possibility of transfusion of the blood.

stood also. He was a mechanist and a comparatist. At the beginning
of his first lecture, he stated bluntly that, far from attempting to win
his audience's approval in the usual way by stressing the differences
between man and the other animals, he intended to point out the
likenesses; he would doubtless be accused of impiety, but so much
the worse! Then comes a contrast between Galen, the finalist and
his theological counterpart Lactantius, on the one hand, and Epicurus and Lucretius on the other. Lamy makes no bones about
agreeing with Epicurus and Lucretius that 'the figure, situation and
number of the parts depend entirely on matter and its motions'. If
we could see the shape, size and motion of the atoms which compose
the semen, we should clearly understand the formation of the foetus
and the constitution of the body. The atoms of human semen must
necessarily form a man of some sort and not a being of a different
species, just as three dice rolled together must produce a number between three and eighteen. Variations are possible, but only between
fixed limits. The parts are formed by the necessary motions of
matter and are not formed for a particular end; we do not have eyes
in order to see, we see because we have eyes. Epicurus admitted no
intelligent cause in the universe and believed that, before the animals
we see were formed, there existed others less perfect, some without
eyes, others without a mouth or some other organ, which could not
survive because they were not fitted to survive. Such a view, added
the lecturer, is manifestly opposed to religion, while Galen's view
leads to manifestly false consequences; as for himself, he believed
that his business was to study 'efficient' causes and not to venture
into the labyrinth of teleology. For instance, why has man no wings?
Is not the need for wings real? How can Galen reply to such a
question? Is it not plain that man originally rose above the beasts by
learning to dress, to use arms and otherwise exercise his superior
intellect? God gave one organ to one species and another to another,
without any consideration as to how they were to be used: he had no
aim outside himself in the act of creation. Such a statement is the
equivalent, in the context of Lamy's lectures, to saying that God and
Nature are one. In Lamy's work one can find that admixture of
Lucretian materialism with suggestions of what was later to be called
pantheism and to be confused in the popular mind with the doctrine
of Spinoza. It is as characteristic of the 'Gassendist' mode of thought
late in the seventeenth century as it was to be of the 'Spinozist' or
'neo-Spinozist' (to use the term adopted by the *Encyclopédie*). Lamy

was not dogmatic on the subject. When it came to discussing the mind and its relation to the brain, he talked of religious faith. It is obvious that faith for him was no more than the acceptance of what one does not believe, but he was not prepared to be dogmatic as to what he did not believe. After a rapid summary of what the ancients taught concerning the soul and the rebuttal of Descartes's 'fashionable' views, he expounds a theory which unites the Epicurean fiery soul, made of rapidly moving atoms, with the Stoic conception of a material soul of the world, drawn from the speculations of the chemists. He continues:

The most likely opinion that we can have concerning the soul, which is the same in all animals and only diversified by differences of their organs and humours, is the one which I shall now relate to you. It is certain that there is in the world a very subtle spirit or very fine matter, always in motion and of which the greater part and, so to speak, the source, is in the sun and the rest distributed throughout all other bodies in greater or less quantity, according to their nature and consistency. It is assuredly the soul of the world, which governs and vivifies it and of which every part has a certain quantity. It is the purest fire of the universe and by itself does not burn, but by the different motions it gives to the particles which make up other bodies, it burns and causes the sensation of heat. Visible fire contains much of this spirit, the air less, water much less, earth very little. Amongst mixed substances, minerals have the least of it, plants more, animals much more. It is what makes their soul and, enclosed in their bodies, makes them capable of feeling. We call this substance 'animal spirits'. It is not enough for this substance to be present in a thing for that thing to be animate; there must be a certain quantity of it and the thing must be a specially organized body. As for man, apart from this soul, which disintegrates at death like that of the beasts, religion tells us that there is in him another soul, immaterial and immortal, proceeding directly from the Creator's hands and united to the body by means of the spirit just referred to. It is this second soul which is the principle of our reason and which contains within itself that inclination, natural to all men, to know the Divinity. But this second soul is known with certainty only by faith; it is the theologian's part to tell us what to believe concerning its nature.[1]

Lamy returned to the same subject in his replies to Cressé's accusation that he talked about the human soul as though he did not believe in its immortality. He made no bones about admitting that he did not believe in its immortality as a philosopher, but he added

[1] *Discours anatomiques*, pp. 228–30.

separated for long periods from her soldier husband, she remained faithful to him and regretted the convention which made a show of affection in her letters to him an exhibition of bad taste. Nevertheless, most of her poetry is love poetry and the love she refers to is not the intellectualized affection of the *précieuses*, it is the passion which seeks the satisfaction of the senses; she made of resistance to such a passion a theme for poetry of a pronounced voluptuous flavour and allowed herself, in exchanges of amorous epistles, flirtations of which the implications were not in doubt. It was a coquettish game, and its limitations were obvious. In order to give it wider scope, she resorted to writing madrigals in which her cat Grisette and the various cats belonging to her friends were the protagonists. One may smile, but a woman poet was at a disadvantage when handling the lyric poets' favourite theme. The tone moreover is light and some of her cats are not unworthy of comparison with La Fontaine's sleek and wily prowlers. These poems are ditties of the Paris roofs and an occasional homely or picturesque expression, reminiscent of Boileau's early satires, keeps the tone well down to the familiar level. Usually, however, Mme Deshoulières avoids imagery in her search for simplicity of expression. Molière writes in a similar style when his young lovers sing together: simplicity and fervour are aimed at, in contrast with the involved puns, witticisms and figures of speech which were the stock-in-trade of the *précieux* poets.

The theme of death occurs repeatedly in Mme Deshoulières's verses. Doomed to suffering, she could look upon death as a release from the world's ills, but the only immortality she could hope for was in the memory of her friends.[1] In the last ten years of her life,

> Quelle erreur a pu faire appeler les humains
> Le chef-d'œuvre accompli de ses savantes mains ?
> Que pour se détromper de ces fausses chimères,
>   Qui nous rendent si fiers, si vains,
> On vienne méditer dans ces lieux solitaires.
>   Avec étonnement j'y vois
>   Que le plus petit des reptiles
>   Cent fois plus habile que moi
> Trouve pour tous ses maux des remèdes utiles.
>   (*La Solitude, Œuvres*, 1753, t. ii, pp. 4–5.)

[1] Courez, ruisseaux, courez, fuyez-nous, reportez
Vos ondes dans le sein des mers dont vous sortez,
    Tandis que, pour remplir la dure destinée,
        Où nous sommes assujettis,

when she was dying of cancer, her catholic education reasserted itself, and she even went as far as to approve of the revocation of the Edict of Nantes; her last poems were on subjects of piety.

One of her admirers was Jean Dehénault (or Hesnault, 1611 ?–82), a *conseiller du roi*, who addressed her as Sappho in his verses. He had the reputation of being witty, erudite, 'debauched with art and delicacy' and of making no secret of his atheism.[1] His translation of the Invocation to Venus at the beginning of the *De rerum natura*, 126 lines, goes as far as 'Tantum relligio potuit suadere malorum', translated as 'Tant la religion put enfanter de maux.'[2] When he died in 1682, he destroyed the remainder of his translation on his

> Nous irons reporter la vie infortunée
>   Que le hasard nous a donnée
> Dans le sein du néant d'où nous sommes sortis.
>   (*Le Ruisseau*, ibid., t. i, pp. 150–1.)

> Que l'homme connaît peu la mort qu'il appréhende
>   Quand il dit qu'elle le surprend!
> Elle naît avec lui, sans cesse lui demande
> Un tribut dont en vain son orgueil se défend.
> Il commence à mourir longtemps avant qu'il meure;
> Il périt en détail, imperceptiblement.
> Le nom de Mort qu'on donne à notre dernière heure
>   N'en est que l'accomplissement.
>   (*Réflexions diverses*, 1686, ibid., t. i, p. 197.)

> Tandis que le soleil se lève encor pour nous,
>   Je conviens que rien n'est plus doux
>   Que de pouvoir sûrement croire
> Qu'après qu'un froid nuage aura couvert nos yeux,
>   Rien de lâche, rien d'odieux
>   Ne souillera notre mémoire;
>   Que, regrettés par nos amis,
>   Dans leur cœur nous vivrons encore . . .
>   N'être plus qu'un peu de poussière
> Blesse l'orgueil dont l'homme est plein
> Il a beau faire voir un visage serein,
> Et traiter de sang froid une telle matière,
> Tout dément ses dehors, tout sert à nous prouver
> Que par un nom célèbre il cherche à se sauver
>   D'une destruction entière.
>   (*Réflexions morales*, 1693, ibid., t. ii, pp. 66, 67.)

---

[1] 'C'était un homme d'esprit et d'érudition, aimant le plaisir avec raffinement et débauché avec art et délicatesse; mais il avait le plus grand travers dont un homme fût capable; il se piquait d'athéisme et faisait parade de son sentiment avec une fureur et une affectation abominables.' (*Furetieriana*.)

[2] Published posthumously in Moetjens' *Recueil de pièces curieuses*, 1694, 1714, t. ii. Text also in F. Lachèvre, *Les Œuvres de J. Dehénault*, Paris, 1922.

deathbed, at the order of his confessor, either because he sincerely
disavowed it, or in order to secure a peaceful end and a decent
burial, but he would have liked to possess the calm courage of the
philosophers in the face of death, and the lines from Seneca's
Troades in which he expressed this quintessence of ancient wisdom
had obviously been rethought and refelt in his translation.

> Tout meurt en nous quand nous mourons;
> La mort ne laisse rien, et n'est rien elle-même:
> Du peu de temps que nous durons
> Ce n'est que le moment extrême.
> Cesse de craindre ou d'espérer
> Cet avenir qui la doit suivre;
> Que la peur d'être éteint, que l'espoir de revivre
> Dans ce sombre avenir cessent de t'égarer.
> L'état dont la mort est suivie
> Est semblable à l'état qui précède la vie.
> Nous sommes dévorés du temps;
> La Nature au chaos sans cesse nous rappelle;
> Elle entretient à nos dépens
> Sa vicissitude éternelle.
> Comme elle nous a tout donné
> Elle aussi reprend tout notre être.
> Le malheur de mourir égale l'heur de naître,
> Et l'homme meurt entier, comme entier il est né.
> La mort, sans souffrir de partage,
> Confond l'âme et le corps et leur fait même outrage.
> Tout ce qu'on nous dit des enfers
> Et du tyran qui règne en ces royaumes sombres,
> Ces cachots, ces feux et ces fers
> Où sont les criminelles ombres,
> Ce monstre si prodigieux
> Et ce portier si redoutable
> Qui rend du noir palais l'entrée épouvantable
> Et qui fait fuir bien loin les mortels curieux,
> Tout cela n'est, ou qu'un mensonge,
> Ou qu'un discours en l'air, ou que l'horreur d'un songe.[1]

Another of Mme Deshoulières's admirers was François Payot,
chevalier de Linières or Lignières. He was the author of a number of
charming songs, epigrams and satirical pieces, some of which appeared in the *Recueil de Sercy*. Mme Deshoulières reproached him

---

[1] *Œuvres diverses*, Paris, 1670, pp. 109–11.

with following Epicurus too blindly, while Boileau, who disliked him, said cattishly that his couplets would be burned before he was.[1] His mistress, Mme de Montbel, was also a devotee of Lucretius.[2]

The abbé de Choisy (1644–1724) was converted in 1685 and became a missionary to Siam. But this son of the chancellor to Gaston of Orleans had lived a wild life in his youth and had worn women's clothes and called himself the duchesse de Barres. The little poem entitled *Les Philosophies*, written in praise of Epicurus, on the theme 'pleasure is the summum bonum', which he left amongst his papers, doubtless dates from the earlier period of his career.

> Vous qui cherchez le délectable
> Venez ici prendre leçon.
> Je donne tout à l'agréable,
> La joie est toujours de saison.
>
> Le plan de mon joyeux système
> Peut se concevoir aisément;
> Le plaisir est la loi suprême . . .
>
> Rendez-vous donc à mon système,
> Mais usez-en tout à loisir;
> Eloignez-vous de tout extrême;
> N'épuisez ni soif, ni désir;
> Le plaisir est le bien suprême,
> Mais l'excès n'est point un plaisir.
>
> Pardonne-moi, grand Epicure,
> Si j'ose commenter ta loi;
> Ne le prends pas pour une injure;
> Chacun travaille ici pour soi;
> Ton système est d'après nature;
> Elle m'a parlé, comme à toi.[3]

---

[1] Pour suivre aveuglément les conseils d'Epicure,
Pour croire quelquefois un peu trop la nature,
Pour vouloir se mêler de porter jugement
Sur tout ce que contient le Nouveau Testament,
On s'égare aisément du chemin de la grâce.
Tirsis y reviendra; ce n'est que par grimace
Qu'il dit qu'on ne peut pas aller contre le sort:
Il changera d'humeur à l'heure de la mort.

(*Portrait de M. de Lignières*, 1658, *Œuvres*, 1753, t. i, p. 8.) Boileau: *Epître VII* and *Poésies diverses*, XIII.

[2] Cf. G. Reynier, *La Femme au XVIIe siècle*, Paris, 1933, p. 168.

[3] J. Mélia, *Inédits et belles pages de l'abbé Choisy*, Paris, 1922, pp. 29–31.

The mercurial Anthony, earl of Hamilton (1646–1720), of Scottish origin, but brought up at the exiled court in France, and his equally witty brother-in-law, the comte de Gramont (1619–1707) were both masters of the epistle in verse and prose which a generation of talented poets used for their private correspondence. When Gramont was on what he thought was his deathbed, the king sent Dangeau to ask whether he had made his peace with his maker; Gramont turned to his wife, who was sitting beside the bed and said, 'Countess, if you are not careful, Dangeau will filch my conversion from you.'[1] Both Hamilton and Gramont were friends and admirers of Saint-Evremond. Gramont counselled the exiled sage to continue to follow the gentle inclinations of his nature, as his master Epicurus would have him do.

> Et là votre maître Epicure
> A certains morts des plus récents
> Demandait par quelle aventure,
> Avec tant d'esprit, tant de sens,
> Vous restiez parmi les vivants;
> Mais n'en déplaise à la figure
> Que font là-bas tous nos savants,
> Puisque c'est par la sépulture
> Qu'on passe à leurs paisibles champs,
> Suivez ici les doux penchants
> Où vous attache la nature,
> Et que dans la demeure obscure
> On vous attende encor longtemps.[2]

Hamilton, in one of his dialogues, drew a distinction between the higher and the lower pleasures in a manner worthy of the *arbiter elegantiarum* himself.[3]

Luillier's illegitimate son Claude-Emmanuel (1626–78), known as Chapelle because he was born at La Chapelle near Paris, was looked upon as the master of light verse. One of Hamilton's correspondents referred to him as the model of amiable simplicity and of charming naïveté.[4] The abbé de Chaulieu looked upon Chapelle as his

---

[1] 'Comtesse, si vous n'y prenez garde, Dangeau vous escamotera ma conversion.' Saint-Evremond to Gramont, in Saint-Evremond, *Œuvres*, 1708, v, p. 198.

[2] *Réponse du comte de Gramont à la lettre de M. de Saint-Evremond* in *Œuvres mêlées en prose et en vers par le C. Antoine Hamilton*, 1749, t. i, p. 228.

[3] *Œuvres diverses*, ed. of 1778, pp. 341–5.

[4] 'Dans le temps que je reçus la première de vos lettres . . . je jurais contre la réconciliation que vous m'avez obligée de faire avec celle des neuf sœurs qui

master.[1] Voltaire reproached him with carelessness and accused him of a predilection for redoubled rhymes found in Richelet's rhyming dictionary, but looked upon him nevertheless as a natural genius and a facile rhymer.[2] Such work of Chapelle as has been preserved to us, and it is very little,[3] is amiable enough, but not more than that; his principal medium of expression must have been conversation, and he seems to have been very popular.[4] That he fre-

> De l'aimable simplicité
> Nous donna le juste modèle,
> Inspirant jadis à Chapelle
> Sa charmante naïveté.

(*Lettre de Monsieur le duc de* [*Foix?*] *à Monsieur d'Hamilton* in *Œuvres mêlées* of Hamilton, t. i, p. 88.)

[1] Chapelle, à qui je dois les premiers éléments, ce maître qui me fait tant d'honneur et à qui je crains de faire si peu.' (Preface to Chaulieu's works.) Cf.:

> Chapelle . . . ce maître qui m'apprit,
> Au son harmonieux des rimes redoublées,
> L'art d'enchanter l'oreille et d'amuser l'esprit
> Par la diversité de cent nobles idées,
> Chapelle, par hasard rencontré dans Anet,
> S'en vint infecter ma jeunesse
> De ce poison fatal qui coule de Permesse
> Et cache le mal qu'il nous fait
> En plongeant l'amour-propre en une douce ivresse.
> Cet esprit délicat, comme moi libertin,
> Entre le tabac et le vin,
> M'apprit, sans rabot et sans lime,
> L'art d'attraper facilement,
> Sans être esclave de la rime,
> Ce tour aisé, cet enjouement
> Qui peut seul faire le sublime.
> (*Epître au chevalier de Bouillon*.)

[2] 'Là se trouvait Chapelle, ce génie plus débauché encore que délicat, plus naturel que poli, facile dans ses vers, incorrect dans son style, libre dans ses idées. Il parlait toujours au dieu du Goût dans les mêmes rimes. On dit que le dieu lui répondit un jour:

> Réglez mieux votre passion
> Pour ces syllabes enfilées
> Qui chez Richelet étalées
> Quelquefois sans invention,
> Disent avec profusion
> Des riens en rimes redoublées.
> (*Le Temple du goût*.)

[3] An account in prose and verse of a journey through the southern provinces, in collaboration with a lawyer friend F. de Coigneux de Bachaumont, and some two dozen epistles and epigrams.

[4] His epistles are addressed to Condé, Vendôme, Effiat, Lonzac, Saint-Aignan, Chaulieu, Dassoucy, Ninon de Lenclos, Nantouillet, Sercelles, Lude, Jussac, the duchesse de Bouillon, while Blot is referred to as a friend in the *Voyage*. Bernier writes: 'Jamais la nature ne fit une imagination plus vive, un esprit plus pénétrant, plus fin,

quented the taverns is not in doubt,[1] but there is no evidence of his having been a thorough debauchee. Perhaps he was indolent, at any rate he did not realize the great project he was reputed to have undertaken, no less than a major philosophical work on the lines of the *De rerum natura*.[2] He seems to have pushed further in the direction of Lucretian materialism than the teaching of Gassendi warranted. At any rate, Bernier, who was just back from India, where he had studied Eastern religions, thought it necessary to lecture him on the subject and remind him that 'though we do not know what we are, we ought yet to affirm boldly that there is something in us not composed of mud and filth'.[3]

Charles-Auguste de la Fare (1644–1711), son of the marquis de Montclar, saw service against the Turks and the Dutch, and showed himself to be a brave man on more than one occasion, but he was of

---

plus délicat, plus enjoué, plus agréable.' (*Journal des savants*, 7 vi 1688.) It is Bernier who tells us that Molière and Chapelle were great friends: 'L'illustre Molière ne pouvait vivre sans son Chapelle' (ibid). Cf. Chapelain to Bernier, 25 iv 1662: 'le comédien Molière, ami de Chapelle.' Saint-Aignan writes: 'O Chapelle, que j'estime Et que j'aime tendrement.' (*Réponse impromptue* in Chapelle, *Œuvres*, 1826, p. 157) and François de Caillères:

> Esprit aisé, naturel, libertin,
> Et possédé d'une douce manie,
> Chapelle fit admirer son génie,
> Sans imiter auteur grec ni latin,
> Comme l'on voit d'une source féconde
> Couler sans art les eaux d'un clair ruisseau,
> Tels les beaux vers coulaient de son cerveau,
> Et s'en allaient errer parmi le monde,
> Y répandant un plaisir tout nouveau.
> (*De la Science du monde*, Brussels, 1717, p. 236.)

> [1] Ce fut à la Croix de Lorraine,
> Lieu propre à se rompre le cou,
> Tant la montée en est vilaine,
> Surtout quand, entre chien et loup,
> On en sort chantant *Mirdondaine* . . .
> Or là nous étions bien neuvaine
> De gens valant tous peu ou prou. . . .

(*Lettre à M. le marquis de Jonzac, Poésies diverses*, 1826, pp. 146–50.) The abbé Boussac, the abbé Le Vayer, Molière and Desbarreaux were amongst the nine (ibid.).

[2] Bernier to Chapelle, 10 vi 1668.

[3] 'Néanmoins, nous devons prendre une plus haute idée de nous-mêmes et ne pas faire notre âme de si basse étoffe que ces grands philosophes, trop corporels en ce point; nous devons croire pour certain que nous sommes infiniment plus nobles et plus parfaits qu'ils ne veulent, et soutenir hardiment que, bien que nous ne puissions savoir de vrai ce que nous sommes, du moins savons-nous bien ce que nous ne sommes pas, que nous ne sommes pas entièrement de la boue et de la fange, comme ils prétendent.' (Bernier to Chapelle, 10 vi 1668.)

an independent spirit and was refused advancement by Louvois. On that account he sold his commission in 1677. He had all the easy charm of manner which distinguished the French at the time as compared with the rougher and hardier men of the north.[1] He charmed the virtuous Mme de la Sablière, who sacrificed her reputation to him. He was indulgent, and self-indulgent, and towards the end of his life took immoderately to drink.[2] His verses have a nonchalant grace about them. They are in honour of love and pleasure and make no claim to serious doctrine, but La Fare had some interesting remarks to make to the effect that the study of one's fellow-men and the experience of social life are the only way to happiness.[3] Like Saint-Evremond, he seems to have held the belief that a purely social ethic was possible, as distinct from a rational or religious one. There is a hint of the same attempt at a positive sociology that Voltaire makes in his *Traité de métaphysique*. He is prepared to defend the passions as being essentially good and maintains that on the whole they do less damage than the reason. He thought of reducing men's actions to the expression of their temperaments and, realizing this was not possible, regretted the fact, putting forward the strange reason that, if everybody followed his own natural bent in a perfectly sincere manner, it would be easy to distinguish the good from the vicious.

Jean de la Fontaine (1621–95) lived for twenty years, from 1673 to 1693, in the house of Mme de la Sablière, because he found life easy there. He was of a malleable, impressionable temperament, a contemplative and receptive spirit and his imagination was filled with fields, running brooks, ponds, angular herons, flapping rooks, long-backed weasels. Like Mme Deshoulières he had a liking for solitary contemplation.[4] He was ready to find voluptuous pleasure in all things, even in gentle melancholy.[5] He could write stories full

---

[1] 'Mes manières, mon humeur et mon esprit, qui était doux, faisaient un tout qui plut assez au monde.' (*Mémoires et réflexions*, Rotterdam, 1716, p. 41.)

[2] The chevalier de Bouillon, in a letter to Chaulieu (1711), describes one of his drinking bouts and says he is a lost man. (Chaulieu, *Œuvres*, 1774, t. i, pp. 107–8.)

[3] *Mémoires et réflexions*, pp. 10 sqq.

[4] The hermits of his stories and fables live in very pleasant places, under oak-trees.

[5] He wrote in his *Amours de Psyché et de Cupidon* (1669):

> J'aime le jeu, l'amour, les livres, la musique,
> La ville, la campagne, enfin tout: il n'est rien
> Qui ne me soit souverain bien,
> Jusqu'aux sombres plaisirs d'un cœur mélancolique.

of sensual charm. His morality was consciously Epicurean,[1] though at times some homespun good sense straight from the French countryside puts a sharp edge on the sensitive poetry of the *Fables*. It is easy to understand why he preferred Gassendi to Descartes. He could not have written his fables had he not been able to credit the beasts with a certain amount of psychical activity: it is unthinkable that a mere machine should be taken as the symbol of a man. So a neat little Gassendist philosophy falls perfectly into place in the poet's life and work. La Fontaine went to church at least once; he went with Racine to matins in Easter week, but the way Louis Racine tells the story in his memoirs makes it very evident that the indolent poet's appearance was something out of the ordinary. He made his peace with the Church in 1693, but there is no reason to doubt that the *Discours à Mme de la Sablière* (Fables, bk. ix) contained all he needed by way of a reasoned metaphysics and religion. It contains just a suggestion of ancient animism or of the new pantheism, enough to light up some of the most poetic of the *Fables*, such as *Le Chêne et le Roseau*, with the mysterious glow of 'something far more deeply interfused'.

With the exception of the abbé de Choisy, who had gone off to the Far East as a missionary, all the Epicurean poets were acquainted with each other or had friends in common; their epistles and other correspondence link them all together. Many of them met in the taverns and at various private houses, that of Mme de la Sablière until she retired into a convent in 1680, at the abbé de Chaulieu's house in the Temple from that time onwards.

Mme de la Sablière (b. 1640) was married to a financier at fourteen, separated from her wayward husband at twenty-eight and lived in the rue neuve des Petits Champs where from 1669 until 1680 her house was open to a great number of friends. Boileau called her a bluestocking, but she seems, all the same, to have been a success as a hostess. She was well-educated, it is true; according to Corbinelli she knew Greek; she had mathematics lessons from Roberval and Sauveur. But she was good-looking and gracious. She continued to preside over her salon until the break-up of her love-affair with La Fare; she then retired to live quietly at the Feuillants' convent in the rue St Honoré and at the Incurables, where she died of cancer in 1693.

---

[1] He proclaimed himself to be a 'disciple of Epicurus' in a scientific poem on the virtues of the new febrifuge quinquina bark (1682).

At the time that Mme de la Sablière went into retirement the abbé de Chaulieu (1636 or 39–1720) became, by the grace of the younger of the two Vendôme brothers, grandsons of Henri IV and Gabrielle d'Estrées, the lessee of a house in the Temple, of which the younger Vendôme, as Grand Prior of the Order of Hospitalers had the giving. This house was to be, for some thirty years to come, a meeting place for Chaulieu's friends, who were mostly poets living on the favours of the great, and 'grands seigneurs' who liked the company of poets; it was to be the centre of the literary world. Chaulieu's guests included, at various times, La Fare, Chapelle, Lulli, La Fontaine, Malézieux, the abbés de Châteauneuf, Courtin, Servien, the duc de Foix,[1] the chevalier de Bouillon,[2] the two Vendôme brothers, Ninon, the duchesse de Bouillon, J.-B. Rousseau, Voltaire, and a good-natured financier named Sonning, who tried his hand at verse like the others. At Chaulieu's house the atmosphere of free and intimate confidence was so well established that it was quite in order to contradict the duc de Vendôme to his face. La Fontaine describes a party at which the wine flowed freely and there was singing until dawn, ending with the affirmation that he

---

[1] Chaulieu called him an amiable disciple of Epicurus:

> Amis, buvons à la Nature
> Dont nous suivons les douces lois;
> Disciple aimable d'Epicure,
>   Duc de Foix,
> Bois, Anacréon de nos jours,
>   A tes amours.

(*Couplets de chanson faits à un souper chez M. Sonning, sur un air des fragments de Lulli*, *Œuvres*, La Haye, 1777, t. I, p. 132.)

[2] Chaulieu wrote of him:

> Elève que j'ai fait en la loi d'Epicure,
>   Disciple qui suit pas à pas
>   D'une doctrine saine et pure
>   Et les leçons et les appas,
> Philosophe formé des mains de la Nature,
> Qui sans rien emprunter de tes réflexions,
>   Prend pour guide les passions,
>   Et les satisfait sans mesure,
>   Qui ne fit jamais de projets
>   Que pour l'instant présent . . .
>   Heureux libertin qui ne fait
>   Jamais rien qu'il ne désire,
>   Et désire tout ce qu'il fait . . .

(*Epître au chevalier de Bouillon*, ibid., t. II, p. 21.)

himself contradicted both the Vendômes.[1] The parties were not debauches, except, perhaps, as far as the exchange of ideas was concerned. The fact that the Vendômes were spendthrifts and that Saint-Simon describes them as degenerates, and the fact that La Fare was a drunkard in his later years, are not grounds for believing that Chaulieu and his guests drank themselves under the table or turned his house into a brothel. The one meal Chaulieu himself describes is a somewhat frugal one, consisting of mutton and an omelette:

> Quand verrai-je ma pauvreté,
> Honorable et voluptueuse,
> Te donner avec liberté
> Un souper où la propreté
> Fait, loin d'une foule ennuyeuse,
> Une chère délicteuse,
> De beaucoup de frugalité?
> Là, le nombre et l'éclat de cent verres bien nets
> Répare par les yeux la disette des mets,
> Et la mousse pétillante
> D'un vin délicat et frais,
> D'une fortune brillante
> Cache à mon souvenir les fragiles attraits.
>
> Quelle injure à l'abondance
> Lorsqu'avec volupté ton appétit glouton
> Borne son intempérance
> A l'épaule du mouton,
> Et qu'avec des cris de joie
> On voit toujours sur le tard
> Venir l'omelette au lard
> Qu'au secours de ta faim le Ciel propice envoie.
>
> Alors l'imagination,
> Par ce nouveau mets aiguisée,
> De mainte nouvelle pensée
> Orne la conversation.

[1] Malgré tout son beau langage
Qu'on était ravi d'écouter,
Nul ne s'abstint de contester;
Je dois tout respect aux Vendômes,
Mais j'irais en d'autres royaumes,
S'il leur fallait en ce moment
Céder un ciron seulement.
          (Œuvres, Grands Ecrivains, ix, p. 451.)

A des maximes de sagesse
On mêle de joyeux propos,
Et l'on jette sur quelques mots
Ce sel que produisait la Grèce
Qui nous fait la terreur des sots.[1]

Chaulieu was the Grand Prior's intendant, which meant that he was
nominally in control of the extravagant spending the younger
Vendôme indulged in, particularly at the Château d'Anet, where he
entertained lavishly, but the abbé was relieved of this responsibility
by the king in 1699 on account of the pressing need to put some sort
of order into the Vendômes' finances, so that from that time forward
he was free to follow his bent for an indolent life. The peace of mind
he enjoyed was that of carefree irresponsibility rather than the
tranquil conscience of the just man; he looked however to philosophy
to complete that peace of mind by ridding him of the one source of
disquiet ever likely to trouble him, namely the fear of death.
Epicurus supplied him with the answer: death brings nothing good
or bad and is nothing in itself; it is merely the end of life's feast:

Plus j'approche du terme et moins je le redoute;
Sur des principes sûrs mon esprit affermi,
Content, persuadé, ne connaît plus de doute,
Je ne suis libertin ni dévot à demi.[2]

Qu'importe que la vieillesse
Vers moi s'avance à grands pas,
Quand Epicure et Lucrèce
M'ont appris que la sagesse
Veut qu'au sortir d'un repas,
Ou des bras de sa maîtresse,
Content l'on aille là-bas?
Pour moi qui crois telles choses
Conformes à la raison,
Sur les pas d'Anacréon,
Je veux couronné de roses
Rendre visite à Pluton.[3]

---

[1] *A La Fare*, La Haye, 1777, pp. 77–8.   [2] *A La Fare*, 1708, ibid., t. I, p. 15.
[3] *Epître au chevalier de Bouillon*, 1704, ibid., t. II, p. 8. Cf.:

Aux pensers de la mort accoutume ton âme;
Hors son nom seulement, elle n'a rien d'affreux.
Détaches-en l'horreur d'un séjour ténébreux,
De démons, d'enfer et de flamme,
Qu'aura-t-elle de douloureux?

He had no doubts as to the mortality of the human soul, nor, apparently, as to its materiality. To Malézieux, who argued, in an epistle which seems to be the echo of a conversation, that no arrangement of subtle atoms could explain the existence of Chaulieu's verses, the abbé merely replied that he would have to consult Epicurus and Lucretius on the subject.[1] He constantly rejected 'superstition' and 'prejudice' and, although he was prepared to worship a God who was master of all things, and laughed at 'the errors of a foolish sect which thought that chance could be the author of the World',[2] he did not distinguish very clearly between such a God and the Nature whose 'gentle laws' he sought at all times to follow and which he imagined as a spirit breathing in the wind and animating all things, a source of fruitfulness and beauty:

> C'est lui qui, se cachant sous cent noms différents,
> S'insinuant partout, anime la Nature,
> Et dont la bonté sans mesure

> La mort est simplement le terme de la vie;
> De peines ni de biens elle n'est point suivie:
> C'est un asile sûr, c'est la fin de nos maux,
> C'est le commencement d'un éternel repos.

(*A madame la duchesse de Bouillon*, 1700, ibid., t. I, p. 20.)

Malézieux to Chaulieu:

> Le plus subtil mouvement,
> La matière la plus pure,
> La plus parfaite figure,
> Le plus bel arrangement,
> Bref, un être périssable
> Ne peut avoir fait tes vers;
> Il faut une âme semblable
> A celle de l'univers.

Chaulieu to Malézieux:

> Pour répondre à tes chansons,
> Il faudrait de la Nature,
> De Lucrèce ou d'Epicure
> Emprunter quelques raisons,
> Mais sur l'essence divine
> Je hais leur témérité
> Et je n'aime leur doctrine
> Que touchant la volupté.

(Ibid., t. I, pp. 272, 274.)

[2] Puis de là, tout à coup, élevant ma pensée
Vers cet Etre du monde et maître et créateur,
Je me ris des erreurs d'une secte insensée
Qui croit que le hasard en peut être l'auteur.

(*La retraite*, ibid., t. I, p. 28.)

Fait un cercle de biens de la course des ans;
       Lui de qui la féconde haleine,
Sous le nom de Zéphyrs, rappelle le printemps
Ressuscite les fleurs et dans nos bois ramène
Le ramage et l'amour de cent oiseaux divers
Qui de chantres nouveaux repeuplent l'univers.[1]

This naturalism was literary rather than scientific; he professed not to have decided whether Copernicus was right or not,[2] and, although such a statement, made in 1700, was doubtless the expression of an assumed poetic attitude, it does mean that he professed not to be interested in the contemporary scientific movement. If the young François-Marie Arouet, who was admitted to Chaulieu's house while still at the Collège Louis le Grand, heard the abbé, who was sixty-seven or seventy years of age at that time, discoursing on the *De rerum natura*, he doubtless heard a more sympathetic commentary than ever his teacher of rhetoric, the Jesuit Father Porée, made in class, but it was in all probability confined to the ethics of Epicurus. The two currents of Epicurean thought, the scientific and the moral, had moved apart from each other and were progressing independently. It remained for Voltaire himself to bring them together again.

[1] *Epître A La Fare*, 1708, ibid., t. I, p. 16. Cf.:

Immense, tout-puissant, équitable, éternel,
Maître de tout, a-t-il besoin de mon autel?
                              (ibid.)

[2] Je contemple à loisir cet amas de lumière
Ce brillant tourbillon, ce globe radieux,
Et cherche s'il parcourt en effet sa carrière,
Ou si sans se mouvoir il éclaire les cieux.
                    (*La retraite*, 1698, ibid., t. I, p. 28.)

Part Two

Descartes and the Rationalists

IX

Nature without Consciousness

DESCARTES succeeded in persuading a large part of the French intelligentsia that consciousness is the special privilege of human minds and that the only connection between human minds and the vast machine of whirling and unconscious matter was a little organ in the brain which he took for a gland and referred to as the 'pineal gland'. Strange as it may seem at first sight, this notion had every chance of pleasing those who were interested only in natural philosophy, because it removed from the scope of their inquiry the embarrassing question of the soul, a most embarrassing question indeed in a land where the faculties of theology had a firm grip on intellectual life. Under the Cartesian dispensation, the soul could be abandoned to the moralists, but as a counterpart to this policy of disinterestedness, nature, including man's corporeal being and the bodily passions, became the apanage of the natural philosopher. It is understandable also that it should have met with success in the small, highly-organized fashionable society which had just constituted itself in Paris and was becoming more and more isolated from a countryside falling gradually into decay. Did it not give undisputed pre-eminence to man's intellectual and moral activities? But whatever links one may seek to establish between this most striking product of French intellectual life in the seventeenth century and other manifestations of that intellectual life, the fact remains that it was startling in its newness and much further removed from traditional ways of thought than the most daring speculations of a Vanini, a Campanella or a Gassendi.

Descartes did not remove consciousness from nature (man apart) by teaching, along with Epicurus, that the world is made of insensible atoms moving in the void. From insensible atoms, Epicurus composed a nature full of consciousness. Descartes removed consciousness from nature by demonstrating the value of the method used by the mathematicians when it is applied to the intellectual and practical problems with which men are faced. A method by which useful distinctions may be made clearly and the resultant separate elements expressed succinctly, so that they may be considered in isolation or reviewed rapidly, appeared quite rightly to Descartes to be a method of inestimable value, and the men who used such a method, namely the mathematicians and, in particular, the geometers, whom he had been taught to look upon as mere technicians, began to appear to him, when he came to see their work in a new light, as better equipped to be philosophers than the teachers of the schools who were philologists and dialecticians. Small wonder was it that in his enthusiasm he should not have stopped to think that the geometer isolates the objects of his study, points, lines, surfaces, volumes, from consciousness at the outset, as the known object is separated from the knowing subject. The practical problems of his generation, the problems of navigation, gunnery, engineering, medicine, were being tackled around him in busy Holland by men who preferred to weigh, measure, dissect, rather than carry on the verbal disputes in which the long days of their lives at school had been spent. Maurice of Nassau, general, statesman, mathematician, was such a man, to look no further. Descartes had a practical bent and was not hampered by scholastic habits as were his possible rivals. A man like Mersenne, well-acquainted though he was with current speculation in mathematics and mechanics, was quite incapable of using the concepts supplied by Galileo for a thorough overhaul of the old philosophy; he got no further than an easy-going eclecticism; the good-natured friar's mind was very tolerant of conflicting theories. Maignan was too respectful of his scholastic adversaries. Thomas Hobbes of Malmesbury imprisoned himself in a sterilizing logic. Gassendi was hampered by his erudition. Pascal's anxious mind turned from physics to religion. Descartes had the necessary enthusiasm, the necessary self-assurance, the necessary scorn for school learning to enable him to develop his idea forcefully and impose its authority far beyond the realm of mathematics.

Descartes left the Jesuit college of La Flèche in Anjou in 1615, at the age of nineteen, with no other philosophical baggage than what the Schoolmen had burdened him with and a rudimentary knowledge of mathematics, hydraulics and fortification, which the Jesuit pedagogues, mindful of their pupils' future careers, added to the academic curriculum with a view to imparting to it a practical bias. It was a bias which suited Descartes. He saw in mathematics a contact with reality which he found in no other branch of study and hydraulics was to provide the basic mental images he applied to physics. The conviction that a properly conducted mathematical argument truly expresses the concatenation of things was to remain with him throughout his life.

There seems to be no reason for doubting that the notion of applying the methods of geometry to fields of inquiry beyond the limits of that discipline was conceived by Descartes as early as 1619, when he was serving with the army of the elector of Bavaria, as a volunteer, at Neuburg on the Danube. He had joined the Dutch army on leaving school and then that of the elector, doubtless as an engineer officer. He was full of enthusiasm for mathematics, and his zeal had been quickened during his sojourn in Holland by personal contact with a mathematician eight years his senior, Isaac Beeckmann, who was later to become the head of the college of Dordrecht. He was also aware of the existence of a secret society of the learned, the Rosicrucians, who believed in the possibility of a universal science. He may well have put together the two notions of a geometrical method and a universal science in his mind. The title of an imaginary book of mathematics, a burlesque apparently, which he copied out in one of his notebooks in January 1619, while still in Holland, seems to suggest it.[1] But whether he formulated at the same time the famous rules of method as given in the *Discours de la méthode* of 1637 is open to doubt. According to the *Discours*, he did, on one and the same occasion, in the solitude of a little room heated by a stove, at Neuburg on the Danube, in the autumn of the year in which the emperor was crowned (1619), formulate four rules of method and three rules of conduct, after which he left his retreat and went on his journeys with the intention of studying his fellow men.

Modern criticism has cast doubts on the complete accuracy of Descartes's account. As early as 1868 Janet suggested that it had been somewhat arranged and systematized, especially with regard to the philosophic intention of Descartes's journeys.[2] Since that time an intermittent debate has been kept up, especially active in the twenties of this century, Espinas and Cantecor developing Janet's thesis,

[1] *Polibii cosmopolitani thesaurus mathematicus, in quo traduntur vera media ad omnes hujus scientiae difficultates resolvendas, demonstraturque circa illas ab humano ingenio nihil ultra posse praestari: ad quorumdam, qui nova miracula in scientiis omnibus exhibere pollicentur vel cunctationem provocandam et temeritatem explodendam; tum ad multorum cruciabiles labores sublevandos, qui, in quibusdam hujus scientiae nodis Gordiis noctes diesque irretiti, oleum ingenii inutiliter absumunt: totius orbis eruditis et specialiter celeberrimis in G. (Germania) F.R.C. (fratribus rosiae crucis) denuo oblatus. (Œuvres, ed. C. Adam and P. Tannery, x, 1908, p. 214.)*

[2] *Revue des Deux Mondes*, 15 Jan. 1868.

Gilson, Gouhier and Sirven attempting to limit the effect of Espinas's and Cantecor's criticism.[1] As Gouhier points out, the *Discours* is the most important piece of evidence we have, and Descartes's account must be accepted in the last resort except where internal contradictions or independent documentary evidence can be shown to invalidate it. But it is none the less inevitable that one should have doubts about the simplicity and purity of the mental processes by which Descartes claims to have reached his conclusions. Did he experience no hesitations, make no false starts, follow no false leads? Furthermore there is documentary evidence to suggest that the notion of a new method did not at first penetrate all his thinking. Such parts of his scrap books for 1619 as have been preserved, in copies made by his biographer Baillet and by Leibniz,[2] show that he classified his notes under the titles *Parnassus* (or *De Considerationibus mathematicis*), *Olympica*, *Democritica* and *Experimenta*. The notes in the section entitled *Parnassus* are chiefly mathematical. It is not known what the few lines of notes headed *Democritica* were, apart from one personal anecdote related by Baillet, or the ten pages of *Experimenta*, though the titles allow of some speculation. As for the *Olympica*, they were notes on matters which their author regarded as spiritual or supernatural,[3] and in particular three dreams, together with suggested interpretations, which, whatever else they may or may not show, certainly do not present the young Descartes as a thorough-going rationalist. A questing reason was however already at work in him; he considered it necessary to explain away the statement in Genesis that God separated the light from the darkness by interpreting the light as good angels and the dark as bad angels.[4] It is also certain that his approach to physics was

---

[1] Espinas, 'Le Point de départ de Descartes' (*Revue bleue*, 10 March 1906); id., *Descartes et la morale*, Paris, 1925, i, pp. 121–2; Gilson, 'Descartes en Hollande' (*Revue de métaphysique et de morale*, July–September, 1921, pp. 551–2); id., 'Recherches sur la formation du système cartésien' (*Revue d'histoire de la philosophie*, iii, 1929, pp. 113–64); Cantecor, 'La Vocation de Descartes' (*Revue philosophique*, vol. 96, 1923, pp. 373–400); Sirven, *Les Années d'apprentissage de Descartes*, Albi, 1928; Gouhier, 'Sur la Date de la Recherche de la vérité de Descartes' (*Revue d'histoire de la philosophie*, 1929, pp. 296–320).

[2] Baillet, *Vie de Descartes*, 1691, i, p. 51; Leibniz's copy was taken in 1676 in Paris; it was published in 1859 by Foucher de Careil. Text in the Adam and Tannery edition of Descartes's works, vol. x (1908).

[3] 'Sensibilia apta concipiendis Olympicis: ventus spiritum significat, motus cum tempore vitam, lumen cognitionem, calor amorem.' (*Œuvres*, ed. Adam and Tannery, x, p. 218.)

[4] 'Deum separasse lucem a tenebris, Genesi, est separasse bonos angelos a malis, quia non potest separari privatio ab habitu. Intelligentia pura est Deus.' (ibid.) In the same

already through mathematics.[1] He may well have glimpsed the philosophical vista which lay before the position he had taken up as a mathematician. Some of his jottings in his scrapbook for 1619–20 have a distinct intellectualist and Platonic flavour, particularly a sentence in which he talks of truth being in us as fire is in stones; the philosopher draws it out by reason and the poet by imagination, or the sentence: 'Una est in rebus activa vis, amor, charitas, harmonia.'[2] When, in 1626, in Paris, in the entourage of Cardinal Bérulle, he came into contact with the Oratorians, great readers of the Platonizing church fathers, he was predisposed to feel, if not their influence, at least the warmth of their approbation. He was ready to lend his intelligence in the campaign against 'libertinage', though wary enough of the theologians of the Sorbonne to prefer to live in the peace and calm of the university town of Franeker in Holland rather than within the jurisdiction of the University and Parlement of Paris. Between October 1626 and July 1629 he drafted a short metaphysical treatise in which conceptual knowledge was placed far above opinions derived from the experience of the senses, and is guaranteed by the existence of a God of truth from whom it flows into the human intelligence created in the very image of God. Having drafted this treatise, he wrote to Mersenne, informing him that the truths of metaphysics were as firmly established as the truths of geometry.

One might say that Descartes's metaphysics were implicit in the method he had worked out the year before. In the incomplete essay entitled *Regulae ad directionem ingenii*, which, by common consent of scholars, was written in 1628,[3] the intellectualist character of this method is strongly marked. In the mind, if we know how to distinguish them, can be found simple ideas, which correspond to the simple essences of nature. The reduction of the complexes of nature to simple essences is identical with the reduction of complex notions

place: 'Tria mirabilia fecit Dominus: res ex nihilo, liberum arbitrium et Hominem Deum', which indicates that his own reason found these three concepts impenetrable.

[1] 'Hic Picto cum multis Jesuitis aliisque studiosis virisque doctis versatus est. Dicit tamen se nunquam hominem reperisse praeter me, qui hoc modo, quo ego gaudeo, studendi utatur, accurateque cum Mathematica Physicam jungat. Neque etiam ego, praeter illum, nemini locutus sum hujusmodo studii.' (Beeckmann's diary, in Descartes, *Œuvres*, ed. Adam and Tannery, x, p. 52.) Cf. G. Cohen, *Les Ecrivains français en Holland*, 1920, pp. 371 sqq.

[2] *Œuvres*, ed. Adam and Tannery, x, p. 217–18.

[3] H. Gouhier, preface to his edition of the *Regulae*, Paris, 1930; A. Espinas, *Descartes et la morale*, Paris, 1925, p. 45; Adam and Tannery, x, pp. 486–8.

to simple ones. The simple idea of extension, which is the object of contemplation in the mind, contains within itself the world which is 'formally' extended outside the mind. In the metaphysical treatise written in the following year, the idea of an all-perfect Being, clearly contemplated in the mind, is also held to prove the existence of such a Being outside the mind. No original text of this treatise has survived, but there is no reason for doubting that it was in substance the work which was summarized in the *Discours de la méthode* of 1637 and finally appeared as the *Meditationes de prima philosophia* in 1641. It is a sketch of a theory of knowledge, and if a good deal of attention is given to proving the existence of God, and if the distinction between the mind and the body is insisted upon, the part these themes play is incidental to establishing that conceptual knowledge, as exemplified in geometry, is certain knowledge, whereas experimental information, while not being necessarily untrustworthy, is not wholly trustworthy either.

Descartes's physics, which he began to sketch out also in 1629, was that of a geometer, like his method and metaphysics. If the simple idea of extension, the object of geometry, contains the reality of the outside world, a complete description of that world can be given in geometrical terms, to the exclusion of such psychological terms as 'hotness', which are not the concern of the geometer. With a clear realization of his position, he began his treatise of physics with an attack on explanations couched in the language of the senses. In discreet terms, but with no lack of determination, he excluded all the 'forms' used by the teachers in the schools, reducing them to the level of 'opinion' or 'prejudice'. A distinction between appearance and reality had nothing in itself to affright the professors, but for them the knowledge of essences was the prerogative of the divine comprehension, whilst man's mind could only infer from the evidence of the senses what realities lay above and beyond the world of sense. Physics belonged to the domain of experience. Descartes claimed physics for metaphysics in the guise of geometry, and drove out the evidence of the senses into the non-philosophical sphere where it might well be useful for man's self-preservation and well-being, but could not enable him to lift even a corner of the veil surrounding truth. For this he offered compensation by allowing reality itself to be contained in the simple idea of extension and thus to be contemplated directly by the mind.

The problem he set out to solve in geometrical terms was that of light, to which his attention had been drawn by the phenomenon of the parhelion, seen at Rome on 20 March 1629 and which had greatly intrigued the learned world. But in order to apply geometry to this problem, he had not only to get rid of explanations couched in the language of the senses, he had also to outline a complete cosmogony. This he proceeded to do, with the result that his theory of light was not expounded until the last part of the treatise. At the beginning of the work he accepted the traditional view of the world's structure, reserving until later to reorganize it to his liking. At first he placed pure fire in the upper regions and even a *primum mobile* surrounding all. Below it he placed the heavier air and, still lower, water and earth which he did not distinguish the one from the other as separate elements. And throughout the heavier elements moved the lighter, so that air and fire moved restlessly through the water and earth, and fire through air, water and earth. His elements were distinguished by size and motion, the particles of fire being smaller and more mobile, the particles of earth larger and less mobile. The smaller particles filled the spaces between the larger, so that what some philosophers took for void was filled with moving particles. Space was full, matter was full space. Void was nothingness and nothingness could not be being, nothingness could not be the object of knowledge. From an indefinite extent of solid space, split up into fragments by motion derived from the prime mover, a world such as ours would evolve.

There was indeed a difficulty here. If space was full, how could motion be possible at all? Descartes was aware of this Lucretian objection and found a reply to it. His argument suggested, it is true, an opposition between God and matter which the reader had not been led to expect,[1] but it had the advantage of suiting very well the system of whirlpools of particles, to be called 'rings of matter', or 'skies', or 'vortices', which he proposed to describe. In principle, or in the intention of God, all motions are rectilinear and bodies continue to move in straight lines until they are prevented from doing so by other bodies, but in a full universe all motions must

[1] 'Il faut dire que Dieu seul est l'auteur de tous les mouvements qui sont au monde, en tant qu'ils sont, et en tant qu'ils sont droits; mais que ce sont les diverses dispositions de la matière qui les rendent irréguliers et courbés. Ainsi que les théologiens nous apprennent que Dieu est l'auteur de toutes nos actions en tant qu'elles sont et en tant qu'elles ont quelque bonté, mais que ce sont les diverses dispositions de nos volontés qui les peuvent rendre vicieuses.' (*Le Monde*, from *Œuvres*, ed. Adam and Tannery, xi, pp. 46–7, spelling modernized.)

combine together to form circular motions, as no particle can move
unless another simultaneously gives way before it and so on in
continuous circuits. Matter, from the mere fact that it is cut up into
parts, must move in circuits.

The effervescence of moving particles sorts itself out into a system
of vortices, through which wander the comets which no vortex has
claimed. Within each vortex, the whirling particles rub together and
wear each other down to three main sizes, which Descartes identifies
as the three elements, fire, air and water cum earth. In the old cosmology the elements were sorted out by weight, the heavier being
in the centre, whilst fire was situated in the highest regions, but
Descartes knew that the sun was in the centre of our vortex, so he
found himself obliged to reason out why the lightest and smallest
particles were in the centre. He managed to describe an intricate
series of pushings and jostlings of particles in order to achieve this
and at length reached the problem he set out to solve, namely that of
the nature of light and its transmission. He had now only to refer to
his diagrams to explain light as a motion, or rather as a pressure
transmitted from particle to particle until it reaches the eye and
presses upon it. The source of the pressure is the sun and the great
stars forming the centres of other vortices. The light of the stars
will be refracted as it enters our vortex, so that it is unlikely that we
see the stars in the places where they really are.

As it stood, without any metaphysical introduction and containing
as it did, in the place of such an introduction, an attack on scholastic
'forms', this treatise of physics might well have been condemned had
Descartes published it in the early thirties. The intellectual movement centred on Galileo was not without its adherents in Paris, and
both Mersenne and Gassendi are to be counted amongst them. Even
at La Flèche, Galileo's name had been in honour during Descartes's
schooldays. But Descartes's work contained an attack on scholastic
methods. At any rate, the condemnation of Galileo in Rome in 1633
decided Descartes against the publication of the work. He published
nothing until 1637, when his *Discours de la méthode pour bien
conduire sa raison et chercher la vérité dans les sciences* appeared, containing his intellectual autobiography and a summary of the work
he had written but had not published. There was no attack on
'forms' in it, merely a statement to the effect that he had imagined
matter without the forms and qualities of the schools. In a short
treatise of optics, written in 1635 and published in 1637, there was

again no mention of 'forms', but merely a rejection of 'intentional species', which were described in the Lucretian manner as 'little images flitting through the air' and a remark to the effect that there is nothing in the objects of the outside world resembling the images we have of them. In the *Météores* (1637) he stated at the end of his first chapter that he did not 'reject' the forms, but merely did not need them in his descriptions. He advised his disciple Regius of Utrecht to say the same thing in 1642.[1] In his later publications he contented himself with a general warning against the evidence of the senses.

The second part of the treatise of physics which Descartes began in 1629 but did not publish[2] was devoted to physiology and psychophysiology. He would have liked, he said later, in the *Discours de la méthode*, to proceed from causes to effects in his physiological demonstrations; that is to say from first principles to their applications, but his physiological knowledge was insufficient for this. It was in fact rudimentary. Harvey's *De motu cordis* (1628) had only just appeared, so it was excusable that he should have persisted in many old errors. He accepted the fact of the circulation of the blood, but he imagined a spontaneous combustion in the heart, something like the heat engendered in wet hay, heating up and vaporizing the blood and sending very rapidly moving particles of it to the brain, where they 'serve to nourish and maintain its substance and principally also to produce a certain very lively and pure flame which is called the animal spirits'. These animal spirits are distributed into the cavities of the brain and it is they which are sent into the nerves and muscles and move the limbs by causing the muscles to swell. The whole process is compared by Descartes with the hydraulic machines in the royal gardens, where people who walked on the grass trod on hidden levers, causing fountains to play. When pressure coming from an outside object affects a sense organ, a thread running along inside the nerve is pulled and a pore in the brain is opened and gives passage to the spirits, which flow into the nerve and then into the

[1] Letter of February 1642.

[2] The work was published at Paris in 1664, in two parts, *Le Monde de M. Descartes ou le Traité de la lumière et des autres principaux objets des sens* and *L'Homme de René Descartes et un Traité de la formation du fœtus du même auteur.*

It was thoroughly out of date by that time. In the editor Clerselier's manuscript the first part ended at chapter xv and the second began at chapter xviii. From the summary given in the fifth part of the *Discours de la méthode* one can conclude that the intervening chapters were devoted to mountains, rivers, metals, plants, fire and some curious effects of fire, such as the making of glass.

muscles and move a part of the body. The condition and motion of the spirits will explain the various moods we find ourselves in, or rather would explain those of a machine which we can imagine in the likeness of a man:

The spirits may be more or less abundant, and their parts more or less large or more or less agitated, more or less equal to each other, at one time than another and it is by these four differences that the divers humours or natural inclinations (at least in so far as they are not dependent on the constitution of the brain or the affections of the soul) are represented in this machine, for if the spirits are more abundant than is their wont, they are suitable for producing motions similar to those which show goodness, or liberality or love in us, and similar to those which show confidence or boldness in us if their parts are stronger and larger, and firmness if they are more equal in shape, in strength and size, and promptitude and diligence and desire if they are more agitated, and tranquillity of mind if they are more equal in their agitation. As, on the contrary, these same spirits are suitable for exciting movements like those which show malignity, humility, vacillation, dilatoriness or anxiety if these same qualities are lacking.

After a meal, the juice of meat is mixed with the blood, so the spirits are sluggish. Dry air taken in by respiration makes them more active than damp air. If the liver is not working properly, the spirits will be unevenly agitated; a change in the blood means a change in the spirits. In the cavities of the brain, the spirits which issue from the pineal gland[1] either enter the pores opened for them by the threads of the nerves, or, if they miss, ricochet backwards and forwards until they enter other pores. In doing so, they provoke divers disturbances such as sneezing or dizziness. When the spirits are plentiful enough to keep the cavities full, the man is awake, but if the pressure drops he falls asleep. When the pressure of light from an outside object affects the eye, the shape of the object is reproduced on the surface of the brain cavities by the opening of various pores, and this shape is also reproduced on the pineal gland by the points from which spirits flow from the gland towards the open pores. In this way the rational soul, which has its seat in the pineal gland, is conscious of all that affects the body from outside. Moreover, the pores do not close at once; they tend to stay open, the more so if they have been opened violently, so that they retain the effect of having been opened, which is why a man remembers things. Furthermore, as the re-

---

[1] An oval-shaped body towards the front of the brain.

opening of certain pores will reopen others which were opened at the same time, one memory will evoke another associated memory. The pineal gland, being very flexible, is easily moved, either by the soul or by the spirits themselves. The movement of the gland affects the flow of spirits into the pores and so influences the movements of the limbs. Thus the soul can direct the movements of the body by moving the pineal gland. There are two kinds of bodily motion, the first being external and suited for the pursuit of desirable things and the avoidance of undesirable things, the second being internal and suitable for disposing the animal spirits towards the first type of movement. Anger is such an internal motion; it agitates the spirits and produces energetic bodily action. Anger is a purely bodily passion. But if the disturbed state of the spirits does not correspond to some desirable object to be attained or some undesirable object to be avoided, the spirits flow hither and thither and produce hesitation in the mind. Hesitation being a state of the judgment, belongs to the mind. Apart from the interference of the rational soul by way of the pineal gland, all the motions of the body follow from

the mere disposition of the organs, neither more or less than do the motions of a clock or other machine from the movements of the weights and wheels, so there is no need in respect of them to conceive of any vegetative or sensitive soul, nor any other principle of motion or life except the blood and the spirits agitated by the heat of the fire which burns continually in the heart and which is not by nature different from the fires which are to be found in inanimate bodies.

Descartes published nothing until 1637, when he was forty-one years of age. He then published the *Discours de la méthode*, together with two scientific essays (the *Dioptrique* and the *Météores*) and a treatise of analytical geometry. The *Discours* was not written as a philosophical treatise; it was written as an intellectual autobiography and strongly reminiscent of Montaigne's essays, being addressed to the ordinary reader and not to the learned. The first part, after a preliminary discussion of the notion of method itself, tells the story of Descartes's schooling at La Flèche and is mainly critical of the teaching there. It ends on a note of uncertainty and scepticism. The second part asserts the necessity of having a philosophy of one's own and tells of the invention of the method in 1619. The third is a little moral essay in which the author proposes a certain number of provisional principles to guide his conduct during his independent inquiries; it has a pronounced Stoic flavour. The fourth and fifth summarize rapidly the unpublished treatises of metaphysics and physics, while the sixth takes up the question of method again and is an essay on the theme of indefinite progress in the sciences. The plan is easy to follow and one can understand the work's having been accepted as a coherent whole. There are however some inconsistencies in it. The scepticism à la Montaigne of the first part conflicts with the Stoicism of the third, and the sixth part goes over much of the ground already covered. The first of these inconsistencies may be explained by the autobiographical development; they are successive phases in Descartes's life. It has been suggested that the sixth part was originally intended as a preface to the *Geometry*[1] and this solution is a plausible one.

When the sketch of his mechanistic physiology appeared in 1637 it occasioned some doubts as to the materialistic consequences which could be drawn from it, as a letter from Froidmont dated 13 September 1637 witnesses. By substituting for the sensitive soul a mere fermentation in the heart, one is reduced, wrote Froidmont, to explaining sensation, which is something noble, by a fermentation which is something gross. 'If one suppresses the vegetative and sensitive soul in the brutes, one opens the door to the atheists, who will attribute the operations of the rational soul to a cause of the same kind and will give us a material soul to replace our spiritual soul. Descartes, who had made it abundantly clear in the *Discours* that he did look upon a brute beast as a machine, was content to reply that the beasts feel as we feel when we do not think about our sensations and resorted to the scriptures to show that no distinction need be made between the rational soul and the sensitive or vegetative souls. The *Philosophical Meditations* when they at length appeared in 1641 made his position abundantly clear as far as materialism was concerned and in the controversy which followed with Gassendi he appeared as the champion of spiritualism.

The first Meditation is given up to banishing for the sake of argument all the beliefs he has ever had, including the belief that he has a body and sense organs. The second advances the argument that even on the foregoing assumption, he cannot but believe himself to be something or other as long as he is thinking, that is to say doubting, conceiving, affirming, denying, desiring, rejecting, imagining and having sensations. He is indeed better known to himself as a

[1] See Gadoffre's edition of the *Discours*, Manchester, 1941 (preface).

thinking being than the outside world is known to him through the senses. In the third Meditation, he puts aside all such impressions of the outside world and considers only the operation of thinking and finds that it is impossible to reject as doubtful those conceptions of the type $2 + 3 = 5$ which he conceives clearly and distinctly. Only the possibility of his being constantly the victim of a deceitful God prevents him from declaring them to be certainly true, a far-fetched objection doubtless, but one which has to be met. There follows a somewhat involved proof of the existence of God as a being in whom there is no falsehood. He has the idea of an all-perfect being or a being containing all reality. His own mind cannot be the cause of it, because there is more 'objective' reality in it than there is 'formal' reality in his limited understanding. The cause of it is therefore outside himself and contains as much 'formal' reality as there is 'objective' reality in the idea.[1] He finds next (fourth Meditation) within himself 'a certain negative idea of nothingness' at the opposite extreme from God and places himself in between as a being composed of reality and nothingness. In so far as his being is derived from God, there is no source of error in it; the error that is in him is a lack and an absence, not a perfection. Error arises from the use of his will, which is the action of affirming or denying the truth of the ideas which he conceives; the will affirms or denies in cases where the understanding (which is limited) does not present clear ideas by which such an affirmation or denial may be made with certainty. Such is the source of error; it can be avoided if judgments are based on clear ideas only. Considering next (fifth Meditation) the notion of extension, he finds it clear in his mind and with it a number of clear ideas concerning number and figure. Some such ideas, such as geometrical figures and their properties, cannot have come from the senses as he has certainly never seen some of the shapes his mind conceives. But they are clear, and therefore true. The idea of an all-perfect Being is equally clear in his mind, and, seeing that the idea of existence is inseparable from it, he cannot

---

[1] The reader who expects from Descartes only the sort of reasoning a mathematician would be content with will be surprised by the way in which he argues in the third Meditation. He says, e.g. 'From the mere fact that God has created me it is believable that he produced me in his own image and semblance.' He makes use of scholastic principles of which he does not establish the legitimacy. He uses scholastic terms ('objective', 'formal' and even the notion of potentiality) as though their use in the schools was sufficient guarantee of their validity. But these notions presuppose a metaphysical substructure at which Descartes only hints.

conceive of the all-perfect Being except as existing.[1] Once he knows that God exists he knows that he has a certain science of geometrical and similar truths. Can he also trust the evidence of the imagination and the senses? His own nature as a thinking being is essentially separate from any extended thing and therefore from his own body. The two faculties of imagination[2] and sensation are therefore not essential to his nature, because he can conceive of himself as thinking, without any reference to them, but they themselves presuppose a thinking being in order to exist, so they are modes of thought. Sensation is however a passive faculty and he himself as a thinking being does not produce its effects. The activity which produces them must therefore be outside the mind and, unless God is deceitful, it must be in things which bear some resemblance to their images. As God is not deceitful, but is on the contrary all truth, these images do indeed bear some resemblance to the things which give rise to them. In what nature teaches there is truth, and by 'nature' is to be understood God himself,[3] or the order created by God. The inner sensations he experiences teach him something of the state of his body and his outward senses teach him something of the outside world, but if he judges hastily he falls into error, as when he thinks that hotness or whiteness are in things. His reason corrects such hasty judgments, which are by no means imposed upon him by nature. The inner sense tells him what the body needs. It is sometimes mistaken, because the nerve which carries an impression from the sense organ to the brain may be affected somewhere along its length, but the evidence of one sense may usually be corrected by the evidence of the other senses, so general doubt as to the evidence of the senses is not reasonable.

Mersenne, whose mission in life was to keep discussion active in the philosophical world, called for comments on the Meditations from various theologians and philosophers to whom they were com-

---

[1] It is surprising that Descartes should come back to a subject he had dealt with in the third Meditation. It is worthy of note also that the argument of the fifth Meditation continues that of the beginning of the third. The supposition that the complex argumentation of the third and fourth was added to a simpler development in an original draft is permissible, but the argument had adopted more or less its final form by the time it was summarized in the fourth part of the *Discours de la Méthode*.

[2] A pentagon may be known to the intellect by its definition, or it may be represented by the imagination. A chiligon may be known with equal clarity to the intellect by its definition, but it cannot be represented by the imagination.

[3] Descartes uses the word nature in two senses in the *Meditations*, (1) as given here (=*Natura naturans*) and (2) to refer to the powers and properties of a particular being

unicated before publication. These critics, being put upon their
mettle made it their business to play the devil's advocate and pick as
many holes as they could in Descartes's logic, at the same time
showing that they could go straight to the heart of the matter. The
Dutch theologian Caterus refused to admit Descartes's contention
that the reality of the outside world is contained in ideas in the mind.
Thomas Hobbes refused to admit that the distinction between the
mind which contemplates an idea and the idea it contemplates is any
more than a logical distinction between subject and object; if the
brutes cannot make it, it is because they cannot use language. An
idea for Hobbes was an image produced by the motion of certain
parts of an organized body; to these images we attach names by
convention and reason by means of names and the connecting word
. Descartes replied that by an idea he meant not the content but the
form of a perception. Arnauld, while appreciating the arguments
Descartes shared with St Augustine, was concerned lest he should
have tried to prove too much; was not there a danger of going back
to the purely Platonic position of seeing man's nature as entirely
spirit, to the total exclusion of the body? As for Gassendi, he was
in his element when engaged on pulling down an audacious construction and almost gleefully maintained that 'Mr Mind' had not proved
that material things cannot think, he had not proved a real distinction between the mental operations of beasts and those of men, he
had not proved a real distinction between intellection and imagination, he had not proved that clear ideas are true ideas, nor that
consciousness of the self is possible without consciousness of what is
not the self. He denied that Descartes had proved the existence of
God, denied that it is possible to attain to the idea of God by the
reason, denied that Descartes could have any idea of an infinite
being and argued that, if being able to use the term 'Infinite' was
proof of the existence of a being corresponding to it, then the fact
that the Greeks talked of an infinite number of first principles
(atoms) in an infinite space was a proof of the truth of Lucretius's
system. Man was but ashes and dust; how could he have any idea
of God? Descartes maintained his positions, being content to reply
that Gassendi had misinterpreted him or had wilfully reproduced
the objections of the uninitiated who cannot rid themselves of the
prejudices of sense. Gassendi replied with his *Instances* and Descartes countered with a letter addressed to Clerselier, neither adding
anything significant to the discussion.

Gassendi was not the only one to object against Descartes's total separation of consciousness and matter. The argument that God may well have granted the power of thought to certain purely corporeal things, and even that thought and motion may be identical, appears in the objections of a group of theologians and philosophers whose names Mersenne did not reveal. To this Descartes replied with his usual argument, namely that the idea of a thinking thing is totally different from the idea of an extended thing. To their further objection that an atheist might refuse man a thinking soul on the ground that the beasts get along very well without one, Descartes replied that man has immediate knowledge of his own power of thought. The first stages of the controversy endëd with a long involved argument by a Jesuit teacher at the Collège de Clermont, named Bourdin, whose attack was directed principally against Descartes's provisional doubt and the characteristically Cartesian, and Platonic, method of proceeding from thought to the outside world. Descartes replied with patience and refrained from inferring (or at least said that he refrained from inferring) that this was a considered criticism by the whole company. He was concerned about the attitude of the Jesuit colleges. In 1640 Bourdin had had one of his pupils sustain a thesis against the *Dioptrique* and Descartes had written to the rector protesting that he had not been warned of it. He was eager for controversy with the Jesuit teachers, in spite of the hazards, and seems to have had real hopes of being able to come to terms with them in public discussion.[1] His ambition was to be officially adopted by the colleges. There is no other way of interpreting the fact that in 1644 he composed a text book in Latin under the title *Principia philosophiae*. He took particular pains to show that, according to his system, the earth did not move, although it was patent that he was on the side of Copernicus against Ptolemy. He used two arguments for this purpose. The first was that the earth does not move in relation to the sky which carries it along. The second was that, in a universe where no point is fixed, it is perfectly legitimate to consider the whole universe as revolving round the earth.[2] These relativistic arguments did not really affect the issue.

---

[1] To Huyghens, 2 viii 1640. His friend Mydorge in Paris prudently held up the letter to the rector, which Descartes had sent to him for delivery, but Descartes insisted (to Mersenne, 30 viii 1640).

[2] 'Nous nous souviendrons aussi . . . de ce qui a été dit ci-dessus touchant la nature du mouvement, à savoir qu'à proprement parler il n'est que le transport d'un corps du voisinage de ceux qui le touchent immédiatement et que nous considérons comme en

To put the earth in the third heaven and yet claim that it is the hub of the universe was like stating that the army manœuvres round the drummer boy. Descartes cannot but have realized this but he was being careful and conciliatory.

In 1649 Descartes composed, in French, for the Princess Palatine a Treatise of the Passions which became one of his best-known works in the Paris salons.[1] The first part of this work begins with a sketch of Cartesian physiology, but ends with the affirmation of the power of the mind over the passions. It begins with a physiological discussion because Descartes looks upon all the passions as corporeal in origin, all, that is to say, except wonderment, which he looked upon as purely intellectual. The others are dependent upon the physical constitution or temperament of the 'patient', but the will can act upon them, and can direct them, provided it is enlightened by clear conceptions of what is truly advantageous or disadvantageous. Even a weak-willed person can, by practice, assume the direction of his passions and motions of the body (such as trembling) which accompany them. The secret lies in the clear perception of the truth and the basing of judgments upon it. The second part of the treatise is an account of the passions—wonderment (*admiration*), esteem, scorn, generosity, humility, love, hatred, desire, hope, fear, jealousy, courage, remorse, etc. It is an attempt to make, in a very general way, that 'anatomy of the human heart' which was to become the main preoccupation of writers and readers in the second half of the century.

Descartes died the following year. He had been persuaded to go to Stockholm by Queen Christina of Sweden and he died there. His ashes were brought to Paris and placed in the convent of Sainte-Geneviève. His reputation was already great, in spite of the expression of official disapproval which was becoming marked. A tremendous controversy began and raged during the rest of the century. All aspects of French intellectual life were affected by it, not perhaps

repos. Or on ne saurait trouver dans la terre, ni dans les autres planètes, aucun mouvement, selon la propre signification du mot, pour ce qu'elles ne sont point transportées du voisinage des parties du ciel qui les touchent . . . il est bien plus à propos de croire que peut-être, au-delà de toutes les étoiles que nous voyons, il y a d'autres corps au regard desquels il faudrait dire que la terre est en repos et que les étoiles se meuvent, que de supposer . . . qu'il n'y en saurait avoir de tels, ainsi que doivent supposer ceux qui assurent en cette façon que la terre se meut.' (*Principes*, III, 28, 29, *Œuvres*, ed.) Adam and Tannery, ix, pp. 113–14 and 115; spelling modernized.

[1] Cf. G. Gadoffre, 'Le *Discours de la Méthode* et l'histoire littéraire', *French Studies*, Oxford, October 1948.

as exclusively as was thought, about a century ago, by such critics as Cousin, Nizard, Bouillier and Krantz, who looked upon French civilization as applied Cartesianism, but profoundly none the less in all domains.[1] The following chapters will attempt to follow the ramifications of Cartesian influence in various spheres.

[1] The following list of authors and places of publication of works on the title pages of which Descartes was expressly referred to will give an impression of the intensity of the debate (f=favourable, u=unfavourable).

1643, Schoock, Utrecht (u); 1644, Gassendi, Paris (u); 1648, Regius, Utrecht (f); 1651, Schooten, Leyden (f); 1652, Clauberg, Amsterdam (f); 1652, Papin, Paris (u); 1653, Lentz, Frankfurt am Main (u); 1653, Lipstorp, Leyden (f); 1654, Du Roure, Paris (f); 1654, Raey, Leyden (f); 1655, Clauberg, Leyden (f); 1655, Du Bois, Utrecht (u); 1656, Du Bois, Utrecht (u); 1656, Velthuysen, Utrecht (f); 1658, Clauberg, Duisburg (f); 1659, Wittich, Leyden (f); 1660, Clerke, London (f); 1663, Heereboord, Leyden (f); 1663, Bulliardus (Boulliau), The Hague (u); 1663, Bruyn, Amsterdam (f); 1663, Spinoza, Amsterdam (f); 1665, Denis, Paris (f); 1666, La Forge, Paris (f); 1667, Ameline, Paris (f); 1668, Bekker, Vessel (f); 1668, Schuler, Utrecht (f); 1669, Amerpoel, Leeuwarden (f); 1669, Des Fournelles (Cordemoy), Paris, (f); 1669, More, London (u); 1670, Des Fournelles (Cordemoy), London (f); 1670, Desmarets, Groningen (u); 1670, Petit, Paris (u); 1670, Bruyn, Amsterdam (f); 1670, A.M., London (u); 1670, Poisson, Vendôme (f); 1671, Andlo (Mansfeld), Leyden (f); 1671, Le Grand, London (f); 1671, Bassecour, Leyden (f); 1671, Gadrois, Paris (f); 1672, Pardies, Paris (u); 1672, Fayol, Paris (u); 1672, Le Grand, London (f); 1674, Gadrois, Paris (f); 1674, Le Bossu, Paris (f); 1675, Decker, Louvain (u); 1675, La Grange, Paris (u); 1675, De Wulf, Louvain (u); 1676, De Vries and Broedelet, Leyden (u); 1676, Pitcairn, London (critical); 1677, Gadrois, Paris (f); 1677, Sturm and Kraus, Altdorf (f?); 1677, Castelet, Paris (u); 1677, Poiret, Amsterdam (u); 1678, van Mastricht, Amsterdam (u); 1679, Le Grand, London (f); 1680, La Ville, Paris (u); 1680, Clauberg, n.p. (f); 1680, Forbes, Aberdeen (u); 1683, De Vries and Welde, Utrecht (u); 1683, Overkamp, Amsterdam (f); 1683, De Vries and Friedrich, Leipzig (u); 1684, Ancillon, Liège (u); 1684, Otto, Rostock (u); 1684, Pasch and Lachmann, Wittenberg (u); 1684, Helvetius (Schweitzer), Amsterdam (f); 1685, Rochon, Paris (u); 1687, Helvetius (Schweitzer), Utrecht (f); 1688, Langenhert, Franeker (f); 1688, Wittich, Dordrecht (f); 1689, Sismus, Rotterdam (u); 1689, Huet, Paris (u); 1690, Daniel, Paris (u); 1690, Jens, Leyden (f); 1691, Hanbury, Cambridge (f); 1691, Foucher, Paris (u); 1692, Du Hamel, J., Paris (u); 1692, Daniel, Paris (u); 1692, Huet, Paris (u); 1692, Régis, Paris (f); 1693, Daniel, Paris (u); 1694, Peripateticus (Daniel), Paris (u); 1694, Froment, Paris (f); 1695, Volder, Amsterdam (f); 1698, Jens, Leyden (f); 1699, Werenfels, Basel (f); 1700, Howard, London (u); 1702, Schelhammer, Kiel (u); 1703, Berger, Wittenberg (u); 1706, Petermann, Leipzig (f); 1708, Andala, Franeker (f); 1708, Dartiguelongue, Amsterdam (u); 1711, Seligmann and Otto, Rostock (u); 1716, Sbaragli, Bologna (u); 1719, Regius, Franeker (u).

X

The Fortunes of Descartes

THE SCHOOLS AND THE PUBLIC

DESCARTES'S precautions were of no avail; the educational world resisted stubbornly. At Leyden, it is true, Cartesian infiltration was rapid and Utrecht, Amsterdam, Franeker, Groningen and Harderwijk tried to come to terms with the new doctrine,[1] but Louvain and Liège were impenetrable; in Germany Clauberg at Herborn and then at Duisburg held a lonely outpost; Oxford showed no interest and Cambridge but a temperate one.[2] In France the teaching of new doctrines was prohibited in the colleges.

At Leyden, according to an anonymous pamphlet published in 1691 under the title *Relation des progrès du Cartésianisme dans l'université de Leyde*, half the professors in the faculty of medicine and many in the other faculties were Cartesians in 1659. At Utrecht, one of Descartes's earliest disciples, Regius (Henri le Roy), raised a hornets' nest about himself. There were riotous scenes during public examinations conducted by Regius and the rector, Daniel Voet, tried to prevent him from teaching. Descartes had done his best to restrain his disciple, and had provided many ingenious arguments by which trouble could be avoided. For instance, Regius had concluded loyally from Cartesian principles that the union of soul and body is 'accidental', not 'substantial' because body and soul can exist apart. 'No,' advised the master, 'it is better to say that in a certain manner the union can be looked upon as accidental.' Descartes became involved however in the dispute; he and Voet discussed each others' characters publicly and the civil authorities of

---

[1] For attempts at compromise see J. Bohatec, *Die cartesianische Scholastik in der Philosophie und reformierte Dogmatik des 17. Jahrhunderts*, Leipzig, 1912, and C. Louise Thijssen-Schoute, *Descartes et le cartésianisme hollandais*, Paris and Amsterdam, 1950, p. 275. The list of publications given above, p. 188, shows that Holland was the scene of intense controversial activity. In 1654 the curators of Leyden University insisted that Raey should remove the name of Descartes from the title page of his *Clavis philosophiae naturalis* or forfeit a prize of 100 florins; the name of Descartes was looked upon as a provocation.

[2] On the very modest success of Descartes in England consult J. Laird, *L'Influence de Descartes sur la philosophie anglaise* in *Descartes* etc., Paris, 1937, pp. 226–56.

Utrecht stopped the quarrel by forbidding the publication of anything concerning Descartes's philosophy (11 June 1645).

By 1674, nevertheless, J. de Bruyn, L. Woltzogen, J. G. Graevius,
R. van Mansfeld, all professors in the University of Utrecht, were
Cartesians, while at Leyden the professors of the University num-
bered many of the most active Cartesians in their ranks, Geulincx,
Craanen, Schuyl, Wittich, Heerebord, Volder, Heidanus, Jens,
Braun.[1] From 1674 to 1676, Hartsoeker was the pupil of 'obdurate
Cartesians' (cartésiens entêtés), in both philosophy and anatomy, both
at Leyden and Amsterdam, according to Fontenelle: 'all they had
done in the schools was to change from one slavery to another',
comments the author of the Eloge d'Hartsoeker.

The University of Paris remained however closed to Descartes.
The teaching of new doctrines had been forbidden by the Parlement
in 1625, on the occasion of De Claves's theses, and the old school
was in complete command at the Sorbonne and the Colleges. When
some danger of Cartesian intrusion was sensed, an attempt was made
to have the Parlement prohibit the teaching of any other philosophy
than that of Aristotle. The attempt failed, partly because of the
reluctance of the Parlement itself to take such action, partly perhaps
on account of a burlesque decree composed by Boileau in legal and
medical jargon and prohibiting inter alia the blood from circulating.[2]
But Descartes was none the less excluded, because the king had
already given a verbal order forbidding the teaching of new philosophies (1671). Philosophy continued to be taught in the old way, and
text-books of the old type continued to appear. Such are those of
Gonet (1658–9), Vincent (1669), Linze (1666), Frassen (1668),
Ladet (1669), Barbay (1675), Baduer (1675), Goudin (1675),
Duhan (1694), Guérin (1695). One cannot however say that the new
philosophy made no headway at all in the University of Paris. A
course given in the Collège de Montaigu in 1679–80 by Jean Courtillier devoted a good deal of time to refuting Descartes.[3] Refutations
are one way by which a doctrine may become known; silence is a

---

[1] Mme Thijssen-Schoute describes the activities of some fifty or more Cartesian
scholars in the Netherlands.

[2] Requeste des maistres es arts, professeurs et regens de l'Université de Paris présentée à
la cour souveraine de Parnasse : Ensemble l'arrest intervenu sur ladite Requeste contre tous
ceux qui prétendent faire, enseigner ou croire de Nouvelles Decouvertes qui ne soient pas dans
Aristote, A Delphe. Par les Imprimeurs Ordinaires de la Cour de Parnasse, 1671.

[3] E. Gilson, Etude sur le rôle de la pensée médiévale dans la formation du système
cartésien, Paris, 1930, p. 316.

far greater enemy. As compared with Ladet, whose course contained no reference to Descartes whatsoever, Jean Courtillier may be looked upon as a propagandist. At the Collège de Plessis-Sorbon the anti-Cartesian Jean Du Hamel seems to have discussed the theory of clear ideas before his class.[1] But there is more to be said. Even in such colleges as d'Harcourt a certain amount of eclecticism could be risked. Fontenelle tells us that in 1668 J.-B. Du Hamel (the ex-Oratorian curé of Neuilly) compounded a course for the use of a young professor at d'Harcourt, Jacques-Nicolas Colbert, second son of the minister. The young professor of twenty-four years of age dictated the course to his class and it was later published under the title *Philosophia vetus et nova ad usum scholae accommodata,*[2] and had a long run of success, being adopted eventually both by the Oratorians and by their rivals the Jesuits. In 1690 the Jesuit Daniel credited Du Hamel with having attempted to reconcile the Cartesians and the schools.[3] Traditional in method, the course incorporated the discoveries of the 'moderns' to the extent that orthodoxy would allow. Descartes benefited by this, but so did the atomists. Du Hamel was nothing if not eclectic. He was well placed for being up to date; he was the secretary of the newly-founded Académie des Sciences and was well acquainted with the work of Malpighi, Vernay, C. Perrault, Mariotte, Toinard, Boyle, Huyghens, who were all mentioned in his course of lectures. At the Collège Mazarin (or des Quatre Nations) Pourchot, at one time rector of the University, was suspected of Cartesianism, and 'Pourchotiste', in Boileau's *Arrêt burlesque*, means partisan of the new philosophy. He does not seem to have gone very far in the direction of Cartesianism; his *Institutio philosophica ad faciliorem veterum ac recentiorum philosophorum lectionem comparata* (1695)[4] is scholastic in plan, but he does explicitly reject 'substantial forms'. Dagoumer, the principal of the Collège d'Harcourt, adopted a similar attitude.[5] In the 1720's, at the Royal College, the abbé de Molières was teaching Cartesian physics and rebutting the attacks of the Newtonians.

[1] *Journal des savants*, 12 May 1692. The course was published in 1705 (*Philosophia universalis sive commentarius in universam Aristotelis philosophiam, authore J. Joanne Du Hamel; Paris, 4 vols.)*
[2] Paris, 1678, 4 vols.; 1684, 6 vols. Amsterdam, 1700, 6 vols.
[3] *Voyage du monde de Descartes*, part II.
[4] Paris, 4 vols. In 1711 the *Journal des savants* said that the *Institutio philosophica* was widely used in France and elsewhere (23 Nov.).
[5] *Philosophia ad usum scholae accommodata*, Paris, 1702–3, 3 vols.

At Toulouse, where Emmanuel Maignan taught, a certain amount of eclecticism seems to have been allowed also. In 1676, a Capuchin friar named Casimir, who held a chair in the University, published a course of the type which, according to the *Journal des savants*,[1] the 'new philosophers held in horror', but which none the less banished 'substantial forms', 'accidental forms', 'universals' and other 'rational entities' from the lecture room. It was at Toulouse also that François Bayle, in a course delivered about 1675, adopted the conception of a world constructed like a vast machine, while scolding Descartes for having followed reason exclusively and not experience.[2]

The Jesuit colleges were hostile. Far from acceding to Descartes's request that Bourdin, the professor at the Collège de Clermont who had attacked him in his lectures in 1640, should be censured, the Company hardened its heart against the new teaching. A few teachers and monitors at La Flèche were favourably inclined from the start, amongst them Noël, Vatier and Mesland, but the College had refused to express an opinion on its old pupil's *Dioptrique* when Descartes sent a copy as a gift in 1638. A teacher at the Jesuit college at Caen, Le Valois (Louis de la Ville) expressed admiration for Cartesian physics while attacking his general principles, in a book published in 1680, and the Jesuit critic, Rapin, adopted a similar attitude in 1676. Fournier used the *Dioptrique* in his *Hydrographie* in 1643 and a 'geometrical spirit' reigned in La Chaise's physics. H. Fabry's *Tractatus de plantis et generatione animalium* held the balance between Aristotle and Descartes according to the *Journal des savants*.[3] But all these Jesuits were conservative as far as general principles were concerned.[4] After the turn of the century Descartes was praised as a mathematician by a Jesuit teacher at Caen, J.-M. Aubert, in the *Mémoires de Trévoux*, which was a Jesuit publication. The same journal published further praise in 1721. A teacher at Louis le Grand, Régnault (1683–1762) defended Cartesian physics in 1734. In 1772 another teacher at Louis le Grand, J. du Baudory, the suc-

[1] 30 March 1676. Casimir's work was entitled *Atomi peripateticae, sive tum veterum tum recentiorum Atomistarum placita ad Neotericae Peripateticae scholae methodum redacta*. Cf. above, p. 109.

[2] *Journal des savants*, 17 June 1675. F. Bayle published a *Systema generale philosophiae* in 1669 and his *Institutiones physicae ad usum scholarum accommodatae* appeared in 1700 (3 vols).

[3] 23 August 1666. Fabry explained the vegetative and sensitive soul of the brutes as a certain disposition of the parts and not as substantial forms.

[4] G. Sortais, S.J., 'Le Cartésianisme chez les Jésuites' (*Archives de philosophie*, vol. vi, cahier III, 1929.)

cessor to Porée (Voltaire's teacher) as professor of rhetoric, combined a defence of Descartes with an attack on scholasticism, and a Jesuit teacher at Avignon, Paulian, published a *Traité de paix entre Descartes et Newton* in 1763. But these developments belong to another age, an age when the Jesuit Gerdil was publishing a long attack against Locke from a Cartesian standpoint and another Jesuit, Antoine Guénard, was winning a prize awarded by the Académie in 1755 for a eulogy on Descartes.[1] A compromise between the old and the new philosophies had finally been reached in the seminaries and was to be still in force when Renan was at Saint-Sulpice in the middle years of the nineteenth century.

As far as general philosophy goes, only Vatier and Mesland at La Flèche can be quoted as being favourably disposed from the first, and Mesland had objections to make, especially in respect of the Eucharist. We must wait till the first years of the next century for further examples. Then we can quote André, who, as a monitor at Louis le Grand, defended Descartes and Malebranche in the quadrangle, and filled the margins of his copies of their works with enthusiastic notes. Again, in 1706, according to a report sent to the General of the Company, two professors and especially the professor of physics, were suspect of Cartesianism. But André was sent away to La Flèche and, in 1713, forbidden to teach. His lecture notes had been used in other colleges and particularly Amiens, Quimper, Caen and Alençon. The teachers who had used them were obliged to dictate refutations of André's opinions to their classes. At La Flèche, Du Tertre was suspended in 1713. In 1721, when the manuscript of André's *Vie de Malebranche* was discovered, André was put in the Bastille for a few weeks. In 1682, and again in 1696, the Congregation of the order forbade the teaching of new opinions. In 1706, and again in 1714, a manual was issued listing the Cartesian propositions, thirty in number, which were not to be taught in the Jesuit schools.[2]

[1] His dissertation was entitled *Discours sur l'esprit philosophique*, Paris, 1755 (text also in A. Cahour, S.J., *Chefs-d'œuvre de l'éloquence française*, Paris, 1854, pp. 421–6); cf. V. Cousin, *Fragments philosophiques pour servir à l'histoire de la philosophie*, 5th edn., Paris, 1866, pp. 418–21; A. G. A. Balz, 'Cartesian Refutations of Spinoza' in *Philosophical Review*, New York, xlvi (1937), p. 464, and in the same author's *Cartesian Studies*, New York, 1951, p. 221.

[2] They included the propositions that it is possible to doubt of everything, that substances are eternal, that essences are dependent on the will of God, that the essence of matter is extension, that the universe is a plenum, that the universe is indefinitely extended, that there is a constant amount of motion in the universe, that the present universal order is the only possible one, that qualitative differences may be reduced to

A similar story can be told of the Oratorian colleges.[1] Although a certain platonizing tendency was tolerated,[2] the old philosophy was given official support rather than the new, and Cartesian doctrines were actively discouraged. In 1652 André Martin, the author of a *Philosophie de Saint Augustin*, was suspended from teaching at Marseilles for Cartesianism. In 1654 Blampignon was refused permission to print his thesis because he proposed to follow the doctrine of Plato and refute that of Aristotle. In the same year the General of the Congregation sent round a circular to all the Oratorian colleges requiring teachers to 'teach the usual and ordinary philosophy and in the manner in which it is taught in all the universities of France, so as not to single themselves out from the others'. In 1658, a similar directive was sent to all the colleges by the general assembly of the Congregation and in 1661 theses in favour of Descartes were forbidden at Le Mans. Such action was doubtless intended to check the spread of Descartes's popularity with the tutors; it is evidence of the existence of such popularity. At Saumur three teachers were censured in 1672. At the college at Angers the teachers resisted and claimed the right to exercise their liberty in the teaching of philosophy. The result was that the college acquired the reputation of being Cartesian and was denounced on this score by the rector of the University of Angers in a letter to the king. The General of the Order, summoned to appear before the king, gave assurances for the future and wrote a letter of reprimand to the principal of the college at Angers. One of the teachers there, Bernard Lamy, having been denounced by the rector of the University of Angers, was dismissed by *lettre de cachet* in 1670.[3] At Vendôme a teacher named Poisson wrote a treatise on Cartesian mechanics[4] and had it printed in 1671. He was at once summoned to Paris by the Council of the

the arrangement of particles, that secondary qualities are subjective, that the brutes are machines. To these was added the theory of 'occasional causes' developed by the Cartesians, and particularly by Malebranche, to explain the co-ordination of thought and physical motion, mind and body.

[1] It has been told by P. Lallemand in his *L'Education dans l'ancien Oratoire de France*, Paris, 1888.

[2] For instance in a work by Father Thomassin entitled *Dogmatum theologicorum prior portio de Verbi Dei incarnatione*, Paris, 1680.

[3] Lamy was an admirer of the Cartesian method, but was aware that much of Descartes's physics was out of date and preferred Malebranche's theory of ideas. His *Entretiens sur les sciences* became a popular book of methodology and was used by both Montesquieu and J.-J. Rousseau.

[4] *Commentaire ou remarques sur la méthode de M. Descartes où l'on établit plusieurs principes nécessaires pour entendre toutes ses œuvres, par le R.P.N. I.P.P.D.L.*, Paris, 1671.

Oratoire and told to bring all the copies of his book with him. They were not actually destroyed; they were locked up in the college library at Vendôme and some of them gradually filtered through to the other colleges. In 1677 another teacher at Angers, Peland, was censured and relegated to Brive-la Gaillarde, after his lecture notes had been examined by the Sorbonne. Both Lamy and Peland seem to have allied a certain amount of political radicalism to their Cartesianism: Lamy was accused of having taught that social inequalities did not exist in the state of innocence and Peland that the royal authority was derived from the people.

As for the Benedictines, the Abbaye de Saint-Vannes ruled against Cartesianism in 1675, but Dom Robert Desgabets, who had propagandized in various abbeys in favour of Cartesian physics, continued to do so in the Cardinal de Retz's château at Commercy after that date, and Dom François Lamy openly taught Cartesianism at Saint-Denis towards the end of the century.[1]

In the learned world outside the schools, the campaign of resistance to the progress of Cartesianism can be followed from 1665 onwards in the *Journal des savants*, a review intended for the educated, but not the specialist reader, though it published some of the most original work of Huyghens and Leibniz. The struggle of the old for survival seems to have reached its greatest intensity around 1690; after that time, such scholastic works as the reviewer takes note of strike him as curiosities rather than as serious contributions to learning. The rearguard action of the traditionalists—fought in French before the general public, on the ground Descartes had chosen—was already under way when the *Journal des savants* began publication in 1665. In 1665 the Oratorian La Grange, in 1670 and 1672 the Jesuit Pardies, professor of mathematics at the Collège de Clermont, in 1680 the Jesuit Valois (Louis de la Ville), in 1685 the Jesuit Rochon, in 1689 the Jesuit Gallimart, in 1690, 1693 and 1694 the Jesuit Daniel, in 1692 Jean (not J.-B.) Du Hamel, all took part in the affair.[2] So did Huet, bishop of Soissons and then of Avranches,

[1] On Desgabets see P. Lemaire, *Le Cartésianisme chez les Bénédictins, Dom Robert Desgabets, son système, son influence et son école*, Paris, 1901; on Lamy, Dom J. Zehnder, *Dom François Lamy*, Zug, 1944.

[2] J.-B. de La Grange, *Les Principes de la philosophie contre celle d'Epicure, de Gassendi, de Descartes, du père Maignan, de Régis . . .* Paris, 1665, 1675; I. Pardies, *Discours du mouvement local*, Paris, 1674; id., *Lettres d'un philosophe à un Cartésien de ses amis*, Paris, 1672; id., *Discours sur la connaissance des bêtes*, Paris, 1672; id., *Sentiments de M. Descartes touchant l'essence et les propriétés des corps opposés à la doctrine de l'Eglise et conformes aux erreurs de Calvin sur le sujet de l'Eucharistie*, Paris, 1683; R. Rochon,

a sceptical fideist after the manner of an older generation, whose dogged efforts to undermine Descartes's logic, especially that of the *Cogito*, were given a good deal of space in the review.[1] So did Foucher, a canon of the cathedral of Dijon, who attempted to revive the critical philosophy of the Greek Academy in face of the new rationalism.

Pardies concentrated on a question which was exciting much interest in the salons, namely whether the beasts are mere machines or not; the Cartesian contention that they were ran counter to common sense and so was an easy prey. Daniel made use of the public's taste for imaginary travel stories in his *Voyage du monde de Descartes*. Jean Du Hamel, by that time a retired professor, had recourse to his old lecture notes in order to participate in the controversy aroused by the Cartesian Régis's *Système de philosophie* (1690).

The journalist rarely mentions scholastic treatises.[2] When he does so it is usually with a remark to the effect that Aristotle 'still' has his defenders, or that 'one would never suspect from this work that the new philosophy existed', or that 'this smacks too much of the schools to be elaborated upon here', or (of a German peripatetician interested in the Kabbala): 'who is more suited than a peripatetician for seeing in the dark, whereas the Cartesians cannot take a single step except in the light?',[3] or again, 'Aristotle is still taught in the schools because he assists the teaching of theology', or 'it is still the fashion apparently in Copenhagen to prove one's thesis (in this case that the seat of the rational soul is in the heart, rather than in the head or liver) by means of quotations'.[4] All these remarks were made in the *Journal des savants* between 1704 and 1713.[5]

Lettre à un philosophe cartésien, Rennes et Paris, 1685; Gallimart, *La Philosophie du prince*, Paris, 1698; G. Daniel, *Voyage du monde de Descartes*, Paris, 1690; id., *Nouvelles Difficultés proposées par un péripatéticien à l'auteur du monde de Descartes, touchant la connaissance des bêtes, avec la réfutation de deux défenses du système général du monde de Descartes*, Paris, 1693; J. Du Hamel, *Réflexions critiques sur le système cartésien de la philosophie de M. Régis*, Paris, 1692.

[1] Especially his *Censura philosophiae cartesianae*, Paris, 1689.

[2] Guérin was given a brief notice in 1695 and Duhan's *Philosophie problématique* was mentioned in 1705 (9 Jan.), but with a scornful remark. In 1692 an anti-Cartesian *Disputatio* (*De existentia Dei et humanae mentis immortalitate secundum Cartesii et Aristotelis doctrinam*) aroused the reviewer's interest, doubtless because of the comparison made between the two systems.

[3] *Journal des savants*, 16 February 1705.   [4] ibid., 12 July 1706.

[5] Cf. Daniel, in his *Voyage du monde de Descartes* (1690): 'On n'imprime quasi plus de cours de la philosophie selon les méthodes de l'école, et presque tous les ouvrages

In 1707 (24 January) one could read in the same review that Genesis was doubtless not meant to teach physics and astronomy. This enlightened attitude on the part of a publication which could not be suspected of anti-religious sympathies, and which excused itself for having mentioned not only Spinoza himself but even refutations of Spinoza, might have prevented much sterile controversy in the eighteenth century had it been widely adopted. The remark was made on the occasion of a book which attempted to reconcile the new physics with the book of Genesis,[1] one of a long series of attempts (inspired originally by Descartes himself) to prove that such a reconciliation was possible. Before the general public, accusations of anti-Aristotelianism carried no weight at all, but the accusation of disrespect for the Bible was a very different matter (was not Spinoza looked upon as a dangerous criminal and an unwholesome villain for having instituted a critical study of the Old Testament?). Polite society had set its face against all erudition since the early days of the Hôtel de Rambouillet, and the rule of the University, however absolute it might be in the Latin quarter, was without force across the bridges, in the Louvre or the Place Royale. In the public mind a professor's language was composed of terms like *baralipton* and *baroco*, the names of the various types of syllogism used in the philosophy classes of the colleges. There were, however, critical issues over which a public scandal could have arisen and wrecked the Cartesians claim to respectability.

The first was that of the Eucharist.[2] How could transubstantiation be explained except by the old ideas of substance and quality? How could the substance change without affecting the qualities, if the substance was reduced to extension and the qualities to the disposition of the parts? Descartes made an attempt to overcome these difficulties, but the edition of the *Méditations* containing the Cartesian theory (that of Amsterdam, 1659) was put on the Index in

de cette espèce qui paraissent maintenant en France sont des traités de physique qui supposent les principes de la nouvelle. philosophie." Daniel's remark was somewhat premature, but its general implication was justified by the facts.

[1] Sébastien Leclerc's *Nouveau Système du monde conforme à l'Ecriture sainte.*

[2] On the occasion of the Jesuit Le Valois's attack in 1680, the *Journal des savants* commented: 'Ce n'est pas d'aujourd'hui qu'on s'est écrié contre la philosophie de Descartes. Dès qu'elle parut dans le monde, on la regarda comme suspecte et dangereuse pour la religion. Mais, lorsque le bruit que fit la foule de ses sectateurs obligea les curieux de l'examiner de plus près, on l'accusa d'être, non seulement un peu suspecte, mais de combattre même un de nos plus saints et de nos plus augustes mystères, celui de l'Eucharistie.' (12 Feb. 1680.)

1661. There were discussions on the subject in Mme de Sablé's drawing-room, and the Cartesian physicist Rohault wrote a dissertation on the question, but not, however, or so it seems, with the intention of publishing it; it was published by an over-zealous friend in 1671.[1] The Cartesians were discreet enough not to press their point or parry their opponents'. There being no opposition, there was no scandal; the Jesuit thrusts flailed the air and the Cartesians remained unscathed.

The other difficulty was presented by the book of Genesis. Descartes had shown himself ready to use his ingenuity on this topic as on the other and interpret Genesis in terms of mechanistic physics. Intermittent attempts to reconcile the biblical account of the creation with the new philosophy kept the discussion alive and the *Journal des savants*'s remark in 1707 that Genesis was not intended to teach physics did not put a stop to it. Of one Cartesian dissertation Pierre Bayle remarked (whether seriously or not it is impossible to tell, as is nine times out of ten the case with Pierre Bayle), 'It is hoped that the author will carry his Cartesian explanation as far as the temptation.'[2] This dry comment was called forth by Théodore Barin's *Le Monde naissant*, published in 1686.[3] Before that time, a *Cartesius mosaisans* had been published by J. Amerpoel at Leeuwarden in 1669.[4] In 1700 came J. F. Vallade's *Discours philosophiques sur la création et l'arrangement du monde* (Amsterdam), in 1707 Sébastien Leclerc's *Nouveau système du monde conforme à l'écriture sainte*, in 1710 an anonymous *Moyse éclairci ou explication littérale et physique du premier chapitre de la Genèse* (Amsterdam) and in 1713 Saint-Rambert's *Essais d'explication physique du premier chapitre de la Genèse* (Utrecht). One may note that none of these books was actually published in France, without however attaching too much importance to the fact, as the presses of the Low Countries were at this time turning out a large proportion of the books published in French. Nor were the later ones Cartesian in any strict sense. According to the *Moyse éclairci* of 1710 for instance, God

[1] *Entretiens sur la philosophie dédiés à Monseigneur le Prince* (Preface).

[2] *Nouvelles de la République des Lettres*, 1685, p. 1308; cf. A. Monod, *De Pascal à Chateaubriand*, Paris, 1916, p. 192.

[3] *Le Monde naissant ou la Création du monde démontrée par des principes très simples et très conformes à l'histoire de Moïse*, Utrecht. Cf. *Journal des savants*, 1 Jan. 1686.

[4] Cf. Bayle, *Histoire de la République des Lettres*, t. iv, p. 332, and Monod, op. cit., p. 192. There was a further edition in 1677 (in *Johannis Amperpoel Bibliotheca sacra et profana*, Rome). The *Journal des savants* (30 Aug. 1677) says this edition was made from a manuscript discovered in the library of Cardinal Brancaccio.

created two substances, the waters and the spirit that moved thereon, or, in other words, matter and light. Light entered into matter and moulded and formed it. In 1708 an English doctor's effort to prove that doctors and naturalists are not necessarily unbelievers was noted by the *Journal des savants*. This was C. Purshall's *Essay on the Mechanical Fabrick of the Universe* (London, 1707), a strange blend of the Bible, Ptolemaic cosmology, chemistry and mechanistic physics. Many different cosmologies were current at the end of the century including those of Leibniz, Woodward, Whiston and Hart-soeker.[1] Descartes was far from being alone in the field. In particular, the *Telluris theoria sacra* of Thomas Burnet (London, 1681) pro-voked attempts to reconcile the 'natural' and biblical accounts of the earth's origin.[2] Both in Paris and in London much ingenuity seems to have been squandered on this topic.

The accusation of irreligion had never weighed seriously upon Cartesianism as such. Descartes was accused of being wrong, not of being irreligious, or it was pointed out that his doctrines concerning animal automatism supplied arms to the materialists. This accusa-tion seems to have been made commonly in discussions.[3] On the occasion of an aggressively styled diatribe by a certain Pieter van Mastricht, *Novitatum cartesianarum gangrena, seu theologia cartesiana detecta* (Amsterdam, 1678), the *Journal des savants* commented imperturbably, 'As M. Descartes is looked upon as having had a proper attitude towards the faith, he will not lack defenders.'[4] One eager defender had indeed already found the theory of beast machines

[1] Leibniz, *Protogea* (1683), Woodward, *An Essay towards the Natural History of the Earth* (1695), Whiston, *A New Theory of the Earth* (1696), Hartsoeker, *Principes de Physique* (1696). The most fantastic is possibly F. Placet's *Corruption des cieux par le péché*, Lyons, 1696.

[2] *Extrait de la théorie sacrée de la terre et des révolutions et changements de notre globe, traduit du latin de Th. Burnet et concilié avec l'écriture sainte par M.D.* and *Extrait de Doutes ou objections de Thomas Burnet sur le premier chapitre de la Genèse conciliés avec l'écriture sainte par M.D.* (Unpublished manuscripts, probably of the early XVIIIth cen-tury in the Mazarine library, Paris, no. 1194.)

[3] Clerselier gives a clear indication of this: 'Si dans une compagnie, quelque personne un peu grave vient à dire d'un ton sérieux, ou plutôt avec cet air que répand sur le visage l'Imagination, lorsqu'elle est surprise et effrayée par quelque chose d'extraor-dinaire: "En vérité les Cartésiens sont d'étranges gens; ils soutiennent que les bêtes n'ont point d'âme: j'appréhende fort que bientôt ils ne disent autant de l'homme." Cela seul sera suffisant pour persuader plusieurs personnes que cette opinion est dangereuse; il n'y a point de raisons qui puissent empêcher l'effet de ce discours sur les imaginations faibles.' (Preface to Rohault, *Œuvres posthumes*, 1690.)

[4] 'Comme M. Descartes a passé pour un homme qui avait de droits sentiments à l'égard de la foi, il ne manquera pas de défenseurs.' (29 Aug. 1678.)

in Genesis.[1] Mastricht's dissertation might well have sounded less aggressive had it not been written in Latin, a pungent idiom compared with the polite and restrained contemporary French. His bark was worse than his bite. When all came to all, the object of his scorn was merely the attempt to prove the truths of religion by reason!

Outside the academic world (where to be a Cartesian involved a real danger of persecution) no risks were run in opting for the new philosophy. Cartesianism had, from the very first, developed in full view of the public, Descartes having appealed to the general reader over the heads of the professors. All Descartes's published works were available in French by 1664. Rohault, La Forge, Régis all lectured to popular audiences. In 1665 a little book called *Physique d'usage* made a great stir in Paris by explaining the plague as being produced by hard, pointed particles of 'subtle matter'.[2] In 1667 an *Art de vivre heureux selon les principes de M. Descartes* appeared as a book of practical precepts.[3] Poulain de la Barre's *De l'Egalité des deux sexes* (1673) argued the cause of feminism according to the Cartesian method.[4] The same Poulain de la Barre included the *Discours de la méthode* and the *Méditations*, along with Rohault's Cartesian physics and the Port-Royal grammar, in a programme of feminine education outlined in his *Education des dames* (1674). The feminist movement was naturally well disposed to Descartes. One of his feminine admirers, Mme de Galland, was known as a mathematician. In 1665, at Toulouse, another feminine disciple defended Cartesian theses in public under the guidance of Régis. The Port-Royal Grammar (1660) used quotations from Descartes as examples. This little book is witness of the hold the intellectual world was beginning to have on polite society. It was written as though grammar were an abstract science, whereas up to that time grammarians, and particularly Vaugelas, had taken polite usage, with all its arbitrary fantasy as the guide.

The polite world was a-buzzing, eager for initiation into the new mysteries. Soon Louis of Condé was walking with Malebranche

---

[1] Cordemoy (?) under the names Des Fournelles and Desfournellis, in a letter addressed to the Franciscan friar François Bayle in Toulouse and published in Paris in 1669. It was translated into English in the following year as *A Discours written to a learned friar by M. des Fournelles showing that the system of M. Descartes, and particularly his opinion concerning brutes, does contain nothing dangerous and that all he hath written of both seems to have been taken out of the first chapter of Genesis*, London, 1770.

[2] *Journal des savants*, 2 Feb. 1665.   [3] ibid., 19 June 1667.

[4] 'Après avoir examiné cette opinion suivant la règle de vérité qui est de ne rien admettre pour vrai qui ne soit appuyé sur des idées claires et distinctes.'

or Régis in the 'Philosophers' Walk' at his château of Chantilly and listening to their talk.[1] The duc de Luynes was inviting Cartesian physicists to his château;[2] in the Marquise de Sablé's salon the guests were discussing whether Cartesian principles can explain the mystery of the Eucharist or whether Cartesianism leads to Spinozism; at Mme de Sévigné's houses in Paris and Brittany, Corbinelli, the sometime secretary of the marquise, was defending Cartesian rationalism against empiricism and scepticism, with the support of the marquise's son Charles. The marquise herself was anxious to learn enough of the new philosophy to take part in the conversation or retail it in her letters to her daughter Mme de Grignan, who was what we should now call a 'militant' Cartesian. The royal historiographer René Bary took upon himself to inform the ladies of what was going on in the intellectual world in his *Fine philosophie accommodée à l'intelligence des dames*[3] and Louis de Lesclache reduced his popular lectures to the form of a handy manual in his *Abrégé de la philosophie en tables* (1675). Attempts to reach a compromise do not seem to have been made before the general public. Father Le Bossu gave the palm to Descartes as a physicist and to Aristotle as a teacher in 1674, but in such a way as to recognize the superiority of the new over the old as far as the attainment of truth was concerned and the general public was concerned only with that aspect of the question.

At the duchesse du Maine's château at Sceaux,[4] Fontenelle was the centre of intellectual activity, a man admirably suited for the work of scientific propaganda which he had undertaken. A man of the world to his finger tips, a writer of pastoral poetry, a master of flowery style, the model of La Bruyère's Cydias in the *Caractères*, a clear, precise mind, dry and analytical, he presented in a lucid prose enlivened by familiar metaphors, the Cartesian picture of the

[1] Bouillier, *Histoire de la philosophie cartésienne*, i, pp. 419, 423; Fontaine, *Mémoires pour servir à l'histoire de Port-Royal*, Utrecht, 1736, ii, p. 59.

[2] 'Le château de M. le duc de Luynes était la source de toutes ces curiosités et cette source était inépuisable. On y parlait sans cesse du nouveau système du monde selon M. Descartes, et on l'admirait.' (Fontaine, ibid., ii, p. 53.)

[3] Bary admits a general debt to Descartes and says he followed Rohault's lectures in the preface of his *La Physique, où, selon les anciens et les modernes, il est traité de tout ce qu'il y a de plus curieux dans la nature* . . . Paris, 1671, 3 vols.

[4] Mlle de Launay (Mme de Staal) said the duchess believed in Descartes as firmly as she believed in God. (*Mémoires*, London, 1755, t. i, p. 19; Bouillier, op. cit., t. i, p. 424.) Mlle de Launay herself studied Malebranche's *Recherche de la vérité* at the convent where she was educated. (Bouillier, ibid.)

material universe. At the time when he published his *Entretiens sur la pluralité des mondes* (1686) an opera by Quinault and Lulli named *Phaëton* had just had a successful run. The Opera House in Paris was distinguished from the Comédie Française in that it gave great importance to scenic effects. In *Phaëton* were portrayed the temple of the sun and the metamorphoses of Proteus, not to mention Phaëton's flight and his fatal fall into the sea. How is Phaëton's flight made possible? If the sages of ancient Greece, Pythagoras, Plato, Aristotle, could have been present at the Opera House, they would doubtless have talked of numbers, sympathies or Nature's abhorrence of a vacuum, but Descartes and the moderns have discovered the ropes and pulleys by which the miracle is worked. 'I hope', says the instructor to his fair companion, with whom he is sitting in the light of the moon, 'that I am not making the world too simple for you and destroying its wonders.' 'No,' replies the marquise, 'I admire it all the more, now that I know it works so simply.'

Fontenelle's universe was like Descartes's. In it, vortices of subtle matter whirled the stars round on their courses. But Fontenelle had also read Lucretius. He did not mention Descartes's metaphysics in his imaginary conversations; he was more concerned with emptying the world of beings created by human fear and fancy than with giving man's mind a pre-eminent place in the universe. On the other hand, he was prepared, not only to suggest, as Descartes had done, that the moon was inhabited, but to fill the whole world with animate beings, postulating that 'all is living, all is animate', and quoting Hartsoeker's discovery of spermatazoa as evidence pointing in the same direction. Such remarks savour more of the hylopsychism of Cyrano than of Cartesian mechanism and it would be natural enough for the author of the *Entretiens sur la pluralité des mondes* to have been attracted by the ideas of the author of *L'autre Monde*. But Fontenelle's mind was essentially incredulous. Why otherwise should he have taken the trouble to adapt for the general public an erudite Latin work by a Dutch scholar A. van Dale on the history of oracles? The erudite world was absorbed by such topics at the time, it is true, and one can quote many dissertations on this subject and the kindred question of the prophecies of the Sybils,[1] but the fact that Fontenelle gave his time and literary talent to proving that the oracles did not cease at the birth of Christ, as the

[1] See below, p. 295, and P. Hazard, *La Crise de la conscience européenne*, Paris, 1935 iii, p. 73.

popular belief, commonly used as a proof of Christianity, maintained, can only mean one thing, namely that Fontenelle agreed with Lucretius in his attitude towards belief in unseen powers: oracles, prophecies, miracles, demons were all vulnerable to historical and rational criticism. The old scepticism, the scepticism which stemmed from Montaigne had sought to abase man's faculties and had been the antithesis of rationalism: Pascal had made great use of it in his apologetic work. With Fontenelle, on the other hand, scepticism and rationalism, far from being mutually exclusive, and far from constituting, as they had done for Pascal, a proof of man's dual and contradictory nature, were complementary and perfectly allied the one to the other. The catalytic agent was the Cartesian method, which Fontenelle looked upon as Descartes's greatest achievement. When Descartes stated that he would accept as true only what he clearly conceived to be true, or could deduce from what he clearly conceived to be true, he made explicit reference to geometry and had in mind the solution of problems such as the philosopher is called upon to tackle. Applied to historical and social questions, such an attitude of mind naturally produces mainly criticism. Applied in an unlimited field, Descartes's rational method becomes identified with a sceptical method, and this is precisely what Fontenelle, Pierre Bayle, Montesquieu, Voltaire, and many lesser scholars like Fréret and Dumarsais, proceeded to make of it. It was Voltaire who invented the term 'historical pyrrhonism', but long before Voltaire used it, the word 'pyrrhonisme' had come to mean a blend of rationalism and scepticism which we may refer to as 'radicalism'.

Rationalism in the field of literary doctrine and criticism worked against the acceptance of authority, just as it did in the philosophical domain. On this score there was no real division of opinion and however much the *Poetics* of Aristotle were quoted in literary controversies, there was general agreement to the effect that Aristotle was right, not because he was Aristotle but because he was reasonable. Authors, the dramatists particularly, accepted the literary theorists' contention that certain principles or rules could be devised in a rational manner, or by experience of stage and public, and that literary productions were subject to such laws by their very nature.[1] These laws related to the form of literary works and particularly to

[1] Consult, for the whole question, R. Bray, *La Formation de la doctrine classique*, Paris, 1927. Cf. my *Literature and the Sciences in the Age of Molière*, International Book Club, 1953, and R. C. Knight, *Racine, convention and classicism*, Swansea, 1952.

the conformity of the various parts to the whole, or the spirit and tone of the work to the audience it was intended for and of the characters and manners depicted in it and the originals, contemporary or taken from ancient poetry and history. An elaborate theory of suitability (propriety, verisimilitude) was worked out by such critics as the abbé d'Aubignac. Form itself was interpreted as meaning the actual structure of a work, the manner in which the 'fable' or subject was handled, and not the externals of literary ornament. Such a conception of form was much nearer to that of the new philosophy (whether Gassendist or Cartesian) than to the scholastic notion. The new philosophy concerned itself only with the disposition of the parts; such for it was 'form'. The literary critics gave an attention to the structure of works of literature such as had never been given before. The assumption that form *is* structure was common to both philosophers and critics.[1] In this respect, Gassendists and Cartesians were on common ground; the new philosophy as a whole was in conformity with classical criticism. But there arose towards the end of the century a controversy which carried some writers, Fontenelle and Charles Perrault especially, into a position in which a pronounced rationalism caused them to scorn that respect for the Ancients, those revered masters who had achieved a perfect imitation of nature, and caused them to flout what was, for their fellows and especially for Boileau, a conviction deeply embedded in feeling.

The dispute began in a committee which was set up in 1663 under the title 'Commission des inscriptions et médailles' and which finally developed into the Académie des Inscriptions et Belles-Lettres (the erudites' academy) in 1701. In 1673 the commission had to decide whether to use Latin or French for inscriptions to be placed on public monuments and opinion was divided on the subject. In 1676 the secretary of the Académie Française, François Charpentier, published a *Défense de la langue française* and in 1783 *L'Excellence de la langue française*, in which he declared that admiration for the ancients had been pushed to the point of superstition; he provoked a reply from Boileau, the *Discours sur le style des inscriptions* (1683). Four years later, at a meeting of the Académie Française, a poem by Charles Perrault was read entitled *Le Siècle de Louis le Grand*. Boileau showed great restlessness during the reading and replied with three epigrams in one of which he described his adversaries as

---

[1] Cf. my *Form and Structure : Cyrano de Bergerac's atomistic conception of metamorphosis* in *Science and Literature*, Oxford, 1955.

barbarians (*Topinambours*). He had the support of the philologists Ménage and Dacier and generally speaking those poets who, along with Boileau, had reacted against the shallow intellectualism and 'préciosité' of the Paris drawing-rooms and whose literary culture was profound—Racine, La Fontaine, Molière, La Bruyère, Chaulieu. The poets spoke in the name of good taste and literary judgment. Perrault and Fontenelle spoke in the name of reason and progress. The ladies were for the Moderns and Boileau railed against them in a bad-mannered Satire (the tenth, 1694). The defenders of the Moderns started an ill-advised campaign against Homer, ill-advised because its perpetrators had scant philological knowledge. Much ink flowed, but the arguments used on both sides were few. On the side of the Ancients they were very few, for the simple reason that Boileau and his supporters relied on their literary experience for the making of judgments. Fontenelle looked to the natural sciences for arguments to prove that men were no better, no stronger, no more handsome in the youth of the world and their brains were not fashioned differently from ours; the ancients had no advantages over us as far as natural gifts are concerned, and we have over them the advantage of long experience; we have profited by their mistakes. Fontenelle wrote off the debt of the Renaissance to the Ancient World. He placed his Golden Age in the future. He took up and developed the thesis of Descartes's sixth part of the *Discours de la méthode*: progress in knowledge is theoretically unlimited—provided always that governments favour the arts and sciences and the advance of civilization is not thwarted by wars and religious prejudice.[1] The 'Moderns' won the argument: their taste was bad and their literary knowledge insufficient, but they destroyed the last remnants of ancient authority.[2]

THE NATURAL SCIENTISTS

Descartes's most faithful disciples were to be found in the private houses where mathematicians and physicists met as private academies, the house of the abbé Bourdelot,[3] that of the lawyer Habert

---

[1] *Digression sur les anciens et les modernes*, 1688.

[2] For the whole controversy see H. Gillot, *La Querelle des anciens et des modernes*, Paris, 1914.

[3] In 1675 appeared Le Gallois' *Conversations de l'académie de M. l'abbé Bourdelot*. Le Gallois gives a list of the members: Dodart, Bailly, Rainsant, Monginot, Lisot, Thibaud, Guide, Tilleman, Tardif, Mermec, Denis (all doctors); Gallois, Auzout,

de Montmor, that of Thévenot,[1] that of Rohault, or the Hôtel de Belingan, where a professor of philosophy at the College de Navarre, named Marion, held a meeting every Thursday.[2]

Jacques Rohault (1620–75)[3] began his career as a private teacher of mathematics in Paris and was a very successful teacher in both the academic and the social senses of the term. The young princes of Condé were his private pupils and teachers from the colleges came to his lessons. His Wednesday meetings, at which he performed experiments and expounded Cartesian physics were an established institution in 1659. 'People of both sexes and all professions' attended them, not to mention many foreigners.[4] The first row was reserved for ladies. In 1667 Rohault organized a sort of Cartesian festival on the occasion of the return of Descartes's ashes from Sweden in 1666. His most important publication was his *Traité de physique* published in 1671. He was a Cartesian in the sense that most of his explanations were Cartesian, and in the sense that he was a warm partisan and defender of the master, nevertheless his methods as a scientist were not identical with those of Descartes. He laid more stress than Descartes had done on experimental, as against rational physics, or rather he combined the two by an altogether modern theory of scientific hypothesis and its place in scientific method. His practical bias may explain his profound respect for Aristotle and the pains he took to show that Aristotle

Pecquet, Borelli, Mariotte, Roberval, Justel, de Launay, Rohault, Cordemoy, Rouxel, Acar, Claquenelle, Fedé (a defensor acerrimus of Descartes), Garibal, de Loberie, de Montpoly, Glazer, Papé, Colin, de Vessière, Steno (Stensen), Boristius, Vormius, Philippeaux, Graaf, Andriano, Fogel, Gayen, Turbier, Bethereau, Morel, Juillet. No sect was given the preference, says Le Gallois, and Aristotle was respected as well as Gassendi and Descartes, but he also gives an account of a debate in which an Aristotelian rejected the scholastic interpretation of Aristotle and claimèd him to be a physicist (or physician) rather than a metaphysician and far more in accordance with Descartes than was usually believed. Such a statement is revealing.

[1] Stensen entitled his dissertation on the anatomy of the brain *Discours de M. Stenon sur l'anatomie du cerveau, à Messieurs de l'académie qui se fait chez M. Thévenot*, Paris, 1669. This discourse is a criticism of Descartes's description of the brain.

[2] Patin never missed these meetings, according to Le Gallois. Marion's reputation survived until the time of Helvétius, who wrote in *De l'Homme*: 'M. Marion, régent de philosophie au Collège de Navarre a soutenu que toutes les opérations de l'esprit s'expliquent par le seul mouvement des esprits animaux et les traces imprimées dans la mémoire. D'où il suit que les esprits animaux mis en mouvement par les objets extérieurs pourraient produire en nous des idées indépendamment de ce qu'on appelle l'âme.' (London, 1773, vol. i, sect. ii, p. 105.)

[3] For the Cartesian physicists consult P. Mouy, *Le Développement de la physique cartésienne*, Paris, 1934.

[4] Clerselier, Preface to Rohault's *Œuvres posthumes*, Paris, 1690.

was not responsible for many notions, including that of 'substantial forms' which the schools had fathered on him. Rohault's treatise of physics had a long run of success. It was not adopted by the schools, but its many editions show that the general public took to it. It was also used at Cambridge until it was displaced by Newton's *Principia Mathematica*.

A doctor from Saumur, Louis de La Forge (?——?), co-editor with Clerselier of *L'Homme* (1664), undertook, in his *Traité de l'esprit de l'homme* (1666) to complete Descartes's description of man by discussing the relationship of soul and body. Taking one of the articles of Descartes's *Principia philosophiae* (Part II, Art. 36) as his starting point, he tried to show that the cause of this union is to be looked for on the level of the First Cause and not on the level of second causes. God is the only true cause; the union of soul and body is to be found in God.

G. de Cordemoy (1620–84), a lawyer, later to become a member of the Académie Française, proceeded on similar lines in his *Discernement du corps et de l'âme*, published in 1666. But Cordemoy took an independent stand on a fundamental question of physics. He denied the divisibility of matter to infinity and accepted the existence of atoms on the purely rational ground that matter would not be a substance if it was divisible to infinity; it would be nothing at all or mere space. For the rest he was as rigorously mechanistic as Descartes in his explanations, which he reduced to terms of the position and transposition of particles.

In the last decade of the century the leader of the Cartesians was Pierre-Sylvain Régis (1632–1707), a pupil of Rohault, who sent him off in 1665 to give a course of lectures at Toulouse where he made a great stir with lectures delivered in French to a popular audience. Then for a time he gave private lessons to the marquis de Vardes, probably at Aigues-Mortes, before resuming his public teaching, this time at Montpellier. In 1680 he returned to Paris and lectured with great success at the house of the chemist Lémery in the rue Galande, until, six months later, he was asked by the archbishop of Paris to suspend his course, 'out of deference to the old philosophy' (according to Fontenelle). Ten years later he published a complete treatise of philosophy in which his physics were framed in a system of logic, metaphysics and morals. Régis reduced Cartesian metaphysics to a very simple doctrine: he is a thinking being; the idea he has of God as a perfect Being proves the existence of God; the idea he has of the external world proves the existence of the external world; the order and arrangement of the world are an added proof of God's existence; man is a mind united to a body; body and soul are united by the will of God; the mind subsists after the death of the body because its knowledge of itself and of God do not depend on the body: so much can philosophy assure us of, but no more; the rewards and punishments awaiting us in a future life are a matter for religion, not for philosophy.

Régis's metaphysics contain the minimum of psychism necessary to prevent his physics from developing into a thorough-going mechanistic materialism—the distinction between consciousness and extension and the existence of God as a perfect Being and as the Maker of the world. These were the two positions around which conflict was to be most severe in the coming years. He made no distinction, as did Descartes, between an idea and a mental image, or, as Descartes expressed the difference in his reply to Hobbes's objections, between the 'form' of an idea and its 'content'. Ideas for Régis were representations or voluntary abstractions. The idea of extension was a representation of a real extension in the outside world. On this question the Cartesian school split; Regis, supported by the theologian Arnauld, simplified Descartes's theory of ideas; the Oratorians Malebranche and Bernard Lamy developed it; on the one side the tendency was towards 'Aristotelian' realism (the realism of the outside world), on the other the tendency was towards 'Platonic' realism (the realism of the intellectual world). The two sides joined issues, in the *Journal des savants*, on the question of why the moon appears smaller at the zenith than when low down in the sky. For Régis it was a simple matter of perception; the moon's disk was made larger on the horizon by the refraction of its light in low-lying vapours: for Malebranche it was a question of judgment; the impression we receive from the outside world is the same in both cases, but when we see the moon on the horizon, the long distance which seems to separate us from it and the presence of houses and other objects in the field of vision lead us to judge that it is bigger than when we see it high in the sky. For Régis, the further off a thing is, the smaller it seems: there is no other term of reference beside the retinal image. For Malebranche the distant object does not seem smaller because the mind constantly judges its size according to the distance. For Régis we have only one vision of the outside world; it is the one we have by virtue of our bodily organs; there are only two factors concerned in the operation, the thing in the outside world and the image corresponding to it in us. For Malebranche, on the other hand, we see 'in God' the Idea of the outside world. The Idea is purely intellectual: it is the object of geometrical and other mathematical contemplation; we also have an image in our imagination and this is a mere appearance. We see a round disk in the imagination, but the circle we see in God.

Rohault, La Forge, Cordemoy, Régis and Malebranche were all philosophers and teachers rather than scientists in the modern sense. They ranged over a wide field and did not concentrate on providing new knowledge and new techniques. The majority of mathematicians, physicists and physiologists, while sharing with Descartes his general attitude of rational inquiry, were not prepared to treat him as an authority in the old sense, after following him in rejecting authorities. On specific issues they had no compunction about proving him to be wrong. Descartes had his defenders, it is true, ready to fight in the last ditch on scientific issues such as the theory of magnetic attraction, the laws of motion, the cause of the tides,[1] but Huyghens, Mariotte, Castelet, Leibniz all contradicted Descartes when observation and calculation proved him to be wrong. They were true to the spirit which animated Descartes in that they believed that there *are* laws of motion, that the phenomena of nature *are* capable of rational explanation, but they rapidly outstripped him as far as actual inquiry was concerned. One of his most radical critics was also one of the first, Blaise Pascal. As impatient of authority in scientific matters as was Descartes himself,[2] and respectful of experience, Pascal practised a kind of positivism as though by instinct. He treated Descartes's 'subtle matter' with no more respect than if it had been a scholastic 'form'. He was not prepared to suppose that the space above the mercury in Toricelli's tube was full of 'subtle matter' because, according to Descartes's principles, the sides of the tube *must* touch if there is nothing between them. Working in this positive spirit he could criticize Descartes correctly on specific points; on the other hand he was incapable of the constructive and systematic thinking which made of his rival a great philosopher. Another contemporary, the mathematician Roberval,

[1] La Montre on the theory of magnetic attraction (*Journal des savants*, 4 August 1696); Le N. on cause of tides (ibid., 23 Feb. 1699); Catelan on the laws of motion (*Nouvelles de la République des Lettres*, various letters in 1686–7).
[2] See the preface he intended for a *Traité du vide*, written probably in 1647.

went so far in the direction of positivism that he ended up in steril
and disparaging criticism of his contemporaries' work.[1]

Christian Huyghens was far more open to Cartesian influence an
made use of characteristically Cartesian theories, such as the ex
planation of gravity by means of a flux of subtle matter round th
earth, but he was an independent observer and calculator. Hi
telescope enabled him to see the rings of Saturn; his observation c
Jupiter's satellites enabled him, along with the Dane Roemer, t
prove against Descartes that light is not propagated instantaneously
If the time of observation of the satellite's entry into and exit from
the planet's shadow varies (and it *does*) according to the position c
the earth on its orbit, then light takes varying lengths of time t
reach the earth in its various positions. In accordance with th
Englishmen Wrenn and Wallis, he corrected Descartes's laws o
percussion (*Journal des savants*, 1669). He was a Cartesian critic c
Descartes, for whom Descartes showed the way 'by his very errors'.

The Academy of Sciences founded in 1666 was organized aroun
a group of mathematicians all (except Roberval) animated by th
desire to apply geometry to physics. In the sense that it share
Descartes's ambition, the Academy can be called Cartesian, but i
had no intention of being Cartesian in the strict sense. One of it
earliest members, Mariotte, talked of the 'sectarians' when referrin
to the strict Cartesians and showed himself ready to call upon suc
notions as 'sympathy' and 'attraction' in his study of gravity, al
though such terms were entirely ruled out by Cartesian principle
and looked upon as relics of the old, non-mechanistic physics.[3]

At this point in the debate the historians of scientific though
introduce Isaac Newton whose *Principia mathematica* appeared i
1687, but for us Newton must be excluded for the time being as th
impact of his new mathematical physics was not felt until after th
turn of the century and the educated public remained in ignoranc
of him until Voltaire's *Lettres philosophiques*. The *Principia mathe
matica* proved eventually to be the most damaging attack of all, bu

[1] P. Mouy, *Le Développement de la physique cartésienne*, p. 182.

[2] Preface to the *Traité de la lumière*, 1690; Mouy, op. cit., p. 204.

[3] L'abbé Edme Mariotte (1620–84), *Discours de la nature de l'air* in *Essais de physiq*
(1676). Mariotte's essays are essays in the use of the experimental method. He also wro
a Logic, in which he attempted to combine reason and experience and has an interestir
section on probability (*vraisemblance*). It also contains a sketch of an Ethics, in whic
reason and the experience of social life are combined in the notion of decorum. (*Ess
de logique*, published anonymously in 1678, and in *Œuvres*, Leyden, 1717, t. ii.) C
above, p. 135.

the triumph of Cartesian physics in the public mind in Paris came after the publication of Newton's book in Cambridge and in the twenties of the eighteenth century the abbé de Molières (an Oratorian) was still defending Descartes against Newton at the Collège de France (the Royal College). The *Journal des savants* (2 August 1688), while admitting that the *Principia mathematica* contained a 'perfect' study of the laws of motion, brushed aside the rest as a purely arbitrary system of the world and not a real physics, misunderstanding Newton's modest assertion that he merely wished to present to his reader a set of general propositions which could account for the particular facts of observation. The *Journal des savants* misunderstood this modest positivism as a renunication of all claim to be describing the real world. No further article followed and the *Journal* continued to mis-spell Newton's name as Neuthon as late as 1691.[1]

Leibniz, on the other hand, established immediate contact with the French intellectual public by using the *Journal des savants* regularly from 1675 onwards, as a medium for criticizing Descartes and for putting forward his own theories. It cannot be said that his articles produced any widespread reaction, and his publications remained fragmentary,[2] but his contribution to the debate in Paris was direct from the first. His first memoir, presented to the Académie des Sciences in 1670 when he was twenty-four, under the title *Theoria motus abstracti*, already shows a tendency to make the distinction between geometry and physics which Descartes tried to eliminate. A physical point is not the same as a geometrical point; a physical point may have direction without actually being in motion; it may have an incipient motion, a *conatus*. Such a quality, whatever it may be, cannot be expressed in geometrical terms, because it is not a question of position only. Leibniz is prepared to use psychological terms in order to speak of it; he is already looking for a means of putting back into nature the psychical activity which Descartes had removed therefrom. Many years previously Gassendi and Beeckmann had discussed the possibility of taking elasticity in bodies as the most rudimentary form of psychical activity. Leibniz proposes to give the same rôle to *conatus*.[3] In Paris, where he stayed

---

[1] For the introduction of Newtonianism into France consult P. Brunet, *L'Introduction des théories de Newton en France au 18e siècle, avant 1738*, Paris, 1931.

[2] Cf. W. H. Barber, *Leibniz in France from Arnauld to Voltaire*, Oxford, 1955, chap. iii, 'Leibniz and the French public 1670–1716.'

[3] Cf. above, p. 86. 'Omne enim corpus est mens momentanea seu carens recordatione, quia conatum simul suum et alienum contrarium ... non retinet ultra momentum;

from 1672 to 1676 and where he was admitted to the Académie des Sciences in 1675, Leibniz continued to develop his study of infinitesimally small quantities into an 'infinitesimal calculus' and also found time to copy Descartes's manuscripts and carry on a controversy with Malebranche, whose *Recherche de la vérité* appeared in 1674–5. The subject was once more the relation of geometry to physics. Malebranche, faithful to Descartes, refused to distinguish between space and matter, except to look upon matter as parts of space which are constantly being transposed. His conceptions were purely geometrical. Leibniz argued that one cannot logically proceed from 'space' to 'parts of space' without taking into account a certain 'requisite', which is the motion of the agent which cuts up the space into parts. He was not satisfied with Descartes's principle that what can be clearly conceived is fully intelligible. 'Parts of space' can be clearly conceived, but not 'adequately' conceived. 'Adequate' conception includes all that is necessary to produce a being, its 'requisites'. Everything, apart from God, comes into being and can only be adequately understood through its genesis. God alone is absolute in the sense that there is nothing prior to him, nothing posterior, either in logic or in time.

Leibniz went on, in his *Brevis demonstratio*, published in the *Acta Eruditorum* of Leipzig in 1686 and translated in Bayle's *Nouvelles de la République des lettres*[1] in the same year, to criticize Descartes's laws of motion, but by now it was no longer a mere question of correcting Descartes: a new system was taking shape. The Cartesian law according to which the quantity of motion remains the same after, as before, any operation of nature is replaced by the more general statement that there is always a perfect equation between the full cause and the full effect, a law which excludes any influence of the mind upon the body and in particular that influence admitted by Descartes himself, who allowed for the *direction* taken by the flow of animal spirits in the brain to be subject to the intervention of the will.

ergo caret memoria, caret sensu actionum passionumque suarum, caret cogitatione.' (*Philosophischen Schriften* ed. Gerhardt, 1880, iv, p. 230, paragraph 17.)

[1] *Démonstration courte d'une erreur considérable de M. Descartes et de quelques autres touchant une loi de la nature selon laquelle ils soutiennent que Dieu conserve toujours dans la matière la même quantité de mouvement, de quoi ils abusent même dans la mécanique.* It is in this essay that Leibniz demonstrated that the correct formula for representing what was constant was not 'size' (=mass) multiplied by velocity (mv), but 'size' multiplied by the square of the velocity (mv^2), a 'something' which could only be represented mathematically and which, as Leibniz candidly admitted, resembled the 'forms' of the old philosophy.

The *Journal des savants* was again the medium in which Leibniz gave a much fuller sketch of his ideas in 1696. His article was entitled *Système nouveau de la nature et de la communication des substances, aussi bien que de l'union qu'il y a entre l'âme et le corps*. He explained how he had first of all been attracted by atomism, but finding that the notion of atoms was incapable of explaining any sort of unity (an aggregation of atoms not making a united thing), he had been obliged to reintroduce the scholastic notion of 'form' and take as his 'unit of substance', not the material atoms of the Epicureans, but 'formal atoms', endowed, even at the lowest level, with a certain 'perfection' in the Aristotelian sense, a perfection which he himself intends to refer to as a 'primitive force'; these 'formal atoms' (which at a higher level in the scale of being are to be called souls) may be looked upon as eternal precisely in the same way that 'the atoms of Gassendi' are looked upon as eternal. Had not Swammerdam explained that the germs of animals are pre-existent in the sperm? Why should not one suppose that, at death, an animal's soul remains associated with a minute body, the gross parts of the animal's body having been cast off? In that case, the succession of generations would be a succession of metamorphoses, different organs of the same animal being developed in a series of periods of activity. Atoms of substance (the term 'monad' is not used in this essay) 'have something vital and a kind of perception' and mirror more or less clearly in themselves the whole universe. But how is one to conceive of any relationship existing between them, seeing that they are individual substances and therefore not dependent on each other in any way? The answer is that there are no relations between them: God has so ordered the world that they act in complete harmony with each other, just as though they acted upon each other. In a similar manner God has so ordered the world that perceptions and acts of will appear in the soul at the exact moments when they coincide with the various purely mechanical motions which take place in the body. This explanation gives 'a marvellous idea of the harmony of the universe'.

The *Système nouveau* does not seem to have caused any considerable stir in French opinion. One reply only was published in the *Journal des savants*. It came from Samuel Foucher, a fideist and defender of the agnosticism of the ancient academics. Foucher pointed out that Leibniz had not explained why perception was to be attributed to his units of substance and further wondered why

God should have squandered so much ingenuity on inventing a system in which it appeared, quite wrongly, that there was communication between individual beings: and between the soul and the body. Bodies would not be necessary at all in such a scheme of things. It was wiser to admit our ignorance in such matters.[1] The more God could create, replied Leibniz, the better; it is better that the perceptions we have should correspond to something outside us, even though there is no connection between our minds and that something, except through the laws of harmony. In ordinary parlance it is right to speak of the action of one thing upon another, provided it is admitted that such action may only be understood by postulating the system of 'pre-established harmony' (if he may be allowed to use such a term). Descartes can give no help here because of the error he committed with regard to the laws of motion. He was wrong in thinking that the direction of the motion of the animal spirits in the brain may be changed by the will without breaking the law of nature which states that the amount of motive force remains constant in any operation. If Descartes's conception of the unity of body and soul is false, how then shall we conceive of that unity?[2]

Leibniz used the *Journal des savants* constantly during the nineties as a medium for criticizing Descartes. In the numbers dated 18 June 1691 and 5 January 1693 he argued that to take extension as being the essence of matter is to make it quite impossible to explain why bodies have a natural resistance to motion, a natural inertia. In the number dated 13 April 1693 he published a letter to the abbé Nicaise accusing the Cartesians of having failed to add anything useful to the work of the master and berating Descartes himself for his shortcomings, the paralogisms which mar his metaphysics, his lack of knowledge of chemistry, his mistaken laws of motion. More serious for the Cartesians was the accusation, contained in the same letter, that they had turned men away from the contemplation of God's goodness by excluding final causes from scientific inquiry and making it appear, as did Hobbes and Spinoza, that all things possible either were, had been or would be, to the exclusion of God's providence. It was on the last point only that a Cartesian reply was forthcoming, at least publicly: Descartes had removed final causes from physics (*Principia*, I, 28), but not from

---

[1] *Journal des savants*, 12 September 1695. Bayle also pointed out that bodies would not be necessary in Leibniz's world. (See below, p. 233.)

[2] *Journal des savants*, 2 April and 9 April 1696.

morals (*Principia*, III, 3).[1] Leibniz countered with profuse expressions of admiration for Descartes and the affirmation that physics must ask the question *why*? as well as the question *how*?[2] He was by this time prepared to give two parallel and independent accounts of the workings of nature, the one purely mechanistic in terms of efficient causes only and the other purely psychical in terms of final causes only. He was by now well outside the Cartesian orbit.

THE PHYSIOLOGISTS AND DOCTORS: MECHANISM AND MATERIALISM

In the medical sciences discoveries were being made so fast, by observers armed with the miscroscope, that systematic thinking was more likely to prove a hindrance than a help, and a measure of eclecticism or positivism was forced upon the physiologists and doctors by the very nature of their studies. All through the century, physiologists such as Harvey, Glisson, Hooke, Wharton, Mayow, Willis in England, Aselli, Malpighi, Wirsung, Borelli, Bellini, Stensen in Italy, Pitcairn, Leeuwenhoek, Hartsoeker, Swammerdam in Holland, Rudbeck in Sweden, Pecquet, Vieussens, Verduc in France accumulated exact information. Descartes's *L'Homme* was years out of date when finally it appeared in 1664. The *Journal des savants* received it along with Willis's *Cerebri anatome* in 1665 (5 January and 12 January) and clearly preferred the latter work, which it classified under 'Medicine', while *L'Homme* was relegated to the section 'Philosophy'.

Nevertheless, two main systematic tendencies existed and were taken account of, namely the iatrophysical and the iatrochemical. J. C. Barchusen, in his *Historia medicinae* (Amsterdam, 1710) counted Craanen, Bellini, Pitcairn, Baglivi, Guglielmini, Thomson, Freind and Boerhaave amongst the 'mechanists' or 'geometers', and Paracelsus, Van Helmont, Severino, Crollius, Tachenius, Sylvius (Dubois) and Willis amongst the 'chemists'. The mechanical analogy was certainly of great assistance to Borelli, Bellini, Stensen, Pitcairn and Pecquet in their inquiries into muscular action, digestion, secretions and respiration, while at the same time leading them into error, as when Borelli affirmed that the effect of air in the lungs is to

[1] By Régis, *Journal des savants*, 17 June 1697.
[2] Leibniz said that he received many replies privately (ibid., 19 August 1697) and also mentions replies 'in the French papers' (ibid.).

transmit to the blood a delicate vibration regulating the rhythm of bodily operations like the pendulum of a clock.[1] The frequency with which the word 'mechanically', or its equivalents, appears in the titles of works by doctors towards the end of the seventeenth century and at the beginning of the eighteenth is evidence of the great popularity of the method, long after it had begun to cause trouble on the forefront of research.[2] Hartsoeker's discovery of living germs in the sperm of male animals upset the mechanical theories of reproduction, but many still held to the mechanical theory, G. Lamy, Verduc and Ango amongst them. Hartsoeker's discovery led to the formulation of a wild hypothesis known as the 'emboîtement des germes'. It was proposed by Swammerdam, accepted by Malebranche and considered favourably by Leibniz. It was a sort of application of the idea of the infinitely small to embryology. The complete animal was supposed to be ready formed in the germ and to contain within itself its own offspring ready formed and so on indefinitely. In 1710 the *Journal des savants* was still balancing the merits of a purely mechanical theory against the 'emboîtement' theory.[3] Mechanics also played a big part in the study of digestion and the process was

[1] M. Foster gives a clear account of these developments in his *Lectures on the History of Physiology*, Cambridge, 1901.

[2] Some examples: *Nouveau Cours de médecine, ou selon les principes de la nature et des mécaniques on apprend le corps de l'homme*, Paris, 1669; *Explication nouvelle et mécanique des actions animales* (by D. Duncan), Paris, 1678; *Explication mécanique et physique des fonctions de l'âme sensitive . . .* (by G. Lamy), Paris, 1678; *Nouvelle explication mécanique des fièvres* (by Landouillette), Paris, 1679; *La Chimie naturelle ou l'explication chimique et mécanique de la nourriture de l'animal* (by D. Duncan), Paris, 1691; *Histoire de l'animal ou la connaissance du corps animé par la mécanique et par la chimie . . .* (by D. Duncan), Paris, 1687; *De corporis humani machina* (by Herfelt), Leyden, 1688; *Traité des vapeurs ou leur origine, leurs effets et les remèdes sont mécaniquement expliqués* (by Lange), Paris, 1689; *De motu cordis mechanicum theorema* (by Scaramuccius), 'Senogalliae', 1689; *Nouvelle Ostéologie où l'on explique mécaniquement la formation et la nourriture des os* (by Verduc), Paris, 1693 (2nd edn.); *Essais d'anatomie où l'on explique clairement la construction des organes et leurs opérations mécaniques* (by Beddévole), Leyden, 1686; *Traité des aliments . . . suivant les principes chimiques et mécaniques* (by Lémery), Paris, 1702; *Explication physique et mécanique des effets de la saignée* (by Hecquet), Paris, 1706; *La Médecine dogmatique mécanique . . .* (by Bellefontaine), Amsterdam, 1712. In 1707 the *Journal des savants* reviewed a *Mechanical Account of the non-naturals*, published in London, and in 1708 a *Mechanical Account of Poisons . . .* (by Richard Mead). One can add a chapter entitled *Mécanique des animaux* in C. Perrault's *Traité de Physique*, Paris, 1680, and a *Tractatus physio-medicus de homine in quo status ejus . . . mechanice demonstratur* by Th. Craanen (*Opera*, t. i, Antwerp, 1689).

[3] *Journal des savants*, 3 February 1710, in a review of a book published in Upsala which supported the 'emboîtement' theory against the purely mechanistic theory expounded by Descartes in an essay published along with *L'Homme* in 1664 under the title *Traité de la formation du fœtus*.

looked upon as one of trituration or grinding, but by 1710 it took a somewhat cranky man to look upon the stomach only as a mill. Such a person was P. Hecquet, who had already cut a comic figure by proposing draughts of cold water and copious blood-lettings as the cure for all ailments, to such an extent that Lesage chose him as the model of his ridiculous doctor Sangrado in his *Gil Blas*. He added further ridicule to his name by an obstinate defence of trituration against Vieussens and Astruc.[1] In 1704, the *Journal des savants* expressed itself as follows on the popularity of mechanistic explanations:

One hears of nothing else nowadays in the schools of philosophy and amongst scientists (*savants*) except mechanistic physics; there is hardly a physicist (*physicien*) who is not engaged in explaining mechanically the phenomena of nature, which are the changes one sees taking place in the universe; but each one does it in his own manner; some believe it is sufficient to explain each phenomenon by the shape and the arrangement of the particles of each body. Others go further; they employ in their explanations the rules of mechanics, that is to say the knowledge we have of each part of mechanics, which deal with motive forces. Others think they have caught the secret of mechanical explanation because they have discovered, or suppose, that each brute only moves as does a machine with a spring: finally some modern doctors claim to explain the maladies of the human body by a certain mechanics of the constituent principles of the mass of the blood, which are, according to them, salts and sulphurs of different kinds.[2]

The chief rival of the analogy of the machine was that of fermentation in a wine vat. This analogy had always been used by doctors, but it had been given considerable development by Van Helmont (1577–1644) who had introduced into physiology the system of the alchemist Paracelsus. Far from explaining the processes of the body by the laws of mechanics, Van Helmont looked upon each operation as being presided over by an 'archaeus' or a 'blas' (both spiritual principles), working on the bodily organs by the agency of an active material 'spirit' or 'ferment'. Coming into contact with its rival, the notion of fermentation looked for a time as

---

[1] *Explication physique et mécanique des effets de la saignée, par rapport à la transpiration, ou traduction d'une thèse soutenue aux écoles de médecine de Paris*, Paris, 1706; *De la Digestion et des maladies de l'estomac suivant le système de la trituration et du broiement sans l'aide des levains ou de la fermentation*, Paris, 1711.

[2] *Journal des savants*, 1 September 1704, in a review of (Peyssonel's) *Histoire de la machine du monde ou physique mécanique par le sieur C.P., docteur en médecine*, Marseilles, 1704.

though it would be annexed by it, the general influence of the 'new philosophy' being to impose upon all the physical sciences a premature reduction to mechanics. It is significant that the *Journal des savants*, reviewing a complete edition of the works of Van Helmont published in 1707 should have reduced the 'archaei' to 'animal spirits' in a few sentences.

The chemist Lémery's attempt to apply mechanics to chemistry was very thorough-going and the deceptive clarity which he thus introduced into chemistry doubtless explains why his public lectures were so popular around 1670.[1] Lémery explained fermentation by the penetration of pointed acid particles into porous alkaline ones; fermentation was thus reduced, like all the other operations of nature, to terms of figure and motion.

The physiologists Duncan, Froment,[2] Caufapé and Rouvière all reduced fermentation to mechanics. Duncan was both a chemist and a Cartesian. Froment explained all illness by acid ferments 'according to the principles of M. Descartes'. 'When the matter of the third element is surrounded by subtle matter, there occurs a fermentation,' wrote the *Journal des savants* in summarizing his book (10 January 1695). Caufapé reduced the fermentation of fever to the motion of particles, some of which are too big, some too small, others too pointed, other too stagnant, but was not sufficiently under the influence of mechanistic thinking to believe that by purging and bleeding one can get rid of these unwelcome particles from the human frame. 'Fifty years ago,' he commented, 'nature was looked upon as a healing force; nowadays one relies on purgings and bloodlettings; the doctor's part should be to help nature to effect a cure, not to oppose her; fever may produce ill effects by causing a too great rarefaction of the spirits, but it is not of itself an ill, it is nature's attempt to get rid of illness.'[3] Rouvière, an apothecary, applied Cartesian principles to chemistry in his *Réflexions sur la fermentation et sur la nature du feu* (Paris, 1708). According to him, fermentation was a violent motion of the particles of a solid immersed in a liquid. Such theories had no future in them; they are interesting only in as

[1] Fontenelle says they were a great popular success (*Eloge de Lémery*); they were published in 1675 under the title *Cours de Chimie*, Paris.

[2] N. Froment, *Hypothèse raisonnée dans laquelle on fait voir que la cause des fièvres, et généralement de toutes les autres maladies vient des levains acres ou salés qui se rencontrent dans les premières voies, le tout expliqué sur les principes du célèbre M. Descartes et confirmé de l'expérience des meilleurs practiciens*, Paris, 1694.

[3] *Nouvelle explication des fièvres*, Toulouse, 1697.

much as they show to what extent mechanics invaded the other physical sciences. The most noted teacher of medicine in the early years of the eighteenth century, Hermann Boerhaave of Leyden (1668–1738), whose *Institutiones medicae* (1708) were for many years the common text-book of the schools of medicine, was cautious and eclectic. He made use of anatomy, physics and chemistry, without allowing any one of these sciences to exclude the others. He tried to reconcile the conflicting doctrines held by his contemporaries. His explanation of digestion was that it was partly a solution by means of the saliva, the gastric juice, the pancreatic juice and the bile, partly a mechanical squeezing out of juices from the food and partly an incipient fermentation. This doctrine was still taught fifty years later by Albrecht von Haller, the most influential teacher of the middle years of the eighteenth century. But although eclectic as a teacher of medicine, Boerhaave has the reputation of audacious thinking as a philosopher. He was said to explain the faculties of the rational soul mechanically and to reject 'metaphysical' causes from natural philosophy. He passed for being a Spinozist. One of his pupils was Offroi de la Mettrie, the future author of *l'Homme machine*, who was, however, a vitalist, in spite of the seemingly dogmatic statement of mechanistic materialism in the title of his book.

At the beginning of the century, a doctor of Montpellier named Maubec and a doctor of Niort named Gaultier were far more thorough-going in their materialism, and so was the English doctor, William Coward, whose work was reviewed by the *Journal des savants*, but all three added to their materialism an equally thorough-going fideism. In various manuscript treatises which circulated in the early and middle years of the eighteenth century the fideistic counterpart of materialistic theories was lacking.[1]

■Maubec published a book entitled *Principes physiques de la raison et des passions de l'homme* at Paris in 1709. He reached his materialist position by a criticism and rejection of Descartes's 'thinking substance', leaving only the other of Descartes's two substances, the

---

[1] *L'âme matérielle* and *Les Opinions des anciens sur la nature de l'âme* (see above, p. 124); *Les Arguments du pyrrhonisme* (Douai 702, later than 1726); *Réflexions sur l'existence de l'âme et sur l'existence de Dieu* (Arsenal 2557, Fécamp 12, Bordeaux 828); *Lettres sur la religion, sur l'âme humaine et sur l'existence de Dieu* (Mazarine 1183); *Dissertation sur la formation du monde* (Mazarine 1168); *Essais sur les facultés de l'âme* (Mazarine 1192); *Dialogues sur l'âme* (Mazarine 1191), a late work seeing that it refers to 'tous les Encyclopédistes'; the *Testament* of Jean Meslier (copies in most public libraries). Cf. below, pp. 277-79.

'extended substance', but he proposed to endow this 'extended substance' with other properties than extension and, in particular, thought. His reason was that Descartes had failed to prove that 'thought' is a separate, immaterial, substance. Thought may well be a property of matter; we do not know what the properties of matter are. A child is not a thinking being when it is in its mother's womb; it begins to think after birth, when the first impulses reach its brain from the outside world by way of the nerves. God has associated thoughts with certain flexions of the fibres of the brain; we do not know how. All ideas come through sensation; *nihil est in intellectu quod prius non fuerit in sensu.* Impressions are made on the brain as on a tablet of wax. Some are pleasant, others unpleasant: hence the child's first passions of desire and aversion. The flow of spirits leaves traces on the brain and when the spirits flow again along those traces the impressions which made them are revived and awaken others in contiguous traces. What we call judgment is a very similar process; it is a juxtaposition of impressions. A child's first judgments are very liable to error, but experience makes them more reliable. Clear ideas are merely vivid impressions. Reasoning is merely the uniting of ideas. It is possible to make rules for the guidance of our reason, but our reason can never set itself up against the scriptures or the decisions of the Church as a criterion of truth. Maubec ends up in a sceptical fideism reminiscent of the early seventeenth century, for all his materialism and sensationism.

Gaultier was a doctor of Niort, who used as a motto the *Talis est religio medici* of Sir Thomas Browne. He published in 1714, at Niort, a *Réponse en forme de dissertation à un théologien qui demande ce que veulent dire les sceptiques qui cherchent la vérité partout dans la nature, comme dans les écrits des philosophes, lorsqu'ils pensent que la vie et la mort sont la même chose, où l'on voit que la vie et la mort des minéraux, des métaux, des plantes et des animaux, avec tous ces attributs ne sont que des façons d'être de la même substance, à laquelle ces modifications n'ajoutent rien.*[1] This work was published with the approbation of the 'gardien du couvent des Cordeliers de la ville de Niort' and the professor of philosophy Verdin, a Minim friar. Nevertheless it was circulated as a clandestine treatise under the title *Nouvelle Philosophie sceptique par M.G. . . . médecin à . . . ou réponse à un théologien sur l'argument des sceptiques qui pensent que la vie et la mort sont la même*

---

[1] Bibliothèque nationale, R. 25743. I. Wade did not identify this work (*The Clandestine Organization of Philosophic Thought*, p. 257).

chose[1] and a partial copy was made under the title *La Parité de la vie et de la mort*.[2] The unknown copyist who summarized Gaultier's book did not fail to compare him with Spinoza (in spite of the fact that he spends some time refuting Spinoza) because he is content with one substance and refuses to admit the reality of any immaterial substance. They both attribute everything to nature, adds the copyist; the only difference between them is that Gaultier submits to the Church and Spinoza does not. Gaultier is a materialist without being an atomist. He does not refute Gassendi with the same disdain as he refutes Descartes and Malebranche, but he is careful to point out that Gassendi cannot explain how insensitive atoms make sensitive souls and concludes that it is not necessary to know the real nature of matter. His scepticism takes the form of positivism. We do not know the outside world except by the impressions we receive through the senses, and much of what we attribute to the real world is, mere illusion, nothingness, modes of our own feeling. There is a strong pessimistic, nominalistic flavour in Gaultier's work. Only the present is real; neither past nor future have any reality. Our knowledge of the world is scanty. But we gain nothing by multiplying essences unnecessarily. There is no contradiction in thinking that an extended substance can be intelligent. We need only assume one constantly changing substance of which we see the outward appearances: air, water, earth are all modes of this one substance and life and death are but outward appearances having no reality. There is no transcendental morality. Man owes his origin to no one, but he is weak and must combine with his fellows. The foundation of all law is the necessity for keeping the given word and this principle has its source in our own hearts, in the self-respect which prevents us from deceiving others: to deceive a man is to make oneself the inferior of that man. One cannot establish the existence of God by reason. To say that the world must have a creator is no proof. Why should God, having existed from all eternity, suddenly create a world unworthy of himself? Yet, in spite of all, Gaultier submits to the Church and abandons all his reasoning in an act of faith.

The English doctor, William Coward, resembled Gaultier in that his books were compendia of free-thought, yet he himself believed not merely in the existence of God but even in the resurrection of the body on the last day. One of his books, the *Ophthalmoiatria* (London, 1706) was given a long review by the *Journal des savants*.

---

[1] Arsenal Library, no. 2239.　　　　[2] Mazarine Library, no. 1192.

In it, as in his other publications, he declared that the Cartesian conception of an immaterial substance was stupid and that life and judgment were powers infused by God into matter.[1] Judgment is a power attached to the brain and is exercised upon the impressions which are transmitted to it from the outside world by the nerves. The reviewer called Coward's opinions extraordinary, but there is no evidence of their having aroused his ire. The *Ophthalmoiatria* was in Latin and was thus accessible to the French intellectual public, but there seems to have been no other reaction to it than the *Journal des savants*'s review. Two years previously the *Nouvelles de la république des lettres* (May 1704, p. 596) had noted that Coward's *Second Thoughts concerning Souls* had been burnt by order of the English Parliament, but there is no evidence to indicate that England was yet looked upon as the home of materialistic philosophers. Locke's works had been translated,[2] and the *Journal des savants* identified the argument that matter may be capable of thought as being Locke's argument (10 September 1703), but the passage from the *Essay on Human Understanding* which Voltaire was later to pick out and highlight[3] can hardly be said to have created a stir. The

---

[1] The *Journal des savants* commented as follows: 'Sa métaphysique n'est pas ordinaire. Cette âme, cette substance spirituelle ou immatérielle que l'on place dans le cerveau, et à qui l'on commet la direction de beaucoup de mouvements qui appartiennent à l'économie animale, lui paraît une pure chimère, une opinion ridicule indigne d'un philosophe et d'un chrétien, et peu éloignée du blasphème; car il prétend que l'immatérialité est un attribut qui ne convient qu'à Dieu seul . . . c'est uniquement au cerveau que Dieu a donné la faculté de juger des différents objets qui frappent ce principe des nerfs par l'entremise des filets nerveux et membraneux.' (30 Jan. 1708.)

[2] Leclerc published extracts of the *Essay on Human Understanding* as early as 1688 (*Abrégé d'un ouvrage intitulé Essai philosophique touchant l'entendement*, Amsterdam, and in the Bibliothèque universelle, viii, pp. 49–142). A translation by Coste appeared in 1700 under the title *Essai philosophique concernant l'entendement humain* (Amsterdam). One of its early readers was Boulainviller (d. 1722); extracts from it are to be found amongst his reading notes at the Bibliothèque nationale (N.Ac.fr. 11071–6).

[3] 'We have the ideas of matter and thinking, but possibly shall never be able to know whether any mere material being thinks or no, it being impossible for us, by the contemplation of our own ideas, without revelation, to discover whether omnipotency has not given to some systems of matter fitly composed a power to perceive and think, or else joined and fixed to matter so disposed a thinking immaterial substance; it being, in respect of our notions, not much more remote from our comprehension to conceive that God can, if he pleases, superadd to matter a faculty of thinking, than that he should superadd to it another substance with a faculty of thinking, since we know not wherein thinking consists, nor to what sort of substances the Almighty has been pleased to give that power, which cannot be in any created being but merely by the good pleasure of the Creator. For I see no contradiction in it, that the first eternal thinking being should, if he pleased, give to certain systems of created senseless matter, put together as he thinks fit, some degree of sense, perception and thought, though, as I think I have proved,

notion was doubtless too commonplace at the very beginning of the century, before Cartesianism had become the current conservative ideology and recourse to Locke's arguments against Descartes had become useful to the 'philosophes'.[1] Were not the purely corporeal beasts capable of sensation and of a rudimentary kind of thought thanks to their 'material form'? So it was taught in all the schools. The idea of thinking matter was familiar enough for Jurieu, the champion of Protestant orthodoxy, to admit, in controversy with the rationalist Saurin, that he could not disprove the possibility of matter being able to think. Bayle himself was Cartesian enough to look upon thought and extension as incompatible qualities, but he refused to draw the Cartesian conclusion concerning the automatism of the brutes from this intuition.[2] In the article referred to above, the *Journal des savants* (September 1703) compared Locke's argument with that used by an Aristotelian professor of Kiel who wished to give a real sense to the word 'Nature' and therefore argued that God could give matter certain powers not implied in the definition of matter, powers by which it could operate independently, without there being a constant need of God's intervention. The work under review was G. S. Schelhammer's *Naturae vindicatae vindicatio* (Kiel, 1702). Schelhammer, in controversy with Sturm, a Cartesian professor of mathematics at Altdorf, attributed a 'motive force' to matter and was content that God should be the prime mover and 'Nature' the operator of his will. Sturm argued that no 'force' was necessary, beyond what the *Journal* referred to as the 'efficacity' of the laws of motion, a theological term reminiscent of the 'efficacity' of grace. Schelhammer held that this implied a separate act of will by God each time motion took place. The *Journal* replied that it merely meant that the 'efficacity' of the first act of will was sustained. The fact that the Cartesian *Journal des savants* compares Locke's

lib. IV, ch. 10, par. 4 etc., it is no less than a contradiction to suppose matter (which is evidently in its own nature void of sense and thought) should be that eternal first-thinking being.' (*Essay on Human Understanding*, 1690, bk. (V, ch. iii, par. 6.)

[1] The advent of Cartesianism to orthodoxy produced a paradoxical situation in 1751 when the abbé de Prades, one of Diderot's collaborators, presented his thesis in the Sorbonne. The professors accepted the sensationism of this thesis as being in accordance with traditional doctrine, but several bishops condemned it from a Cartesian standpoint as being a Lockean innovation and the thesis was finally rejected.

[2] Jurieu in *La Religion du latitudinaire*, Rotterdam, 1691, p. 388; Bayle in the article *Dicéarque* of his dictionary (1697) and below, p. 230. Jurieu's book is an attack on the 'rationaux' (as he called the rationalist theologians, his adversaries). He went as far as to state (p. 391) that there is no rational reply to the 'Spinozists' who maintain that the world is not added to God.

argument with Schelhammer's argument implies that the journalist looked upon Locke as continuing the scholastic tradition.[1]

By the time Voltaire published his letter on Locke (letter xiii of the *Lettres philosophiques* or *Lettres anglaises*) Cartesianism had established its position and the situation was changed. Voltaire made much of Locke's argument. The abbé Prévost wrote a reply which he developed into a general onslaught on the English deists, Collins, Toland, Tindal, Wollaston, Woolston, asserting that 'for the last thirty years' they have been trying to suppress the soul and 'all immaterial substances'.[2] Even so, no tendency to stake all philosophical and religious issues on whether matter is capable of thought or not was evident outside Cartesian writing. The *Bibliothèque britannique* refused to take sides.[3] Prévost himself fell back later upon the argument that God could give immortality even to a material soul[4] and such was also the position adopted by the *Bibliothèque raisonnée* in 1744, when reviewing a Cartesian attack on Voltaire's letter.[5] At no time did the contention that matter is capable of thought provoke the same horror and fear that Spinoza's conception of the single substance gave rise to. In itself the notion that matter is capable of thought has nothing Spinozist about it, but it was, in certain clandestine writings such as the abbé Meslier's *Testament*, associated with radical thinking of a Spinozistic flavour and takes on a meaning very different from the significance it had for the physiologists. Meslier's philosophy was a monistic material-ism or true atheism, as distinct from the merely physiological materialism of the doctors. There were numerous clandestine trea-tises of philosophical atheism in circulation in the eighteenth cen-

---

[1] The *Journal des savants* did not have a high opinion of Locke's capacity for meta-physics. It brushed aside his complaint that he could not understand Malebranche's conception of God as a purely intelligible substance as being entirely Locke's affair, the notion being clear enough. (27 February 1708, review of Locke's *Posthumous works*, London, 1708.)

[2] 'C'est à l'existence de l'âme et de toutes sortes de substances immatérielles qu'ils en veulent depuis trente ou quarante ans.' (*Le Pour et le contre*, iv, p. 227, Sept. 1734.)

[3] Oct.–Dec. 1733, ii, p. 113.

[4] Towards the end of his *Cleveland*, when Clarendon undertakes to convert Cleveland. There is a contradiction, says Clarendon, in the idea of thinking matter, but, even sup-posing that the soul is material, that does not prevent God from giving it immortality if He so desires. The argument had been used by Sherlock against Locke and reproduced in the *Journal des savants* (Supplement for 1709, 30 Sept.).

[5] Vol. xxxiii, pp. 134 sqq. The work under review was Reinbeck's *Réflexions philo-sophiques sur l'immortalité de l'âme raisonnable, avec quelques remarques sur une lettre dans laquelle on soutient que la matière pense*. Amsterdam and Leipzig, 1744.

tury, and we shall return to them later. The physiologists and doctors generally had a reputation for impiety, if one is to take the evidence of a work written by one of them to prove that such a reputation was unfounded,[1] but in any case the doctors seem at all times to have been allowed to be materialists to their hearts' content without the remainder of the community being disturbed thereby.

[1] G. Purshall's *Essay on the Mechanical Fabrick of the Universe*, London, 1707, reviewed in the *Journal des savants*, 3 Sept. 1708.

XI

Animal Automatism and its Critics

As long as the terminology used in the philosophy classes remained intelligible, it was possible to attribute to the brutes a soul which was neither material nor spiritual with the appearance of talking sense, but the general abandonment of the scholastic vocabulary, and of Latin itself as the philosophical language, made unintelligible jargon of scholastic definitions and explanations. Bossuet attempted to maintain the traditional attitude, although he was Cartesian enough to agree that a substance must be either material or spiritual: the result was that he merely wrapped up the problem in words:

It is not a body, because it is not extended in length, breadth and depth; it is not a spirit, because it is without intelligence . . . So by giving sensation to animals, it is evident that one attributes nothing spiritual to them; their soul will be of the same nature as their operations, which, in us, though they derive from a principle which is not a body, are considered nevertheless as carnal and corporeal because of their total dependence on the body.[1]

Brute soul is 'of the same nature as' the 'operations' which derive from a 'principle' which is a body. What is it then but the name attached to the operations of the body? And why 'in us' should these same operations come from a principle which 'is not a body'? Stripped of its scholastic expression and context the question was starkly simple. Are the purely material beasts capable of feeling and thought or not?

The Cartesians faced the question squarely and did not hesitate to draw the logical conclusions from their premises. Matter and consciousness are incompatible; the brutes are purely material; therefore the brutes are entirely unconscious. The difference between a clock and a dog is the difference between a simple and a complicated mechanism.

It is doubtful whether Descartes himself intended that he should be understood exactly as he was in fact understood. His starting point was a long way back beyond the principles which his disciples took for premises. He was concerned with the application of geo-

[1] *De la Connaissance de Dieu*, ch. v.

metrical methods to physiology, and he used his ingenuity to carry him as far as possible into the ramifications of the subject. His object was not to prove that dogs are like complicated clocks, but to prove that physiology as well as mechanics can be treated by his method. Replies he made to correspondents, such as, for instance, that the beasts feel as we feel when we do not think about our feelings, suggest that he was not anxious to flout common sense to the point of absurdity. One of his earliest disciples, the Oratorian teacher N. Poisson, seems to have understood perfectly well that Descartes looked upon animal automatism as a question of scientific method and that his prime concern was to show that animal motions can be fully accounted for in terms reducible to those of geometry.[1] Most Cartesians however were prepared to accept the straightforward belief that animals are unconscious machines. When the 'hermits' of Port-Royal des Champs nailed animals on boards and opened them to watch the circulation of the blood,[2] they acted in a way that leaves no doubt whatsoever of their having believed in the very letter of the doctrine of unconscious automatism, whereas there is no evidence that Descartes himself ever practised such vivisections. A long succession of Cartesian controversialists preferred logic to common sense: Le Roy (Regius) in 1646, Arnauld in 1662, Schuyl in 1662, Clauberg in 1664, La Forge in 1665, Cordemoy in 1666 and 1668, Langenhert in 1668, Rohault in 1671, Malebranche in 1675, Le Grand in 1675, Dilly in 1676, Darmanson in 1684, Geulincx in 1688 (posthumous), Pourchot in 1695, Vallade in 1700, and the series continues into the eighteenth century with Louis Racine in 1728, Macy in 1737, the cardinal de Polignac in 1747 (poem composed *circa* 1700), Lignac in 1751, Kéranflech in 1765, Guidi in 1782, Cailleau in 1783, Brémont in 1785 and Cotte in 1799, the

---

[1] *Commentaire ou remarques sur la méthode de René Descartes*, Vendôme, 1670.

[2] 'Combien aussi s'éleva-t-il de petites agitations dans ce désert touchant les sciences humaines de la philosophie et les nouvelles opinions de M. Descartes? Comme M. Arnauld, dans ses heures de relâche, s'en entretenait avec ses amis plus particuliers, insensiblement cela se répandit partout et cette solitude, dans les heures d'entretien, ne retentissait plus que de ces discours. Il n'y avait guère de solitaire qui ne parlât d'*automate*. On ne faisait plus une affaire de battre un chien. On lui donnait fort indifféremment des coups de bâton et on se moquait de ceux qui plaignaient ces bêtes comme si elles eussent senti de la douleur. On disait que c'étaient des horloges, que ces cris qu'elles faisaient quand on les frappaient n'étaient que le bruit d'un petit ressort qui avait été remué. On clouait de pauvres animaux sur des ais, par les quatre pattes, pour les ouvrir tout en vie et voir la circulation du sang qui était une grande matière d'entretien.' (Fontaine, *Mémoires pour servir à l'histoire de Port-Royal*, Utrecht, 1736, ii, pp. 52-3.)

names becoming more and more obscure as the theory is followed through a century which has lost interest in it.[1]

One of the favourite arguments of these controversialists was that the opposite view leads to materialism. If the brutes are conscious without having an immaterial soul, then man also can be conscious without having an immaterial soul. A solution could, of course, be found by granting the brutes a spiritual soul, and from time to time this step was taken—by the abbé Villars in 1670, Thomasius Phillips in 1713, Boullier in 1728, Beaumont in 1733, Pernetti in 1746, Condillac in 1755, Bonnet in 1769 and Aumeur in 1781. If this solution was not more often resorted to, the reason doubtless lies in the metaphysical implications of it. If the brutes have immaterial souls, are those souls also immortal by the self-same argument which is used to establish the immortality of the human soul?

The Jesuits maintained their scholastic position as long as the controversy was sharp. Two of the most widely read discussions on the subject were by Jesuits, Pardies, a professor at the Collège de Clermont (1672) and Daniel, the theologian (1693). As late as 1731 a professor of mathematics at the Collège Louis le Grand, N. Régnault, was defending the old positions.[2]

The conception put forward by Gassendi and by Maignan of a material soul composed of fiery particles spread throughout the body and capable of feeling and a rudimentary form of thought, was from time to time resorted to. Cureau de la Chambre may have had such a conception, but his animal psychology could be equally well served with a scholastic definition of the sensitive soul.[3] The English physiologist Willis adopted Gassendi's conception and so did G. Lamy of the Faculty of Medicine in Paris. Colonna reconstructed around it the hylozoic metaphysics without which it cannot stand up to Cartesian criticism. La Fontaine adopted it, as was natural enough; the Cartesian attitude to the beasts made nonsense of his work. How could he ask his readers to take interest in the antics of mechanical toys? The step from the human to the mechanical was

---

[1] Bayle quotes many of these writers in his article on Rorarius. The list may be completed from L. C. Rosenfield, *From Beast-machine to man-machine*, New York, 1941 and H. Hastings, *Man and Beast in French thought in the eighteenth century*, John Hopkins Press, 1936.

[2] I. G. Pardies, *Discours de la connaissance des bêtes*; G. Daniel, 'Preuves de la connaissance des bêtes' in *Difficultés proposées par un Péripatéticien à l'auteur du 'Voyage du monde de Descartes'*; N. Régnault, *Entretiens physiques*.

[3] 'De la Connaissance des bêtes' in *Les Caractères des passions*, Paris, 1645.

too great to be bridged and the essence of the fable was its power to blend the human and the animal kingdoms. Consider how a Cartesian lady, Mme de Grignan, daughter of Mme de Sévigné, talked of a pet dog: 'Please do not bring a dog for Pauline; we want only rational creatures here, and belonging to the sect we belong to we refuse to burden ourselves with these machines: if they were constructed so as not to have dirty business to perform, well and good, but what one has to put up with makes them unbearable.'[1] For this lady at any rate, Cartesian ideas had become Cartesian modes of sensibility. No record of her attitude to La Fontaine's Fables has been preserved, but it would be difficult to imagine her enjoying them.

La Fontaine was in many places content with a poetic animism such as he could, and doubtless did, find in the ancient poets. Nevertheless he seems to have taken his philosophical opposition to Descartes seriously. The last fable but one of the whole collection (*Les Souris et le Chat huant*) is accompanied by a note in which the poet distinguishes carefully between what is allowed to the poetic fancy and what may be seriously argued from a philosophical point of view and in his *Discours à Mme de la Sablière* he presents his case in a systematic way.[2]

Mlle Descartes, the philosopher's niece, thought that a piece of 'rarified matter' was to provide a pet warbler with a soul.[3] But the

---

[1] Translated from a letter of 17 December 1690 in Mme de Sévigné, *Lettres*, Grands Écrivains (1862-6), t. ix, p. 605.

[2] Je subtiliserais un morceau de matière,
Que l'on ne pourrait plus concevoir sans effort,
Quintessence d'atome, extrait de la lumière,
Je ne sais quoi plus vif et plus mobile encore
Que le feu; car enfin si le bois fait la flamme,
La flamme en s'épurant, peut-elle pas de l'âme
Nous donner quelque idée? et sort-il pas de l'or
Des entrailles du plomb? Je rendrais mon ouvrage
Capable de sentir, juger, rien davantage,
        Et juger imparfaitement,
Sans qu'un singe jamais fît le moindre argument.
                                        (*Fables*, bk. ix.)

[3] In a madrigal written in reply to Madeleine de Scudéry's *La Fauvette à Sapho* between 1685 and 1689; cf. Rosenfield, op. cit., p. 159. The madrigal contained the following lines:

Voici quel est mon compliment
Pour la plus belle des fauvettes,
Quand elle revient où vous êtes.
Ah! m'écriai-je alors avec étonnement,
N'en déplaise à mon oncle, elle a du jugement.

notion of a thinking material fluid in the blood and nerves had no future in it. It was looked upon as absurd in the eighteenth century. A thesis sustained at Wittenberg in 1712 disposed of it in the following simple way: 'Si anima propagatur ex materia, erit materialis. Qualis causa, talis effectus. Sed posterius est absurdum. Ergo et prius.'[1] The eighteenth-century materialists were prepared to state that the body thinks or that the brain thinks, but they had no use for parcels of elementary fire whose function was to serve as souls.

Pierre Bayle[2] treated the subject in his usual thorough way, but was as tantalizing here as elsewhere and proffered no positive solution. He pitted the Schoolmen against the Cartesians and used the arguments of each against the other, but he was not tempted by the idea of a thinking material soul. Leibniz at one moment seemed to offer him a way out of the maze, but the avenue opened up by Leibniz had no light of certainty at the end of it; the difficulties closed in again, the obstacles became more and more formidable and finally arrested progress.

Bayle's pretext for the discussion was a book first published in the Grisons in 1548 and re-edited by Naudé in 1648 at Paris and reprinted again in Amsterdam in 1654 and 1666. It was the work of an Italian doctor named Rorario. Rorario tried to prove a thesis common enough in his own day and made much of by Montaigne, namely that beasts are more intelligent than men. Bayle thinks this notion preposterous (and rare indeed in Bayle's time must have been the people who took it seriously), but he plays up Rorario's arguments to the full against the Cartesians. Common sense was sufficient for him, however, to rule out the Cartesian theory, which was a pity, he added, because it would have been very helpful to religion if it could have been proved! The contrary opinion favours materialism, because, if the material brutes can feel, the immateriality of man's soul is jeopardized. If the brutes feel pain, St Augustine's proof of original sin falls to the ground. Man's suffering cannot be a proof of his guilt if the innocent beasts suffer likewise. 'One must therefore agree that M. Descartes's automata are extremely favourable to the principles by which we form our judgment of the eternal Being and by which we defend orthodoxy' (Remark C). It is a great pity,

[1] M. E. Wendius, *Novam animae humanae propagatione sententiam*, Wittenberg, 1712.
[2] We shall deal here only with Bayle's contribution to the subject under discussion; for a study of him as a sceptical erudite, see below, pp. 283-5, and for his criticism of Spinoza's metaphysics, pp. 262-5.

adds Bayle, that the theory cannot be proved! And he instances the Cartesian Darmanson's book *La Bête transformée en machine* (1684), the author of which argues that to allow the beasts feeling and knowledge would be to accuse God of injustice: if the beasts are capable of suffering God makes innocent creatures suffer, and if they are capable of knowledge, God is unjust in refusing the beasts knowledge of Himself. Bayle's comment was that the Cartesians were trying to rally religion to their side; he had already made it in the *Nouvelles de la République des lettres* when the book came out. One may add, looking at this conflict from a distance, that the Cartesians were succeeding far better than Bayle seems to have suspected.

As for the Schoolmen, their 'confused and impenetrable verbiage' filled Bayle only with the desire to confound them with their own arguments. They argue that a dog fears a stick once it has been beaten. What does this prove if not that the dog reasons? But they will not agree that a dog reasons; they only allow him sensation, memory and the passions, without the power of reflection, without the power of comparing two ideas and drawing a conclusion from them. In refuting the Cartesians they prove far too much for their own good; they prove that the beasts are capable of gratitude, equity, morality, but will not allow them reason. One could reply, as Pereira did, long before Descartes, that the beasts perform many acts which presuppose sensation, yet they have no sensation. And, turning the argument the other way round, one can say that if the beasts perform actions which presuppose reflection, it is unreasonable to say that the beasts are incapable of reflection. How can anyone believe that a dog can see a bird without knowing that it sees it? The animals certainly reflect upon their actions and if they do not reach the human level, in this, as in other things, it is because their organs are not the same as ours. Is the soul of a child or a madman different from ours? Of course not! But their organs are different. And similarly, if our organs were more perfect, our thoughts would be more sublime, but our souls would be the same. A soul that is capable of one thought is capable of all thoughts. So the Schoolmen cannot prove that the soul of the beasts is different from our own, however much they talk of knowledge, or lack of knowledge of universal ideas and of the Good. The possession or lack of such knowledge can only establish an accidental, not a substantial difference. Again, which is the more difficult—to know one's thoughts or to know the things which happen outside us? The latter, assuredly! That being so, the vaunted power of reflection, or knowledge of the self, does not establish any superiority of man over the beasts. The soul of a dog in the body of an Aristotle or a Cicero would have acquired all the knowledge possessed by these great men. If, then, the souls of animals are material forms, so are the souls of men. If, on the other hand, they are immaterial and immortal, how many immaterial and immortal souls must God have created! One look in a microscope will give an idea of their number!

So does Bayle reduce the Scholastic position to materialism. If the soul is the same in all living creatures and all differences between souls are to be explained by reference to their bodily organs, the soul is a constant factor which may be disregarded altogether. It resembles that intelligence which, according to Aristotle, comes from without and operates wherever bodily organs are so disposed as to allow of its operations, as the wind produces music in organ pipes.

However, the fact that the Schoolmen cannot establish their own thesis does not mean that they cannot inflict great damage on the thesis of their Cartesian adversaries! Daniel has shown that if a Cartesian is logical he is forced to believe that he alone is a thinking being and that all other beings are mere machines. He knows himself by the act of thought, but he does not know anyone else in this way; he only knows other men as he knows the beasts, by observation. Daniel has found the weak spot in the Cartesian defence, and, as in the Trojan war, counter-attack has succeeded where attack failed. Who, asks Bayle, giving the *coup de grâce*, can claim that he alone is a thinking being without being fit for the madhouse?

Daniel's strength, however, is in his criticism, not in his own thesis. His contention that the sensitive soul in brutes is neither matter nor spirit but an intermediary substance between the two cannot stand, for if the sensitive soul is extended in space, how is it to be distinguished from matter? And if it is not, how is it to be distinguished from spirit? And if it is spirit why is it incapable of thought? Why should it be mortal? How can the remarkable actions of the beasts be explained if the brute soul does not reason?

So finally Daniel's thesis is reduced to the bare claim that the Schoolmen are at present in possession of the field and cannot be driven out unless the Cartesians establish a better right to it. Twenty-five years ago, says Daniel, a great statesman was advised not to have his son learn the old philosophy because it contained nothing but foolishness. 'They say the same of the new,' replied the statesman, 'and if I am forced to choose between an old and a new folly, I may as well stick to the old.'

Leibniz's theory as expounded in the *Journal des savants* in 1695 tempted Bayle, but difficulties at once sprang to his mind. According to Leibniz, the psychical life of any being is independent of its physical life, the two being regulated in perfect harmony with each other by God. But, says Bayle, if the animal's body is suppressed its soul will go on feeling as though nothing has happened. Leibniz says that one feeling follows another in the soul without any interference by the body, but how can that be? How can there be succession or variation in the soul, which is a simple being, if there is no interference from outside? If the soul had several parts, each part could act on the others and produce vraiety, but the soul has no parts, it is a simple being. Leibniz replied in the *Histoire des ouvrages des savants* in 1698, but Bayle was not satisfied. In a further note added to his Dictionary he came back to the two most troublesome points. If God had chosen to annihilate Julius Caesar's soul on the day when he was going to the Capitol, would his body have gone there all the same and have made the speech he had prepared? Again, can one feeling be replaced by another feeling in the soul without any new faculty of feeling being called upon, or any outside influence? Our feelings change rapidly. The child Caesar when pricked by a pin while feeding at the breast changes rapidly from one mood to the next. Would Leibniz explain the change by the gradual modification of one and the same feeling? Or are there several little souls in the soul each with its own particular mood? If the soul is of itself to make the changes suited to the changes taking place in the body, it must know what these changes are to be, it must *know* the future states of the body.

Leibniz's rejoinder to the effect that the soul does indeed know, albeit confusedly, its future perceptions, and that the soul's perceptions are multiple even though the soul itself be simple, and, being multiple, can act upon each other as the parts of a machine act upon each other, satisfied Bayle to some extent, but he maintained his cautious attitude towards 'pre-established harmony' relegating it, as he did Malebranche's 'occasional causes', to the level of unproved speculation.

Bayle places Cartesian analysis at the service of scepticism. Bayle was a sceptic, in spite of his position in the Reformed Church, and maintained his right to be a sceptic by means of the distinction he drew between philosophical conviction on the one hand and religious belief on the other. But his habits of mind were Cartesian. He could only accept clear ideas clearly connected with other clear ideas and underestimated the value of hypotheses which probe tentatively into the unknown. Such hypotheses need encouragement and forebearance in order to flourish and fructify. Bayle knew only how to reduce them to the absurd by implacable logic. He did not know how to place himself at the starting point of his victim's inquiry and face the problem from that modest position. It was legitimate to confront the Schoolmen with the dilemma of thinking matter on the one hand or immortal brute souls on the other. Their theories had held the field for generations and had had ample time in which to show their worth. But Leibniz was at a disadvantage. He could not bring his main arguments to bear on the terrain chosen by Bayle.

At bottom, Leibniz's view of the world was more like that of Gassendi, Maignan and the Schoolmen than it was like Descartes's. He shared with them the assumption of a universal scale of being and separated man from the beasts in the order of perfection. It is the knowledge of necessary and eternal truths which distinguishes man from the creatures which come below him in the scale, and which constitutes 'what we call the rational soul or spirit'. 'It is also by the knowledge of necessary truths and by their abstractions, that we rise to acts of reflection, which make us think of that which calls itself "I", and to observe this or that within "us": and it is thus that, thinking of ourselves, we think of "being", of "substance", "simple" and "compound", of the immaterial and of God himself, conceiving that what is limited in us is, in him, without limits. And these reflective acts furnish the principal objects of our reasonings.'[1] But knowledge of eternal truths and reflective cognition are not the only forms of cognition recognized by Leibniz. Both in man and in the beings placed below him there are 'perceptions' and "appetitions". 'Perception' he distinguishes carefully from 'apperception' or consciousness. By 'perception' is meant what Maignan meant by 'sensitive cognition', while Leibniz relates 'perception' to his theory of the 'monads' in the following manner: 'monads' are the simple substances which make up the compounds there are in the universe.[2] There *are*

---

[1] *Monadologie* (a short account of the system composed in 1714 but not published), para. 29.

[2] Cf. letter to Lady Masham, 1704: 'Our perceptions are sometimes accompanied by *reflection* and sometimes not, and, as from reflection come *abstractions* and *universal and necessary truths*, no traces of which are seen in the brutes and still less in other bodies

compounds in the universe because otherwise there would be no such thing as division into parts. And if there are compounds those compounds must be made up of simple substances, because a compound is nothing else than an aggregation of simple substances. If there were no simple substances to add together there would be no compounds at all. But if the substances are simple they cannot influence each other in any way whatsoever, for if something could go out of one into another they would not be simple. Therefore the changes which take place within the simple substances must derive from an internal principle. Now changes there obviously are in the monads; that fact is one of the starting points of the inquiry. I have one feeling and then another; that is, a change takes place in me. Change implies plurality, so there is plurality in the simple monads. The *state* of the monad at the time when the plurality is present is what Leibniz calls 'perception'. One such state is followed by another such state. The *action* by which one state is replaced by another is what Leibniz calls 'appetition'. Perception and appetition are the basic psychical operations; they are found throughout nature, with the exception of 'primary matter', which is merely passive, merely extended, without any perfections. This notion of matter unites that of the schools with that of the Cartesians. The absence of perfections corresponds to the absence of 'form' but matter for Leibniz is a really existing substance. It flows shapeless and featureless through organisms in an endless stream. The Scholastic notion of form is replaced by that of organization, which becomes the criterion of perfection and determines the place of a being in the scale. Above 'primary matter' are ranged (1) the simple monads, having spontaneity and perception but no organic capacity, memory or self-consciousness, (2) living monads, having spontaneity, perception and organic capacity, but neither memory nor self-consciousness, (3) animal souls, having spontaneity, perception, organic capacity and memory, but not self-consciousness, (4) rational souls, having all these perfections and, in addition, the power to recognize eternal

which surround us, there is reason for believing that this simple being which is in us and which is called soul is distinguished by this from those of other known bodies. Whether now these principles of action and of perception be called Forms, Entelechies, Souls, Spirits or whether the terms be distinguished according to the motions one would like to attribute to them, the things will not thereby be changed. You will ask what these simple beings or the souls which I place in brutes and in other creatures as far as they are organic, will become; I reply that they must not be less inextinguishable than our souls and that they cannot be produced or destroyed by the forces of nature.'

truths, (5) the 'genii' or intellectual beings possessed of all the fore-going perfections and probably also that of changing their outward form at will, and, at the top of the scale, God, who alone is pure perfection.

All the monads have perception and in a certain sense one may say that they have perception of the whole of the universe,[1] for any whole must be presupposed in all its parts, as the whole circle is presupposed in any part of its circumference, however minute.[2] But the degree of clarity with which each monad 'mirrors' the whole universe will depend on the perfection of the organs with which it is associated. In the simple monads all perceptions will be unconscious. The possibility of unconscious perception is proved by the fact that when I am *conscious* of the colour green I *perceive* the colours yellow and blue (in a mixture of yellow and blue powders, for example). Animals have heightened perceptions as compared with simple monads; they have organs which collect rays of light and undulations of air, but neither rays nor undulations enter the soul: 'that which takes place in the soul represents that which takes place in the organs'.[3] The 'soul' is the name given to monads of the third and higher degrees in the scale of being. Like all monads, a soul is a simple substance; no influence from without can act upon it. So the cleavage between soul and body remained as complete in Leibniz's system as in Descartes's and in order to explain why 'that which takes place in the soul represents that which takes place in the organs', Leibniz was obliged to invent the theory of 'pre-established harmony' by which he was principally known in France on account of his articles in the *Journal des savants*.

The beasts have memory, which furnishes the soul with a sort of consecutiveness like enough to reason itself, but none the less to be carefully distinguished from it.[4] A dog, when shown a stick, whines and runs away because it remembers the pain it has suffered from previous beatings. 'Men act like the brutes in so far as the consecu-tiveness of their perceptions results from the principle of memory alone',[5] but men are separated from the brutes by having a rational soul, that is to say by their knowledge of eternal truths gained by reasoning of which mathematical reasoning is the type.

[1] In his *Essay on the Universal Spirit* (1702) he described each monad as a 'mirror of the universe'. When he wrote this essay he was inclined to think that each animal develops from a minute germ, no bigger than a physical point, and returns to the same condition after death.   [2] *Monadologie*, para. 25.
[3] ibid., para. 25.   [4] ibid., para. 26.   [5] ibid., para. 28.

As presented in the *Monadologie*, Leibniz's system preserves, outside the Cartesian orbit, conceptions common to the Schoolmen, Gassendi and Maignan. Leibniz sees the capacity for perception and desire spread throughout nature. Every material object, every plant, every animal, and also every part of every material object, plant, animal, enjoys these powers in some degree. Every plant is full of living plants, every animal of living animals, each sharing the corporate life of the whole, each enjoying an individual existence.

Looked upon in this light, Leibniz's philosophy might be taken for a pure naturalism, but there is no evidence of its having been looked upon as such. The *Monadology* was unpublished, the articles in the *Journal des savants* conveyed the strange theory of 'pre-established harmony' to the French public. Leibniz was known as a theologian on account of the *Théodicée* published in French in 1709.[1] But later in the century disciples of Leibniz, and particularly Maupertuis, were to play a part in constituting. a new hylozoic materialism which was to be that of Diderot.

[1] The impact of this work in France has been studied by W. H. Barber in his *Leibniz in France*, Oxford, 1955.

XII

Monopsychism and the Reaction to Spinoza

THE true Spinoza remained almost unknown in France, not only in the years immediately following the publication of his works but during the whole of the following century. His most important book, the *Ethica ordine geometrico demonstrata* published in the *Opera posthuma* in the year of his death (1677) was not reprinted anywhere until 1802. Theological writers either refused to mention his name or used it with the addition of some such epithet as 'misérable'. Pierre Bayle was almost alone in claiming publicly that, atheist though he was, Spinoza was none the less an upright and virtuous man.[1] There was a French translation of the *Tractatus theologico-politicus* of 1670, but it appeared in the Low Countries (in 1678) and the fact that it was given three different titles,[2] none of them resembling the title of the original, indicates to what extent it was a clandestine enterprise; it cannot possibly have reached a wide audience in France where it could only penetrate by contraband. Some of those who decried Spinoza with most scorn can justifiably be suspected of never having read him: Arnauld and Malebranche are two such persons.

Small wonder is it therefore that both adversaries and would-be disciples had an erroneous idea of what they were arguing about. The battle raged over two notions which were familiar enough in France, but which had no very close connection with Spinoza himself. One of these notions was the age-old idea of the World Soul, the other was the definition of God as the totality of the universe,

---

[1] In the *Lettre sur la comète de* 1680 (1682), chs. 161 sqq., J. M. Lucas, Spinoza's first biographer, represented him in the same light, but his account was not actually published until 1719, although it was written some thirty years before that date and was known by Bayle when he wrote the article *Spinoza* of his dictionary. Cf. P. Vernière, *Spinoza et la pensée française avant la Révolution*, Paris, 1954, i, pp. 24–7.

[2] *La Clef du sanctuaire, Traité des Cérémonies superstitieuses des Juifs, Réflexions curieuses d'un esprit désintéressé*, the first at Leyden, the second at Amsterdam, the third at Cologne, but they are all the same edition. The translator was called Gabriel de Saint-Glain, a captain of Angevine origin in the service of the Dutch (cf. Bayle, *Œuvres diverses*, iv, p. 570 n.).

'le grand Tout'. In the dispute which arose over these topics around the name of Spinoza, the Cartesian theologians figured as the new champions of religion, equipped with bright and shining weapons, stepping boldly into the gap left by the Schoolmen whom they themselves had discomfited. Cartesianism became the main ally of theology[1] after being accused of connivance with the enemy. But, in the hour of its triumph, it became the object of a clandestine campaign carried on by means of manuscript tracts and treatises and failed to win the approval of the new generation of the French intelligentsia in the opening years of the eighteenth century, the first generation of 'philosophes'. It became instead the philosophy of the bishops and finally of the Jesuits and was used to stem the spreading influence of sensationism.

'Spinozism', or the popular misconception of Spinoza's teaching, began to exist as early as 1673, when a Swiss adventurer from the Grisons, by the name of Stouppe, or Stoppa, who held the rank of lieutenant-colonel in the French forces in Holland, published a book under the title *La Religion des Hollandais*, in Paris. Stouppe was in all probability a French intelligence agent. He had been a Calvinist minister in London and was, according to Bishop Burnet, 'much trusted by Cromwell in foreign affairs'; he was, again according to Burnet, 'more a frantic deist than either a protestant or a christian' at that time, 'though he adhered to the protestant religion as to outward appearances'.[2]

Before the publication of Stouppe's book it is impossible to pick up any trace of Spinoza's reputation in France. The fact that Saint-Evremond went to visit him at Voorburg in 1669 or at The Hague in 1670 does not prove that Saint-Evremond heard of him before leaving for Holland. In any case he had at that time no idea of what Spinoza's teaching was and it is unlikely that Spinoza revealed his mind to the visiting Norman gentleman. The date 1673 remains therefore the date at which French public opinion became aware of what purported to be an account of Spinoza's doctrine.[3] Stouppe's book was published in Paris and so was readily accessible, and in any case Moréri's dictionary quoted the passage dealing with Spinoza from 1688 onwards and Bayle's dictionary from 1697 onwards, so

[1] Cf. A. G. A. Balz, 'Cartesian Refutations of Spinoza', *Philosophical Review*, New York, xlvi (Sept. 1937), and in *Cartesian Studies*, New York, 1951.

[2] *History of his own time*, Oxford, 1823, i, p. 111. Cf. L. Feer, 'Un Pamphlet contre les Hollandais', *Bulletin de la société de l'histoire du protestantisme français*, xxxi (1882), p. 78.

[3] See G. Cohen, *Le Séjour de Saint-Evremond en Hollande*, Paris, 1926.

this supposed account of Spinoza's doctrine was constantly paraded before the public.

Stouppe was with the French army at Utrecht when he wrote his book, which was doubtless intended as an act of psychological warfare against the Dutch seeing that he had official support in his enterprise. He managed to get in touch with Spinoza through Graevius, one of the philosopher's correspondents, and to persuade him that he would be serving the cause of peace if he went through the lines and met Condé. Condé was not there when Spinoza arrived in the French camp at Utrecht, but he was well received by the comte de Luxembourg and doubtless Stouppe had the opportunity of conversing with him. If so, he put the opportunity to poor use, judging by the account he gave of Spinoza in his book. After calling Spinoza 'a bad Jew and no better a Christian', he claimed that Spinoza had many disciples in Holland and then referred to what he called the *Tractatus theologico-positivus*, summarizing it by means of the well-known theory, which Vanini was accused of having held and which the author of the *Theophrastus redivivus* certainly did hold, namely that all religions have been invented as a means of government, with the added theme that virtue is its own reward and has no need of the rewards and punishments of a future life, a belief which we have already met in the *Quatrains du déiste* of 1619–23. While not being positively opposed to the teaching of the *Tractatus*, these are current ideas which the 'libertins' were supposed to profess and they cannot be looked upon as an adequate account of a book in which they are not in fact put forward and whose importance is quite different: it was the *Tractatus*, a philological treatment of certain biblical questions, guided by a strictly deterministic philosophy and coupled with a firm plea for liberty of the conscience, which forced Christian apologetics on to the defensive for the first time. Be that as it may, the *Tractatus* became associated, whether on account of Stouppe's efforts or not, with the old legend of the *Tractatus de tribus impostoribus*, and throughout the following century there circulated scores of manuscript and printed copies of a work entitled sometimes *l'Esprit de Spinoza* and sometimes *Traité des trois imposteurs*[1] of which the first part only had any connection with the

---

[1] See my article entitled 'La Diffusion des idées matérialistes et anti-religieuses au début du XVIIIe siècle' (*Revue d'histoire littéraire de la France*, April–June 1937). The *Esprit de Spinoza* existed by 1706 and perhaps earlier; it was described in 1706 by G. B. Struve in his *Dissertatio de doctis impostoribus* and according to Struve's description it still lacked its third part, entitled 'De l'âme'. Manuscript copies of it are to be found in

Tractatus theologico-politicus. It could have been written by almost any of the college regents, or by a man like Guillaume, the son of a peasant who became regent at the Collège de Navarre and then curé of Fresne-sur-Berry and was imprisoned for several years (1728 –) in a monastery for having written a work which by all accounts resembled the *Trois Imposteurs*, or the abbé Leblanc who was imprisoned in the Bastille for having written something similar in 1749.[1] This particular work was written by 1706 by a man of some scholarship, well read in the ancient philosophers and ancient history, acquainted with contemporary accounts of oriental religions, not unfavourably disposed towards Moses, whom he looked upon as the leader of a popular revolt, and not unfavourably disposed towards Christ, whom he considered to have been a patriot Pharisee executed by the Romans, but very antagonistic towards Mahomet whom he condemned as a demagogue who played successfully on the base passions of the mob. There are echoes of the *Tractatus* and even of the *Ethics* in the first part of the work in which popular notions of the deity based on the fear of unknown natural forces are brushed aside and replaced by the definition of an infinite and eternal Substance, and there are echoes again of the *Tractatus* in the section on prophecies, but the author did not rely on Spinoza for his information and made no use of Spinoza's philological criticism. As for the chapter entitled 'De l'Ame', it does not figure in all the manuscript copies and may well be an addition made by a copyist; it does not fit in with the rest of the work and comes, perhaps by way of another clandestine treatise entitled *L'Ame mortelle*, from Guillaume Lamy's *Discours académiques*, stemming originally from the alchemistic tradition.[2] With the *Esprit de Spinoza* was usually coupled, both in the manuscripts and in the editions, the life of Spinoza by Lucas, from which the French public could at least obtain a fairly accurate account of the quiet, studious and virtuous

---

the public libraries of Aix, Arras, Auxerre, Avignon, Carpentras, Châlons-sur-Marne, Chaumont, Fécamp, Grenoble, Laon, Lyons (Palais des Arts), Nantes, Orleans, Paris (B.N., Arsenal, Mazarine, Sorbonne, Ste-Geneviève), Périgueux, Reims, Rouen and Strasburg. Editions were published in 1719 and 1721 in Holland and much later (1775 and 1776) in France. The Dutch editions were probably very rare and the work was handed round mainly in manuscript form until 1775.

[1] G. Lanson, 'Questions diverses sur l'histoire de l'esprit philosophique en France avant 1750' (*Revue d'histoire littéraire de la France*, January–June 1912, pp. 21–4 (Guillaume); J. S. Spink, 'A *prêtre-philosophe* in the XVIIIth century', *Modern Language Review*, xxxvii (1942), pp. 200–2 (Jacques-Joseph Le Blanc).

[2] Cf. above, p. 118.

life of the philosopher of Amsterdam; but very little of his real thought reached the French public through the combination of the two works, which was usually entitled *La Vie et l'Esprit de Spinoza*.

Far more information could be obtained from the attempted refutations of the *Tractatus*, and, although that information was necessarily fragmentary, it could not fail to make a deep impression because of the obvious embarrassment of the controversialists, who had somehow or other to explain away the precise points of textual criticism raised by Spinoza and try to prove, to a public before which such questions had never been raised previously, that Moses was indeed the author of the Pentateuch. Believers and unbelievers had so far managed to reach their respective positions without any serious controversy as to the authenticity of the biblical texts. It is hardly to be wondered at that Spinoza's name became a sort of taboo word: it became the rule to refute Spinoza without mentioning him. But at first this precaution was not taken: Huet attempted, in his *Demonstratio Evangelica* (1679) to fight Spinoza openly and with the same weapons, arguing on the meaning of words, as in the first verse of *Deuteronomy* in which it is clear that whoever wrote this account did so after the crossing of the Jordan, which Moses did not cross: the reading of Huet's book must have made doubts germinate in minds where previously no doubts had arisen.[1]

The rest of Stouppe's account was even more likely to mislead his readers than the first part. He professed to know that Spinoza, in private conversation, maintained that God was a being devoid of intelligence and was merely the spirit of nature diffused throughout all things. The persistence with which this misinterpretation of Spinoza's doctrine was put forward in the next fifty years is only equalled by that with which it was affirmed that Spinoza considered God to be simply the sum total of things in the universe. The

---

[1] For an analysis of Huet's argumentation see A. Monod, *De Pascal à Chateaubriand*, Paris, 1916, pp. 86–90, and P. Vernière, *Spinoza et la pensée française*, i, pp. 129, sqq. Cf. below, p. 291. Most of the numerous refutations of the *Tractatus* were published in Holland. The list includes those by J. Conrad Dürr (Durrius), a professor at Altdorf in Bavaria (1672), Jacob Batelier (Batelarius) (1674), Dr. Musaeus, a professor at Jena (1674), William Blyenburg, a merchant of Dort (1674), Isaac Naeranus (1675), Francis Kuyper (1676), Lambert van Veldhuis (1676), Régnier de Mansfeld (a professor at Utrecht) (1676), Korthold (1680), Pierre Yvon, a protestant minister at Wiewaarden (1687), Van Til (1694). Bayle tells the story of John Bredenburg, an elder of the Lutheran church at Rotterdam, who set down Spinoza's arguments for the purpose of refuting them and then found, to his great affliction, that he was incapable of finding any fault with them (1675).

explanation lies in the fact that both these notions were familiar at the end of the seventeenth and the beginning of the eighteenth centuries: to be able to reduce Spinozism to either of them was a simple way of disposing of it. This seems to have been Bayle's attitude; but Bayle also seems to have been convinced that he was not betraying Spinoza's thought in reducing it first to the one and then to the other, though how Spinozism could have been both one and the other of these quite distinct doctrines is rather difficult to comprehend.

The Spirit of Nature and the Soul of the World had always been familiar themes in European thought. In the schools the word 'nature' itself had often the same significance and some of the definitions given by the dictionaries of the late seventeenth and early eighteenth centuries reflect this fact. In the first dictionary of the Académie Française (1694) the word is defined, in one of its senses, as the universal spirit which is diffused throughout all created things and by which everything has its beginning and its end.[1] It is significant that in the 1762 edition this definition is replaced by a far more Cartesian one: it means also that order which is in all created things and according to which everything has its beginning and its end.[2] Robert Boyle, in a work which was probably not noticed in France at the time of its publication (1685), but which was mentioned later by the *Journal des savants* (10 September 1703) and by Leibniz in his *Essay on the Universal Spirit* (1702), reduced the definition of nature to the working of the laws of motion; the Cartesians, Cordemoy, La Forge, Malebranche, had no real meaning to give the word at all, seeing that, according to their theory of occasional causes, the action of God was immediate in all created things and dispensed with secondary agents; but Leibniz stood out against the Cartesians, arguing that there are 'forces' in things which work for certain periods of time; he refuted a Cartesian professor at Altdorf, named Sturm, and approved the arguments of a doctor at Kiel named Schelhammer, who took up the cudgels in favour of the traditional notion of Nature taught in the schools.[3] So the word 'nature' con-

---

[1] 'Il se prend aussi pour cet esprit universel qui est répandu dans chaque chose créée et par lequel toutes choses ont leur commencement et leur fin.' The Trévoux dictionary of 1704 has a similar definition.

[2] 'Il se prend aussi pour cet ordre qui est répandu dans toutes les choses créées et suivant lequel toutes choses ont leur commencement, leur progrès et leur fin.'

[3] *Naturae vindicatae vindicatio*, Kiel, 1702; reviewed at length in the *Journal des savants*, 10 Sept. 1703 (p. 569). Cf. above, pp. 141 n.1 and 223.

tinued to mean a spirit or force or virtue acting in things and also ordering and guiding the general scheme of the world.

The chemists made much of it. Lémery (1645–1715) gave as one of the 'first principles of chemistry' a 'universal spirit diffused through everything which produces divers things according to the divers matrices or pores of the earth in which it is engaged', but finding this principle 'un peu métaphysique', he went on to give other 'more tangible' principles, meaning thereby water, spirit, oil, salt, earth and mercury 'the very subtle and active principle of growth in animate things'.[1] We find it in an unpublished treatise by the historian and alchemist, count Boulainviller (1658–1722) written in 1683 under the title 'Idée d'un système général de la nature', for which he took his information from the works of Van Helmont. Boulainviller describes 'ferment' as 'that spirit of life diffused throughout nature by the impression of the spirit of God'.[2] The cautious and empirical Mariotte rejected the notion in 1679, but the Dutch physiologist Boerhaave of Leyden, who trained so many eighteenth-century doctors, believed that a very fine and pure material spirit directed the growth of plants, a 'spiritus rector' or 'quinta essentia' which evaporated at death and roamed about amongst the elements diffused in the air until it returned to animate other organisms; it had, wrote Boerhaave, the power of generating a spirit like itself and is called by the alchemists 'filius solis' or 'spiritus inter-alens'.[3] Hartsoeker believed in 'plastic natures' or non-mechanical 'intelligences' whose functions were, in animals, to grow a new limb, for instance, or form the spermatic animalculae in the testicles of the male. These 'natures' derived in his opinion from the 'Anima Mundi'; they were portions of the Soul of the Universe, or first element, which he looked upon as being extended like matter but 'perfectly fluid'.[4] The Cambridge Platonists believed in a Spirit of Nature which resembled the Anima Mundi, except in that it worked in a perfectly regular and predictable manner, being an extended spiritual substance but not a free agent and acting always in a necessary and regular manner, rationally but not spontaneously.[5]

---

[1] *Cours de Chimie*, Paris, 1675, p. 5.

[2] Cf. R. Simon, *H. de Boulainviller*, 1939, p. 364.

[3] *Elements of Chemistry*, translated by Dallowe, London, 1735, i, p. 282, ii, pp. 10–11.

[4] *Recueil de plusieurs pièces de physique où l'on fait principalement voir l'invalidité du système de M. Newton*, Utrecht, 1722, p. 197.

[5] 'It may well be concluded that there is a plastic nature under him (God) which, as

Mersenne had admitted, in his *Impiété des Déistes*, that he was attracted by the notion of a World Soul, because of the similarity between this conception and the One in whom, according to Acts xvii. 28, we live, move and have our being, but on the other hand he disliked it, because it had the stamp of radicalism upon it; he was afraid of its levelling implications; he candidly admitted that it was bad for social discipline: a servant might claim to be as good as his master on the ground that their souls were both parts of the Universal Soul, clothed by the accident of birth in different bodies.[1] Gassendi was prepared to use the expression 'Soul of the World' in various figurative senses. His disciple De Launay included an essay on the Soul of the World in his *Essais de physique* (1667), giving it a far more positive rôle to play in his philosophy than ever Gassendi had done. He recalled that both Plato and the Stoics looked upon the world as an animate being and declared that he was prepared to accept the notion in two possible forms, either as a synonym for God himself as the governing soul of the world (but not as the 'informing' soul of the world) and, secondly, as it was understood by the chemists, namely as the natural heat diffused throughout the earth, inherent in it or coming from the sun, the 'heart' of the world.[2] Guillaume Lamy believed that individual souls are parts of a world soul.[3] He added this belief to his Lucretian physiology, with which it was not incompatible; the only current ideology with which it was incompatible was Cartesianism, and it disappeared wherever Descartes's influence was felt; all the same it was very widespread, or at least widely known at the end of the seventeenth century. When accounts of oriental beliefs became common, from 1660

---

an inferior and subordinate instrument, doth grudgingly execute that part of his providence which consists in the regular and orderly motion of matter.' (Cudworth, *The True Intellectual System of the Universe*, III, xxxvii, 5.) 'The Spirit of Nature . . . is a substance incorporeal, but without sense and animadversion, pervading the whole matter of the universe and exercising a plastic power therein according to the sundry predispositions and occasions in the parts it works upon.' (More, *The Immortality of the Soul*, ch. xii.)

[1] Paris, 1624, ii, pp. 402 and 419.

[2] 'Les uns veulent que cette chaleur soit particulière, comme la chaleur qui se rencontre dans la terre, causée par les feux souterrains, les autres disent que cette chaleur universelle procède du soleil, qui est comme le cœur du monde, qui la répand dans toutes les parties de l'univers, ainsi que le cœur distribue sa chaleur vivifiante dans tous les membres de l'animal. Cette opinion est défendue par nos Lullistes [meaning alchemists, disciples of Raymond Lulle the thirteenth-century alchemist], sous le nom d'archée [Van Helmont's term], ou d'esprit universel, et par les chimistes sous le nom de feu central, ou concentré dans la nature de tous les êtres.' (Vol. i, no. iii, pp. 39–40.)

[3] See above, p. 118.

onwards, along with the first plans for colonial establishments, they usually gave a prominent place to notions which travellers and missionaries alike readily assimilated to the traditional notion of the World Soul. Bernier did so when writing to Chapelain from India, in a letter intended to be read in the Paris drawing-rooms. So did works on China, which appeared in great numbers. In the one year 1688 the *Journal des savants* published three articles on Confucius, while two books on the subject appeared and Bernier composed a third which was not published.[1] They were all occasioned by the Jesuit missionary Couplet's *Confucius Sinarum philosophus* which appeared in 1686–7. In the same year 1688, the *Journal des savants* also reviewed three books on Siam. Rarely did a year pass without an article on Chinese religious beliefs or some kindred topic appearing in the review, whilst the great dispute between the Jesuit missionaries and their rivals kept the presses busy for many years with pamphlets on Chinese beliefs and ceremonies. All these books and articles used such terms as 'the material soul of the world' to describe oriental religious conceptions. La Loubère wrote that in Siam God was 'the material soul of the world or of the finest part thereof, which is the heavens'.[2] Magailan wrote that the Chinese worshipped the sky, which had no visible shape and was the first principle of all things.[3] An unpublished account of the religion of the 'Malabars', composed about 1700, referred to God as the Soul of the World or 'that substance which is diffused throughout all beings and is the intrinsic principle of motion'.[4]

---

[1] 5 Jan., review (by Régis) of Couplet's *Confucius Sinarum philosophus*; 8 June, Bernier's *Introduction à la lecture de Confucius*, originally written for Mme de la Sablière; in it Bernier echoes La Mothe le Vayer's 'Sancte Confuci ora pro nobis'; 26 July, review of Simon Foucher's *Lettre sur la morale de Confucius*, Paris, 1688; Foucher's *Lettre* and an anonymous work (by Brune? Louis Cousin?) entitled *La Morale de Confucius, philosophe de la Chine*, Amsterdam, 1688, are the two books. Bernier's unpublished *Confucius ou la science des princes* is at the Arsenal library, MSS no. 2698 and no. 2331 (2 copies); the information is drawn chiefly from Couplet (p. 6 of MS 2331).

[2] 'L'âme matérielle du monde entier ou de la plus belle partie qui est le ciel.' (*Du Royaume de Siam par Monsieur de la Loubère, envoyé extraordinaire du roi auprès du roi de Siam en 1687 et 1688*, Paris, 1691, i, ch. xxiii.)

[3] *Nouvelle Relation de la Chine* (*Journal des savants*, 12 July).

[4] 'Ils n'entendent autre chose par cette divinité que le plus subtil des cinq éléments, l'eau, le feu, la terre, l'air et le vent, mais pour ne pas faire une divinité aveugle et insensible, ils disent qu'il est intelligent et qu'il a des perfections qui vont jusqu'à l'infini. C'est, disent-ils, cette excellentissime puissance qui contient et renferme en soi tout l'univers et en est comme l'âme, le soutien et la force pour y produire et conserver toutes choses dans un ordre merveilleux. C'est cette substance répandue dans tous les êtres qui est le principe intrinsèque du mouvement. Rien ne peut être comparé à cette

The doctrine of the universal spirit plays a part in a curious imaginary travel story and utopian novel entitled *Histoire des Sévarambes* (1677) by an obscure rationalist named Denis Vairasse or Veiras[1] whose only other work was purely grammatical. His utopia, the land of the Sévarambes, was situated in lat. 42° S. and presumably in the far East. It was inhabited by a very rational people whose laws and customs were based on reason, not on tradition, and whose language was the expression of reason itself, so simple and so clear was it, and in such perfect keeping with the essences of things. Their religion had originally been that of the sun-worshipping Parsees, and in their temples are great flaming orbs and many-breasted statues symbolic of nature's abundance. But a philosopher of Venetian origin taught them that above the sun is a Being from whom all blessings come, via the sun's heat, into this world and this Being is represented by a black veil in their temples. Their philosophers believe the world to be infinite in extent and admit neither vacuum nor any privation or nothingness in it; the world is full of being. The majority of the inhabitants believe that the souls of men migrate after death to the sun, or are relegated to some cold planet if they have merited punishment, but some of their wise men look upon the soul as immortal only in the sense that it is part of the eternal first matter which takes on innumerable forms but subsists eternally. The religion of the country was founded originally by

divinité; elle existe par elle-même; elle ne dépend d'aucune chose et toutes choses dépendent d'elle. Elle a été de toute éternité et sera éternellement.' (Arsenal Library, MS no. 2242, p. 215. The manuscript belonged at one time to a certain Series, almoner on the ships of the Compagnie des Indes (p. 1). It was written after 19 May 1698 (p. 534).)

[1] Born *c.* 1635, of a Protestant family, Vairasse spent some years in London (1665–74) and visited Holland (1672). See E. Von der Mühl, *Denis Veiras et son Histoire des Sévarambes*, Paris, 1938. Vairasse was not the only one to use the imaginary travel story as a means of expressing ideas without taking the responsibility for them. A teacher of mathematics at Deventer in Holland, named Tyssot de Patot, published anonymously at Bordeaux in 1709 the *Voyages et aventures de Jacques Massé*, in one chapter of which a judge and a priest in a strange land express themselves very freely on the mortality of the soul and the social origin of the ideas of right and wrong. In 1727, on the occasion of his *Lettres choisies*, Tyssot de Patot was accused of deism before the Consistory court of Deventer and suspended from his post. He was seventy-two years of age at the time. The following declaration of orthodoxy, in the preface of his *Œuvres poétiques* in 1727, did not save him: 'Quand j'ai parlé de l'âme, ce n'est que dans la vue de faire voir aux fidèles que quelques arguments que Zénon, Origène, Tertullien, Spinoza et une infinité d'autres ont employés pour prouver qu'elle est corporelle et par conséquent mortelle' ... cannot outweigh the scriptures. (Cf. F. Lachèvre, *Le Libertinage au XVIIIe siècle*, x, pp. 236 sqq.) Foigny and Marana also used a literary disguise (see below, p. 270 n. 1) and the tradition was continued by Montesquieu's *Lettres persanes*.

Sévérias, but after his death there arose a false prophet named Omigas, who claimed to hold converse with the beings of the elementary sphere. Omigas gave himself out to be the son of the sun and performed false miracles by trickery, so that the Sévarambes were deceived by him and fell into all manner of superstitions. However, at the time when the European travellers were in the country, a wise and modest philosopher named Scroménas,[1] speaking on the occasion of the festival of the sun, expounded a new philosophy devoid of superstition. The world is eternal, said Scroménas, and it is both material and spiritual, according to the way it is looked upon. Matter and spirit are inseparably united together. Spirit is diffused throughout nature and moulds and forms the things of nature in relation to the Whole.[2] When it departs from a body, that body decomposes; the spirit goes to form some other being. After referring to Pythagoras, Plato and 'many great philosophers, Greek, Arab and Indian' in support of this doctrine, Scroménas goes on to talk about the age of the world according to the Egyptians, the Indians and the Chinese and explains that the Universe is composed of many suns like our own, all of which will one day perish and be replaced by others: his philosophy is a mixture of Pythagorean spiritualism and seventeenth-century astronomy.

Leibniz invented the term 'monopsychites' to describe those who believed in the Universal Spirit. In 1702 he composed an essay on the subject in which he says that 'many ingenious people' believe in the existence of one universal spirit which animates the universe in all its parts, each according to its organic structure, just as the same wind produces different sounds in different organ pipes. When an organic structure is healthy, the universal spirit serves as its individual soul, but when the organs become corrupt the spirit goes back to the boundless deep from whence it came. Aristotle's *intellectus agens* could be interpreted in this way, and both Pomponazzi and Naudé did so interpret it; Queen Christina of Sweden

---

[1] Spinoza? As described by Stouppe? It is not impossible, but nothing justifies us in affirming it.

[2] 'Le grand Tout', ii, p. 225 of the 1702 edition. The words used by Scroménas to describe the universal spirit resemble those used by G. Lamy (see above, p. 118): 'La vertu formatrice de cet esprit étant répandue par tous les corps, elle y agissait diversement et . . . se plaisait à une admirable variété . . . elle aimait à quitter des corps pour passer dans d'autres et . . . cela était la cause de la destruction et de la naissance de certains composés, de la mort et de la vie . . . dans la dissolution des corps il n'y avait que leur forme qui pérît pour en prendre une nouvelle sans qu'il se perdît rien de leur matière' (pp. 223–4 of 1702 edition).

believed in it, so did Spinoza and so do those Cartesians who adopt the system of occasional causes. Leibniz is nothing if not sweeping in his application of the principle, but his explanation of the recent spread of the belief is very apt. One can understand why many intelligent men believe that individual souls return to the universal soul if one takes into account the mistaken efforts made by some (Cartesians) to prove that the soul performs its functions without the aid of the body, forming abstract ideas without the aid of material ones. 'Those who rejected this state of separation and independence as contrary to reason and experience, were all the more disposed on that account to believe in the extinction of the individual soul and the preservation of the universal spirit only.'[1] In his *Théodicée*, in 1710, Leibniz complained that the doctrine had found all too much approval amongst the 'esprits forts' and added that a certain de Preissac had professed it publicly.[2] This Preissac was doubtless Jean-Aimeric de Preissac, marquis d'Eslignac, who fought at Maestricht in 1673, the year of Spinoza's visit to the French camp at Utrecht, and was so seriously wounded that he had to spend the rest of his days on his estates in Guyenne, where he died in 1721. He had originally been intended for the church, but had joined the musketeers on acceding to the title; Leibniz says that he 'dabbled in philosophy': he seems to have resembled in many ways the 'Militaire philosophe' of whom we shall speak later.[3]

Stouppe described the belief in the Universal Soul as the 'ordinary belief' of the Libertins in Holland.[4] Bayle, in his dictionary tried to reduce Spinoza's doctrine of substance to it. The system of the Soul of the World, which was so common amongst the ancients, he

---

[1] *Œuvres philosophiques*, ed. Janet, 1866, ii, p. 573: 'Or ceux qui rejetaient cet état séparé et cette indépendance comme contraire à l'expérience et à la raison, en étaient d'autant plus portés à croire l'extinction de l'âme particulière, et la conservation du seul esprit universel.'

[2] 'Cependant quelques modernes n'ont point fait difficulté d'adopter cette âme universelle et unique qui engloutit les autres. Elle n'a trouvé que trop d'applaudissements parmi les prétendus esprits forts, et le sieur de Preissac, soldat et homme d'esprit, qui se mêlait de philosophie, l'a étalée autrefois publiquement dans ses discours. Le système de l'harmonie préétablie est le plus capable de guérir ce mal. Car il fait voir qu'il y a nécessairement des substances simples et sans étendue, répandues par toute la nature.' (*Œuvres philosophiques*, ii, p. 42.)

[3] See below, p. 293.

[4] 'Quant aux Libertins, il semble qu'autant qu'il y en a, ils aient chacun leur sentiment particulier. La plupart croient qu'il y a un esprit de Dieu qui est dans tous les vivants, qui est épandu par tout ce qui est et qui vit dans toutes les créatures; que la substance et immortalité de notre âme n'est autre chose que cet esprit de Dieu, que Dieu lui-même n'est rien autre chose que cet esprit.' (*La Religion des Hollandais*.)

wrote, and which was the essential part of the Stoics' system, is the same as the doctrine of Spinoza.[1] If, he added, the ancients had used the geometrical method to express their ideas, the similarity would have been apparent. It is not clear what Bayle was driving at. If he meant that, expressed geometrically, the doctrine of the Soul of the World would be a rationalistic doctrine, there might be something to be said for his comparison, but he goes off into a long extract from Bernier's account of Indian religions, in which occurs the metaphor of the phial of water immersed in the ocean, and this way of expressing the relation between the individual soul and the World Soul turns the reader's attention away from the suggestion of immanentist rationalism.[2] The World Soul was not the only familiar conception to which Bayle sought to reduce Spinozism, and indeed it would have been difficult for him to sustain his comparison in any detail. Spinoza's extreme rationalism could hardly be reduced to visual imagery concerning the sea and the wind. One can, it is true, find something to be said for the comparison between the World Soul and Spinoza's 'Substance'. It is that Spinoza used the scholastic distinction between 'Natura naturans' and 'Natura naturata', that is to say the distinction between Nature looked upon as cause and Nature looked upon as effect. This distinction could be compared with the one implied in the belief in a World Soul, namely the distinction between the World as a material mass, and its Soul, or the intelligence diffused throughout it. But where the comparison is misleading is in the emphasis placed upon the dualism of the two. To emphasize the dualism of matter and intelligence leads to taking intelligence out of nature and making it transcendent, whereas Spinoza strove in the opposite direction, towards the realization of perfect unity. Such had been his starting point, in the two dialogues written before 1661 and which are included in the *Short Treatise* in modern editions of his works. They were unknown to the French public in Bayle's time, but there is no reason why we should not refer to them in attempting to assess the degree to which the common notion of a World Soul could provide a means of understanding Spinoza's thought. The two dialogues are full of the influence of Giordano Bruno, and Bayle did not fail to see a likeness between Spinoza and Bruno (Article *Bruno*, rem. D), although Bruno had not by any means been kept before the gaze even of the erudites and rarely had mention been made of him since Mersenne devoted a

[1] *Dictionnaire historique et critique*, article on Spinoza, rem. A.   [2] ibid.

large proportion of his *Impiété des Déistes* to refuting him. Giordano Bruno had not looked in nature for a reflection of an intellectual world; on the contrary he had looked inside nature for nature's cause and the principle of nature's unity. And Spinoza had begun likewise by saying 'is Nature one or is Nature many?' And the reply was that Nature was one, and that, if people failed to realize the fact and divided Nature into matter and spirit, it was because they had a wrong conception of causality; they imagined causes to be outside things and they were actually inside things. He had taken up the notion of immanent causality again in the second dialogue. The theologians looked upon God as the immanent cause of himself, but as the transitive cause of the world. But what if this distinction were a false one? What if God were the cause of the world in precisely the same way as he is the cause of himself? If so, God is the immanent cause of the world; the world is not added to God; the effect is not added to its cause; the world is the manifestation of God.

The doctrine of the immanence of the divine had never been looked upon with favour in the schools of theology. It is true that a change was in preparation at the end of the seventeenth century and that the most widely read demonstration of the existence of God, that by Fénelon, published in 1713, was to begin with the definition of the Being who is the cause of himself. But Fénelon made great use of Platonic and Cartesian themes and so did not have to take the precautions against pantheistic naturalism which the scholastic theologians had had to take. Malebranche similarly. Malebranche could even place the extended objects of geometry, ideal squares, circles, spheres, in God, without identifying God and the extended universe. The Cartesians could always fall back, in the last resort, on the fundamental distinction between thought and matter.

Malebranche composed, in 1708, a series of Dialogues in which he set out professedly to refute the immanentist rationalism of the Chinese doctrine of the 'Li', but with the real intention of refuting Spinoza without naming him.[1] The 'Li' is defined as an immutable order or eternal law to which the Christian God, if he existed, would be obliged to submit. The definition reminds one of the statements made by Uzbek, one of Montesquieu's Persians in the *Lettres persanes*: 'If there is a God, Rhédi, he must necessarily be just' (Letter 83), and 'Justice is a relationship of suitability really existing between two things'. Here the rationalism of the seventeenth century

[1] Cf. Malebranche to Dortous de Mairan, 29 Sept. 1713.

as a whole is implied and Montesquieu could have quoted Grotius for example: 'The propositions of natural law would retain their validity even if we were to assume that there was no God.'[1] But when Montesquieu put together such rationalism with natural science and defined laws in general as the necessary relationships which derive from the nature of things, he was, unknown to himself, stating the fundamental principle of an immanentist rationalism which Spinoza alone had consciously and systematically preached. The nearest the Cartesians got towards such thoroughgoing rationalism was when they defined Nature as the actual working of the laws of nature and denied the need for any separate entity entitled 'Nature' to preside over the workings of such laws. The doctrine of occasional causes, which dispensed with such a third entity between God and the World and saw in each operation of nature an active expression of God's will, came as near as dualism can come to making reason immanent in nature, but, far from wishing to suppress the distinction between the two substances, its chief exponent, Malebranche recoiled in horror from such an idea. Spinoza on the other hand affirmed explicitly that there can be no more than one substance and, although such a contention shocked Malebranche, it was attractive to many minds. It became the centre of controversy, to the almost total exclusion of all other aspects of Spinoza's philosophy. The fact that Descartes and Spinoza did not use the word 'substance' in the same sense made little impression on the dispute. The unity of substance became a tenacious theme in the free-thought of the eighteenth century and Christian apologetics became Cartesian in order to resist its appeal.

---

[1] *De Jure belli et pacis* (Preface). Pufendorf preferred to say that God had placed in all men's hearts the precepts upon which sociability depends (*De Jure naturae et gentium*, II, iii, 19).

XIII

Le Grand Tout

THE belief that all things are *parts* of God was foreign to Spinoza himself. 'Part' and 'whole' are indispensable concepts in our ordinary thinking, and Spinoza made constant use of them; but he denied that they could be applied to 'Substance', that is to say to reality itself.[1] He was not concerned with showing that all things are parts of one whole, though he did sometimes talk of the universality of things, or the sum total of existing things, carefully distinguishing between such a notion and that of Substance, Nature or God. He was not concerned with the 'stuff' of which the universe is made; he was concerned with the causes of things. He was concerned with showing that there is only one and the same order or concatenation of causes, whether we look upon nature under the aspect of extension or under the aspect of thought, whether we consider things or the true ideas (true definitions) of those things.[2] Such an approach to

[1] 'To this [*viz.* that God would be divisible] we reply: (1) that "part" and "whole" are not true or real entities, but only "things of reason", and consequently there are in Nature neither whole nor parts. (2) A thing composed of different parts must be such that the parts thereof, taken separately, can be conceived and understood one without another. Take for instance a clock which is composed of many wheels, cords and other things; in it, I say, each wheel, cord, etc., can be conceived and understood separately, without the composite whole being necessary thereto. Similarly also in the case of water, which consists of straight oblong particles, each part thereof can be conceived and understood, and can exist without the whole; but extension, being a substance [a word which Spinoza replaced later, in the *Ethics*, by the word "attribute"], one cannot say of it that it has parts, since it can neither diminish nor increase, and no parts thereof can be understood apart, because by its nature it must be infinite. And that it must be such follows from this, namely because if it were not such, but consisted of parts, then it would not be infinite by its nature, as it is said to be; and it is impossible to conceive parts in an infinite nature, since by their nature all parts are finite.' (*Short Treatise on God, Man and his Well-being*, trans. A. Wolf, London, 1910, pp. 28-9.)

[2] 'The order and connexion of ideas is the same as the order and connexion of things.' (*Ethics*, Everyman edn., part II, prop. vii.) Cf.: 'Thus also a mode of extension and the idea of that mode are one and the same thing, but expressed in two manners, which certain of the Jews seem to have perceived but confusedly, for they said that God and his intellect and the things conceived by his intellect were one and the same thing. For example, a circle existing in nature and the idea of an existing circle which is also in God is one and the same thing, although explained through different attributes. And thus, whether we consider nature under the attribute of extension or under the attribute of thought or under any other attribute, we shall find one and the same order and one and the same connexion of causes: that is the same things follow in either case. . . . As long

the study of nature implies a belief in its complete rationality and comprehensibility. It implies the belief that our knowledge of nature is, or can be, consistent with itself, that incoherence is not installed in the heart of things. In order to believe that, we must be able to believe that there is only one Substance, the cause and ground of all that is. We must be able to take as our starting point the definition of a Being, to be called God or Nature, *Deus sive Natura*, beyond whom and outside whom nothing can be thought of as having the least reality, a Being having all possible attributes.[1] A Being defined in this way must be a Substance[2] and must be self-caused;[3] such a Being cannot be thought of except as existing. A Being defined in this way must also be unique. Any other substance we might posit could only be known under one or other of the attributes of the Being we have defined and would therefore be indistinguishable from that Being.

All that exists exists by virtue of the one Substance thus defined. All that is produced is produced according to the laws of the divine nature. These productions are the ways in which the two attributes of thought and extension may be known to us. They are the effects of which the one Substance is the cause. Some of the modes[4] of Substance are infinite modes, such as the idea of God and universally true ideas, under the attribute of thought, and motion-and-rest, under the attribute of extension. The others are finite, such as the definition (or true idea) of the circle, under the attribute of thought, and the circle, under the attribute of extension. Individual things are modes of extension and thought actually existing. Men are individual things. The human body is a mode of extension actually

as things are considered as modes of thought, we must explain by the mere attribute of thought the order and connexion of causes of all nature; and in so far as things are considered as modes of extension, the order also of the whole of nature must be explained through the mere attribute of extension.... Wherefore of things as they are in themselves, God is in truth the cause, forasmuch as he consists of infinite attributes.' (ibid., note.)

[1] 'God I understand to be a being absolutely infinite, that is, a substance consisting of infinite attributes, each of which expresses eternal and infinite essence.' (ibid., part I, definition VI.)

[2] 'I understand Substance to be that which is in itself and is conceived through itself: I mean that, the conception of which does not depend on the conception of another thing from which it must be formed.' (ibid., definition III.)

[3] 'I understand that to be cause of itself whose essence involves existence and whose nature cannot be conceived unless existing.' (ibid., definition I.)

[4] Spinoza's definition of this term is as follows: 'By mode I understand the modifications (*affectiones*) of a substance or that which is in something else through which it may be conceived.' (ibid., definition V.)

existing, and the human mind is the idea of which the body is the object.[1]

God is the cause of all things, the source of all power; God's power is identical with his essence; the two concepts 'God's power' and 'God's essence' are the same. Most men, being used to considering mainly the utility of the things they desire, are satisfied with explanations of natural events couched in terms of an end in view, which they attribute to God. They say, for instance, 'We have teeth so that we may be able to bite', or, 'The sun shines so that we may see.' Thus men imagined gods whose intention was to reward or punish human beings, and when they saw that misfortune fell upon the good as well as upon the wicked, they supposed that the gods had plans which men were not able to comprehend. But mathematics and the other scientific disciplines[2] have taught men to search for the essences and properties of things and disregard their supposed utility.

On the face of it one might have expected the partisans of the new philosophy, headed by the Cartesians, to acclaim the first part of Spinoza's *Ethics* as a systematic statement of their principles. Spinoza himself did not fail to realize that the new science of the seventeenth century was the beginning of modern civilization, and he gave Descartes the credit for it.[3] But in fact the Cartesians, far from acclaiming Spinoza as a master, drew in their raiment and shunned him. 'The dull-witted Cartesians,' wrote Spinoza to Oldenburg as early as 1675, 'because they are believed to be in my favour and in order to free themselves from the suspicion, continued, and even now continue, to denounce my opinions and writings everywhere.' His first biographer, Lucas, echoed, 'The partisans of this great man (Descartes), in order to justify him against the accusation of atheism, have done all they could to bring down the lightning on the head of our philosopher.'[4]

---

[1] 'The object of the idea constituting the human mind is the body, or a certain mode of extension actually existing and nothing else.' (*Ethics*, Part II, prop. XIII.) For a systematic exposition of Spinoza's thought the reader is referred to H. F. Hallett, *Benedict de Spinoza: The Elements of his Philosophy*, London, 1957.

[2] 'And besides mathematics there are other causes (which need not be enumerated here) which enabled men to take notice of these general prejudices and to be led to the true knowledge of things.' (ibid., Appendix to Part I.)

[3] Cf. L. Brunschvicg, *Le Progrès de la conscience dans la philosophie occidentale*, Paris, 1927, p. 568.

[4] 'Les partisans de ce grand homme, pour le justifier de l'accusation d'athéisme, ont fait depuis tout ce qu'ils ont pu pour faire tomber la foudre sur la tête de notre philosophe.' (Quoted by G. Friedmann, *Leibniz et Spinoza*, Paris, 1946, p. 178.) A variant reads: 'Les partisans de ce grand homme, accusés d'athéisme. . . .' (Wolf, *The Oldest*

The very first attempt at a refutation of Spinoza's *Ethics* was indeed intended to prove that Spinozism was a product of Cartesianism. This was a frivolously inadequate dissertation by an obscure French controversialist named Aubert de Versé, who was living in the Netherlands and trying to put his spoke into every wheel.[1] The source of the trouble, according to this writer, was the notion of an all-perfect Being, which could only lead to the belief that the world is an emanation from God, as is believed in India. De Versé preferred to suppose the existence of two distinct substances, the one a perfect Being, the other imperfect, lifeless and unconscious. But he did not stop to explain how a substance that is *im*perfect, life*less* and *un*conscious can be conceived in and through itself. He disliked Spinoza's conception of a substance, and thought that the God Spinoza defined would not exist outside the human mind. He took no account of the elaborate reasoning whereby Descartes sought to establish that the 'objective' reality of the idea of such a Being in the mind presupposes the 'formal' reality of that Being. He was not therefore in a position to estimate the extent to which the conception was purely intellectual. Nor did he stop to consider that a system of knowledge must be an intellectual system. Knowing is an act of the mind; there is no knowing except in minds. We may change the world, or adapt ourselves to the world, without intellectualizing it, but it is difficult to see how we can *know* it without doing so; one cannot *know* the world by means of a builder's trowel, however immediate be the contact established by a builder's trowel between us and the world outside.

Pierre Poiret, a Protestant minister of Amsterdam, who published his *Fundamenta atheismi eversa* there in 1685, was only half a Cartesian; he had fallen under the spell of mysticism after the manner of Jacob Boehme and quietism *à la* Antoinette Bourignon, but he attempted to overthrow Spinoza by purely rational and logical arguments. Unfortunately for the success of his attempt, his thinking was far from having the sharp precision of his adversary's. He tried to show that Spinoza's 'Substance' was merely a universal collection of individual things, but he did not use the words defined by Spinoza with the same meanings as Spinoza had given to them. Spinoza's mathematical mind conceived of 'finite' things as things

Biography of Spinoza, London, 1927, p. 110.) The sense of this second version is not very clear.

[1] *L'Impie convaincu ou dissertation contre Spinoza*, Amsterdam, 1684.

bounded, or determined, by other things, and of 'infinite' things as things not bounded or determined in such a manner. But Poiret used the word 'finite' of things 'in which something is lacking' and 'infinite' of things 'in which there is full and pure reality', expressions of which the sense is far from clear, and which indeed have an emotional rather than a rational content. He made great play with subtle distinctions quite unconnected with Spinoza's definitions. He distinguished *substantia individualis*, *substantia summa*, *substantia idealis* and *substantia conceptualis*; nevertheless his language lacked real precision, and he resorted constantly to invective.

Christopher Wittich was a professor at Leyden. He had been a thoroughgoing Cartesian for years when he undertook to refute the *Ethics*, and had already published, in 1682, an attempt at reconciling Cartesianism with theology. His *Anti-Spinoza sive examen Ethices* appeared at Amsterdam in 1690, three years after his death. The preface, written by an anonymous editor, placed all philosophers in two groups, those who look upon God as the immanent cause of the world in the one, and those who look upon God as the transient cause of the world in the other. In the first group figured Democritus, Epicurus, Seneca and Spinoza, in the second, Descartes 'who first established this system with mathematical certainty'. The first group 'confused God with the world'; the second distinguished God from the world. Wittich himself began with an attack on Spinoza's logic. He tried to break through the argument concerning the unity of substance, making use for the purpose of distinctions current in the philosophy classes, but which had no place in the *Ethics*. The schools made use of the terms *genus*, *species* and *individual* in classifying the things to be found in nature. These were not terms used by Descartes, whose system was not classificatory, and Wittich cannot be said to be arguing as a Cartesian in making use of them, but he used them none the less in an attempt to show that two or more substances of the 'same' attribute may be granted. A thing may be the 'same' as another thing because it belongs to the same species; but it may at the same time be different, because it is a different individual in the same species. It was a distinction which Bayle was to reproduce with a flourish in his Dictionary. But it neglects the fact that Spinoza's definition of Substance makes nonsense of the expression 'a substance of the same species'. Such a substance could only be conceived with the aid of the notion 'species', and, according to Spinoza's definition, a substance is that which is conceived in and through itself. Spinoza gave no reality to the terms 'genus' and 'species' and he distinguished individuals from each other only in so far as they are causes of different effects. Spinoza's philosophy was a theory of causality, not a system of classification. He was not interested in knowing whether all things add up to one Thing or not; he was interested in knowing whether all things are the effects of one cause or not.

In France silence was kept for a long time. The first overt references came indirectly, as part of a controversy between Arnauld and Malebranche in the eighties; Malebranche avoided mentioning Spinoza's name in the eighth of his *Entretiens sur la métaphysique*, although this dialogue was intended to be a refutation of the *Ethics*; he referred only to 'that impious man of our times who made of the universe his God'.[1] When he did finally mention him in the thirteenth, he added the epithet 'misérable' to his name. A Benedictine monk named François Lamy composed a 'geometrical' refutation as early as 1684, but he was persuaded not to publish it, in spite of the appreciation expressed by 'illustrious prelates', of which he speaks in his preface, until he could add a more 'popular' refutation to it. Later he came to realize that the proper approach to the subject was not through geometrical reasoning, but through the study of human nature, a fact which he appreciated 'after reading' a *Traité de la connaissance de soi-même*, which he himself, though he does not tell us so, had written and begun to publish anonymously in 1694. When he finally published his *Le nouvel Athéisme renversé* in 1696, he quoted letters from Bossuet and Fénelon expressing approval of his work, and a sketch of a proposed refutation of the *Ethics* sent to him in a letter by Fénelon. There are two letters from Bossuet. The first approves of Lamy's 'popular' refutation and states that Bossuet has not yet read the 'geometrical' one; the other approves of the whole work. Bossuet seems to have been cautious in expressing approbation of Lamy's 'geometrical' refutation and, indeed, it is surprising that he should have given it countenance at all, seeing that it is very poor from a technical point of view. For the most part Lamy merely replaces Spinoza's carefully worded definitions by others less carefully worded. For instance he replaces the sixth definition of the first part, by the following: 'I call God the sovereign perfect Being, that is to say the Being who, in sovereign simplicity, possesses an infinity of perfections.' The terms he uses smack of the

[1] 'Cet impie de nos jours qui faisait son Dieu de l'univers.'

rhetoric of the pulpit rather than of exact science. This was not the style in which an argument could be carried on with the author of the *Ethics*. Spinoza had written: 'God I understand to be a Being absolutely infinite, that is to say a substance having infinite attributes each of which expresses eternal and infinite essence.'

Lamy was at great pains to rebut the accusation that Spinozism was a product of Cartesianism. He was himself an adept of the new philosophy, particularly of Cartesian physics, and had written a book in 1680 (published in 1689) in an attempt to justify the use of natural science in restraining popular fears and vain superstitions, a praiseworthy initiative for which he has not received all the credit he deserves. In his 'popular' refutation of Spinoza he relied to a great extent on Descartes's distinction between 'extended' things and 'thinking' things, but he worked this demonstration of the immateriality of the soul into an account of the human predicament. The Christian religion teaches the renunciation of the pleasures of this world, but the unbelievers, eager to enjoy this world's goods, claim that religion was invented for political reasons. One has only to study oneself for a while to understand that man's nature is dual, that he is a mixture of high and low, and Christianity alone can provide the remedy for the malady from which human nature suffers. But what if Spinoza's system were adopted? There would be no redemption, no rewards or punishments in a future life, no morality. Is it not obvious that the world is governed by providence? Why are our eyes at the front of our heads? Why have we molars at the back of our mouths?

In the sketch of a refutation sent to Lamy and published at the end of Lamy's book, Fénelon accepted the notion of an infinite Being as the starting point of the argument, and was content to argue within the scope of that conception, just as was Spinoza, but Fénelon insisted on interpreting the word 'infinite' in a 'nongeometrical' sense, an 'intensive', not an 'extensive' sense. He also argued that created things are not modes of the infinite Being. It is more perfect to be able to create something different from oneself than not to be able to do so. Therefore the perfect Being is able to create things different from himself. His creation must be imperfect by reason of its being separated from the perfect Being. The created world does not add anything to the infinity of God, because that infinity is 'intensive'. The argument obviously depends upon one's being able to read a sense into the word 'intensive' as used here, and, if one starts from Spinoza's own interpretation of the terms 'finite' and 'infinite' it is not possible to read any meaning into Fénelon's expression. But there is no flagrant misinterpretation of Spinoza's doctrine here, as there was to be in the same Fénelon's *Démonstration de l'existence de Dieu* of 1712. In this latter work Fénelon attributes to Spinoza the belief that the universe as given to sense, a composite assemblage of material things, is the perfect Being, in order to oppose to this pseudo-Spinozistic notion his own conception of a God who has drawn all bodily and thinking things from nothing and is all that is real in them, but without communicating his own substance to them in any way.

Malebranche's interpretation of Part I of the *Ethics* was similarly a gross misrepresentation. In his *Entretiens de métaphysique* (1688), he wrote:

The infinitely perfect Being is the universe, the assemblage of all that is . . . What a monster, Ariste, what a terrible and ridiculous fantasy! A God necessarily miserable or senseless in the greatest number of his parts or modifications, a God punishing himself or avenging himself, in a word an infinitely perfect Being composed nevertheless of all the disorders in the universe: what notion could be more full of obvious contradictions![1]

To be accused by Arnauld of agreeing with Spinoza was doubtless very painful for Malebranche, but neither of them made any serious attempt to express Spinoza's real thought in the long controversy they carried on and the name of Spinoza was little more than a term of abuse. Their real quarrel was a quarrel between two Cartesians concerning the nature of ideas. Arnauld refused to distinguish between 'intellectual' space, as conceived in the mind, and space as it is formally extended in the outside world. For Arnauld there was only one space, and if, as Malebranche said, 'intellectual' space was in God, then God was divisible into parts. Arnauld refused to read the *Ethics*, so it is not surprising that his knowledge of it was slight.[2]

---

[1] 'L'Etre infiniment parfait, c'est l'univers, c'est l'assemblage de tout ce qui est . . . quel monstre, Ariste, quel épouvantable et ridicule chimère! . . . un Dieu nécessairement ou malheureux ou insensible dans le plus grand nombre de ses parties ou de ses modifications, un Dieu se punissant ou se vengeant soi-même, en un mot un Etre infiniment parfait composé néanmoins de tous les désordres de l'univers: quelle notion plus remplie de contradictions visibles!' (Ninth *Entretien*.)

[2] 'Je n'ai point lu les livres de Spinoza, mais je sais que ce sont de très méchants livres et je suis persuadé que votre ami ferait très mal de les lire. C'est un franc athée qui ne croit point d'autre dieu que la nature. Il est de droit naturel de ne point lire de tels livres à moins qu'on ne les voulût absolument réfuter et qu'on eût du talent pour cela.' (To Vaucel, 30 xi 1691, *Œuvres*, 1775–85, III, p. 406.)

Many years later, when Malebranche was seventy-five years of age and was ill and tired, he was obliged by the inquiries of an ardent young physicist, Dortous de Mairan, to attempt to find an error of logic in the first part of Spinoza's *Ethics*, but it went very much against the grain with him and he soon asked his young correspondent not to pursue the topic. Mairan wrote first in 1713, from Béziers, asking Malebranche to point out where the first paralogism in Spinoza's reasoning lay. Malebranche replied that he had only read part of the *Ethics* and had been so put off by the first pages that he had not read any further. The chief error lay in confusing the intellectual world with the material world. But Mairan came back to his point, insisting, where exactly did the first paralogism occur? To this Malebranche replied with definitions of substance and mode: 'I can conceive, imagine and feel a single cubic foot of space without thinking about anything else; so that space is the substance and the cubic figure is a modification of it.' Malebranche's conception of 'substance' as exemplified here has, of course, no resemblance with Spinoza's. For Spinoza, only one of the three concepts 'space', 'foot', 'cube' can be thought of alone, namely 'space'. In order to pass from 'space' to 'cubic foot', a determination must take place.[1] But the next paragraph in his letter to Mairan shows that he was not prepared to discuss the doctrine of Spinoza seriously with the young physicist: 'He does not show that the reason which enlightens him is the universe or that the sky, the earth, men and himself are modifications of that reason.' Mairan asked again, where was the first paralogism? but got no further answer except that the axioms at the beginning of the *Ethics* were unacceptable and the fifth proposition (*viz.*, in the nature of things, two or more things may not be granted having the same nature or attribute) false.[2] Malebranche broke off the correspondence at this point.

Pierre Sylvain Régis, the Cartesian physicist and metaphysician, did at least face up to the problem of pure logic involved in Spinoza's definition of a substance. He tackled the question at the end of his

---

[1] It was the same point which had arisen between Leibniz and Malebranche concerning 'clear' and 'adequate' ideas (see above, p. 212). Malebranche doubtless saw his cube clearly in his mind; but he had no 'adequate' idea of it because he did not take into account the process by which it was generated.

[2] 'Il ne prouve nullement que cette raison qui l'éclaire soit l'univers, et que le ciel, la terre, les hommes et lui-même soient des modifications de cette raison.' (*Méditations métaphysiques et correspondance avec J.-J. Dortous de Mairan*, published by F.-S. Feuillet de Conches, Paris, 1841.)

L'Usage de la raison et de la foi (1704) and concluded courageously by saying that God should not be defined as a 'substance' at all. The essential function of a 'substance' is to be the subject of 'modes'; the terms 'substance' and 'modes' are correlative (p. 483). But God is not the subject of any 'modes'; he is 'pure Thought, existing by itself, eternal, infinite'. For Régis, as for all the Cartesians, 'thought' and 'spirit' are synonymous and his expression 'Une Pensée parfaite' could be rendered literally by 'A perfect Thought', but the meaning is 'A Spirit of which the essence is Thought', a 'Mind', and the Spinozistic equivalent would be 'God conceived under the attribute of thought.'[1]

In the Low Countries, Jean Leclerc, in his *De l'Incrédulité* (Amsterdam, 1696), Isaac Jaquelot, in books published in 1697 and 1699 at The Hague, where he was a minister of religion,[2] Peter Jens, a Cartesian doctor of philosophy and medicine of Leyden University, who published his book at Dordrecht in 1697,[3] all maintained that Spinoza's God was the material world as given to the senses. For Leclerc this was the essence of 'libertinage'. Pierre Bayle[4] concentrated on the same issue. He used against Spinoza the arms he used against any other sort of dogmatism, the reduction to the absurd, and the final position he adopted, in his revised edition of 1702, was that Spinozism was either a monstrosity or an uninterestingly orthodox and tiresomely obscure theological system. He was convinced that it had many adherents who were attracted only by its apparent newness and his chief object was not to show to what extent it departed from Christian beliefs, but to ridicule it and destroy its

---

[1] 'Une Pensée parfaite, c'est-à-dire qui existe par elle-même, qui est éternelle, infinie, etc.' (p. 499). Copies of an unpublished reply to Régis are to be found in the libraries of Aix-en-Provence, Auxerre and Fécamp; this work attempts to identify Spinoza's position with that of Malebranche.

[2] Jaquelot, *Dissertation sur l'existence de Dieu où l'on démontre cette vérité par la réfutation du système d'Epicure et de Spinoza* (they are the same according to the author), 1697; *Dissertation sur le Messie*, 1699, preface: 'J'apprends que ceux qui veulent soutenir Spinoza disent en secret qu'on ne l'entend pas, afin que le prétendu mystère de leur système serve d'asile à ceux qui se plaisent à contredire la religion sans savoir pourquoi ... Pour moi, je comprends que Spinoza, ayant appris de Descartes que l'espace ou l'étendue est une seule et même chose que le corps, il fait de cet espace une substance simple, unique, indivisible et éternelle qu'il nomme Dieu parce que notre imagination se forme cette idée de l'espace lorsqu'on le considère par abstraction sans rapport à aucun corps particulier.'

[3] *Petri Jens Phil. et Med. Doct. Examen philosophicum sextae definitionis Part. I Et. Benedicti Spinoza* (British Museum).

[4] We shall deal here only with Bayle's criticism of Spinoza; for an account of his career and his activities as a sceptical erudite, see below, pp. 283–5.

prestige; his arguments were so framed that, if successful, they would leave his reader's mind in a sceptical, rational and positive disposition like Bayle's own usual frame of mind. He did not dispose of Spinozism easily; it was never far from his thoughts for a quarter of a century. By 1677 he had heard of the *Tractatus theologico-politicus* and of two refutations of it, but he had as yet seen none of these works. It was in 1679 that he first read the *Tractatus*, in Saint-Glain's translation; he had not seen the original and could only suppose that the work he had before him was indeed a translation of Spinoza's work.[1] The account he wrote of the book at that time shows that he understood clearly enough all its implications as far as the criticism of the Old Testament was concerned, but towards the end of the book what caught his eye was not the claim to freedom of thought, but the right of the sovereign to decide the religion of a country, a notion which was not likely in any case to please a French Protestant. The next year he bought the *Opera posthuma* in Paris,[2] but the *Ethica* struck him merely as a 'big book of morals . . . not so orthodox as that of Henry More'. When the *Pensées diverses sur la comète de 1680* appeared in 1682, Spinoza already figured in it as an example of a virtuous atheist, but he was placed second to Vanini, and it was only in the second edition, in 1683, that an account of Spinoza's calm fortitude in the face of death was added, possibly to make up for Vanini's failure to remain unmoved in his appalling agony. By that time Bayle was in Holland and had doubtless heard the story of Spinoza's exemplary life. He had no doubts about Spinoza's atheism. In reviews in the *Nouvelles de la république des lettres* and in his correspondence all the way through the eighties, he constantly discussed the *Tractatus* and the *Ethics*, or, at any rate, refutations of the *Ethics*. He rebutted the attempt made by Aubert de Versé to make Cartesianism responsible for Spinozism. He collected arguments from Cartesian refutations such as that by Wittich. He accumulated around the name of Spinoza a vast store of information, a bibliography of refutations, a host of references and quotations by which the philosophies of the ancient atheists, of the Hindus, and of the Chinese could be shown to have preceded that of the *Ethics* on the way to dusty death or remained to serve as the expression of primitive mentalities. He knew of everything connected with Spinozism and convinced himself that there was nothing new

[1] *Œuvres diverses*, t. iv, pp. 570–1 (letter to Minutoli, 26 May 1679).
[2] ibid., p. 573 (to same, 1 Jan. 1680).

in it except the 'geometry'. The belief in a single substance was an old error. That Spinoza should have been an unbeliever and at the same time a kind and virtuous man, well and good! but that his system should be taken seriously, no! Bayle devoted a score of in-folio pages, the matter of a book of considerable size, to ridiculing it. He referred to Moslem sects who had identified God with the material world; he referred to the Sadducees, to a certain Alexander Epicurus who taught that God and matter were identical, to Straton, to a certain David de Dinan in the twelfth century who taught that God and primary matter were the same. He quoted from Cicero's *De natura deorum*. He argued that if God is material he is changeable and corruptible like the gods of Ovid and Virgil, like Proteus, or Thetis or Vertumnus. If God is the one substance, God is responsible for all crimes; he commits all crimes; he is the killer and the killed; he is the army of the victors and the army of the vanquished; when the Germans slaughter the Turks or *vice versa*, it is God who does the killing on both sides and who is killed; it is God who eats God when one animal eats another; God has diseases, the stone, colic, fever, madness; why trouble about the difficulties of the Christian belief if one is prepared to accept absurdities of this kind? Bayle obviously felt some warmth in writing this, and had a Spinozist replied: 'Yes, indeed, when German fights Turk, God is in the one as he is in the other and neither has any strength without God', it is doubtful whether Bayle would have been convinced, for he had in his mind the notion that an extended substance was something which could be cut up and sold by the pound. He did not rely only on ridicule; he was convinced that he could destroy Spinoza's argu-ments by logical weapons, but his blows fall so wide of the mark that one is driven to wonder whether Bayle, who had read everything even remotely connected with the question, had read the *Ethics* with care. His application of Wittich's argument went particularly wide of the mark. He assumed that Spinoza described man as a 'species of modification' and Socrates an individual in that species, whereas nothing could be more foreign to Spinoza's way of thinking than to give any sort of reality to such a term as 'species' or any merely classificatory term. Bayle sensed that the problem of individuation was unresolved in Spinoza's book, but far from approaching the problem with sympathy and far from realizing that Spinoza had worked back from the many to the One, from effects to causes, from causes to the One cause, and was now attempting the great movement in the other direction which Descartes had dreamed of, from causes to effects, Bayle vulgarized the whole dispute.[1] At no time did he come near to the Spinozistic conception of immanent causality, which presents the modes as the effects of which God, under the aspect of thought or under the aspect of extension, is the immanent cause. Even in the 1702 edition, in which Bayle replied to the accusation of having misrepresented his adversary's thought, he still wrote as though he were describing some primitive religion. As for Spinoza's theory of ideas, in Part II of the *Ethics*, and the psychological doctrine contained in Part III, Bayle showed no interest in them, and in this he resembled the Cartesian metaphysicians. The only aspect of Spinoza's work which attracted him was the scholarship of the *Tractatus*; at no time did he speak slightingly of that; but the metaphysics of the *Opera posthuma* troubled him unpleasantly. It is doubtless not surprising that a man whose historical and critical bent disposed him primarily to an interest in the peculiarities of individual consciences should have resisted the unifying impulse of Spinoza: Bayle was not inclined to lose his individual consciousness in the infinite.

Many of Bayle's contemporaries felt, however, the lure of cosmic unity. The same idea of the Totality of all things from which Bayle shrank did not repel all men in the same way. The author of the *Histoire des Sévarambes* (1677) seems to have been the first to use an expression which was to represent one of the key ideas of the next century: *le grand Tout*. In an infinite universe, says the wise Scroménas, in Vairasse's novel, innumerable suns, each one of which is the source of life and animation for the planets which surround it, are all 'lieutenants du grand Tout'.[2] It may be that Scroménas represents Spinoza, and that the author is seeking to distinguish Spinozism from the deism which is described elsewhere in the book and is the worship of a Supreme Being, not of the universality of things. But it is more likely that the expression 'le grand Tout' represents the All of the ancients and that Vairasse was not thinking particularly of Spinoza. One may say the same of another rationalist writer of a travel story and utopia, Gabriel Foigny, an unfrocked

---

[1] 'Mais selon Spinoza les créatures sont en Dieu, ou comme l'effet dans sa cause matérielle, ou comme l'accident dans son sujet d'inhésion, ou comme la forme du chandelier est dans l'étain dont il est composé. Le soleil, la lune, les arbres, en tant que ce sont des choses à trois dimensions, sont en Dieu comme dans la cause matérielle dont leur étendue est composée; il y a donc identité entre Dieu et le soleil, etc.' (Rem. DD.)

[2] vol. ii, p. 225 of the 1702 edition.

Franciscan monk, who lived by giving lessons.[1] Foigny was the author
of *La Terre australe connue* (1676), which he attributed to a M.
Sadeur, supposedly a great traveller. In his book, which mingles
fantastic adventures with botanical observations and philosophical
discussion, an Australian sage explains that one must distinguish
between 'being in general' or 'general existence', on the one hand,
and 'particular existence', on the other. In so far as we participate in
'being in general', we are immortal, but in so far as we are particular
beings, we perish. When Foigny's Australians are tired of their particular existence, they eat the fruit of a certain tree and die happy.
Were it not for this induced demise, they would live for ever as
'particular beings', because their perfectly healthy mode of life has
eliminated disease from amongst them. They are nudists and paci-
fists, and, as they are hermaphrodites, jealousy is unknown amongst
them. Their language is perfectly simple and comprehensible because
it is rational and corresponds to the nature of things. There is no
doubt about Foigny being a radical rationalist, and it is not impossible that he had heard of Spinoza; perhaps he had read Stouppe?
He may even have read the *Tractatus* in the original; but it would be
gratuitous supposition to suggest that his ideas came from Spinoza;
they are in line with the tradition of radical rationalism to which
Vanini and Cyrano belong.

The idea of 'le grand Tout' was expressed again very clearly in
the Niort doctor Gaultier's work entitled *La nouvelle Philosophie
sceptique* (1714), which we have already analysed.[2] In that work, the
unity of all that is, and the multiplicity of all that is, are said to be
the same thing, the All, which is perfect in its totality, without being
infinitely perfect, unless it be in extension, seeing that it is of infinite
extent. It is being without restriction, being of every sort, no matter
what it is or may be.[3] It is found in the abbé Meslier's criticism of
Fénelon's *Démonstration de l'existence de Dieu* and in Meslier's

[1] At Geneva. See F. Lachèvre, *La Vie de Gabriel de Foigny*, in *Le Libertinage au XVIIe
siècle*, x, p. 21.

[2] See above, p. 220.

[3] John Toland, in his *Origines judaïcae* (1706), had attributed to Moses the belief that
God and the universality of things were the same (p. 117). Toland had invented for this
conception a word which in later years was to be adopted generally, namely the word
pantheism. He used it first in 1705, in *Socinianism truly stated*. Toland referred to Moses
as a 'pantheist' or a 'Spinozist': 'Mosem enimvero fuisse Pantheistam, sive ut cum
recentioribus loquar, Spinozistam.' (*Origines judaïcae*, p. 117.) Gaultier may have known
Toland's work, but he made no mention of him, and he declared against Spinoza. The
idea of the All was 'in the air' at the time both in France and England.

'Testament', where no doubt is left that the one universal substance is matter. The theory existed outside the scope of Spinoza's influence and united a pronounced opposition to Cartesian dualism with the original radical tradition from which it stems.

In one case at least, however, it was either looked upon as a faithful interpretation of Spinoza's doctrine of substance or wittingly used as an improvement on Spinoza's doctrine. This was Count Henry de Boulainviller's *Essai de métaphysique*, of which the popularity is vouched for by the fact that manuscript copies of it are to be found in eleven French public libraries, despite the fact that it was published in 1731 in the guise of a refutation of Spinoza, along with those of Lamy and Fénelon.[1] Whatever it may be, it is certainly not a refutation of Spinoza. It is, in fact, a system of philosophy worked out by Boulainviller himself and combining with elements taken from the *Ethics* philosophical themes taken from many different traditions. Boulainviller (1658–1722) had become interested in Spinoza around 1696. His first philosophical essay dated from 1683,[2] and was a scholastic exercise with a strong admixture of notions taken from the 'chemists' and astrologers, Van Helmont particularly; Boulainviller remained an astrologer all his life. He also borrowed from Locke; he was nothing if not eclectic. His first acquaintance with Spinoza came through the *Tractatus*. Among his reading notes, preserved at the Bibliothèque nationale, is a careful analysis of the first six chapters of this work, made either by Boulainviller himself or by a secretary. It is accompanied by a commentary which consists of a conventional refutation; for instance, commenting on the chapter on miracles, he opposes Spinoza with the remark: 'the order of the world depends on a free power and not on the necessity of nature'. But he was aware of the problem: 'If God and nature are the same thing or if the fixed order of the world is a consequence of the divine order, Spinoza is right.'[3]

---

[1] Angoulême (29), Arsenal (Paris) (2235 and 2236, 2 copies), Auxerre (235–6 and a partial copy in 237), Besançon (418), Bibliothèque nationale (fonds fr. 9111 and 12242–43, 2 copies), Fécamp (24–25), La Flèche (Prytanée nationale, 6), Laon (514), Mazarine (Paris) (3558), Troyes (2820), Vire (295). It was published in 1731 at Brussels by Lenglet du Fresnoy under the title *Réfutation des erreurs de Benoît de Spinoza*.

[2] Boulainviller revised his essay in 1700, for his son. Renée Simon gives an analysis of it in her *Henry de Boulainviller*, Paris, 1939, pp. 358–417. There is a copy of it in the library at Vire and another in the library of the Chambre des Députés.

[3] This analysis of the *Tractatus* is preserved with Boulainviller's other reading notes at the Bibliothèque nationale; the manuscript came from the library of the Saint-Sulpice seminary. There are six volumes of reading notes (MS n. acq. fr. 11071–6), the

Boulainviller did not however, or so he says, concern himself with the *Ethics* until 1704, when he came across a copy of it (in a book shop doubtless) while he was hunting for a Hebrew grammar. He had heard Spinoza discussed in the learned circles he frequented, where some said he was dangerous and others that he was too unintelligible to be dangerous, but he had not studied the matter seriously. He now did so, and at the same time an account of Chinese religions published by the Jesuit missionaries made him realize the similarity between Spinoza's doctrine and that of the Chinese, and contributed to arouse his interest.[1] There is doubtless a good deal of invention in this account. Boulainviller must have known that Bayle made the same comparison with Chinese religions.[2] There is, moreover, in the same volume of reading notes which contains the analysis of the *Tractatus*, an analysis of the first part of the *Ethics*, made doubtless by a secretary, with Boulainviller's commentary added. The analysis suggests that Spinoza's two attributes of thought and extension presuppose two distinct substances. Boulainviller, in his added comment, resolves this problem in a manner which enables us to foresee the way in which he was to interpret Spinoza's doctrine in his *Essai de métaphysique*. Instead of saying that the two attributes are two ways in which God is known, he argues that that 'attribute' should be taken to mean 'mode'; they are 'modes' of something he calls 'existence'. He did not approach the problem as one of causality or of theory of knowledge; he asked what the 'stuff' of the universe is, with the result that he made of 'existence' the equivalent of the 'primary matter' of the schools. On the other hand, in the same volume of reading notes, along with notes taken from Locke in which all knowledge of 'substances' is denied to us, are other notes, taken apparently from the *Ethics*, in which the relationship between Substance and Attribute according to Spinoza is quite correctly stated.[3] In the *Essai de métaphysique* one finds both the incorrect and the correct interpretations. Boulainviller says quite explicitly that 'God and the universality of things are the same', but

Extrait du Traité théologico-politique is in vol. ii, pp. 53–255. There is a summary in Renée Simon, *Henry de Boulainviller*, pp. 461–94, p. 245 (Simon, p. 490): 'Si Dieu et la nature sont la même chose ou si l'ordre fixe du monde est une conséquence de l'ordre divin, Spinoza aura raison.'

[1] Prefatory remarks.

[2] He declares in the same place, at the beginning of the *Essai*, that Bayle did not understand the *Ethics*.

[3] 'L'étendue n'est ni une modalité, ni une substance, . . . elle est un attribut de la substance.' (Quoted by Renée Simon, *Henry de Boulainviller*, p. 455.)

he also maintains that 'Substance' is indivisible, and explains the relationship between 'Substance' and 'Attribute' as one of knowledge, our knowledge of 'Substance', and the relationship between 'Substance' and 'mode' as one of cause and effect, not as one of subject and adjunct. He also gave a place to Spinoza's moral doctrine in his work, without deforming it; he prescribed obedience to the rules of conduct one finds within oneself, because to transgress those rules is to deny the very principle of one's being. He prescribed the love of God untainted by any mercenary aim.

Boulainviller's work does not begin like a summary of the *Ethics*. It begins with the Cartesian assertion that he is a thinking being, and then proceeds, in a very un-Cartesian way, to the assertion that other beings exist also, some of them thinking beings like himself, others with the power of feeling and perhaps also, but not certainly, the power of thought, others which are merely extended in space and having neither feeling nor thought. Experience, which comes from sensations stored up in his memory, teaches him that all three of these categories of things share the property of being extended, not only because they can all be seen to be extended, but also because, after a certain time, those belonging to the thinking and feeling groups lose those properties and fall together with the third kind, devoid of thought and feeling. There is therefore another distinction to be made, a distinction between living things on the one hand and non-living things on the other. But in all these beings, living and non-living, thinking, feeling and the merely extended, there is one common property: they all enjoy the common property of existence. From this common property of existence, the mind proceeds to the universal idea embracing all that exists, the idea of 'being taken abstractly' or 'being in general'. The first property of 'being in general' is existence: it would not otherwise be 'being'. Particularly things are not this Being; they are seen to be corruptible and to perish. Is the matter which composes them, and which is transferred from the one to the other, this Being? No, because neither thought nor incorporeal space are included in matter. So there must be a Being more all-embracing than matter and which includes all ways of existing within itself. Now, everything that exists exists either in itself or in something else. Some things appear at first sight to exist in themselves, men; for instance, or trees. Other things obviously exist in something else; colours, for instance, or shape. A thing may be (1) a substance, (2) a 'mode', (3) an 'accident'.

A man is a 'mode' of being, his shape is an 'accident'. A round object is a 'mode' of being, its roundness is an 'accident'. We have no positive idea of Substance. It is not extension, because extension excludes thought; it is not thought, because thought excludes extension. Thought and extension are 'attributes' of absolute being. Absolute being is unique, infinite, independent, indivisible, eternal, extended, thinking. Each idea in my mind is the form of my mind, as figure is the form of wax; I have no mind apart from my present idea. An idea is not added to thought; an idea is not an adjunct of which thought is the subject. An idea is a 'mode' of thought, just as figure is a 'mode' of extension. The relation between thought and an idea is one of cause and effect, not one of subject and adjunct. Substance is self-caused, and is therefore 'free', in the sense that its determination is in itself; were this not so, Substance would be contingent and therefore not self-caused. Thoughts are separate 'modes', but that does not mean that Substance is divisible under the attribute of thought; similarly, bodies are separate 'modes', but that does not mean that Substance is divisible under the attribute of extension.

God is the universality of things. Therefore, the God I have looked upon as a creator and as a judge has no reality. But this does not mean that there is no God. The Universal Being has given me my being and I must love the source of my being with a pure and untainted love, worship him without fanatical zeal, follow the precepts he has placed in my reason.[1] It may be objected that the ideas of good and evil are merely experimental and derive from the need of self-preservation, but in seeking my own self-preservation I am indeed following the laws of my own being, and in that sense I am seeking the Good. Here Boulainviller replies to a whole series of possible objections, leading up to the statement[2] that the only way of under-

---

[1] The theme is developed in a somewhat similar way by G. P. Marana's 'Turkish spy' in the *Espion turc dans les cours des princes chrétiens* (published in Italian and French in Paris, 1684, and in English in London, 1694, under the title *Letters writ by a Turkish Spy who lived five and forty years undiscovered at Paris*): 'To speak the truth, I am wavering in all things but this, that there is an eternal mind everywhere present, the root and basis of all things visible and invisible, whom we call Allah, the support of infinite ages, the rock and stay of the universe. Let thou and I, dear friend, persevere in adoring that superlative essence of essences with internal and profound devotion; let our thoughts be pure, our words few, and those full of innocent and grateful flames (*sic*), for assuredly God delights not in the babbling of the tongue; as for the rest, let us live according to our nature and reason as we are men.' (Letter xix of vol. iv, p. 358.)

[2] p. 176 of Part I of the 1731 edition.

standing the union of body and soul is to see them as modes of two attributes which have been looked upon as two separate substances for the last two thousand years. They are not two substances, but one, known under the two attributes of thought and extension. The mind is the idea of the body. A mind is an 'objective' idea in the infinite mind, that is to say, the object of an idea in the infinite mind; the body is the thing of which it is the idea.

But all bodies are not the objects of minds,[1] only such as have a certain degree of flexibility, depending upon their organization. From the lowest form of organized life to the highest development of the reason, innumerable degrees exist. Boulainviller comes near here to Leibniz without mentioning him, and similarly when he defines the 'idea' of an unconscious being as an 'incomplete act' in the infinite mind. The greater the degree of consciousness in an individual being, the more complete the act in the infinite mind.

The exposé then turns towards sensationism. The body receives impressions, which are stored in the brain as images and are revived by memory. The mind does not know itself; it does not know the things outside the body; it knows only the sensations caused in the body by those things. The comparison between two sensations is what we call judgment; what we call an obvious truth is merely a very clear perception.[2] The brutes reason by means of the juxtaposition of images, and the only difference between us and them is that our bodies are better organized than theirs. All our ideas are true in the sense that they have existence, but when we say that an idea is true we usually mean that it conforms with its object. A very clear perception assures us that an idea conforms with its object. Confused conceptions cannot be true. Soon we come to the principle: *nihil est in intellectu quod prius non fuerit in sensu*, and we are far from Spinoza. The rest of the work is actually a discussion on method,

---

[1] Here begins a very non-Spinozistic development.

[2] 'N'est-ce pas évident que, quand il s'agit de comparer deux idées ou deux images, e seul sentiment nous découvre ce qu'elles ont de commun ou de différent, et que la conclusion n'est autre chose que la sensation plus ou moins parfaite de leur convenance ou disconvenance, laquelle, si elle atteint jusqu'au degré que nous nommons évidence et conviction, n'est qu'une perception plus vive, et qui en grave d'autant mieux son image dans la mémoire que toutes les autres de même espèce?

'Il est donc vrai que nos plus subtiles pensées, pourvu que ce soient des pensées (car il est souvent des assemblages de paroles qui ne signifient rien) ne sont que les images de nos perceptions, pareilles aux plus simples dans le principe commun, qui est la sensation, mais plus délicates dans les portraits qu'elles nous peignent, parce qu'elles sont tirées par réflexion et conséquemment plus dégagées de la matière.' (p. 121 of Part I of the 1731 edition.)

which is an empirical method and includes instructions for the checking of the evidence of one sense against the evidence of another.[1] We are far also from le grand Tout, but return to it at the end of the first part of the *Essai* with the assertion that, at death, the body returns to universal matter and the soul remains in the infinite mind as an idea of what an individual person has been, and could be again, if the body were restored to life. The rest is called 'On the Passions' and occasionally makes use of the fourth part of the *Ethics*, but most of it is unlike the original it is supposed to be following. There is nothing in the *Essai* corresponding to the fifth part, 'On the Power of the Intellect', which contains the essence of Spinoza's moral doctrine; the moral doctrine, in the *Essai*, is confined to the developments on love of self, desire and aversion as in any naturalistic treatise of morals. In fine, Boulainviller's effort centres on the establishment of the notion of a single substance, coupled with a sensationalist psychology and a naturalistic morals.

Boulainviller's notion of 'Substance' resembles that of the English free-thinker John Toland, but there is no mention of Toland's *Letters to Serena* (1704) in the *Essai* and no mention of Toland in his reading notes. Nor is there any trace of Toland's characteristic doctrine, the theory by which he aimed at correcting Spinoza, namely that motion is essential to matter. Toland's *Letters to Serena*, containing as they do an account of ancient beliefs concerning the immortality of the soul, coupled with a sketch of a non-spiritualistic philosophy, might well have served as a compendium of free-thought in France in the early years of the eighteenth century, but it is actually easier to prove that Toland was acquainted with speculation in France (he knew of Dehénault's translation of a passage from Seneca's *Troades*, for example),[2] than it is to discover any trace of him at all in France at the beginning of the century.[3]

[1] There is little to be gained by comparing it with the intellectual method described in Spinoza's *Tractatus de intellectus emendatione* which appeared in the *Opera posthuma*.

[2] At the end of book II of the *Letters to Serena*; cf. above, p. 157.

[3] There are manuscript copies of translations of the *Pantheisticon* at Carpentras, Paris (Sénat) and Vire, but the earliest possible date for these is the year of publication (1720). There is also one in the University library at Ghent; it mentions the date of Toland's death (1722) in the preface. Huet attacked Toland in 1714 (*Dissertations sur diverses matières de religion et de philosophie*, publ. by de Tilladet at The Hague, 5th *dissertation*). Huet remarks that 'La machine du monde est le seul être éternel reconnu par Toland.' The *Journal littéraire* of 1714 (iv, p. 252) remarked on the fact. Fréret had a copy of the *Letters to Serena*, but Voltaire seems to have made little use of Toland (N. L. Torrey, *Voltaire and the English Deists*, New Haven, 1930, p. 18 (Fréret)). Voltaire may have known Desmaizeaux's *Life of Toland* (1722). At Rouen there is a manu-

The abbé Jean Meslier seems to have been indebted neither to Spinoza nor to Toland and to have found it necessary neither to suppose two infinite attributes of Substance, nor to adopt a religious attitude towards the universality of things. He was content that one material substance diversely formed and infinite in extent should compose the total sum of being, a simple creed which he reached, as far as argument goes, by pulling to pieces the loose logic of Fénelon's *Démonstration de l'existence de Dieu*. Fénelon's book, which appeared first in 1712 and ran through seventeen editions by 1740, exercised a subtle influence on eighteenth-century thought, but not as a piece of close reasoning.[1] One of his most affectionate readers was Jean-Jacques Rousseau. Fénelon's sincerity, his human-heartedness and feeling for the majesty and mystery of the world appealed to those who sought a religion of the heart and yearned to lose themselves in a universe filled with God, but not to understand the nature thereof. Nevertheless, it claimed to be a demonstration and unfolded long strings of proofs of both a popular and a meta-physical kind, not always in a coherent manner, and not altogether above the reproach of stringing together pulpit phrases where logical argument had been promised. His book was just the kind to provoke angry marginal notes from a reader enamoured of rigorous demonstrations.

After a series of 'popular' proofs drawn from the spectacle of nature and enumerating the marvels of the world and of the human frame, Fénelon confronted the Epicurean contention that nature was not made for man and that the present ordering of things is merely one of an infinite series occurring in a universe composed of an infinite number of atoms in motion. If atoms are in motion, claimed Fénelon, who gave them that motion? If they move according to certain laws, who established those laws? Is it not necessary to assume that in everything that has been created there is a nothing-ness, a void and an imperfection, as well as the mark of the giver of all being?

In the second part Fénelon unfolds his metaphysical proofs against Spinoza, or rather against the popular notion of Spinozism. His argument begins in a Cartesian vein with the knowledge of

script entitled *Mémoires touchant la vie et les écrits de M. Jean Toland* (MS no. 1554). Prévost attacked Toland in vol. xx of *Le Pour et le Contre*, pp. 310–11. The clandestine tracts do not mention him amongst their innumerable references. In short Toland seems to have caused little stir in France before d'Holbach became interested in him.

[1] Cf. A. Chérel, *Fénelon au XVIIIe siècle*, Paris, 1917.

himself as a thinking being and the doctrine of clear ideas, pushed to the point at which he judges God by a standard of truth independent of God, but, as truth and being are the same thing, God, Truth and Being become identified, and Fénelon begins to pursue a course which takes him alongside that pursued by Spinoza, without apparently suspecting the presence of Spinoza in the discussion. Our intelligence only exists in so far as its object is true; if God has created me as a thinking being, he has created nothing unless he has given me some real knowledge. That real knowledge consists in clear ideas. I have the idea of infinite perfection. Such an idea cannot be derived from nothingness, so there must be a really existing source of it outside myself. Moreover, my idea of a perfect being includes existence by definition, as the definition of 'man' includes 'reason'. Who has put this idea in my mind if not God? Spinoza confuses this Being with the universality of things, and says that, although the parts of the universe change, the whole does not. But internal motion is contrary to infinite perfection and an assemblage of things cannot be a unity; the All cannot be the infinitely perfect Being. The All cannot know itself; the perfect Being has the perfection of self-knowledge. The perfect Being has drawn the created world from nothingness; he is all that is positive in his creation while all that is imperfect is nothingness. A little examination reveals the pit of nothingness that there is in the things of this world. All that is positive is in God. Immensity is in God, but not extension, which is limited and divisible. God is all being, or, more simply, he is.[1] He watches over his creatures and expects to receive their worship. He has given man an immaterial soul. Can matter think? And what reason is there for supposing that the non-material soul dies when the material body dies?[2]

Jean Meslier was born in 1664 or 1667 and was ordained in 1688. He served as a country curate (*vicaire*) until 1692 and was then given the living of Etrépigny in Champagne, where he served until his death in 1729. He had acquired considerable erudition, and his reading, as illustrated by the numerous quotations with which he supported his arguments, was vast, stretching from the ancient poets and philosophers to Bayle and Malebranche by way of the

---

[1] 'Il n'est précisément aucune chose singulière et restreinte; il est tout; il est l'être, ou, pour dire encore mieux en disant plus simplement, il est; car moins on dit de paroles de lui, et plus on dit de choses. Il est: gardez-vous bien d'y rien ajouter.' (p. 167.)

[2] There follows the text of Fénelon's letter to François Lamy containing a refutation of Spinoza (cf. above, p. 259).

Church fathers: judging by the frequency with which he quoted the *Essais*, his favourite author was Montaigne.

He read Fénelon's *Démonstration* in the 1718 edition and covered the margins with angry rebuttals of the author's arguments.[1] These scattered observations are not difficult to piece together into a coherent whole. Meslier's main contention is simple. It is that the eternal and infinite being, which is self-caused and necessarily existing, is none other than nature itself. Being, nature, matter, substance are all one and it is useless to invent an 'all-perfect Being', for such a Being, separate from matter, would be featureless, motionless and impotent, incapable of acting in any way on the material world. Only matter can give motion to matter; a non-material cause could never have set matter in motion at the beginning. There is no point in asking who made matter and set it in motion. Such a question leads merely to another, namely: who made the being who made matter and set it in motion? One can save one's breath by saying that matter is what it is by itself, an eternal and infinite being. It is divisible, and it is divided into particles. Meslier calls these particles atoms, but makes it quite clear that he does not look upon even the smallest particles as indivisible. The particles move according to certain laws which are inherent in matter and have not been prescribed by any outside being. They are not arbitrary laws and are merely what they are. This does not mean that chance motion can manufacture a clock. The present ordering of the world may be looked upon as one of innumerable possible orderings of matter, but a clock can only be made by human hands. It is not claimed that atoms suddenly come together to form things; what is claimed is that, over a period of time, bodies are constituted, which may become organic bodies, living bodies, beasts and men who think. Men seek the good; men act freely. One gains nothing by inventing a Perfect Being, whom one is then obliged to make responsible for both good and evil; unless, that is to say, one invents another being called nothingness in order to make of it the source of evil. And why should nothingness be called a 'being'? Fénelon has declared that nothingness cannot be the object of knowledge; is he now going to make of it the very substance of the world?

[1] There is a copy at the Arsenal library (S1109); Nodier described three copies in 1829 (*Mélanges tirés d'une petite bibliothèque*, pp. 178–82). Many of Meslier's notes are reproduced in A. Chérel, *Fénelon au XVIIIe siècle*, 1917.

The foregoing is Meslier's reply to Fénelon's 'popular' or anti-Epicurean first section; what follows is his criticism of Fénelon's Cartesian and Platonic second section. The essence of man, says Meslier, does not consist in thought; otherwise he would cease to exist when he was asleep. Man is not a mind placed in a body. He is matter in a certain form, which means that what was not a man becomes a man, just as what was not a house becomes a house, or what was not a chicken becomes a chicken. Fénelon talks of degrees of 'being' and 'not-being' and of 'being' which is 'drawn out' of 'not-being'. There are no 'degrees of being', there are only changes, modifications of the same matter, which persists always in different forms. *Nil novi sub sole.* The idea of the infinite is not a difficult idea to conceive and is not different from other ideas. 'Infinite' means unbounded, and that only. It does not mean 'absolutely perfect'; an 'absolutely perfect' being is a fiction of the mind. It is useless to claim that existence is a necessary quality of such a being, except in the mind. Even as a conception of the mind it would be absurd to look upon non-extended being as perfect; such a conception is more limited than any other. What exists outside our minds is the All, an infinitely extended quantity of divisible matter. It has neither perfections nor imperfections: it is. Many of the ancients thought that the All was conscious of itself; there is no means by which we can know whether this is so or not; but in any case there is no thinking without extension; only an extended thing can think. The one Being that *is* makes all particular things by taking on different shapes. It is infinite in extent, in duration, in the number of its parts; it exists independently of our thoughts; time is its duration; motion is inherent in it. Atheism is the only true philosophy. There are more atheists than is commonly believed. Atheists are as capable as any other men of being virtuous. True piety does not consist in believing blindly in errors, nor in inventing gods and idols. This world is an imperfect world and vice is rampant in it. One gains nothing by saying that the present order of things is the work of a wise and beneficent providence. The world is governed by the laws of motion. It is in the work of man's hands only that we can look for perfection. The laws of necessity govern all things, and would govern God himself if he existed, but man can be said to act freely when he acts without constraint.

When Meslier died in 1729, he left behind a manuscript work which was widely distributed with the other clandestine tracts of which we shall speak in the next chapter. It was known as Meslier's 'Testament'.[1] In 1735, Voltaire's friend Thieriot mentioned it to him in a letter. Voltaire was intrigued by the news of a French village curé as 'judiciously inclined as Locke' and asked to have the manuscript sent to him. This was the time when he was still writing, or had just finished, his own *Traité de métaphysique*, and there is every reason to assume that the active and tenacious Voltaire, once having heard of Meslier's work, managed to obtain a copy of it soon afterwards. What use he made of it for his own purposes at the time is a matter for conjecture; he certainly kept it in mind. He made extracts from it which he dated '1742' and in 1762 he published these extracts in an edition which sold out immediately and was followed in the same year by a further edition of 5,000 copies.[2] It was widely circulated towards the end of the century. D'Holbach published extracts under the title *Le Bon Sens du curé Meslier* (1772) and Sylvain Maréchal *Le Catéchisme du curé Meslier* (1789). It was condemned by the Parlement of Paris in 1775 and further condemnations followed between 1824 and 1838.[3]

The work is a rationalistic criticism of religion as such and of the Christian religion in particular. Religions on the whole are claimed to be a fabric of error and illusion fostered for political reasons by governments. They all claim their miracles; they all have their sacred writings. The Christian writings carry within them no more certain signs of truth, no greater evidence of wisdom than other similar writings. The notion of a specially favoured people which is the main theme of the Old Testament is an unjust and immoral notion. The Christian revelation is false, as are all supposed revelations. Sacrifices are barbarous, prophecies vain, the Trinity and the Incarnation mere errors. The Christian religion began as the creed of a fanatical sect. The eating of bread as a sacrament is a monstrous superstition; it opens the door to all manner of idolatry. Christian morality, if by that is to be understood the praise of suffering, the rejection of pleasure, submission to one's enemies and non-resistance

---

[1] Copies of it are to be found in the libraries at Aix-en-Provence (58 and 59–61), Arsenal (Paris), (2237 and 2559); Bibliothèque nationale (f. fr. 6337 and 19458–60), Chartres (775), Fécamp (17–18), Orleans (1115), Reims (652), Rouen (1572, 1573, 1574, M. 74). There are also copies of extracts at Arras (253), Arsenal (2558) and Reims (653). The complete text was published by R. Charles, Amsterdam, 1864, 3 vols.

[2] According to the preface.

[3] Cf. preface to the Charles edition and A. R. Morehouse, *Voltaire and Jean Meslier*, New Haven, 1936.

to crime, is a bad morality. It aids and abets tyranny and oppression
by the great and powerful. The position of the great and powerful is
not justified by reason; all men are equal by nature. Nobility is based
on brigandage and rapine. The clergy lives in idleness and luxury;
it would be better for all if the monks and mendicants worked for a
living. If all men put together all their wealth and enjoyed it in
common, a state of happiness would be possible. The primitive
Christians did share their goods, but that primitive community no
longer exists. The world is ruled by tyrants. The kings of France are
tyrants. The 'taille' and taxes are unjust. All this injustice, all this
tyranny are founded on the belief that there is an all-powerful
Being who must be adored and served. It is true that many learned
and wise men, from antiquity to the present time have rejected this
belief, including Socrates, Plato, Aristotle, Pythagoras, Pliny,
Lucian, Averroes, Julius III, Leo X, Rabelais, Vanini, Spinoza
and Philip of Orleans, the late regent, but the stupid have usually
been gulled by the cunning. The conception of an immaterial all-
perfect Being, lately expounded by the 'archdeicole' Fénelon, is
drawn entirely from the archbishop's imagination. The only 'being
in general' is matter itself; no other being is necessary for understanding the ordering of things; the first and fundamental truths are
eternal and independent of any will or cause; motion is inherent in
matter itself. If a good God exists, why are his creatures vicious and
unhappy as we see them at present? No, the world is not governed
by an all-perfect Being; it is governed by the motions of matter.
The deformities existing in things are not to be explained away by
reference to the will of an all-wise Being. Nor can man believe that
he has an immortal soul, or that the wrongs of this world will be
righted in the next. Good and evil are modifications of the minds of
men and beasts, of their pleasure and pain. Evil is inescapable in
this world of ours.

I would that I could make my voice resound from one end of the kingdom
to the other, or rather from one end of the earth to the other, crying with
all my might, 'How foolish are ye, O men, that ye allow yourselves thus
to be led astray and believe thus blindly such foolish things.' I would say
to them that they are in error and that those who govern them deceive
and hoodwink them. I would uncover this fraud of iniquity which renders
them wretched and unhappy and which will most certainly be, in years
to come, the shame and disgrace of our times. I would reproach them with
their folly and weak-mindedness in allowing themselves to believe so

blindly in all these errors, illusions, gross and ridiculous impostures. I would reproach them with their cowardice in allowing tyrants to live so long and in not shaking off completely the odious yoke of their tyrannous rule.[1]

Thus arose the embittered cry of the frustrated country priest, to whom no Savoyard curate had preached a consoling religion of the heart, in a land which, throughout his long career, had been devastated by war, by the dragonnades, by the depredations of the tax-gatherers; a land in which the police exercised a terrible and purely arbitrary control over intellectual life, lest dangerous ideas from the enemy Low Countries should creep in and spread.

[1] From Charles edition, iii, pp. 372-3.

XIV

Clandestine Erudition

IN spite of rigorous police supervision, innumerable copies of free-thinking treatises were handed round in the first half of the eighteenth century.[1] A brisk and very dangerous trade was carried on in clandestine literature. On 16 February 1725 a raid was made on the bookshop of a certain Le Prévost in Rouen, a port through which much printed contraband came from Holland. The books seized were examined by Leullier, the curé of St John's church, who found nothing incriminating except *Robinson Crusoe*, 'a very bad book for religion and morals' and the picaresque novel entitled *Lazarillo de Tormès*. *Robinson Crusoe* was indeed banned; a 'tacit permission' was given to import such copies of the book as were at Amsterdam in 1720, but in 1721 this was not renewed, and in 1723 a 'tacit permission' was given to print a 'corrected' version only.[2] The police at Rouen was doubtless not aware of the secret tolerance that had been accorded to Defoe's masterpiece. At the beginning of 1725, two journalists, named Bonnet and Lecoulteux, and seven of their clerks were arrested; 300 folio sheets of the *Esprit de Spinoza* were seized at Bonnet's house and several copies of Boulainviller's works were found at Lecoulteux's house. Bonnet admitted having made three copies of the *Vie et Esprit de Spinoza*. Lecoulteux said he had sold copies of it to the comte de Toulouse, the bishop of Blois and a certain M. de Caraman.[3] About 1729, a man named Mathieu or Morléon, who lived at a café on the corner of the rue Saint-

---

[1] The best guide to this clandestine literature is I. O. Wade's *The Clandestine Organization of Philosophic Ideas in France from 1700 to 1750*, Princeton, 1938. There are some gaps in it. Professor Wade did not know of the existence of the *Theophrastus Redivivus* manuscript; he did not know that Gaultier's book was published (p. 257), or that the *Curiositates philosophicae* were published (p. 100). He greatly exaggerates the influence of Spinoza, and in a general way his bibliographical work is more valuable than his exegesis.

[2] *Registre des livres d'impression étrangère présentés* (à d'Argenson, garde des sceaux) *pour la permission de débiter*, Bibliothèque nationale, fonds fr. 21990). The *Lettres persanes* (2 vols., Cologne) were refused on 1 July 1721. Ditton's *Religion chrétienne démontrée* in 1728, the abbé de St. Pierre's *Paix perpétuelle*, in 1729, Boulainviller's *Vie de Mahomet* and Chaulieu's works in 1731.

[3] *Archives de la Bastille*, ed. Ravaisson, xiii, pp. 473–6; G. Lanson, 'Questions diverses sur l'histoire de l'esprit philosophique en France' (*Revue d'histoire littéraire*, 1912, p. 4).

Dominique, sold copies of 'works full of impieties and maxims contrary to the existence of God, the divinity and morals of Jesus Christ'. Many people, including ecclesiastics, bought them from him at high prices. The inspector of police Haymier visited the place and bought a manuscript dealing with the history of the first man, the history of Egypt, of the patriarchs from the vocation of Abraham to the exodus of the Israelites, and sent it to Hesnault, the lieutenant of police. 'There are others', said Haymier, 'dealing with the life of Christ, his origin and the errors introduced since his death. I could not get hold of them because he would not let them go for less than 20 pistoles. He said there was not an officer of the Parlement but had copies of all these manuscript writings.'[1] In 1741 a certain La Barrière, living in the rue des Porcherons, was found to be supplying the itinerant booksellers with 'dangerous' books and manuscripts, including the *Liberté de penser* (Collins) and Meslier's *Testament*. In 1747 a teacher and an usher at the Collège de la Marche were denounced by a printer for having tried to sell him a history of the Inquisition in Rome, Spain and Portugal, with critical reflections of a sceptical author, 'an upholder of the rationalist system in religion', and a 'Système de raison sur la religion' in which all religions were attacked.[2] In 1749 a Franciscan monk named Jacques-Joseph Le Blanc, living in a monastery at Versailles, was arrested for having written and tried to sell a work entitled *Le Tombeau des préjugés sur lesquels se fondent les principales maximes de la religion*.[3] In 1766 the same police officer who arrested Le Blanc, D'Hémery, seized 48 parcels of books 'against religion and morality' at Avignon.[4]

But in spite of the efforts of Haymier, D'Hémery and their colleagues, scores of free-thinking works were in circulation in manuscript copies from the early years of the century and many of them were published in the middle years of the century, in the form of collections of essays, at Amsterdam, Geneva, or 'London', that is to say secretly in France, under the titles, *Dissertations mêlées, Nouvelles Libertés de penser, Recueil nécessaire, L'Evangile de la raison, Recueil philosophique, Bibliothèque du bon sens portatif*.[5] They fall into two

---

[1] *Archives de la Bastille*, xiv, p. 222, Lanson, loc. cit.
[2] *Archives de la Bastille*, xx, p. 220; Lanson, loc. cit.
[3] Cf. my 'A *prêtre-philosophe* in the xviiith century', *Modern Language Review*, xxxvii (1942), pp. 200–2.
[4] *Archives de la Bastille* (Arsenal Library), no. 22098 f. 27.
[5] 1. Amsterdam by Bernard, 1740; 2. Amsterdam, 1743; 3. Geneva by Voltaire, 1766; 4. Geneva by Voltaire, 1767; 5. 'Londres' by Naigeon, 1770; 6. 'Londres' by

main groups of which the bigger consists of works devoted to the history of religions and particularly of Christianity, usually written from the point of view of critical deism. The other group consists of essays which are atheistic, deterministic and materialistic. The clandestine tracts are all anonymous and many of them were added to and changed by the various copyists through whose hands they passed in such a way that they give the impression of being collective productions, the common property of all who took part in the underground dissemination of prohibited ideas. Some of them were ascribed by the copyists or editors to various erudites of the first half of the century, particularly Nicolas Fréret (1688–1749) of the Académie des Inscriptions et Belles-Lettres, the author of numerous articles on such topics as the cult of Bacchus, the worship of heroes, the oracles, the religious feasts of the Persian year, published by the Academy, and also Jean-Baptiste de Mirabaud (1675–1760), secretary of the Académie Française, and the grammarian César Chesneau Dumarsais (1676–1756), but there is no unanimity amongst the copyists and editors as to which works should be ascribed to which erudites and none of them can be attributed with any degree of certainty. It is plausible however to believe that they were the work of erudites of the calibre of the three mentioned above, and they may be taken as a reflection of the activity which went on in the erudites' academy, the Académie des Inscriptions et Belles-Lettres. Erudite activity at the end of the seventeenth century and the beginning of the eighteenth was intense. The age of Louis XIV is often portrayed as an age of great stability in all domains, politics, religion, literature and the arts, and, indeed the leaders of opinion, Bossuet particularly, strove to convey an impression of solidity and agreement, but, in point of fact, beneath the surface, or out of the public view, active inquiry was burrowing its way about in all directions. This activity was not constrained by any national frontiers as long as it avoided criticism of Christianity, so that the work of Egyptologists such as Marsham and Kircher, the work of Hyde the historian of Zoroastrianism, of Kuster the biographer of Pythagoras, of Prideaux and Basnage historians of the Jews, of the ecclesiastical

D'Holbach, 1773. Many of the manuscripts are already collections of essays similar to these published 'recueils'. Such are: Aix 816 and 818, Arsenal 2091, 2239, 2558, Bordeaux 828, Carpentras 954, Douai 702, 703, Fécamp 12, Institut 567, Lyon 169, Mazarine 1189, 1190, 1192, 1193, 1194, 1195, 1197, 1198, 1199, 3560, 3561, 3564, Orleans 1115, Reims 651, Rochefort 4–7, Rouen 1569–70, 1572, 1574, 1575, M. 74, Sénat 144, Sorbonne 760, 761, Tours 971, Troyes 2320, 2376, Vire 152.

historians, Tillemont, Fleury, Leclerc, and of Van Dale the historian of Oracles, whose work was popularized by Fontenelle, were all accessible. Pierre Bayle's *Dictionnaire historique et critique* of 1697 condensed it all into handy form. Bayle enjoyed enormous authority amongst the erudites. When Fréret was imprisoned in the Bastille in 1714–15, he spent his time reading the Dictionary from A to Z.

Bayle was born a Protestant at Carlat, near Foix, in 1647, but he abjured and became a Catholic in 1669, impressed by the idea of the unity of the Church, and followed his philosophy courses at the Jesuit college at Toulouse. However, unable to reconcile certain dogmas with his human reason, he returned to the Reformed Church in 1670 and being now a 'relapsed heretic' enjoying no privileges under the Edict of Nantes, he was in danger of imprisonment and fled to Geneva. Five years later (1675) he was appointed to a chair at the Protestant academy at Sedan. At Geneva he had replaced his Scholastic learning by a knowledge of Descartes, and, while never becoming a disciple of Descartes in any strict sense, he had assimilated certain characteristically Cartesian notions and methods which he applied to the defence of Malebranche against the Jesuit Pardies on the subject of the Eucharist, in a dissertation on the essence of bodies (1680).[1]

When the Protestant academy was suppressed by royal order (1680), he accepted a call to a new chair at Rotterdam to teach philosophy and history. It was there that he published (1682) the *Lettre sur la comète de 1680*, containing the daringly new claim that atheists are not necessarily villains, whilst some very devout persons are. Vanini and Spinoza were the chosen examples of virtuous atheists. The theme was to be echoed in the clandestine tracts and the virtuous unbeliever was eventually to become an accepted social type, exemplified by the Baron de Wolmar in the *Nouvelle Héloïse*. Bayle's polemical works showed the real bent of his nature. He wished to influence public opinion far beyond his lecture room. He was a questioner of accepted ideas, an unearther of unexpected facts, a lover of unpalatable truths, with an insatiable *libido sciendi*. He was a born agitator and he became the greatest journalist of his time, in the printer's paradise that was Holland at the end of the seventeenth century. He limited himself to news of the intellectual world and entitled his review *Nouvelles de la république des letters*, but he had that 'insatiability for news', as he calls it, which would

[1] Published in 1684 in *Recueil de quelques pièces curieuses*, Amsterdam.

also have made him a good gazeteer, had he desired to become one. All ideas, of whatever colouring, were of interest to Pierre Bayle. No man was ever more curious, more at home amidst conflicting opinions, orthodox, heterodox, old, new, European, oriental: he was prepared to make acquaintance with them all. Nevertheless he had a touchstone with which to test them, a touchstone for which he had two names, the one being Reason and the other Conscience. With the Cartesians he shared the notion of the clear idea; from the Protestant tradition he took his respect for the individual conscience, the criterion of the good, the stern daughter of the voice of God. Under either name it was a severe touchstone with which to test contemporary doctrine, but Bayle desired to remain within the Reformed Church and speak as one of its champions. He carried on a dispute with Maimbourg who had used the expression 'La France toute catholique sous le règne de Louis XIV' in a pamphlet published in the year before the revocation of the Edict of Nantes. The year after the revocation, Bayle replied with a violent indictment of France the Catholic under the reign of Louis XIV, castigating the bloody oppression of the Protestants and claiming that no honest man could wish to be a Catholic as long as villains called themselves by that name. He followed it with a commentary on the expression *Compelle intrare*,[1] a forthright affirmation of the rights of the individual conscience. This was going too far in the opinion of some of his colleagues, who, led by Jurieu, the champion of Protestant orthodoxy, forced him to resign from his chair in 1693. From then onwards he gave himself up to his critical and historical dictionary, of which he conceived the plan in 1690. His original aim was to correct the errors made by his predecessors, Moréri in particular, a great perpetuator of prejudices, but he quickly went beyond that limited ambition and packed the columns of the big folio volumes which appeared in 1695-7 with the most brain-teasing problems of biography and philosophy. Bayle refused to stop short of the facts. No pious story, however conducive to good morality, is to be pre-

---

[1] *Commentaire philosophique sur les paroles de Jésus-Christ: 'Contrains-les d'entrer', où l'on prouve . . . qu'il n'y a rien de plus abominable que de faire des conversions par contrainte* (1686). Bayle stated his position as follows: 'A Dieu ne plaise que je veuille étendre ce principe (la lumière naturelle) autant que les Sociniens, mais s'il peut avoir certaines limitations à l'égard des vérités spéculatives, je ne pense pas qu'il en doive avoir aucune à l'égard des principes pratiques et généraux qui se rapportent aux mœurs. Je veux dire que, sans exception, il faut soumettre toutes les lois morales à cette idée naturelle d'équité qui, aussi bien que la lumière métaphysique, illumine tout homme venant au monde.' (*Commentaire*, I, i.)

ferred to the facts, if the facts can be come by. No unfounded belief, however encouraging, must parade as a rational one. Facts and clear ideas are all that our thinking has of real substance in it. By all means let us believe the doctrines of the Christian religion which are compatible with our conscience, but let us not delude ourselves into thinking that they can be established by philosophy as rational convictions! This point of view was put quite openly in the *Réponses aux questions d'un provincial*, which Bayle published in parts, from 1704 to 1706. The freedom of the will, the immortality and immateriality of the soul, the existence of a beneficent providence in a world where suffering is so prevalent, were here described as beliefs which it is impossible to give one's adhesion to rationally, because they are contradicted by clear conceptions. The belief in a beneficent providence seemed especially to Bayle to be beyond reasoned proof. It was impossible to accept that a loving father should stand by while his son ate food he knew to be poisoned. Bayle's arguments were at all times pitched on the level of experience and when Leibniz replied in his *Théodicée*, arguing that God is Being and Goodness, and evil a lack of being or imperfection necessary in any created world, his metaphysics were no reply to Bayle's protests and had but little effect on the French public.[1]

Bayle remained a Christian writer, and his criticism, though pushed as far as any non-Christian writer could have pushed it, did not take him outside the Christian orbit, because his point of view and base of operations were placed within the Reformed Church and he always looked upon the unbelievers as 'them', not as 'us'. But the readers of his Dictionary were not to know the niceties of Bayle's attitudes of mind. How could they be understood in a Paris where to say the things that Bayle said could well mean a sojourn of indefinite duration in the Bastille ? In Paris, when Fontenelle published his *Histoire des Oracles*, drawn from the work of the Dutch erudite Van Dale, he had to trust his readers to read between the lines and ask why he had taken the trouble to write the book at all. What Fontenelle actually said in 1688 was that the oracles of antiquity were pious frauds practised on a gullible public by unscrupulous priests. The early Christians who attributed them to daemons were mistaken, and there were no daemons anyway. They did not stop at the birth of Christ, and belief to the contrary provided no proof of Christianity. One would be better occupied in seeking to establish

[1] Cf. W. H. Barber, *Leibniz in France*, Oxford, 1955, pp. 91-2.

the facts of history, or, for that matter, of any problem, than in putting forward theories concerning supernatural interventions in the affairs of men. A false religion cannot be bolstered up indefinitely by such fabrications and the true religion does not need them. Limited severely to the question in hand, and written in a light vein, Fontenelle's book appeared without difficulty. The subject was one of 'profane' erudition. It was quite possible to indulge an interest in the history of non-Christian religions to one's heart's content without incurring the reproof of unbelief, and a large proportion of the scholars who conducted researches in this field were 'abbés'. When the Académie des Inscriptions et Belles-Lettres was constituted in 1701, from the old Commission des Inscriptions, ecclesiastics were admitted to it freely and throughout the century were always well represented in it. The serenity with which the Academy's publications on Egyptian, Indian, and Greek ceremonies and mythology handled these topics is in marked contrast with the atmosphere of danger and taboo in which eighteenth-century discussions on Christianity were carried on. Such discussions had to be conducted in private or in the coffee houses. We have, fortunately, from the pen of Duclos, the future secretary of the Académie Française, and a member of the Académie des Inscriptions et Belles-Lettres, an account of the way he, Fréret and Boindin,[1] another member of the

---

[1] Nicolas Boindin (1676–1751) was interested particularly in the ancient theatre. 'Il fut reçu en 1706 de l'Académie des Inscriptions et Belles-Lettres, et l'aurait été de l'Académie Française, si la profession publique qu'il faisait d'être athée ne lui eût donné l'exclusion . . . On lui refusa les honneurs de la sépulture. Il fut enterré . . . sans pompe, à trois heures du matin. Un bel esprit fit cette épitaphe épigrammatique: Sans murmurer contre la Parque /Dont il connaissait le pouvoir,/ Boindin vient de passer la barque,/ Et nous a dit à tous bonsoir./ Il l'a fait sans cérémonie./ On sait qu'en ces derniers moments / On suit volontiers son génie: / Il n'aimait pas les compliments . . . Les mœurs de Boindin étaient aussi pures que peuvent l'être celles d'un athée; son cœur était généreux; mais il joignait à ces vertus la présomption et l'opiniâtreté qui en est la suite, une humeur bizarre et un caractère insociable.' (Chaudon, *Nouveau Dictionnaire historico-portatif*, Amsterdam, 1770.) The edition of 1804 adds: 'Il échappa à la persécution et au châtiment, malgré son athéisme, parce que, dans les disputes entre les Jésuites et leurs adversaires, il pérora souvent dans les cafés contre ceux-ci. De la Place rapporte qu'il disait d'un homme qui pensait comme lui et qu'on voulait inquiéter: "On vous tourmente parce que vous êtes un athée janséniste; mais on me laisse en paix parce que je suis un athée moliniste".' J.-B. Rousseau in one of his satirical poems also referred to Boindin as an atheist. (*Œuvres*, Paris, 1797, v, p. 216.) So do the authors of three epitaphs quoted by the police inspector D'Hémery in his *Journal de la Librairie*, MS in the Bibliothèque nationale, Fr. 22156, f. 164 vo). I: Ci-gît le célèbre Boindin,/ Si l'athéisme rend célèbre; / Plus dangereux que l'Arétin, / Voici son oraison funèbre. / L'Arétin d'un style effronté, / Et par ses peintures lascives, / Effraya les grâces naïves,/ Et fit rougir la volupté./ L'autre toujours plein d'artifice, / Par ses sophismes séducteurs /

erudites' academy, used to discuss at the café Procope in 1725. There were two cafés which were often the scene of free arguments amongst scholars. One was the Procope, in what is now the rue de l'Ancienne Comédie, and the other was Gradot's on the quai de l'Ecole. Duclos describes one such argument.

I went to the Procope and found them arguing a point of metaphysics when I went in. Fréret and Boindin were the protagonists. The first was a man of vast and profound erudition, the most learned man I have ever known and his learning was based on a sound philosophical knowledge; the other, with far less sagacity, talked with vehement eloquence, though with no loss of stylistic correctness. He was never so brilliant in dispute as when he was in the wrong, which often happened when he did not speak first, because he had a natural urge to contradict. If a play was ill received, he pointed out its good qualities and defended them vigorously; if it was applauded, he used considerable finesse in revealing its smallest faults. He liked most of all to attack current opinions concerning the most serious questions, a bent which had earned him a reputation for impiety, which he regretted, as he admitted to me one day, because it greatly upset the peace of his existence, adding that one should never reveal such opinions and it was better for one if one did not have them at all. It is no secret that he is called an atheist in some couplets ascribed to the poet Rousseau. The wise Fontenelle, who esteemed Boindin in many ways and was respected by him, asked him one day why he liked contradicting people so much. 'Because I see reasons against everything,' replied Boindin. 'I see reasons in favour of everything,' returned Fontenelle, 'and if I had my hand full of truths, I should not open it for the public.' I always found Boindin very reasonable, but as soon as he was in the midst of an audience, as at the café, he aimed at applause for his eloquence. Even when he was over sixty he still had this puerile ambition. He was a member of the Académie des Belles-Lettres and would have been elected to the Académie Française, where his great knowledge of the language would have distinguished him, had not the Cardinal de Fleury opposed his election. Unfair use was made against him, so it is said, of a tribute he paid to three philosophers. It was a cornelian on which he had had engraved three

Corrompit l'esprit et les mœurs / D'une jeunesse encor novice. / Il prêcha pendant quarante ans; / Un café lui servit de temple; / Ses disciples à son exemple / Exercent encor ses talents; / Mais d'une secte sans principes, / L'erreur à la fin se dissipe./ Le célèbre Boindin est mort. / Sa secte aura le même sort. II: Boindin gît je ne sais où; / Mais en quelque lieu qu'il repose, / Il fut bien sage, ou bien fou; / Je vous laisse à juger la chose. III: Deux apôtres de l'athéisme, / La Mettrie et Boindin passent au sombre bord; / Mais à l'approche de la mort, / Le premier, oubliant son matérialisme, / En lâche abjurant ses erreurs, / Prouve qu'il n'eut jamais solidité ni mœurs;/ L'autre, sans remords, sans faiblesse, / Soutenant jusqu'au bout la même hardiesse, / Montre que son esprit fermement convaincu/ N'errait que par principe et même par vertu.

profiles very much like those of Descartes, Bayle and Fontenelle, and the indiscreet motto 'sunt tres qui testimonium perhibent de lumine'.[1] I have dwelt in some detail on Boindin because he is the only member of the Académie des Belles-Lettres not to be spoken of in a public session at his death. They could at least have done for him what they did for the notorious Father Letellier, whose panegyric was reduced to the dates of his birth, his nomination as the king's confessor and his death. Both custom and decency would thus have been observed.

As I was saying, I arrived at the café in the thick of a dispute on metaphysics. After listening for a while to the two disputants, I hazarded a few words on the subject which drew their attention. The audience appeared surprised that a young man should dare to measure his skill with that of such champions, but they both gave me a good reception none the less and invited me to come again. I did not fail to do so and, as I was always sure to find Boindin there, I soon became his antagonist and shared with him the attention of the audience, who showed a preference for me because Boindin was so dogmatic in his way of contradicting whilst I adopted a gay manner. One day he and I had a set-to on whether the order of the universe was as explainable by polytheism as by the belief in a single supreme being. I upheld the unity of the necessary being and Boindin claimed that everything could be reconciled with a plurality of gods. Every sophism he could think of was used to bolster up his case. The assembly was numerous and attentive. Boindin, out for their support, was in the heat of his eloquence when I burst out laughing. He was put off by this and snapped that laughing and replying were two different things. 'I admit it,' I said, 'but I couldn't help laughing to see you trying to prove the plurality of the gods; there's nothing like a miser's feast, as the saying goes!' As he had the reputation of not believing in any god at all, everybody laughed at the proverb being applied to him; he took it in good part and the argument dropped.

The characters of the men of letters who frequented the café were very varied. Boindin held forth and never conversed; Fréret reasoned, always supporting his arguments by quotations from authorities, not to establish the facts in an erudite manner, but in order to develop his principles philosophically. He had written a work which would be dangerous if it was available to the general reader; he would have been very annoyed if it had been made public.[2]

Amongst Boulainviller's reading notes at the Bibliothèque nationale is an account of 'a conversation imperfectly remembered' on the

---

[1] Confirmed by Boindin's account of his own life given in D'Hémery's *Journal de la Librairie* (year 1753, MS in the Bibliothèque nationale, Fr. 22158, f. 186 vo). D'Hémery gives the text of several passages which were suppressed in the Parfaict edition of Boindin's works (1753).   [2] From Duclos, *Mémoires secrets*, Paris, 1864, i, pp. 34-8.

question of mechanical causes versus final causes, which doubtless took place at Boulainviller's own house. Boulainviller's table was a centre for such discussions judging by the fact that Voltaire entitled one of his stories *Le Dîner du comte de Boulainvilliers*.

A certain amount of public discussion of the biblical texts had been possible towards the end of the seventeenth century, but after the turn of the century only works written in defence of their authenticity could appear. In the previous century serious criticism had been rare, but half a dozen books had nevertheless been published in which doubts concerning the integrity of the text had been formulated. Only one, or at most two, had actually been published in France, it is true, and both of these were condemned, but it was possible for scholars to get hold of the volumes published in French and Latin in the Low Countries. The beginning of the eighteenth century witnessed both attempts to disseminate knowledge more widely on the one hand and a stricter and more active police control on the other.

The first serious textual criticism had come from a French Protestant at Bordeaux, named La Peyrère, in 1655. La Peyrère pointed out that a passage in Romans (v. 12–14) seemed to indicate that there were men on the earth before Adam.[1] His book was burnt and he was arrested by order of the archbishop of Reims and abjured the Protestant faith. In 1670 there appeared a Latin version of Hobbes's *Leviathan* (1651). It does not seem to have left any trace of positive influence in France at the time, nor indeed at the beginning of the eighteenth century, as far as biblical criticism goes; it was not until the time of Diderot and Naigeon that Hobbes was to be looked upon as a forerunner by the Philosophes; but Huet refuted it in his *Demonstratio evangelica* (1679) and Hobbes figured in Kortholt's *De tribus impostoribus magnis liber* (Kiel, 1680) along with Spinoza and Herbert of Cherbury, so the idea was abroad that he was an enemy of the faith. Hobbes had collected together[2] those passages of the Old Testament which make it clear that many of the books were written long after the events related in them, and had also studied, by means of comparisons between various passages, the meanings carried by such words as Spirit, Angel, Inspiration, Kingdom of God, Holy, Sacred, Sacrament, the Word of God, Prophesy, Miracle. Here were the beginnings of a philological

---

[1] *Prae-Adamitae, systema theologicum ex Praeadamitarum hypothesi*, n.p., 1655.
[2] Part III, ch. 33–8.

method of inquiry. Hobbes proceeded without asking whether the texts should be rejected or not as unauthentic, because such a question was one for the head of the Church and State, namely the king, in Hobbes's opinion. He reserved the right to believe or not to believe to the individual conscience, but he considered it the duty of the citizen to act as though he did believe the doctrines prescribed by the sovereign. He thus took up a radical point of view, but placed it well within the Christian orbit, in that manner characteristic of seventeenth-century Protestant countries which was not countenanced in France.[1] Spinoza's *Tractatus theologico-politicus* caused a stir while *Leviathan* passed almost unnoticed. Whether it would have had much effect on the French public had not Huet undertaken to refute it is open to question. Be that as it may, interest in biblical criticism was certainly roused. Bossuet remarked at the end of the century that it was the fashion and the only sort of criticism that could satisfy the curious.[2] Spinoza raised the problems already raised by Hobbes and proceeded in a similar fashion, by the confrontation of passages, the study of references to places and times, but he also brought to the study a sound knowledge of Hebrew and he was prepared to push his arguments to conclusions far more systematically than Hobbes had been. He concluded that the books up to Kings were a compilation made by a pious historian, Ezra probably, just after the captivity, and that the remaining books dated from the time of the Maccabees. He denied the possibility of miracles in a universe whose laws themselves express the nature of God and he used his knowledge of Hebrew to explain that many expressions which seemed to imply the intervention of God were current idioms not implying any special divine action. As for the prophets, the scriptures describe them, not as learned men of high intellectual capacity, but as men of great imagination, animated by zeal for the good and whose teaching was intended as a moral exhortation.

A great many books appeared in Holland to anathemize Spinoza[3] nevertheless it was possible in that country to carry on straightforward critical work on the biblical texts, and Jean Leclerc (1657–1737), professor of philosophy and Hebrew at the University of

---

[1] J.-J. Rousseau's attitude might be compared with it, but Rousseau fully realized that his *Emile* could not be published in France.

[2] Letter to Rancé, 17 March 1692, with reference to Rancé's *Réponse au traité des études monastiques*. 'Vous attaquez la fausse critique qui est la maladie et la tentation de nos jours avec une efficace invincible.' (Grands Ecrivains edition, v, p. 62.)

[3] They are described by A. Monod in his *De Pascal à Chateaubriand*, Paris, 1916.

Amsterdam continued to do so, but in France discussion was soon driven underground, Bossuet declaring that all was lost if niggling criticism was to be allowed to undermine the structure of religion. He took a sweeping perspective which reduced the activities of the scholars to a small compass and then brushed them aside.[1] But before discussion became impossible, Pierre Daniel Huet, the future bishop of Avranches, a man who in many ways continued the erudite traditions of the Du Puy brothers' circle, and had stayed resolutely aloof from the 'new philosophy', opposed Spinoza with arms worthy of his adversary, but it was evident that he was fighting a rearguard action. Richard Simon, a teacher at the Oratorian school at Juilly, admitted the truth of Spinoza's criticism, but without actually mentioning him, and whilst maintaining the complete authority of the biblical texts. It was scholarly give and take of this kind that offended Bossuet. Simon's book was condemned and Simon was expelled from the Oratorian congregation. Biblical criticism appeared to be stifled, but actually it took refuge in the clandestine tracts, where, by the very nature of things, erudition was at the mercy of every anonymous copyist.[2]

Spinoza's rejection of miracles could not but have a profound effect on minds which had habituated themselves to the new physics. Before the question was put in a critical form both François Lamy and Malebranche showed themselves disposed to use Cartesian physics against popular superstitions.[3] But Arnauld protested, affirming that God suspends the laws of nature when a miracle takes place. Far from losing their importance as weapons in the hands of the apologists of the Christian faith, the miracles of the Bible were to be put to greater and greater use in the eighteenth century. As long as the doctrine of redemption and grace had been the central feature of Christian thinking, the miracles and prophecies had been little called upon. But the questioning of the biblical texts and the

---

[1] In the last four chapters of his *Discours sur l'histoire universelle* (1681).

[2] The *Journal des savants* did however summarize the state of the dispute (in its supplement for September 1708) in reviewing a book by a professor of Wittenberg named L. S. Deyling: according to La Peyrère, the Pentateuch was fragments only, the rest having been lost; Hobbes thought that Moses was the author of Deut. ii to xxvii only; Spinoza that the Pentateuch and historical books were probably by Ezra; Simon, that Moses was the author of the laws, but they were written down by scribes; Leclerc that the Pentateuch was written down by a priest sent from Babylon to instruct the people at the time of the captivity; Huet, Heidegger, Schomer, Kidder and now Deyling, that Moses was the author of all the Pentateuch.

[3] Lamy, *Conjectures physiques sur deux colonnes de nues qui ont paru depuis quelques années*, Paris, 1689; Malebranche, *Méditations chrétiennes*, 1683.

historicity of the Christian revelation caused these 'external' proofs to be brought into play just at a time when they were under attack from the standpoint of the new science. The title of one of the most-read works of Christian apologetics of the eighteenth century, the abbé Houtteville's *La Religion chrétienne prouvée par les faits* (1722) indicates the methods that were used. A similar development took place in England, witness Sherlock's *Trial of the witnesses of the resurrection* (1729). In London the debate went on openly. Locke, while maintaining the value of miracles as proofs of Christ's mission, refused to look upon them as supernatural happenings; they were merely new and strange for some people: a miracle for one man could be a perfectly natural event for another. Toland attempted to use Spinoza's philological method: when Isaiah says that God will strike water from the rocks in the desert, he means that water will be found in the desert; when the scriptures say that the sun stood still for Joshua, they mean that darkness was late in coming. Woolston, a Cambridge professor, explained the miracles of the Gospels as allegories. He was imprisoned for a while, but on the whole the criticism of the English deists could be openly expressed and the debate went on in public. In Paris the situation was different. Only the works of the apologists were published; the numerous deistic treatises were clandestine. The apologists affirmed doggedly not only the possibility of miracles, but also the historicity of the miracles related in the Bible, and the usefulness of miracles as proof of the Christian revelation. Houtteville and Buffier,[1] the two most popular apologists, argued that God makes and breaks the laws of nature as he wishes, that the miracles of the Gospels were solidly authenticated by contemporary witnesses, and that they constituted a sound proof of the divinity of Christ's mission, in spite of the existence of false miracles worked by the devil, from which true miracles are sometimes difficult to distinguish. The efforts of the eighteenth-century apologists, both Catholic and Protestant, were concentrated on defending the revelation; the picture painted by them of the human predicament was not the picture of sinful man, corrupted by Adam's fall and saved by the redemption; it was the picture of natural man, guided merely by his natural reason and uncertain of the truth, suddenly enlightened and assisted by a divine revelation of the good and the true. The miracles of the Gospels

---

[1] Houtteville, *La Religion chrétienne prouvée par les faits*, Paris, 1722. Buffier, *Exposition des preuves les plus sensibles de la religion chrétienne*, Paris, 1732.

took on the importance of credentials guaranteeing the authenticity of Christ's mission. And this just at the time when the new physics excluded miracles and historical criticism questioned whether they ever took place! The clandestine treatises in which the revelation was rejected were numerous, and two of them in particular, one entitled *Examen de la religion* and the other *Analyse de la religion*, were very widely disseminated, to judge by the number of manuscript copies in public libraries. Some of the treatises were devoted to biblical criticism, others attempted a sort of natural history of religions and society. Of those devoted to biblical criticism, the earliest probably dates from before the turn of the century. It carries the title *Examen et censure des livres de l'Ancien Testament*, but only one copy of it is known and it may never have been intended for circulation. It is very critical of Huet's *Demonstratio evangelica*, but was written by a man who looked upon himself as a Catholic and disliked the Protestants, an ecclesiastic almost certainly.[1] The author was not prepared to go further than admitting that 'whole sentences' had been intercalated into the Pentateuch, and he believed that Moses was the main author of it, but his defence of Moses as a purely political leader and his denial of any sort of divine inspiration in the Old Testament show a very radical mind at work.

Another manuscript work, composed between 1706 and 1710, bears the title *Difficultés sur la religion proposées au père Malebranche* and was usually referred to, in the eighteenth century, as *Le Militaire philosophe*.[2] The author of this work gives us a certain amount of

---

[1] Dijon, MS no. 89, p. 376: 'Il répond dans le 14ᵉ chapitre aux arguments de Spinoza, de La Peyrère, de Hobbes contre la vérité du Pentateuch que nous avons. La plupart de leurs raisons sont faibles, mais il y a quelques-unes qui forcent d'avouer qu'on a fourré dans le texte des phrases entières qui ne sont point et ne peuvent être de la façon de Moïse, mais de celle d'Esdras. Il l'avoue de plus. Ce chapitre mérite d'être examiné à loisir si l'on veut juger exactement qui dit vrai. Il y a sans doute beaucoup de malignité et de chicanes de la part de nos adversaires, mais il y a peut-être de la crédulité de la nôtre.' (p. 367.) This discussion of Huet's book (1679) is topical in tone, making it legitimate to date the manuscript from not long after 1679, before the end of the century at latest.

[2] Date established by G. Lanson, op. cit. (*Revue d'histoire littéraire*, 1912). In the Mazarine MS no. 1163, p. 36, 'Mon fils est devant Barcelone.' There were three sieges of Barcelona about this time, 1696, 1706, 1714. A reference to 1701 on p. 53 eliminates 1696; the words 'l'année passée' on p. 103 eliminate 1714 and indicate 1710 as the date of the latter part of the work. Mazarine no. 1163 is the only known complete copy of this work, but there are two copies of a shortened version in the same library, no. 1192 and no. 1197. A partial edition, probably due to d'Holbach, was published in 1768 ('Londres'). Voltaire made its acquaintance in this edition. Cf. I. Wade, op. cit., p. 45.

information about himself, whilst hiding his identity very effectively. He was born about 1665 and was very pious in his youth. At the age of six he was tonsured. At the age of seven he was taken to see Our Lady of Ardilliers and was disappointed to find a small and dirty statue. When he was twelve he heard a priest say that the real presence is like an image seen in all the pieces of a broken mirror and was not satisfied. At eighteen, although still devout, and 'wearing crosses from head to foot', he became a soldier and soon learnt to fear physical danger more than the devil. Shortly afterwards he took part in the persecution of the Huguenots and saw a sick old man dragged out of bed and made to dance in the street. Later he learned that the philosophy of Descartes was excluded from the colleges because it could not be reconciled with the traditional explanation of the Eucharist. Things of this kind made him decide to examine the religion he had been brought up in.

Religion is a matter for the individual conscience, not for the government and every person should examine his religion in the light of his reason. Religions cannot be established on facts, unless it be by a continuous sequence of miracles. Reason and conscience are sufficient guides for conduct. The books of the Old Testament were not divinely inspired and were written by rabbis long after the events related in them; they are full of stories impossible to believe and the persons one is expected to admire in them are guilty of abominable crimes. As for the New Testament, though there are many excellent precepts in it, there are also many things contrary to good morality, many impossible happenings, and much verbiage, particularly in the Epistles. The history of Christianity and the conduct of the priests are not likely to satisfy a reasonable man. Only one miracle is satisfying to the reason, that is the miracle of God's creation. The claim that Christianity alone can explain the human predicament is false. If there are contradictions in man's nature, they are like the bow which stretches the bow string; they provide the driving force of his nature; his nature is not corrupt. He pursues his self-interest as does every other living thing, but his reason restrains him in the pursuit of pleasure when he comes in conflict with the requirements of society. It is true that some men experience a sense of liberty when they defy the law; it is true that men do evil in pursuit of pleasure, but they do not do evil gratuitously. Pascal accuses human justice of being worthless, but what shall be said of a justice that condemns all men because of Adam's sin?

A religion worthy of God can be founded on reason, a religion devoid of the mummeries of the Church. It would teach that man has an immortal soul, and, although it would reject miracles, it would teach that nature's laws are in themselves a divine providence.

The book of Genesis was given a good deal of attention. One essay claims to consists of extracts from a book entitled 'Doutes et objections de Thomas Burnet sur le premier chapitre de la Genèse' and comes directly or indirectly from Burnet's *Archaeologiae philosophicae* of 1692.[1] It figures in a collection of short essays (Mazarine 1194), of which one is a rejection of the story of the creation on historical grounds because of the great antiquity of the Egyptians, the Chaldeans, the Indians and the Chinese, all nations older than the supposed creation of the world, another is on miracles, a fourth on oracles, a fifth on Moses and a sixth on the theme of the virtuous unbeliever. The attitude adopted towards Moses is the same as in the *Examen et censure* mentioned above: Moses was a courageous and capable barbarian. This seems to have been a usual attitude; it is reflected also in the *Esprit de Spinoza* and in a little prose satire entitled *La Moïsade*.[2] The little dissertation entitled *Des Miracles* appears also in another collection of essays (Arsenal, 1195), in which it claims to be a translation of part of the *Theophrastus redivivus*.[3] It is certainly not that, and judging by a long run of references which ends with the thirteenth volume of the *Bibliothèque choisie* (1707) it was doubtless written soon after that date, an indication which allows us to suggest that the essays on oracles, prophecies and the virtuous unbeliever may be productions of roughly the same period. The method used in the essay on miracles is that of a comparison between the miracles described in the Bible and those attributed to Pythagoras, Apuleius, and Apollonius of Tyana, in a manner which was common in the works of the English deists, but there is no identifiable trace of English influence in the essay and the references and allusions it contains are usually French. The essay on oracles might have been taken from Fontenelle, but there is nothing to show conclusively that it was. The essay on non-religious morality quotes as examples Vanini, Hobbes and Spinoza

---

[1] It is followed by notes taken from Burnet's *Sacra Theoria telluris*.

[2] Published in the works of Fréret, but probably not by him; for the verse *Moïsade* see below, p. 313 n.

[3] This claim was repeated when the manuscript was published in 1775 ('Londres'); it reappears in the copy preserved in the University of Lille (219).

and proposes a morality based on the love of God and one's fellow men and the dictates of reason.

The *Opinions des anciens sur les Juifs*, which is often found together with the *Opinions des anciens sur la nature de l'âme*, the *Examen critique du nouveau testament* and, occasionally, the *Opinions des anciens sur le monde*,[1] is also claimed, in one copy,[2] to be a partial translation of the *Theophrastus redivivus*, which was known, it appears, at least by name. The *Opinions des anciens sur les Juifs* is not, however, a partial translation of the *Theophrastus redivivus*. Nor is it a résumé of Basnage's *Histoire des Juifs* (1706); the author refers to Basnage's work, but he is independent of Basnage's plodding erudition. He has the quality which was to secure a hearing for the French Philosophes everywhere, namely a certain freedom in the handling of a discussion which was nourished by scholarship but managed to be rapid and brisk. These authors of clandestine tracts carried their erudition lightly; their aim was frankly polemical, but on the other hand they showed none of the bad temper which marked English polemics at the time. The general theme of the *Opinions des anciens sur les Juifs* is that the Jews had no good claim to be a 'chosen' people; they had no special quality which would prepare men for thinking that a revelation would be made to them. The *De Jésus-Christ* or *Examen critique du nouveau testament* supplies information on the canonical and non-canonical gospels, discusses the Platonic element in the fourth gospel, points out that Philo and Josephus are silent concerning Christ and claims that Christian morality, far from being an improvement on natural morality, is an unpractical interference with it. The title of the *Opinions des anciens sur la nature de l'âme* is sufficient indication as to its contents. The *Opinions des anciens sur le monde* is directed against the story of the creation in Genesis.

The interconnectedness of the three *Opinions des anciens* and of the *Examen critique du nouveau testament* makes it likely that they all came originally from one pen. They have often been ascribed to Jean-Baptiste de Mirabaud (1675–1760), and Mirabaud's biographer, Paul de Mirabaud,[3] does not contest this attribution. Jean-Baptiste de Mirabaud belonged to the Boulainviller-Fréret circle; he was the duchess of Orleans's secretary and had charge of the education of her

---

[1] In nearly every public library manuscripts which contain at least two of the four are to be found.

[2] Mazarine 1195.　　　[3] *Notice sur Jean-Baptiste de Mirabaud*, Paris, 1895.

daughters. Later in life (1742), he was to follow the abbé Houtte-ville as secretary to the Académie Française. The *Opinions des anciens* can be dated with some degree of accuracy, seeing that Boulainviller, who died in 1722, had a copy of the *Opinions des anciens sur le monde*.[1] The *Opinions des anciens sur les Juifs* makes use of Basnage's *Histoire des Juifs* (1706), so the period 1706–22 is the most likely time at which these essays were written.

The most widely disseminated treatises were the *Examen de la religion*, also referred to as *Les Doutes*, and *La Religion chrétienne analysée*. There are no less than forty-two copies of the *Examen de la religion* still extant in French public libraries.[2] It varies a good deal from copy to copy and seems to have been looked upon as common property by the copyists. In 1748 a certain De la Serre, who was hanged as a spy at Maestricht, confessed to having written a sequel to it. It was in circulation about 1710, according to one copy and about 1720 according to another. Voltaire thought that part of it at any rate was by the grammarian Dumarsais. It lists a great many inconsistencies in the biblical texts, rejects the doctrine of original sin as contrary to justice, and of the Trinity as contrary to reason, criticizes the clergy for their riches and proposes the worship of the Supreme Being without any fixed ceremonies.

The *Religion chrétienne analysée* or *Analyse de la religion*, of which there are copies in various French libraries,[3] is a similar work, varying similarly from copy to copy and containing critical matter of the same kind. It was written after 1739.[4]

The *Préface ou examen critique du livre de l'abbé Houtteville ayant pour titre la Religion chrétienne prouvée par les faits* was probably written soon after Houtteville's book came out in 1722. It is not actually a refutation of Houtteville however; it is a straightforward statement of deism: religions are institutions created by clever legislators as a means of preserving public order; Christ was not the messiah expected by the Jews.[5]

---

[1] D'Argenson's son, the marquis de Paulmy, says that his father received a copy of it from Boulainviller (Paulmy's catalogue of what is now the Arsenal library, Arsenal MS no. 6299, f. 239ro).

[2] For bibliographical details see Wade, *The Clandestine Organization . . . of philosophic ideas*, ch. iii.

[3] In the following libraries: Aix, Bibliothèque nationale, Fécamp, Mazarine, Monti-villiers, Orleans, Rouen, Troyes. Cf. Wade, ibid., ch. iv.

[4] It contains a reference to an edition of the Bible published in 1739.

[5] Arsenal 2239. It refers to La Monnoye's dissertation on the *Trois Imposteurs* (1716) as having appeared 'il y a quelques années'.

The *Histoire critique du Christianisme ou Examen de la religion chrétienne*, of which at least nine copies are still extant under various titles, was usually attributed to Fréret in the eighteenth century. It was composed after 1733.[1] It examines the authenticity of the Gospels and attributes the successful establishment of the Christian church to the support given to it by the Christian emperors. It refuses to admit that the coming of Christianity produced any general improvement of morality and devotes a final chapter to refuting Pascal's argument on the Wager.

At the municipal library at Troyes are five manuscript volumes under the titles *Examen de la Genèse* and *Examen du nouveau testament* which are attributed to Mme du Châtelet and can be assumed to have been written at Cirey in the late seventeen-thirties and during the seventeen-forties, when she and Voltaire made a serious and lengthy study of the biblical texts.[2] Mme du Châtelet was an intelligent and industrious woman, but this was a field in which she had no competence as compared with professional erudites, so one is not surprised to learn that she put to good use the work of the professional scholars, especially the *Commentaire littéral sur tous les livres de l'Ancien et du Nouveau Testament*, published in twenty-four volumes between 1707 and 1716, by the Benedictine monk A. Calmet, who supplied her both with the historical and philological information of which she was in need and with many naïve remarks upon which to sharpen her wit. Mme du Châtelet's commentary is very often a commentary on Dom Calmet.[3] The time had come when the study of the biblical texts and their history was no longer a province reserved for scholars. When Voltaire, who presumably took part in Mme du Châtelet's studies, came to write

[1] This is the title of Mazarine no. 1198. It was published under the title *Examen critique des apologistes de la religion chrétienne*, n.p., 1767, and in the works of Fréret (1785). On p. 107 of Mazarine 1198 is a reference to a pastoral instruction by the bishop of Montpellier dated 1 February 1733.

[2] Troyes no. 2376–7. The *Examen de la Genèse* actually covers the whole of the Old Testament. The handwriting is not that of Mme du Châtelet as the Troyes manuscript states. However we have Grimm's statement to the effect that at Cirey a chapter of the Bible was read and commented upon every day (*Correspondance littéraire*, ed. Tourneux, xi, p. 348), and Mme de Graffigny's statement that Voltaire and Mme du Châtelet were reading Dom Calmet with great interest and amusement when she was staying with them. (*Vie privée*, Paris, 1820, p. 187.) Cf. I. O. Wade, *Voltaire and Madame du Châtelet, an Essay on the Intellectual Activity at Cirey*, Princeton, 1941, pp. 128, 44, 115.

[3] Meslier's *Testament* and Woolston's *Six Discourses on the Miracles of our Saviour* are also made use of. Cf. Wade, ibid., ch. iii and R. Pomeau, *La Religion de Voltaire*, pp. 154–79.

and publish his *Sermon des Cinquante* (1749), his *Dictionnaire philosophique* (1764), his *Examen important de Milord Bolingbroke* (1767), his *Dîner du comte de Boulainvilliers* (1767), his *Bible enfin expliquée* (1776) and his *Histoire de l'établissement du christianisme* (1777), it was no longer a question of convincing the learned but of confounding the enemy and Voltaire's methods are those of satire, not those of scholarship. Once it is admitted that the biblical texts are to be treated by the ordinary methods of historical and philological inquiry, Voltaire's pamphlets become superfluous, and even impertinent, but the corner had to be turned, the change of approach had to be made. Spinoza's quiet voice had been silenced; Voltaire's shrill clamour had become necessary.

XV

Clandestine Sociology

MANY of the clandestine tracts concern themselves with questions of ethics and psychology and constitute a rudimentary natural history of religions and societies.

The first of these in date is called *Lettre d'Hypocrate à Damagette* and was written by 1700 at latest.[1] It claims to be an authentic letter from Hippocrates to an unknown correspondent, using a device which was to be common in an age of strict censorship. Its author adopts an entirely sociological attitude towards religion: in the beginning men did not need religions; they lived according to pure nature in perfect innocence; the passions, ambition, avarice, love other than physical love, were unknown to them; there were no masters, no slaves; but the formation of societies gave rise to the passions, to social inequalities, to conquests and resistance thereto: such a state of affairs produced religion and the cult of the gods as a necessary instrument of government. No religion is of divine origin, but all should be respected for their social utility.

Another of the manuscripts is a translation of a book published in London in 1713, but written probably in Holland, judging by numerous references to events and places. The title of the printed book, which is in Latin, is *Curiositates philosophicae* and in the French translation it is called *Recherches curieuses de philosophie*.[2] In many ways it is a good half-century behind the times; its materialism and sensationism are scholastic and in astronomy it claims to take up a position mid-way between Copernicus and Tycho-Brahe, but in one way it establishes a continuity between the previous century and its

---

[1] It was published at Amsterdam and Cologne in 1700, but it seems to have circulated in manuscript form in France; there are copies at the Bibliothèque nationale (MS français 25393 and n. acq. fr. 22156) and Rouen (1846).

[2] The full title is *Curiositates philosophicae sive de principiis rerum naturalium dissertatio selecta*, Londini, 1713 (British Museum 717 g i). It was reviewed by the *Journal des savants* (3 Aug. 1713). The French title: *Recherches curieuses de philosophie ou dissertation sur les principes des choses naturelles, dans laquelle, par le secours d'une méthode nouvelle, on traite de la génération des hommes, des animaux, des arbres, des plantes, de la formation du monde et de sa durée, des causes des vents, du tonnerre, de la foudre, de l'esprit, du raisonnement*, par T.S.J.F. (=T.F., S.J.?), imprimé à Londres au dépens de la Compagnie, 1713, traduit en 1714. On p. 490 of the MS the words 'aujourd'hui en 1704' seem to give a clear indication of the date of composition (Bibliothèque nationale, MSS fr. 9107).

own quite outside the Cartesian orbit: it contains a sketch of a history of man in primitive times which is purely imaginary, but which describes the *process* of man's development, as Rousseau's *Discours sur l'inégalité* was to do later; it is not, that is to say, an abstract discourse on the state of nature as compared with the civil state of the type philosophers of law were addicted to; it is an attempted natural history of man.

A manuscript entitled *Suite des Pyrrhoniens: qu'on peut douter si les religions viennent immédiatement de Dieu ou de l'invention des politiques pour faire craindre et garder les préceptes de l'homme* dates from soon after 1723, judging by the fact that a long run of references to authorities stops at that date.[1] It is the sequel to a 'little treatise' in which the author has already discussed the 'causes of friendship and enmity between men', and given a short account of the origin of societies. Men join together to resist the most powerful amongst them; they sacrifice some of their liberty in order to retain the rest; their laws vary according to the different climates in which they are to be found; the observance of these laws is virtue and brings with it honour; the non-observance thereof is vice and is punished. Legislators have also looked upon religion as an efficacious way of persuading men to observe the law. Numa Pompilius claimed to have received the laws from Egeria, Solon from the oracle of Apollo, Moses from God, Mahomet from the angel Gabriel, the Chinese from Foe or Xa. But the most important precepts of morality are inscribed by God in the hearts of all men; they can be called 'humanity'. Whether one thinks of God as the substance of the universe or as a Supreme Being separate from nature, his only direct instruction to man is the social instinct which enables man to live in society. The will of God is identical with the nature and powers of the various things which exist. The number of different religious beliefs is bewildering. (Here follows a rapid history of the belief in the immortality of the soul and of Egyptian, Greek, Mahometan, Indian, Siamese, Chinese and Japanese ceremonies): the only adoration God requires is that he should be recognized as supreme; no ceremonies, no clergy are necessary. A society can very well exist without religion. Men act according to their physical complexion anyway, their 'temperament'; they are restrained in

---

[1] They run as follows: 1663, 1667, 1672, 1696, 1699, 1705, 1721, 1723. I know of only one copy of this manuscript; it is in private hands in London. It is a small octavo volume of 274 pp.

society by punishments; it is true that the fear of punishments after death, such as is instilled by religion, acts as a deterrent to some persons, but the evils engendered by religion far outweigh this social advantage. Monasticism, monkish intrigues and idleness, not to mention human sacrifices and other extreme manifestations of clerical dominance are some of these evils. England and Holland have an advantage in respect of tolerance over other countries. Some Pyrrhonians would like to see religion abolished altogether; others would prefer the cult of a Supreme Being celebrated in a single temple in the capital city at midday or one p.m. The work ends with a plea for the codification of laws, which differ according to climate and a final statement to the effect that everything that happens happens by the will of God.

One of the most systematic of the clandestine treatises, containing a natural history of religions, a sketch of sensationist psychology and naturalistic morals, is also one of the most widely disseminated. It is entitled *Lettre de Thrasibule à Leucippe*[1] and is often attributed to Fréret in the various copies of it, doubtless because Fréret was capable of the erudition it displays and was known as a free-thinker. It is difficult to date it, except to say that it was in circulation in the first half of the century; J.-J. Rousseau knew of it by the time he wrote his *Discours sur l'inégalité*, while there is an expression in it which seems to be a verbal reminiscence of the *Lettres persanes*.[2] If Fréret is indeed the author of it, it was composed before 1749 as Fréret died in that year. It could then have been written at any time from 1721 to the middle of the century. It combines a Cartesian liking for clear ideas with a sensationist theory of knowledge and a rejection of innate ideas. It combines sensationism with a theory of morals based on the notions of pleasure and pain in the usual manner. We pursue at first the objects which give us immediate pleasure and avoid those which cause us immediate pain, but experience at length teaches us to look for those things which give

---

[1] Arsenal (5805), Bibliothèque nationale (MSS français 15288), Carpentras (954), Château-Thierry (1), Douai (703), Grenoble (919), Mazarine (1193), Rouen (1570), Sorbonne (762). The Mazarine copy says that 'some people' claim to have read it in 1723. It was published in the second half of the century (London, n.d.; *Œuvres de Fréret*, London, 1775, vol. iv).

[2] p. 519 of vol. iv of the *Œuvres de Fréret*, Londres, 1775. The expression is 'rapport de convenance'. The author asks whether God's will is the perception of the 'rapports de convenance ou de disconvenance' between things. Montesquieu defines justice as a 'rapport de convenance' between two things and says that the idea of it is anterior to the idea of God. (*Lettres persanes*, no. 83.)

lasting pleasure and avoid those things which cause lasting sorrow. We wonder whether the world is formed for our well-being, and we often use the words providence, divinity, destiny, without attaching clear ideas to them. Religious beliefs usually arouse our passions and destroy the calm that comes of reason. Religious beliefs have sprung from man's ignorance and his desire that nature shall favour him. The religious systems of the world fall into two groups, that of polytheism, including the Egyptian, the Greek and western religions generally, and that of monotheism, including those of the Chaldeans, the Jews, and eastern religions generally. The new Christian sect has affinities with both groups, writes Thrasibule, who is supposed to have lived at the time of the Roman Empire. It has been influenced by the beliefs of the Jews, and has added to them a sort of Stoicism, placing supreme beatitude in the knowledge of the truth and the practice of virtue. Like the other sects it has books full of un-believable stories. When we consider ourselves and the world in a rational manner, we find that our knowledge of the world comes to us from our sensations and we realize that we have often taken our fancies for realities. The atomists have imagined indivisible particles and say that the world is composed of them; the geometers have imagined points, surfaces and lines and take them for realities. Others have imagined universal ideas, still others a universal cause of all things. Such a 'universal cause' has only an 'objective exis-tence', that is to say it exists only in our minds. All we have the right to assume is that there is something outside ourselves which causes continually changing impressions in us; we have not the right to say that the changes themselves are real in the outside world, any more than we have the right to say that things which appear to us differ-ently in different lights are really different. There are, however, certain truths, those of mathematics, which all men accept as soon as they become aware of them. They are truths of the reason. The reason can also guide our conduct towards the attainment of true pleasure. Reason guides men to form societies and establish laws amongst themselves. Men in society look upon as virtue any act which is conducive to the general well-being and reprove those actions which are noxious to the interests of all. It is true that all the laws established by men cannot be related directly to this prin-ciple, but it must be remembered that differences of habit, educa-tion, government, climate, religion, circumstances must all be taken into account together with innumerable other physical and moral causes to explain the existing laws of various countries. This treatise gives ample proof that Montesquieu was not alone in thinking as he did concerning the science of laws: there is but one step to be taken from the *Lettre de Thrasibule* to the general theory of law stated in the first chapters of the *Esprit des lois*, where Montesquieu proposes a formula which combines reason with experience.

In the Arsenal library (no. 2557) is a dissertation entitled *Traité de la liberté*, which a note attributes to Fontenelle, adding that it was burnt by order of the Parlement in 1700.[1] There is nothing in it which rules Fontenelle out; on the contrary, at least one of the leading ideas expressed in it, namely the dependence of thinking on the material constitution of the brain, is stated similarly in Fontenelle's *Digression sur les anciens et les modernes*. It is a deterministic and materialistic work. It begins by saying that when the material constitution of the brain gives rise to two conflicting desires of equal strength, the will is incapable of deciding between them. It conducts the argument as a problem of mechanics in such a way that it might well have been the original thesis of which Bergson's *Données immédiates de la conscience* is the antithesis. All our motions are determined. But that does not mean to say that some of them cannot be described as voluntary. I write because I wish to write. But there is a material disposition in my brain which determines me to wish to write. Moreover the succession of thoughts in my brain is determined by associations of ideas materially based on traces in the brain. If the same sequences of associations do not take place in sleep as in my waking life, that is merely because the spirits in the nerves are more distended during sleep and the motions are not communicated so readily from trace to trace. The moral quality of our actions appears in a very different light when we realize to what extent they are physically determined; but the realization also allows us to understand by what means the vicious may be corrected and made to conform their actions to the well-being of society. Criminals who cannot be influenced in this manner must be destroyed as monsters, because of the harm they do to society,[2] but

[1] It was first published in the *Nouvelles Libertés de penser* (1743). Professor J.-R. Carré, the author of the best book to date on Fontenelle's philosophy, believes that Fontenelle was indeed the author of it (*La Philosophie de Fontenelle*, Paris, 1932, p. 333).

[2] There is an echo of this story of a monster who has to be stifled in Diderot's *Encyclopédie* article on *Droit naturel* to which Rousseau replied in the first draft of his *Contrat social*.

this necessary action should be taken without hatred towards them. One should not be vain about one's virtue, if one is lucky enough to be born with virtuous instincts; it is a matter of temperament. The wise man looks without passion upon the conduct of his fellows. It may not be good that men whose instincts are vicious should know the truth of this, but it is not the only truth God has taken care to hide from men in case they used it for their own ill.[1] It is a simple truth, and one which integrates human conduct into the general mechanism of the universe.

An equally deterministic essay is called *Le Philosophe*, which was written before 1728 and testifies to the popularity of the term 'philosophe' by that date.[2] The 'philosophe's' conduct is determined like that of other men, but he reflects on its causes and can influence those causes, producing in himself the states of mind he wishes to produce. Reason plays the same part in the scheme of the 'philosophe' that grace does in the equally determined world of the Jansenists. The theory outlined in this little essay was to be used later in the century by J.-J. Rousseau in a work of ethics which he planned but did not complete entitled *La Morale sensitive ou le matérialisme du sage*.

The *Essai sur la recherche de la vérité*[3] was probably composed early in the century seeing that its mechanistic theory is Cartesian. A later copyist has added the remark that Newtonian mechanics may easily be substituted for Cartesian mechanics in this work. It is determinist in more than one sense. First it claims that human actions are always motivated by the desire for happiness or advantage, even when these motives are not fully conscious. Secondly the education we receive forms our habits, instills prejudices into our minds. Thirdly the circumstances we find ourselves in have an influence on our actions and our thoughts. The outside world is a succession of events produced by a fixed and immutable principle which is self-caused and may be called the slave of itself. This is followed by a sketch of a sensationist psychology. We receive impressions from the outside world through the senses. They are stored in

---

[1] Another idea characteristic of Fontenelle according to Duclos (cf. above, p. 287).

[2] Sénat no. 145, Troyes no. 2320 and Ghent no. 503. In the Ghent manuscript is a note dated 15 March 1728 (p. 667). The Ghent manuscript also contains a copy of a translation of Toland's *Pantheisticon* (1720) and a copy of the *Opinions des anciens sur la nature de l'âme*, It was published in the *Nouvelles Libertés de penser* (1743). There is a modern edition by H. Dieckmann. It was commonly attributed to Dumarsais in the eighteenth century. [3] Arsenal no. 2558. It was not published.

the memory. A comparison between a remembered impression and a present impression is called a judgment. Such comparisons are the substance of our thought. The same operations occur in beasts as in men; their soul is of the same nature as ours. No immaterial principle is necessary to make these operations explicable. It is believable that pain arises from the rough passage of the animal spirits in the delicate passages of the body, whilst a gentle motion of the spirits causes pleasure. The operation of the memory may be explained mechanically by the widening of certain passages in the brain through which the spirits have flowed. A child has few ideas because his organs are not yet developed. After the prime of life, the organs degenerate and ideas become less distinct. The dependence of thought on the body is obvious, but man's pride prompts him to believe that he is an immaterial substance superior to other beings. It is true that the materialist explanation has its difficulties, but that is no reason for not facing up to the facts. Then follows a rejection of the proof of the existence of God drawn from the beauty and order of the world: 'beauty', 'order', these are relative terms; the world is neither beautiful nor ordered in itself. The world does not exist for man any more than the sea exists for the fishes which swim therein. Final causes are useless as explanations as soon as the mechanical causes are understood. It is idle to look upon the human body as perfectly organized. If man had had ten fingers on each hand he would have done many things he could not do with five. The existence of God cannot be shown this way. The earth is obviously not ordered for man's well-being; there are more noxious plants than wholesome ones. Epicurus was right in refusing to see a providence in nature; nature acts according to necessary principles. There is no first being except matter, infinite and eternal matter. Motion is implicit in it. We cannot always perceive the motion that is implicit in matter, but the fact that all things continually change and decay is proof enough. Either matter has always been in motion, or motion is an eternal substance coexistent with matter. It may be difficult to understand just how motion and matter are related to each other, but it is more reasonable to believe in the existence of eternal matter and a fixed sum of motion[1] than it is to invent an

[1] This Cartesian affirmation of the constant sum of motion indicates an early date. It is worded as follows: 'Quelque parti qu'on prenne, le mouvement doit être éternel, comme la matière, et il doit toujours avoir existé dans la même quantité étant seulement modifié et déterminé à tout moment par les accidents particuliers de la matière.' (p. 107 of Arsenal 2558.)

imaginary being whose function is to create matter and set it in motion. All that happens happens according to simple mechanical laws which govern the motion of matter. The smallest parts of matter, the *quinta essentia*, constitute the souls of animals and of men; these particles move far more rapidly than the larger particles because of their smallness. They constitute also the semen of animals and their rapid agitation, seeking an outlet, drives male and female to seek each other. The reproduction of their kind is an element in the general mechanism of the universe.

At Douai (no. 702) is a manuscript album which it is difficult to date, but judging by the kind of topic dealt with and the run of references, of which the last in date is to an edition of Sextus Empiricus 'newly translated into our language in 1726', it seems to date from early in the century and probably soon after 1726. The reference to Sextus Empiricus is in the second essay in the collection. The first is a refutation of Darmanson's Cartesian *La Bête transformée en machine* (1684) and is sensationist and materialist; its main contention is that the soul is not a being which thinks, but a being which feels and its author turns to Aristotle (not to Locke) when in need of an authority. The second is entitled *Arguments du Pyrrhonisme pour une demoiselle qui voulait apprendre les principes philosophiques de cette secte* and resembles the *Lettre de Thrasibule* by its argumentation. Our knowledge comes through the senses; the senses deceive us; there is only one substance in the outside world; it is homogeneous, it has no qualities; there is no hot, cold, right, left, light, heavy, pleasant, unpleasant in nature; these words are conventional, they describe modifications of our own being. This is followed (p. 80) by advice to the unbeliever, who is urged not to play the 'esprit fort' and by a little dissertation on the golden mean. Finally there is a summary of the opinions of the ancients on the nature of the soul and the statement that we cannot know what the nature of the soul is. The next item is Stouppe's *Religion des Hollandais*. This is followed by a letter on Indian religions describing the 'one being susceptible of a great number of modalities forming the things we see'. The author thinks that Indian religious beliefs are no less 'defective' than other religious beliefs and no less 'absurd'; the 'universal cause' which he is willing to believe in is not a 'metaphysical cause' and the only 'cult' he is prepared to observe is that which the laws of the land prescribe; this he will submit to because, without such observance, one cannot live at peace in society. The whole of this notebook has an acquiescent flavour reminiscent of the Epicurean tradition of the previous century. It came from one of the religious houses established by the English in Douai; on the fly-leaf are two names, Thomas Ulgate of the Parish of Covent Garden and J. Day, Esq. of St George's Coffee House near Temple Bar.

The *Réflexions sur l'existence de l'âme et sur l'existence de Dieu* were published in the *Nouvelles Libertés de penser* in 1743 and were written, in all probability, not long before that date. This work begins by insisting on the importance of the early formation received by the child in the constitution of his beliefs and concludes from that observation that only a rational re-examination of religious and philosophical opinions can bring enlightenment. The author then arrives at materialism by the rejection of Descartes's immaterial substance. To suppose two substances is of no assistance. An immaterial substance could have no relationship with the body at all. An immaterial substance of which the essence was intelligence would be incapable of error. Error comes from mistaken perceptions of relationship. If the intelligence fails to perceive a relationship correctly it is no longer intelligence and ceases to exist. It is no answer to say that the body obstructs the intelligence and causes it to err; such a contention merely makes the 'soul' dependent upon the body. And such a dependence is inconceivable, because all actions of the body are motion, and the 'soul' is incapable of motion. Moreover, if the body can interrupt the working of the intelligence, it thereby destroys the 'soul' of which the essence is intelligence. So nothing is gained by positing an immaterial substance: one must conclude that the operations we attribute to the soul are to be attributed to matter. We do not know the material substance we have always before us; we do not know what it is capable of. Our vanity has induced us to imagine a distant cause or principle of all things, a principle we call God. But the idea of God varies from people to people. Each people makes God in its own image. The idea of God usually put before us is unacceptable. Why, for instance, should he punish his creatures for infringing his laws seeing that he has not afforded the means of observing them? It is said that he produced the universe merely for his own glory, but what is this glory? And why did he not produce an infinitely more perfect universe than the present one? How, moreover, can one understand the act of creation? In order to create the material universe he needed to know it already, and how could he know nothingness? If he knew it already, it existed already. From these observations one must conclude that man owes his existence to no one and is independent. But he is weak and cannot exist in isolation, so he has created societies, each individual giving his help on the understanding that he shall receive help. This 'traffic in help' is the basis of society and of all laws. The golden rule of society is that contracts shall be observed. It is a rule which has its sanction in our hearts. Our self-esteem (*amour-propre*) causes us to feel shame if we fail to observe the promises we have made; by deception we admit our inferiority to the person we deceive. Our self-esteem is a sufficient guide for our conduct, but it is admitted that it may well be that this moral philosophy is not suited for general use; it should only be preached to the 'honnêtes gens'; the populace would not be restrained by this delicate sense of self-esteem.[1]

The *Dissertation sur la formation du monde* is dated 1738. Its epigraph is Virgil's *Felix qui potuit rerum cognoscere causas*, and it does indeed owe much to Lucretius's sixth book, but it also reminds the reader of Coward, Gaultier of Niort, Meslier, the *Theophrastus redivivus*, Vanini and the manner in which it proclaims at the outset that Montaigne was 'the most enlightened and perhaps the most sceptical of all men', helps us to understand why works of this kind could be entitled 'Nouvelle philosophie sceptique' or 'Suite du pyrrhonisme'. The author claims that he doubts about everything that is not 'mathematically true'; one could hardly hope for a better illustration of the manner in which the radical naturalism of the seventeenth century was maintained in the eighteenth. His first contentions are that God cannot have created the world and that the world has its principle within itself. The creation is inconceivable: if the world was created to 'fill a gap in the Grand Tout', then the spiritual essence which existed before the creation was not infinite; it was limited by the gap which was to be filled. If Space is an idea in the Divine Mind, it must have been 'in actu' from all eternity. But there is no space without matter; so matter must have been in existence from all eternity. Is motion inherent in matter? No, because some things are in repose, but it is a property of some 'modes' of matter. All things are modes of matter. At one time, in all probability,

---

[1] It was doubtless the reading of such conclusions as this which made J.-J. Rousseau, in whom the popular instinct was strong, cry out against secret doctrines suitable only for the 'philosopher' and unsuited for popular consumption.

things were all confounded together in a semi-solid, semi-liquid mass, the 'Grand Tout' (here follows a sketch of a cosmogony which is certainly pre-Newtonian in inspiration; it describes our world as a hollow sphere, outside which chaos still reigns). Forms appeared first on the planets nearest the sun, but they did not evolve from a single prototype, in spite of the similarities of structure discovered by the anatomists between the various species; the species appeared separately. For a long time the surface of the earth was covered with water. When the water drained away, simple molecules were pulled towards each other by heat and made the first forms and a harmonic arrangement of the molecules constituted sensation. 'The earth is the matrix, water is the germ, fire is the vivifying and productive principle.' All things have a degree of life. Stones have a certain degree of life, passive life. They grow. The small particle of earth may one day be an enormous rock. If stones had less earth and more fire in them, they would be capable of motion. The first living things appeared in the mud when the water drained away; probably big animals at first because the 'spermatic mud' was more active at first. The more active a germ was, the more capable it was of assimilating surrounding particles to itself. The reptiles must have appeared later, when the spermatic power had diminished. The lessening of the action of the sun has destroyed most of the germs, but if one turns up the soil one finds many still left in the earth which come to life if heat is applied to them. It may be that all forms have the power of sensation, but we cannot tell whether stones and plants have it because they give no sign by which we may know. The first animals must have been witnesses of the appearance of the forms, but they were gross and uncomprehending. Doubtless the human race has not always been as it is now. Men were probably strong and dull-witted; humidity must have dominated the fire within them. The first men probably had no more power of thought than an oyster. Their mental powers must have been co-terminous with their needs, and their needs were few: perhaps the only one was hunger and little intelligence was needed to satisfy it. The first men probably had little power of feeling: the lack of sensibility in some savages nowadays confirms this conjecture. As ideas are dependent on sensations, primitive man, born of the earth, must have had few ideas. Their offspring, born of women, must have been more delicate, more impressionable, possessed of more ideas. But how many myriads of centuries must have elapsed for men to acquire their present degree of sensibility! The question has been obscured by the belief that feeling was something independent of matter, but it is only one of the 'ways of being' of the universal substance. The yoke of an egg has no feeling, it is true, but after three weeks of incubation a heart begins to beat in it: feeling is the effect of a certain correspondence between fibres, membranes, vessels. In one and the same species differences of sensibility can be observed, and they depend on the degree of hardness or flexibility of the organs. The first men were rough and hard and must have had little feeling: those of heat, cold, hunger, thirst and sex-desire only. As their needs increased, so did the scope of their imagination. If our limbs were as flexible as is our brain we should have ideas in our limbs. Life and death are the same exactly as far as the universal substance is concerned. Death is in no wise an evil. The only real evil is pain. The fear of death is merely the fear of pain, but there is no pain after death, so death is not to be feared.[1]

In many ways this treatise does not get far beyond the sixth book of the *De rerum natura*, but there are parts of it in which a sense of the passage of time and the cautious proposal of theories as working hypotheses give it the manner of modern evolutionary science. It is true that it refuses to admit the possibility of a prototype from which many different species may have developed and sticks to the conception of separate species, but on the other hand it supposes that many important changes have taken place and are continually taking place, not only in the organization of the various species, but also in the appearance of the earth itself. The word 'transformism' can very well be applied to the system sketched out here; it is but a step from this clandestine treatise to the picture of nature and its history held by Denis Diderot at the time when he wrote the *Rêve de d'Alembert* or the *Voyage à Bourbonne*. The way forward to Lamarck, Darwin and Haeckel was clear of major obstacles.

[1] Mazarine library, no. 1168.

XVI

Voltaire versus Pascal

THE picture of man and his place in the scheme of things which constituted Voltaire's philosophy during the first half of his long career was as different from that painted by Blaise Pascal in his *Pensées* as a positive is from a negative photograph, white for black and black for white. And Voltaire soon came to realize the fact, although Pascal was far from being in the public gaze at the time and had attracted but little notice. It is indeed difficult for a modern reader to appreciate the obscurity into which Pascal had fallen at the end of the seventeenth century and the beginning of the eighteenth. Since the time of Victor Cousin, Pascal has been in the limelight and his place in the history of his generation has become a dominant one, but that was by no means so when Voltaire singled him out as the enemy. Neither Bossuet nor Malebranche paid any attention to him; the only theologians to make any considerable use of the *Pensées* were Mauduit, an Oratorian, and Abbadie, a Protestant. The only other names of disciples one can quote are those of unknown, or scarcely known, men—Filleau de la Chaise, Vallant, Périer, Villemont, Dubois—not half a dozen in all.[1] The Jansenists themselves were far from being enthusiastic about the *Pensées*. They were pessimists, but they preferred La Rochefoucauld's brand of pessimism to that of Pascal. Antoine Arnauld frowned on his scepticism and thought that it smacked of 'libertinage'.[2] The result was that the posthumous Port Royal edition (1670) was an unfaithful rendering of the author's manuscripts: it attentuated the radical element of Pascal's thought, accentuated its anti-humanism and played up the lamentable arguments by which he tried to persuade his readers to bet on the possibility of a future life because the odds were good.[3]

[1] Cf. B. Amoudru, *La Vie posthume des Pensées*, Paris, 1936.   [2] Cf. above, p. 74.

[3] The wager, with the stake laid firmly on the other side, was first attributed by Garasse to Cardano, Vanini and Théophile: 'Après tous ces malheureux écrivains sont venus ces nouveaux libertins de notre siècle qui ont enchéri sur le marché de Cardan et de Lucilio en ce que publiquement et sans honte ils avancent cette maudite maxime qu'il n'est pas assuré que l'âme de l'homme soit immortelle et que, par conséquent, il vaut mieux tenir le présent qu'aboyer à l'avenir et prendre en ce monde ses plaisirs que de courir après une félicité incertaine et imaginaire de l'autre monde.' (*Doctrine curieuse*,

Voltaire's elder brother Armand Arouet, who was educated at the Oratorian seminary of St Magloire and followed the paternal profession of the law, chose Jansenism and became austere and strict. François-Marie, on the other hand, came early to the hatred of the Jansenist creed, seeing in it the worship of a cruel God, the unknown and unknowable ruler of an incomprehensible universe. Had he been better acquainted with the Jansenist lawyers, he would perhaps have appreciated a certain reforming zeal which made them hostile towards the worship of relics and images, but he disliked the law, which his father attempted to make him follow, and there is no trace in his writings of any warm sympathy towards the Jansenists at all. He had ample opportunities for learning other conceptions of God and man. During his early childhood, two benign friends of his mother, the abbé de Châteauneuf and the abbé Gédoyn, both members of Chaulieu's entourage, took an interest in him, and Châteauneuf is reputed to have taught him a deistic poem entitled *La Moïsade*.[1] Furthermore he was educated by the Jesuit

p. 885.) But the bizarre notion of treating the question mathematically seems to belong entirely to Pascal.

[1] According to Duvernet (*Vie de Voltaire*, Geneva, 1789, p. 11), Châteauneuf taught him *La Moïsade* when he was three years of age and first took him to Chaulieu's when he was twelve. The text of the *Moïsade* is to be found in certain editions of the works of J.-B. Rousseau, such as the Rotterdam, 1719 edition, ii, pp. 25 sqq. From about 1707 to 1720, Rousseau showed himself very anxious to please Chaulieu and La Fare and composed half a dozen epistles in the manner of the Temple on the theme of pleasant indolence, but he strenuously denied having written the *Moïsade* and declared that he had seen a copy of it as early as 1684, when he was a pupil of thirteen years of age at the Collège de la Marche, attributing it to a certain Lourdet. For the text of Rousseau's statement, which is dated 1712 and is to be found at the library of Chartres, no. 1591, see Grubbs, *J.-B. Rousseau*, Princeton, 1941, pp. 9-10. The title *La Moïsade* is to be explained by the fact that in some versions Moses is mentioned as having deceived the people of Israel in order to govern them; usually the reference is to Numa Pompilius. The poem is a straightforward declaration of deism. It begins as follows: 'Votre impertinente leçon/ Ne détruit point mon pyrrhonisme./ Ce n'est point par un vain sophisme/ Que vous surprendrez ma raison:/ L'esprit humain veut des preuves plus claires/ Que les lieux communs d'un curé./ Ce fatras obscur de mystères/ Qu'on débite au peuple épaté/ Avec le sens commun n'est pas bien mesuré./ La raison n'y peut rien connaître/ Et quand on les croit il faut être/ Bien aveugle ou bien éclairé./ En vain je cherche et j'envisage/ Les preuves d'une déité./ J'en connais l'excellence et la solidité;/ J'adore en frémissant cette divinité/ Dont mon esprit se forme une si belle image,/ Mais quand j'en cherche davantage,/ Je ne trouve qu'obscurité./ Le vérité cachée en un épais nuage/ A mon esprit confus n'offre point de clarté./ Rien ne fixe mon doute et ma perplexité;/ En vain de tous côtés je cherche quelque usage/ Qui du bon sens ne soit point écarté;/ De mille préjugés chaque peuple entêté/ Me tient un différent langage./ Et la raison prudente et sage/ Ne découvre qu'erreur et qu'ambiguité./ Papistes, Siamois, tout le monde raisonne./ L'un dit blanc, l'autre noir; on ne s'accorde point./ Chacun dit sa créance bonne./ Qui croirai-je du Talapoin,/ Ou bien du Docteur de Sorbonne?'

pedagogues of the Collège Louis le Grand, moralists for whom man was still in the place God had assigned to him in an understandable universe, exactly as he had been before the new science had stretched the limits of the world to infinity, and in 1714, at the age of twenty, he became an habitué of Chaulieu's house in the Temple.

Voltaire became acquainted at an early age with contemporary biblical criticism, or at any rate had the reputation of adopting an outspokenly negative attitude towards the biblical texts. An anonymous denunciation made to the lieutenant of police at the time of his arrest in 1726, but referring to 'more than twenty years' previously, and more particularly to 'ten or twelve years previously', reproached him with having 'preached deism at the dressing tables of young noblemen' and of having called the Old Testament 'a tissue of stories and fables', the apostles 'simple credulous idiots' and the fathers of the church 'charlatans and deceivers'.[1] There is no reason for doubting that this anonymous denunciation reflects Voltaire's reputation accurately, or even for doubting that it represents his actual beliefs accurately. In his writing at the time, which consisted of epistles after the manner of Chaulieu and his friends for the most part, little evidence of such beliefs appears, it is true, but it would have been surprising had this not been the case; the police was very active and young Voltaire was a marked man. However, a good deal more meaning than at first appears may occasionally be read into some of his couplets; sometimes doubt concerning the immortality of the soul is hinted at; elsewhere the poet affirms with slight overemphasis that he accepts some miraculous story or other related in the Old Testament. An occasional remark in his correspondence is also revealing. In 1721 he asked his friend Thieriot to perform for his writings the service Ezra had performed for the scriptures and write them all down from memory.[2] Such a remark can mean only one thing, namely that Voltaire was aware of the controversy concerning the Pentateuch and accepted the point of view of the rationalist critics. His first plays also, without being *pièces à thèse*, showed a sceptical mind at work. *Œdipe*, played in 1718, is rebellious in respect of unreasonable gods and priests who gull the people. Jealous gods are a useful theme for any tragic author, it is true, but Voltaire made a point of claiming that his play was interpreted as being anti-Jansenist. And

---

[1] Text in R. Pomeau, *La Religion de Voltaire*, Paris, 1956, p. 80.
[2] 2 June 1721 (*Correspondence*, ed. Besterman, Geneva, i, 1953, p. 91).

so it is, though only incidentally, so to speak; a deist and frequenter of the Temple was hardly likely to favour the Jansenist creed. In 1722, Louis Racine's poem *La Grâce*, which contained many Pascalian developments on the human predicament, provoked a vigorous response.[1] In *La Ligue* (1722), which was later to become *La Henriade*, he refused to damn the virtuous bonzes, brahmans, disciples of Confucius and Zoroaster and inhabitants of the new world for not having received the Christian revelation and refused to admit any revelation from God, the creator and ruler of myriads of worlds, other than the natural law engraved in human hearts and minds.[2] *La Ligue* is enthusiastically royalist, but it is openly anti-clerical, whilst monks are described with relish as fanatical murderers of lawful kings: the poet's mentality as revealed in *La Ligue* is very like that of the 'politiques' who supported Henri IV at the end of the wars of religion, and the description of the libertine given by Garasse a hundred years previously would have suited Voltaire very well. He related the massacre of St Bartholomew's day with intense horror and disgust. According to his friend Cideville, he shut himself up without food or sleep to compose this passage,[3] and the description given by the marquis de Villette[4] of the revulsion of feeling which the poet felt each year on the anniversary of the

---

[1] *Œuvres* (Moland), x, p. 479. Professor Pomeau states (*Religion de Voltaire*, p. 100) that a reference to Pascal in the prefaces of the tragedy entitled *Mariamne* shows that Voltaire had read the *Pensées* by 1725. He may well have done so, but this reference does not prove it, because it occurs in the second preface which dates from 1730.

[2] Henri IV is transported to heaven by St Louis:

> Quelle est, disait Henri, s'interrogeant lui-même,
> Quel est de Dieu sur eux la justice suprême?
> Ce Dieu les punit-il d'avoir fermé leurs yeux
> Aux clartés que lui-même il plaça si loin d'eux?
> Pourrait-il les juger, tel qu'un injuste maître,
> Sur la loi des chrétiens qu'ils n'avaient pu connaître?
> Non, Dieu nous a créés, Dieu nous veut sauver tous.
> Partout il nous conduit, partout il parle à nous;
> Il grave en tous les cœurs la loi de la nature,
> Seule à jamais la même et seule toujours pure.
> Sur cette loi, sans doute, il juge les païens,
> Et si leur cœur fut juste, ils ont été chrétiens.

[3] Oubliant de manger et sans avoir dormi,
> Dans une chambre obscure,
> Il évoquait, peignant à la race future,
> Les diables de la Saint-Barthélemy.
> (Text in J. Noury, *Voltaire inédit*, Paris, 1895, p. 5.)

[4] Cf. R. Pomeau, *La Religion de Voltaire*, p. 108.

massacre makes it clear that he experienced intensely the feeling with which we are so familiar in our own times and which has no necessary connection with the knowledge that atrocities which have been committed have been committed by the 'other' side or by our 'own' side. It was a new mode of sensibility, and one may recall that the same generation of the beginning of the eighteenth century also adopted a new attitude towards the killing of Vanini.

Voltaire's mind was still running on Louis Racine's Jansenist poem when he wrote the epistle usually entitled *Le Pour et le Contre* which he read to Mme de Rupelmonde and J.-B. Rousseau, in 1722, during a drive in a carriage on the outskirts of Brussels. His mind still revolted against a God who could make men evil and punish them for their wickedness. He could recognize only a God who had written his law in the hearts of all men. He had by now separated himself consciously from Christianity and declared in favour of a universal natural religion.[1]

When Voltaire came to England in 1726, it was with the intention —so he said—of 'learning to think', but it would not do to read too much meaning into this expression; he already had in his mind a set of convictions which he owed to French masters and a long tradition of French free-thought. Nevertheless London could offer him much and he began to read the English authors without delay. So far he had had the benefit of Bolingbroke's conversation and correspondence, and particularly a letter sent to him by Bolingbroke on 27 June 1724 informing him of Newton's criticism of Descartes and recommending him to read Locke.[2] He now read Tindal's anticlerical *Rights of the Christian Church asserted*, Gordon and Trenchard's

---

[1] Il créa les humains à lui-même semblables,
   Afin de les mieux avilir;
   Il nous donna des cœurs coupables,
   Pour avoir droit de nous punir.
   Il nous fit aimer le plaisir,
Pour nous mieux tourmenter par des maux effroyables . . .
Songe que du Très-Haut la sagesse éternelle
A gravé de sa main dans le fond de ton cœur
   La religion naturelle . . .
Crois que devant son trône en tout temps, en tous lieux,
   Le cœur du juste est précieux;
Crois qu'un bonze modeste, un dervis charitable,
   Trouvent plutôt grâce à ses yeux
   Qu'un janséniste impitoyable.

[2] *Correspondence*, ed. Besterman, Geneva, i, 1953, p. 247.

Independent Whig, Woolston's *Discourses on Miracles*, and, with Samuel Clarke, who was to contribute so much to his own *Traité de métaphysique*, he made the acquaintance of English liberal theology, and began to study the physics of Newton upon which Clarke had drawn so freely in his *Demonstration of the Being and Attributes of God*. Reading and conversation in London could no longer reveal the main themes of free-thought to Voltaire, because he was already familiar with them before he came, but reading and conversation in London could, and did, help him to elaborate them in his own mind, supplied him with information, served as models for the development of arguments, reinforced his deistic position and gave him a positive creed distinguishable from the mainly critical deism current in the clandestine literature of his own country. In the *Lettres philosophiques* or *Lettres anglaises*, which he wrote after his return and published in 1734, his religious and philosophic attitudes showed themselves as having more complexity than before the English visit. In the *Lettres* he treated the Quakers with amused sympathy, the Anglicans and Presbyterians with dislike, but less dislike than the Church in his own country, and he reserved a word of approval for the antitrinitarians or unitarians. He admired the tolerance exhibited by the English in their religious life and even exaggerated it by omitting any reference to the Test Act. The omission may have been due to ignorance, it may have been due to design, but in any case it does not noticeably weaken the impression of living experience conveyed by the *Lettres*. Problems which had been abstract in Voltaire's mind were now related to men living in their different ways in a real society. *Alzire*, a tragedy written just after the *Lettres philosophiques*, portrayed Christianity as Voltaire would have liked it to be, a religion of pure charity, that is to say, and in his correspondence with his friend d'Argental on the subject of this play he let it be understood that the approval of certain 'dévots' would give him pleasure.[1]

There was one attitude however which had never been theoretical in Voltaire's mind and that was his dislike of the Jansenist moral philosophy, which he found in its most irritating form in Pascal's *Pensées*. He returned to the *Pensées* after the trip to England and in an *Epistle* which was published in the *Mercure de France* in 1732 he declared that one of his occupations was reading the 'formless works' of the 'dévot satirique' who made it his business to teach men to hate

---

[1] Nov.–Dec. 1734, *Correspondence*, ed. Besterman, iii, pp. 326–7, 334.

their very nature.[1] When the *Lettres philosophiques* appeared, he added some of his reading notes on the *Pensées* at the end of the text. He did not add them all; the most dangerous he kept in reserve, saying, in a letter to Maupertuis, that he could not mention Pascal's defence of miracles and prophecies until he was safe in Basel.[2]

Pascal's mathematical argument in favour of the Wager seemed to Voltaire, as it had to others before him—Gilbert, Boulainviller, the marquis de Lassay—and as it did to the authors of two of the clandestine tracts—the *Histoire critique du christianisme* and the *Réflexions sur l'argument de M. Pascal et de M. Locke concernant la possibilité d'une autre vie à venir*—worthless and indecent.[3] Claude Gilbert, in his *Histoire de Calejava* (1700)[4] and the marquis de Lassay, in his *Recueil de différentes choses* (1727), had pointed out that the argument could be equally well used in favour of Mahometanism. So did the author of the *Histoire critique*[5] who traced it back to Arnobius, found it again in Mauduit's *Traité de la religion contre les athées, les déistes et les nouveaux pyrrhoniens* (1677) and La Bruyère's

---

[1] Je cours après Newton dans l'abîme des cieux . . .
    J'en entends raisonner les plus profonds esprits,
    Maupertuis et Clairault . . .
    De ces obscurités je passe à la morale . . .
    J'examine avec soin les informes écrits,
    Les monuments épars, et le style énergique,
    De ce fameux Pascal, ce dévot satirique.
    Je vois ce rare esprit trop prompt à s'enflammer;
       Je combats ses rigueurs extrêmes.
    Il enseigne aux humains à se haïr eux-mêmes;
    Je voudrais, malgré lui, leur apprendre à s'aimer.
                                    (*Œuvres*, ed. Moland, x, pp. 275–6.)

[2] 'Ce sont ces *lettres anglaises* qui vont m'exiler! Cartésiens, Malebranchistes, Jansénistes, tout se déchaîne contre moi! . . . Savez-vous bien que j'ai fait prodigieusement grâce à ce Pascal? De toutes les prophéties qu'il rapporte, il n'y en a pas une qui puisse s'expliquer honnêtement de Jésus-Christ. Son chapitre sur les miracles est un persiflage. Cependant je n'en ai rien dit, et l'on crie! Mais laissez-moi faire; quand je serai une fois à Bâle, je ne serai pas si prudent.' (29 April 1734; *Correspondence*, ed. Besterman, iii, pp. 235–6.) Cf. 'Vraiment, puisqu'on crie tant sur ces fichues *Lettres*, je me repens bien de n'en avoir pas dit davantage. Va, va, Pascal, laisse-moi faire! tu as un chapitre sur les prophéties où il n'y a pas l'ombre du bon sens. Attends, attends!' (To d'Argental, *c.* 23 May 1734, ibid., p. 257.)

[3] Cf. J.-R. Carré, *Réflexions sur l'anti-Pascal de Voltaire*, Paris, 1935. Professor Carré, who accepts the *Réflexions sur l'argument de M. Pascal* as being 'probably' by Fontenelle, analyses this work in his *La Philosophie de Fontenelle*, Paris, 1932, pp. 459 sqq.

[4] *Histoire de Calejava ou de l'île des hommes raisonnables, avec le parallèle de leur morale et du christianisme*, n.p., 1700.

[5] Fréret? Cf. above, p. 298. The *Histoire critique*, also called *Examen des apologistes de la religion chrétienne*, was written after 1733.

chapter on the 'Esprit forts', declared that Nicole and Jaquelot were against it because interest can never decide between truth and falsehood, and himself rejected it because to believe what is not founded in reason is to have a false idea of God.[1] Boulainviller said it was a bad bet; it amounted to staking one's all against nothing.[2] The author of the *Réflexions*[3] argued that any bet must be bad if the chance of winning is infinitely small, even if the prize is infinite.[4] Voltaire preferred non-mathematical arguments. The mere suggestion of playing heads and tails seemed to him unworthy of such a subject; the interest one may or may not have in whether God exists has nothing whatever to do with the truth of that existence; in any case it ill becomes a Jansenist, who professes to believe that only a handful of souls will be saved in any event, not one in a million, to try and inveigle his readers into so fraudulent a lottery: if Pascal has any arguments of weight to bring forward, let him bring them forward and not waste time in proposing games of pitch and toss!

It was not merely Pascal's dialectics that Voltaire could not stomach; it was the conception of life he found in the *Pensées*. In this, whether he was aware of it or not, he was in agreement with the 'Militaire philosophe' and the author of the *Histoire critique*. Pascal's insistence on describing man as a stranger in nature, out of place, lost, unhappy, incapable of discovering the truth and obliged, in a desperate bid for a little comfort and solace, to humiliate his reason and accept the tutelage of priests, was offensive to Voltaire, unhealthy and wrongheaded. Man is as he should be, as he was intended to be, in his place in the order designed by providence, neither entirely happy nor entirely unhappy; he is neither a monster nor corrupt; he bears no mark of Cain upon his brow; he is no angel either; he is to be accepted as he is. So much Voltaire dared to say in the *Lettres philosophiques*, which he had some hope of being able to publish without undue danger.[5] But there were some things he

---

[1] p. 241 of the Mazarine MS no. 1198.   [2] *Réfutation des erreurs* . . . (1731), p. 160.

[3] Arsenal no. 2557. A note attributes it to Fontenelle. Also in *Nouvelles libertés de penser* (1743) and Fontenelle, *Œuvres*, Paris, 1818, vol. ii. Condorcet attributed it to Fontenelle in his edition of the *Pensées* (1776); Voltaire was uncertain when he republished Condorcet's edition (1778).

[4] Pascal had argued that the bet was a good one even in the limiting case, i.e. when the chance of winning was only one in an infinite number.

[5] 'Pourquoi nous faire horreur de notre être ? Notre existencen'est point si malheureuse qu'on veut nous le faire accroire. Regarder l'univers comme un cachot et tous les hommes comme des criminels qu'on va exécuter est l'idée d'un fanatique; croire que le monde est

knew he could not say in public. Having written a first version of his letter on Locke, a short essay on the theme that a child's intelligence develops in the same way as a young animal's, only more slowly to begin with and much more rapidly later, without there being any need whatsoever to suppose the presence of an immaterial substance in the child, he abandoned it and replaced it by a more prudently worded letter on the theme 'many have written the romance of the soul, at last Locke has written its history'. The second version prudently placed on Locke's shoulders all the responsibility for having said that it was in God's power to endow matter with thought. The first version was independent of Locke and developed a naturalistic thesis in as simple and straightforward a way as any of the clandestine treatises, albeit with more humour. Suppose that on the same day a child, a canary, a cat and a dog are born. At the end of three months the canary can be taught a minuet; in six weeks a cat learns all its tricks and a dog becomes a good hunting dog in a year and a half. But the child can do nothing at the age of four. One might well take the child for an automaton and the beasts for intelligent creatures. Later the child acquires far more ideas than the others, but this is no reason for concluding that he is a twofold being; it is reason for thinking, as was commonly thought before the Egyptian politicians encouraged the belief in a spiritual soul to further their own designs, that God has associated the power of thinking with various material bodies, differently organized and of differing degrees of sensitivity: on other planets there may well be beings endowed with twenty or thirty different sense organs and far more ideas than we possess. Locke will be accused of impiety for having said this, but so were those who believed long ago in the antipodes. It is not the philosophers, Montaigne, Locke, Bayle, Spinoza, Hobbes, Shaftesbury, Collins or Toland who have caused strife and upheavals in history; it is the leaders of religious sects.[1]

un lieu de délices où l'on ne doit avoir que du plaisir, c'est la rêverie d'un sybarite. Penser que la terre, les hommes et les animaux sont ce qu'ils doivent être dans l'ordre de la Providence est, je crois d'un homme sage.' (*Lettres philosophiques*, ed. Lanson, ii, p. 193.)

[1] There is a manuscript copy at the Arsenal library (no. 2557) in a collection of six clandestine tracts. It was published first in 1738 in *Lettres de M. de V.* (The Hague). It forms part of the article *Ame* of the *Dictionnaire philosophique*. Manuscript copies were in circulation before 1738 according to a statement made in 1745 by the author of an anonymous *Réflexions philosophiques sur l'immortalité de l'âme raisonnable*. For the text of this statement and a critical text of the *Lettre sur Mr. Locke*, see Lanson's edition of the *Lettres philosophiques*, i, pp. 190 sqq.

The first draft of the letter on Locke was a sketch of the *Traité de métaphysique* which Voltaire wrote shortly afterwards for Mme du Châtelet. We have taken the *Traité de métaphysique* as the final stage in our study because Voltaire's philosophic outlook as expressed therein was already stable and consistent and not destined to change radically during the whole of his long career. It is true that he lost, during the second half of his career, some of the faith he had had in the rational organization of the universe, and as the years passed he found it increasingly difficult to believe that man was a free agent in nature and master of his own fate: he finally turned away from philosophical speculation altogether and threw all his energy into practical action in favour of the victims of miscarriages of justice. But the darkening of the picture which took place in his mind did not alter its design. The design was fixed by the time he wrote the *Traité de métaphysique* in June 1734; he was forty years old at the time and his thinking had acquired the stability that becomes a mature mind. It is no more than a sketch of a system and the title Voltaire chose was a misnomer. It is actually an essay on man in which the author attempts to use a non-metaphysical method of inquiry but fails to apply it systematically and falls back upon the current metaphysical themes. It begins as anthropology and ends as sociology, but sandwiched between the beginning and the end are chapters on the existence of God and the nature of the human soul. The first chapters approach the study of man with all the freshness and ingenuousness of which Bayle, Fontenelle and Montesquieu had made such an effective satirical device. It replaces very aptly the objectivity of the experimental sciences:

Coming from Mars or Jupiter, I land on the coasts of the Atlantic Ocean, in the Kaffir country, and straightway begin to look for a man. I see monkeys, elephants, negroes, all of which seem to have some glimmer of imperfect reason. They all use languages I do not understand, and all their actions seem to be motivated equally by an end in view. If I judged things by the first impression they made on me, I should be inclined to believe that of all these animals the rational one was the elephant; but to avoid jumping to hasty conclusions, I take the young of these various beasts; I examine a negro child at six months, a little elephant, a little monkey, a little lion, a little dog; I see beyond all doubt that these young animals have incomparably more strength and skill, more ideas, more passions, more memory than the little negro, that they express all their desires in a more intelligible way; but a short time afterwards the little

negro has more ideas than all the others put together. I even observe that
these negro animals employ a better articulated and much more flexible
language than all the other beasts. I have had time to learn this language,
and at length, actuated by the consideration of the slight degree of superiority which they acquire finally over the monkeys and the elephants, I
hazarded the conclusion that these were men, and I worked out the following definition: 'A man is a black animal having wool on its head, walking on two legs, almost as clever as a monkey, less strong than the other
animals of the same size, with a few more ideas than they have and more
facility in the expression thereof; subject none the less to all the same
needs, being born, living and dying just as they do.'

This was a good beginning, but Voltaire did not keep it up. His
second chapter is drawn from Samuel Clarke's *Demonstration of the
Being and Attributes of God*, the third ('Que toutes les idées viennent
par les sens') summarizes the beginning of Locke's *Essay on human
Understanding*, the fourth replies to Berkeley's criticism of the
common-sense belief in the existence of material things, but without
naming Berkeley himself. With the fifth we return to the Kaffirs and
the monkeys:

Some philosophers tell me 'Make no mistake, man is entirely different
from the other animals; he has a spiritual and immortal soul, for (be
careful to observe) if thought were composed of matter it would necessarily be the same as that which it was composed of; it would be divisible,
capable of motion etc., but thought cannot be divided, so it is not composed of matter; it has no parts, it is simple, immortal, the work and image
of God.' I listen to these masters and I reply with my usual diffidence as
regards myself, but not with any confidence in them, 'If man has a soul,
as you assure me he has, then doubtless this dog and this mole have one
just like it.' They all swear that this is not so. I ask what difference there is
between the dog and them. Some reply that the dog is a substantial form;
others tell me to believe nothing of the kind because substantial forms are
products of the imagination, the dog is a machine like a roasting jack and
nothing else. I ask the inventors of substantial forms what they understand by this term and they reply with a lot of grandiloquent nonsense, so
I turn again to the makers of roasting jacks and say, 'If these beasts are
pure machines, you yourselves are certainly nothing more than repeater
watches by comparison with the roasting jacks of which you speak, so if
you have the honour to possess a spiritual soul, the beasts have one too,
for they are all that you are; they have the same organs by means of
which you receive sensations and if these organs do not serve them for the
same end, God performs a useless task in giving them those organs, and

God, according to you yourselves, does nought in vain. So choose, either to give a spiritual soul to a flea, a worm, a microbe, or to be an automaton as they are.'

The sixth chapter leaves no doubt that the belief in immortality is unacceptable to Voltaire's mind, but the seventh claims to be able to give some meaning to the freedom of the will, drawing on Clarke and Locke for the purpose, and it is not until the eighth and ninth that the tone of the naturalist reappears. These last chapters deal with man as a social animal and put forward a sketch of a social ethics.

Man has no gregarious instinct, like the ants, but sexual love, the presence of children, the founding of a home replaced such an instinct at the beginning and explain the origin of societies and the source of the arts. Man has, moreover, a feeling of affection for his fellows which other animals have not; he is naturally capable of pity. Self-love, which is strong in man, just as it is in other animals, often stifles the cry of pity, but that pity exists none the less. It would not suffice, however, by itself, to create order amongst men. It is men's passions, and particularly pride, emulation and the desire to command which perform this function. Avarice and envy may also serve the general weal by inspiring industry.[1] The passions are the wheels which make the machines go round. From one society to another laws differ considerably; in all societies what is called virtuous is what is in accordance with the general well-being and what is called vice is contrary to the general good. There are, however, certain feelings which are common to all men, wherever they may be found, such as an affection for one's own species, and pity for one's fellows. Certain general principles also apply to all societies: one must, for instance, abide by the given word, otherwise social

---

[1] It is not known whether Voltaire read Mandeville's *Fable of the Bees* before writing the *Traité de métaphysique*, but he certainly knew it by 1736. He made use of it in *Le Mondain*, a half-serious eulogy on luxury and Mme du Châtelet translated parts of it and introduced into her rendering some of the ideas expressed in the *Traité de métaphysique* which are not Mandevillian, e.g. that sexual love and the bearing of children produced the earliest social life and that there are feelings and principles common to all men. Mme de Graffigny saw parts of the translation when she stayed at Cirey in the winter of 1738-9; it may have existed for some time before that date and Professor Wade thinks that Voltaire was influenced by Mme du Châtelet and not Mme du Châtelet by Voltaire in the matter of the modifications introduced into Mandeville's doctrine (*Voltaire and Mme du Châtelet*, pp. 24-33). They were doubtless entirely in agreement with each other in seeking to preserve a certain rationalistic and universalistic basis for their moral philosophy.

order is impossible. These are not absolute rules in the sense that they are dictated from on high; there is no absolute moral code enacted by God: good and evil are human concerns; it is for man to suppress anti-social acts by means of punishments. There is no moral law applying to the whole of nature: 'Woe betide the fly that falls into the spider's web, the bull that is attacked by a lion, the lamb that falls in with wolves.' It is for man to establish order in society, and he does so by the expression of approval or disapproval. The knowledge that there is no absolute morality does not necessarily make a man immoral; the philosophers who have commonly been called unbelievers or libertines have been at all times the most scrupulous of men; La Mothe le Vayer, Bayle, Locke, Spinoza, Shaftesbury, Collins were all men of rigid virtue. Those who need religion to inspire them with the feelings which nature should inspire them with are to be pitied; they are made of inferior stuff.

This little treatise is well within the limits of the French libertine tradition. It is true that it borrows from Clarke and Locke and brushes aside the arguments which Descartes had to offer on the same subject: these English elements characterize Voltaire amongst the free-thinkers of his own generation; they are the direct result of his English trip. So also was the interest which Newton had aroused in him and which was to inspire his *Eléments de la philosophie de Newton* in 1738. They provide some of the striking and vivid features of his mental stock-in-trade, the positive religious element, the theism of Newton and Clarke, the famous sentence on 'thinking matter' from Locke, and Mandeville's identification of private vice with public good, but it is doubtful whether Voltaire's mind ever assimilated them perfectly. The substance of his thinking remained independent of these English additions; it consisted of the combination of scepticism, Epicureanism and rationalism which the 'libertins' had compounded and which provided also the substance of the 'philosophic spirit'.

Postscript

ON the surface calm still prevailed during the twenties and thirties of the eighteenth century. College pupils wrote down lessons dictated in Latin just as they had done a century before. The content of the lessons had not changed much; the space allotted to the new physics had increased, that was all: the old framework of teaching still remained intact.[1] Readers of the memoirs published by the various academies, and readers of the reviews—the *Journal des savants* and those imported from Holland—were aware of the intense activity which scholars and men of science everywhere, and especially in Holland and England, were pursuing, but the ordinary book trade in France had little to offer that was new and exciting by way of ideas: the censors saw to that!

On the flat plain of orthodoxy two small but intriguing outcrops commanded attention. Two books, both published abroad in the first place, but both written in France and intended for the French public at large, achieved an immediate success. Voltaire's *Lettres philosophiques*, first published in an English translation in London (1733) and then clandestinely at Rouen (1734) was one of them. The other had appeared thirteen years previously; it was Montesquieu's *Lettres persanes*, published at Cologne in 1721. Both were master-

---

[1] D'Alembert, who was educated at the Collège des Quatre Nations, made the following scathing remarks in the *Encyclopédie* (Collège): 'Après avoir passé sept ans à apprendre des mots et à parler sans rien dire, on commence enfin, ou on croit commencer, l'étude des choses, car c'est la vraie définition de la philosophie. Mais il s'en faut bien que celle des collèges mérite ce nom. Elle ouvre pour l'ordinaire par un *compendium* qui est, si on peut parler ainsi, le rendez-vous d'une infinité de questions inutiles sur l'existence de la philosophie, la philosophie d'Aristote, etc. On passe de là en logique. Celle qu'on enseigne, du moins dans un grand nombre de collèges, est à peu près celle que le maître de philosophie se propose d'apprendre au bourgeois gentilhomme . . . enfin, dans la physique, on bâtit à sa mode un système du monde; on y explique tout ou presque tout; on y suit ou on y réfute à tort et à travers Aristote, Descartes, Newton.' Diderot, who was educated at the Collège Louis le Grand, was less damning at the beginning of his adaptation of Shaftesbury's *An Inquiry concerning Virtue and Merit*, published in 1745: 'Un jeune homme, au sortir de son cours de philosophie, est jeté dans un monde d'athées, de déistes, de sociniens, de spinozistes et d'autres impies, fort instruit des propriétés de la matière subtile et de la formation des tourbillons . . . mais à peine sait-il des avantages de la vertu ce que lui en a dit un précepteur . . . Il faut espérer que ces professeurs éclairés qui ont purgé la logique des *universaux* et des *catégories*, la métaphysique des *entités* et des *quiddités*, et qui ont substitué dans la physique l'expérience et la géométrie aux *hypothèses frivoles* . . . ne refuseront pas à la morale quelques-unes de ces veilles qu'ils consacrent au bien public.'

pieces of the clearest of clear French prose. Nevertheless both left so much to be read between the lines that echoes in the reader's mind contributed as much to the sense as did the printed word. In the midst of *badinage* concerning fashions, coquetry, the Opera, Montesquieu's Persian tourists commented with such charming naïvety on morals and politics that it was difficult for anybody to profess to be shocked or to take offence. All the same the bland assumption that things were not as they should be, the disrespectful air, could not be mistaken. Old idols had received sufficient incense and the reader was assumed to be as well aware of the fact as the author. The naïvety was the naïvety of irony. Moreover the reader was assumed to be well aware, and needing only to be reminded, that religious intolerance was a curse, that slavery could in no way be defended, that justice was the highest of all values and that a state could only flourish if its institutions were respected by its citizens. All this was said rapidly, as though in passing, and interspersed with complaints emanating from a Persian harem concerning the tyrannical conduct of eunuchs and the insubordination of wives. Voltaire was just as oblique and tantalizing in the *Lettres philosophiques*. Was he not merely describing the manners and ideas of a foreign country? So at least he could claim. But the implied strictures on the French counterparts of all he praised in England were not difficult to perceive, and if, in all literary matters, he weighted the balance at the other end and heaped his praises on all that did not offend his Gallic taste, the fact served mainly to show how the scale turned elsewhere in the book. In spite of a ceremonial laceration and committal to the flames by the public hangman—or perhaps, in part, because of it[1]—the *Lettres philosophiques* ran through twelve editions by 1739. The French reading public was ready to understand and appreciate them to the full.

In the forties the intellectual stratum that had been laid down beneath the surface emerged into full view, and how solid it proved to be! The year 1746 saw the beginning of the *Encyclopédie* and the publication, at Amsterdam, of Condillac's *Essai sur l'origine des connaissances humaines*. In 1748 *L'Esprit des lois* was published in Geneva. La Mettrie's *L'Homme machine* also appeared in that year

---

[1] Voltaire was certainly aware at a later date of the fact that censorship can make for literary success. At the end of *La Princesse de Babylone* (1768) he wrote: 'Tâchez surtout d'engager le père Riballier à faire condamner la *Princesse de Babylone* par la Sorbonne; vous ferez grand plaisir à mon libraire, à qui j'ai donné cette petite histoire pour ses étrennes.'

at Leyden. With 1749 came from the Imprimerie Royale the first volume of Buffon's *Histoire naturelle*, condemned by the Sorbonne in 1751, but approved of generally. The same year (1749) saw the anonymous publication of Diderot's *Lettre sur les aveugles* and their author's prompt imprisonment in the Château de Vincennes. The director of the *Encyclopédie* was in gaol! But the first volume was already being prepared for the press. It appeared in 1751 amid public acclaim. The era of the wide diffusion of French free-thought had begun.

Select Bibliography of General Studies

ASCOLI, G., *La Grande Bretagne devant l'opinion française au* XVIIIe *siècle*, Paris, 1930.

ATKINSON, G., *The Extraordinary Voyage in French Literature before 1700*, New York, 1900.

BARBER, W. H., *Leibniz in France*, Oxford, 1955.

BÉNICHOU, P., *Morales du Grand Siècle*, Paris, 1948.

BONNO, G., *La Culture et la civilisation britanniques devant l'opinion française, de la paix d'Utrecht aux Lettres philosophiques*, Philadelphia, 1948.

BOUILLIER, F., *Histoire de la philosophie cartésienne*, Paris, 1868.

BURTT, E. A., *The Metaphysical Foundations of Modern Physical Science*, London, 1928.

BUSSON, H., *Les Sources et le développement du rationalisme dans la littérature française*, Paris, 1922.

—— *La Pensée religieuse française de Charron à Pascal*, Paris, 1933.

—— *La Religion des classiques*, Paris, 1948.

CASSIRER, E., *The Philosophy of the Enlightenment*, Princeton, N.J., 1951.

CHARBONNEL, J.-R., *La Pensée italienne et le courant libertin*, Paris, 1917.

GUYÉNOT, E., *Les Sciences de la vie aux* XVIIe *et* XVIIIe *siècles : l'idée d'évolution*, Paris, 1941.

HAZARD, P., *La Crise de la conscience européenne*, Paris, 1935.

LACHÈVRE, F., *Le Libertinage au* XVIIe *siècle*, Paris, 1904–24.

LANGE, F. A., *A History of Materialism*, London, 1877.

LANSON, G., 'Origines et premières manifestations de l'esprit philosophique dans la littérature française de 1675 à 1748', in *Revue des cours et conférences*, 1907–10.

—— 'Questions diverses sur l'histoire de l'esprit philosophique en France avant 1750', in *Revue d'histoire littéraire de la France*, 1912.

LOVEJOY, A., *The Great Chain of Being*, Cambridge, Mass. 1948.

MONOD, A., *De Pascal à Chateaubriand : les défenseurs français du christianisme de 1670 à 1802*, Paris, 1916.

MORNET, D., *Les Sciences de la nature au* XVIIIe *siècle*, Paris, 1926.

—— *Les Origines intellectuelles de la Révolution*, Paris, 1933.

MOUY, P., *Le Développement de la physique cartésienne*, Paris, 1934.

PERRENS, F.-T., *Les Libertins en France au* XVIIe *siècle*, Paris, 1896.

PINOT, V., *La Chine et la formation de l'esprit philosophique en France*, Paris, 1932.

PINTARD, R., *Le Libertinage érudit dans la première moitié du* XVIIe *siècle*, Paris, 1943. (Good bibliography.)

ROSENFIELD, L. C., *From Beast-Machine to Man-Machine*, New York, 1941.

SAGNAC, P., *La Formation de la société française moderne*, Paris, 1946.

SORTAIS, G., S.J., 'Le Cartésianisme chez les Jesuites', in *Archives de philosophie*, 1936.

STEPHEN, L., *English Thought in the Eighteenth Century*, London, 1876.

TORREY, N. L., *Voltaire and the English Deists*, New Haven, Conn. 1930.

VARTANIAN, A., *Diderot and Descartes*, Princeton, N.J. 1953.

VERNIÈRE, P., *Spinoza et la pensée française avant la Révolution*, Paris, 1954. (Good bibliography.)

WADE, I. O., *The Clandestine Organization and Diffusion of Philosophic Ideas in France from 1700 to 1750*, Princeton, N.J. 1938.

Index

A. Anonymous Manuscript Works

B. Themes, Catchwords, Phrases

'Supreme Being', 167, 168, 247, 297, 302, 316n 1; *see also* 'Being'
'Supremum infimi attingit infimum supremi', 76, 80, 83
Sybils, 4, 202

Teleology, *see* Finalism
Transformism, 77, 110n, 275-6, 310-11

Utopias and imaginary voyages, 48-66 (Campanella, Cyrano), 196 (Daniel), 247-8 (Vairasse, Tyssot de Patot), 265-266 (Vairasse, Foigny), 270n (Marana), 325-6 (Montesquieu)

Vacuum, 92, 209; plenum, 177-8, 193n, 309
'Verisimilitude', 204; = probability, 210n (Mariotte)
'Virtue', self-sufficient, 21, 46, 49, 240; conformity with the natural order, 46; disinterested, 269; *see also* Atheist
'Voluptas', 69, 101, 133, 139, 140n, 143, 144n

c. Persons, Institutions and Books

Abbadie, J., 312
Académie des Inscriptions et Belles-Lettres, 282, 286, 287
Académie des Sciences, 110, 191
Acar, 206n
Adam, A., 44n
Agrippa, Cornelius, 7, 55
Alembert, d', 325n
Amoudru, B., 312n
Ameline, C., 188n
Amerpoel, J., 188n, 198
Anacreon, 166
Anaxagoras, 79
Ancillon, P., 188n
Andala, R., 188n
Andlo, P., 188n
André, Jesuit, 193
Andriano, 206n
Ango, P., 216
Anti-Bigot, 45-6, 47, 48, 240
Apel, J. W., 34n
Apollonius of Tyana, 295
Apuleius, 295
Archives de la Bastille, 280n
Argenson, d', 280n
Argental, d', 317
Aristotle, 15, 23n, 35n, 67, 70n, 75-84, 85, 94, 112, 119, 128, 130, 131, 132, 138, 194, 196, 201, 202, 203 (*Poetics*), 206, 232, 248, 278, 307, 325n
Arnauld, A., 16, 74, 123
Arnauld d'Andilly, 13n
Arnobius, 318
Arouet, Armand, 313
Arpe, P. F., 34
Asclepiades, 131

Ascoli, G., 144n
Aselli, G., 215
Astruc, J., 217
Aubert, J. M., 192
Aubignac, abbé d', 46, 204
Aumeur, 228
Augustine, St, 46, 185, 194, 230
Auzout, 205n
Averroes, 35n, 278

Bachaumont, 160n
Bacon, 7, 94, 110, 111, 112n
Baduer, 190
Baglivi, 215
Bagny, cardinal, 25n
Baillet, A., 20
Bailly, a doctor, 205n
Balz, A. G. A., 193n, 239n
Balzac, Guez de, 10n, 27, 28, 32
Barbay, P., 140, 190
Barber, W. H., 211n, 237n, 285n
Barchusen, J. C., 215
Barclay, W., 13
Barin, T., 198
Barker, J. E., 70n
Barres, duchesse de, 158
Bary, R., 201
Basnage de Beauval, J., 20, 282, 296, 297
Bassecour, F. de la, 188n
Basso(n), 109
Bassompierre, maréchal de, 13
Batelier, J. (Batelarius), 242n
Baudouin, A., 28n, 33n